POLITICAL ECONOMY

Political Economy

A COMPARATIVE APPROACH

Second Edition

Barry Clark

PRAEGER

Westport, Connecticut
London

Library of Congress Cataloging-in-Publication Data

Clark, Barry Stewart, 1948–
    Political economy : a comparative approach / Barry Clark. — 2nd
ed.
        p.   cm.
    Includes bibliographical references and index.
    ISBN 0-275-95869-8 (alk. paper). — ISBN 0-275-96370-5 (pbk. :
alk. paper)
    1. Comparative economics. I. Title.
HB90.C52   1998
330—dc21   98-15657

British Library Cataloguing-in-Publication Data is available.

Library of Congress Catalog Card Number: 98-15657
ISBN: 0-275-95869-8
        0-275-96370-5 (pbk.)

First published in 1998

Praeger Publishers, 88 Post Road West, Westport, CT 06881
An imprint of Greenwood Publishing Group, Inc.

Printed in the United States of America

The paper used in this book complies with the
Permanent Paper Standard issued by the National
Information Standards Organization (Z39.48-1984).

10   9   8   7   6   5   4   3   2   1

Contents

Introduction

Political economy was the original social science. Theorists such as Adam Smith, John Stuart Mill, and Karl Marx developed broad visions of the social system. Not until the latter half of the nineteenth century did political economy splinter into economics, political science, sociology, social history, social psychology, and social philosophy. The motives for this reorientation were mixed. By partitioning the study of human behavior and society into narrower subdisciplines, social scientists hoped to emulate the analytical power and precision of the natural sciences. However, ideological motives also played a role in the disintegration of political economy. The all-encompassing visions of Smith, Mill, and Marx revealed conflict and tension in society. As political resistance to free-market liberalism mounted in the mid-nineteenth century, social scientists attempted to establish a body of objective knowledge from which to formulate reasoned arguments for particular social policies. By adhering to strict logic and factual data, they hoped to resolve divisive political issues.

Proponents of each of the new social sciences recognized the importance of defining their scope and method of analysis to establish boundaries separating the disciplines. As the most immediate heir to the legacy of political economy, economics held the greatest potential for emulating natural science because its scope was confined to behaviors most amenable to observation and measurement. The political, social, cultural, historical, and psychological dimensions of human existence were relegated to other disciplines, while economists focused on the individual pursuit of material well-being in the market. The assumption of individual rationality and the use of money as a yardstick for measuring cause and effect enabled economists to construct an impressive theoretical edifice borrowed largely from nineteenth century physics.

Modern economics often elicits skepticism from other social scientists. Criticism is directed toward its simplistic assumptions about human behavior, its focus on material and pecuniary interests, its blindness to social relationships, and its esoteric jargon, graphs, and mathematics. Yet, simultaneously, many social scientists tacitly proclaim their admiration of economics as they increasingly borrow concepts, theories, and methods of analysis from the so-called "dismal science."

These conflicting attitudes are evident even among economists. On one hand, economics has been labeled the "queen of the social sciences," and economists have extended their scope of analysis to include issues ranging from government and law to family life and sexual behavior. Yet, underlying this hubris is a caldron of internal dissension. In addition to the expected attacks by non-mainstream economists, various Nobel prize winners and widely respected theorists have expressed qualms about the direction in which modern economics is moving. The focus on mathematics and theoretical rigor, they charge, has pushed aside questions of relevance or applicability. Until recently, economists were faced with the discomfiting fact that as their models gained elegance, the real economy was relatively stagnant and a wide range of social problems were actually worsening. A question poses itself: how can a discipline in such internal disarray merit emulation by other social scientists?

The answer to this paradox lies in the allure of science. Scientific analysis carries tremendous weight in settling intellectual disputes and formulating public policy. In the social sciences, the quality of scholarship is often judged by its resemblance to the physical sciences, and no other social science has been able to match the rigor and elegance of economic theory. Economists have been successful in large part because their simplistic assumptions and narrow focus permit them to borrow mathematical techniques from the physical sciences.

Historians, political scientists, sociologists, and psychologists have been unable to reach consensus on a single scientific paradigm within their respective disciplines. Economists, however, formed such a consensus from the 1950s to the early 1970s, and their advocacy of Keynesian policies propelled them into positions of influence at the highest levels of government. Yet the breakdown of the Keynesian consensus during the 1970s and economists' inability to converge on a new paradigm have diminished the scientific status of economics even as other social scientists increasingly rely on its reputed scientific models and methods.

The quest for a science of economics has not been futile. The sophistication with which empirical data is gathered and analyzed, the construction of elaborate models of the macroeconomy, and the application of microeconomic theory to decisionmaking have all been impressive. Yet the public image of economics remains clouded. If economists are indeed scientists, citizens expect the same expertise and objectivity exhibited by engineers or medical professionals. When economists pronounce widely divergent assessments, forecasts, and policy prescriptions, public reaction ranges from skepticism to disdain. However, economists disagree not because they are inept, but because they are humans who embody the conflicting values present in modern societies.

The claim that value judgments underlie economics does not necessarily imply that economists consciously seek to advance their personal visions of the good society. For the most part, economists are committed to scientific research in which the facts are permitted to speak for themselves. However, values enter into economics even before research commences. Values affect the choice of issues to be investigated, the theoretical concepts to be used, and the selection of variables to be measured. Although the scientific method of controlled experimentation is designed to keep values out of research, this method has limited applicability in economics, where the laboratory is human society with its complex interaction of innumerable and often unmeasurable variables.

Economists may deny or suppress ideological disputes within their profession for several reasons. First, the reasoning and conclusions of economists lose the aura of scientific authority if they reflect the same unresolved value conflicts confronting all citizens. Most economists view themselves as social scientists seeking to objectively analyze and improve the workings of the economy. Any admission of value commitments might undermine their status as experts possessing higher forms of knowledge.

Second, economic education is transformed when alternative values are introduced into the classroom. The principles and applications of neoclassical microeconomics and Keynesian macroeconomics that now occupy a substantial portion of the curriculum can no longer be treated as the whole of economic wisdom. Students face the challenge of grasping several competing perspectives from which to understand the economy, and professors can no longer rely on their own mastery of a single theoretical approach if students are to be fully exposed to the breadth of economic thought.

Finally, many economists suppress the ideological dimensions of their discipline because they believe that ideological debate can have no resolution. Without scientific appeals to objective evidence, disagreements may degenerate into open conflict. If economics were perceived as merely sophisticated ideology, authoritative decisions by policymakers could be replaced by chaotic struggles for power among competing interests.

Despite these concerns, maintaining the myth of value-free economics poses corresponding dangers. First, economics embodies ethical judgments that would be controversial if made explicit. When these judgments are introduced into policy under the guise of science, one set of values prevails without public debate, violating the principles of a democratic society.

Second, in the realm of economic education, students may gain impressive technical sophistication while remaining naive about the values underlying their knowledge and skills. Lacking this awareness, students believe they have acquired a genuinely scientific technique for analyzing social issues and making policy recommendations. Those students who become professional economists or policy analysts may be baffled when their scientific prescriptions are regarded by others as simply one viewpoint among many.

Third, the effort to minimize public dissent by maintaining the scientific status of economists' advice reflects a low opinion of citizen participation in democratic societies. By promoting one set of values and portraying other values as merely "special interests," economists narrow the scope for popular input into political decisionmaking. Citizens biased by personal interests are portrayed as incapable of making responsible choices in political matters. However, by sealing important decisions from democratic input, "scientific" policymakers offer little incentive to develop citizenship skills or to engage in public dialogues concerning competing visions of the good society. Moreover, scientific analysis of social issues contains an inherent bias. Policymakers relying on scientific methods will inevitably focus on observable aspects of an issue while de-emphasizing or ignoring intangible or ethical considerations. The method of science tends to limit the scope of analysis to that which can be measured.

This text provides a balance to the currently dominant focus on scientific technique in economics education. Integrating economic analysis with material from history, political theory, sociology, psychology, and ethics reveals the underlying value commitments fueling debates over public policy. Social science cannot be value-free, but the values underlying various theories and techniques can at least be made evident and open to discussion.

The purpose of textbooks is to present a body of knowledge nearly universally accepted within a particular academic discipline. In the case of political economy, however, even the most basic terms and principles are subject to debate. The many contending perspectives in political economy dictate a comparative approach to the subject. In this text, four perspectives—Classical Liberal, Radical, Conservative, and Modern Liberal—are covered. Political economy is introduced in the first two chapters; the next four chapters are devoted to the theorists and ideas associated with each of the four perspectives. Chapters seven through fifteen cover major issues in modern political economy and, for each issue, examine the analyses and policies offered by these perspectives. Finally, chapter sixteen examines the roles of science and ideology in political economy.

The contending perspectives struggling for dominance in political economy represent dramatically different visions of the good society. Theoretical debates over economic and political issues are ultimately based on these visions, and citizens need to be aware of and consider the value commitments underlying alternative policies before choosing among them.

PART I

POLITICAL ECONOMY:
AN OVERVIEW

Chapter 1

Politics, Economics, and Political Economy

In all the political systems of the world, much of politics is
economics, and most of economics is politics.
Charles Lindblom

Economics does not usefully exist apart from politics.
John Kenneth Galbraith

There is no such thing as a purely economic issue.
Milton Friedman

POLITICS AND ECONOMICS

As a prelude to the study of political economy, a firm grasp of the words
politics and economics is essential. Unfortunately, these widely used terms
lack clear definition. As depicted below, politics and economics can be distinguished with reference to three characteristics: the primary goal being
pursued, the institutional arena within which the goal is pursued, and the
primary actor who chooses the goal.

	Economics	Politics
Primary Goal	Prosperity	Justice
Institutional Arena	Market	Government
Primary Actor	Individual	Community

Using these distinctions, economics might be defined as the individual pursuit of prosperity through the market, while politics is the communal pursuit of justice through government. Closer scrutiny of each of the three distinguishing characteristics, however, will reveal the unsatisfactory nature of these definitions.

Primary Goals

Economics is associated with efforts to achieve the highest possible material standard of living from available resources. The primary economic goal of prosperity has three dimensions: efficiency, growth, and stability. Politics, on the other hand, is linked with efforts to establish and protect rights so citizens can receive and hold that to which they are entitled. The primary political goal of justice, too, includes three dimensions: individual freedom, equity in the distribution of benefits and burdens, and social order.

However, distinguishing between economics and politics solely by referring to their respective goals is ultimately unsatisfactory because prosperity and justice are inextricably linked. A prosperous society is more likely to be perceived as a just society because the range of individual choice is broadened and order tends to prevail. Conversely, a just society fosters prosperity by providing open opportunities, fair rewards, and individual security to motivate production and accumulation of wealth. Because prosperity and justice are often mutually reinforcing, distinguishing between economic and political processes by referring to their different goals is inconclusive. Both economics and politics are concerned with promoting human well-being by maintaining prosperity and justice.

Institutional Arenas

Politics often refers to activities associated with government, while economics deals with activities occurring in the market. We use this distinction when we label campaigns, elections, and lawmaking as "political activity," while referring to exchanges of commodities and money as "economic activity." This method of distinguishing between politics and economics is certainly common, but it also leads to ambiguity. Like economic transactions, political activity often consists of mutually beneficial exchanges among self-interested persons or groups. For example, citizens consent to obey laws in exchange for governmental protection of their rights. Politicians provide particular programs or laws in exchange for votes or money. Indeed, with the possible exception of establishing a constitution, government activity can be viewed as a series of exchanges in a political market. Government also functions as an economizing agent when it seeks to achieve public goals at minimum cost and directs resources toward their optimal use.

Conversely, the market has various political dimensions. The prevalence of the corporate form of enterprise demonstrates that economic activity is often pursued by large groups of people collectively focused on a common goal. Within a corporation, workers are subject to the sometimes arbitrary power of their employer. Just as governments punish those who violate the law, employers rely on sanctions such as dismissal or demotion to maintain control over workers. Corporate executives establish goals and rules with little input from workers, and corporate power is often exercised to influence government policy. In addition, many market activities have public consequences and, therefore, become political issues of concern to the community as a whole. Finally, when income and wealth are highly concentrated, the power of the rich to command others resembles the prerogatives of a political dictator. Based on these observations, sole reliance on distinct institutional arenas does not provide an adequate basis for distinguishing between economics and politics.

Primary Actors

From this perspective, economic activity is pursued by persons acting as autonomous individuals, while political activity represents the efforts of an entire community to collectively pursue goals. This distinction is observable in the origins of the words "economics" and "politics." Economics derives from the Greek words *oikos*, meaning household, and *nomos*, meaning principle or law. As the principle of household management, economics deals with efforts to attain private goals with available resources. Economizing behavior can be directed toward any goal and practiced in any institutional arena. Reflecting this approach, economics is sometimes defined as the science of rational choice or the use of scarce means to achieve specified ends.

Politics, on the other hand, derives from the Greek word *polis*, meaning community or society. According to Aristotle, the public life of the *polis* is the arena within which true freedom and human development occur. Although economic activities are essential to human survival, they fail to engage the uniquely human capacities for cooperation and collective decision-making based on reasoned argument, dialog, persuasion, and compromise.

Distinguishing between economics and politics by reference to the primary actor is problematic due to the porous boundary separating the private and public spheres. In democratic societies, the collective choices of the community should largely reflect aggregated individual preferences. Much of the public choosing of goals through government consists of registering citizen preferences through voting or poll-taking. Moreover, public choice often reflects the influence of private individuals and groups exerted through lobbying, campaign contributions, and control over the selection of candidates for public office.

Conversely, the quality of public life affects the goals that individuals choose or are able to pursue. The material and social environments within which people live shape their language, self-image, desires, and goals. Given this interaction between public and private spheres, the distinction between individual and community as primary actors is not fully sustainable.

If politics and economics cannot be clearly distinguished, perhaps these terms are simply two names for the same process. Both are concerned with organizing and coordinating human activity, marshalling resources, managing conflict, allocating burdens and benefits, and providing for the satisfaction of human wants and needs. However, to completely collapse politics into economics or vice-versa would gloss over important differences between political and economic goals, institutional arenas, and actors. While prosperity/justice, market/government, and individual/community may be interrelated, they are not identical. Therefore, despite the considerable overlap between politics and economics, they can initially be analyzed as distinct processes.

THE MARKET AS AN ECONOMIC INSTITUTION

The market is a system of exchanges in which individual choices to supply or demand resources or products interact to determine prices. To assess the market's potential for achieving the economic goal of prosperity, one must examine each of the three dimensions of prosperity: efficiency, growth, and stability. For each dimension, arguments both for and against the market are presented.

Efficiency

For the market. A perfectly competitive market will, with some exceptions, direct resources toward their most highly valued use, resulting in a "Pareto optimal" or efficient economy in which no person can be made better off without making someone else worse off. The market coordinates vast numbers of transactions with minimal political supervision as prices provide information and incentives to guide individuals and businesses in making rational choices about employing resources and purchasing products.

The market achieves efficiency by allowing individuals to make mutually beneficial transactions. Individuals will exchange with one another until they have reached the maximum level of utility permitted by the resources with which they enter the market. Competition also promotes market efficiency. Firms and individuals are under constant pressure to adopt the most efficient technology, enabling them to produce at the lowest possible cost.

Against the market. Competition is imperfect due to barriers to entry, immobility of resources, lack of information, product differentiation, and concentrations of power caused by both technical conditions of production and the efforts of individuals to protect themselves from competition. These imperfections cause inefficiency.

Transaction costs also reduce efficiency. A transaction cost is any cost associated with conducting a transaction, as opposed to the actual cost of the commodity being bought or sold. Transaction costs include the costs of gathering information, specifying contracts, and enforcing the terms of contracts. High transaction costs sometimes prevent the formation of markets for certain goods. For example, a market for clean air does not exist because citizens would have to devote considerable time and expense to organizing themselves and negotiating with firms to reduce pollution. When some markets are missing, external costs and benefits arise from existing market transactions. Without a market for clean air, the production of steel imposes the cost of pollution on local residents. When external costs are present, government may be able to improve efficiency by taxing or regulating the industry. On the other hand, when the external benefits of a good are very large, government can increase efficiency by providing the good at public expense. Examples of "public goods" include national defense, highways, and police and fire protection.

The competitive individualism underlying market behavior may also be detrimental to efficiency. Intense competition may weaken social bonds, causing alienation, apathy, or hostility. These psychological conditions often manifest themselves in lower productivity, crime, and civil unrest, all of which interfere with efficiency.

Even if the market achieves economic efficiency, it may fail to attain the broader notion of social efficiency. Whereas economic efficiency refers only to the fulfillment of individual preferences backed by money and capable of satisfaction through commodities, social efficiency also recognizes goals adopted by society through government that may not be backed by individual purchasing power, or may be attainable only through collective action. For example, a handicapped person's need for public access or a homeless person's need for housing will be ignored by the market, but a community that values decent treatment of all citizens can increase social efficiency by using government to direct resources toward these needs.

Growth

For the market. The market is a powerful mechanism for increasing both the availability and productivity of economic resources. By placing both negative and positive consequences of decisions directly on the individual, the market provides strong incentives for prudent and industrious behavior. When individuals know they will personally reap the rewards or suffer the consequences of their actions, they are motivated to consider their choices more carefully. As a result of the market's incentives, additional resources are made available, the quality of resources is upgraded, and innovation and risk-taking are encouraged. The combination of technological development and expansion of resources provides an impetus for economic growth.

The market also fosters psychological changes conducive to growth. By minimizing the constraints of moral and cultural norms, the market encourages individuals to create their own identities by transcending the bounds of traditional roles and expectations. Self-reliant individuals may experiment with diverse lifestyles and forms of expression. Formerly dormant talents and desires are awakened. This process of self-discovery and self-renewal becomes a significant source of the dynamism of market societies. The productivity and innovation flowing from energized individuals contributes to rising standards of living that, in turn, broaden the range of individual opportunities and renew the motivation essential to economic expansion.

Against the market. The market's capacity for growth may be constrained by an inability to establish adequate social and economic infrastructure. Growth requires transportation systems, education, and other public goods that the market is ill-equipped to provide because of the difficulty in charging individuals for benefits received. Another constraining factor is uncertainty due to lack of information. Investors may be reluctant to finance ventures essential to growth when they are unable to accurately assess the degree of risk involved. Growth may also be hindered by insufficient demand if wealth and income become so concentrated that spending on consumer goods lags.

The competitive individualism associated with markets may also function to obstruct growth. Competition for social status may entail excessive consumption in order to display affluence. While high levels of consumption contribute to immediate expansion of the economy, the corresponding low level of saving may impede investment and therefore undermine long-term growth. Competition may also foster frustration and envy that interfere with productivity and growth. Finally, because competition creates insecurity, individuals may attempt to protect themselves by forming organizations and interest groups to suppress the flexibility and dynamism of the market.

Stability

For the market. The market is extremely flexible in responding to changing patterns of consumer preferences, technology, and resource availability. Through the price mechanism, these changes quickly elicit appropriate reactions as businesses and consumers adjust their production and consumption decisions, respectively. The market contributes to stability by adjusting quickly before serious imbalances arise. Competitive pressures reward prompt and effective responses to a changing business environment. Financial markets also contribute to stability. When the economy slows, interest rates fall until borrowing and investing are again attractive. Conversely, when the economy begins to overheat, rising interest rates choke off borrowing and spending until stability is restored.

Against the market. "Boom and bust" cycles have persisted since the market became the dominant institution for organizing economic activities. In earlier years, these cycles were often confined to a particular market in which a "speculative bubble" would develop as buyers anticipated ever-rising prices. Eventually, the bubble would burst, bringing financial ruin to some speculators. In modern times, however, the connectivity of markets and the emergence of financial markets have created national and even global cycles of instability.

This instability is partially explained by the role of expectations. A psychological shift toward pessimism among investors may create a financial crisis that spills over into the real economy, resulting in recession and unemployment. Conversely, optimism leads to new investments and higher spending that may trigger inflation.

THE MARKET AS A POLITICAL INSTITUTION

Although the market is usually viewed as an economic institution, it also performs important functions in achieving the political goal of justice. The market's role as a political institution can be understood by assessing its capabilities in promoting three dimensions of justice: freedom, equity, and order.

Freedom

For the market. The market provides a wide range of freedoms. Individuals have the right to make choices concerning employment, place of residence, consumption patterns, and social relationships. Competing alternatives constrain the power of any single person or firm to oppress and manipulate others. The sense of freedom offered by the market may partly explain the popularity of shopping. Consumers tend to enjoy the experience of being able to select from an array of alternatives—the power to choose with whom they shall transact. The market also provides citizens with opportunities to engage their resources, including entrepreneurial talent, in the most advantageous way. Finally, the market potentially protects individuals from abuses of governmental authority by establishing decentralized bases of power from which citizens can express opinions and organize opposition.

Against the market. While the market offers a considerable range of choice, it also limits choice. The market provides only commodities that can be sold at a profit and therefore fails to respond to demands for goods such as national defense, a clean environment, or public transportation. Since only a subset of human interests is expressible in the market, the freedom of individuals to pursue their goals is correspondingly narrowed.

Not only does the market limit the range of interests capable of fulfillment, it also conditions individuals to tailor their interests to suit the capabilities of the market. A social environment in which profitable commodities are the major source of satisfaction causes humans to develop capacities oriented toward consumption of commodities and diminishes their freedom to establish self-directed goals.

Although individuals in a pure market are largely free of legal restrictions on exchange, the freedom of persons with few marketable assets will be limited by their financial inability to pursue personal goals. Moreover, the prospect of hunger and deprivation effectively coerce individuals to seek employment. Once on the job, workers surrender much of their autonomy and self-direction to the authority of employers.

Even as consumers, citizens may not experience genuine freedom in the market. In real-world markets, consumers have only limited information and producers tend to be well-organized. Instead of being sovereigns of the market, consumers may feel like the prey, surrounded by manipulative advertising, inflated prices, shoddy merchandise, and deceitful sellers.

Historically, the link between markets and freedom has been based on the assumption that the interests of different individuals are ultimately harmonious. If no transactions are coerced, then all transactions must benefit both buyer and seller and hence increase the overall well-being of society. However, the record of real-world markets amply illustrates that the freedom of one individual may restrict the freedom of another. Markets allow practices such as monopolization of industries, pollution of the environment, and discrimination, all of which narrow the choices available to citizens.

Equity

For the market. With the forces of supply and demand establishing resource prices, the market distributes rewards according to each person's ability to provide valuable resources. The market permits individuals to decide how many of their resources to make available and how much time and expense to engage in upgrading the quality of their resources. By placing much of the responsibility for personal income in the hands of individuals, the market distributes the benefits and burdens of society's productive activities in a manner seemingly independent of political authority.

The market's potential for achieving equity is also enhanced by the presence of opportunity. In a perfectly competitive market, individual characteristics such as race, gender, religion, or ethnicity should be irrelevant in determining a person's success. For less successful individuals, resentment is dampened by awareness of opportunities to offer resources and by the perception that rewards accrue to resources in accordance with productivity.

Against the market. Concentrations of wealth and power typically appear in a market economy either because technological conditions favor large producers over smaller businesses or because individuals intentionally create large organizations to suppress competition and gain some control over market forces. These concentrations change the market's prices and allocation of resources. As a result, personal income reflects not only the productivity of resources provided to the market, but also an individual's status in the power structure. Those persons belonging to powerful groups are likely to receive income in excess of their productivity, while members of disadvantaged groups are likely to receive lower incomes than they would in a competitive market.

Even if the market is perfectly competitive, the distribution of income will reflect the pattern of ownership of productive resources. Wealthy owners of land or capital may be richly rewarded without any current personal contribution to production. Since various unethical and illegal means have been used in the past to accumulate property, the current distribution of income is unlikely to be equitable.

Equity in a market society requires equal opportunity, but when competition generates substantial inequality of property holdings, the opportunities of some people are restricted. Individuals enter market competition with burdens or advantages bequeathed by their family backgrounds, neighborhoods, schools, and cultures. When these conditions vary widely in preparing individuals for productive employment, genuine equality of opportunity cannot exist.

Finally, the market may be inequitable because it responds only to those human needs and desires backed by money. The market neither recognizes nor allocates resources toward the protection of human rights entitling individuals to certain benefits regardless of ability to pay. Examples of human rights might include the right to legal counsel for accused criminals, the right to public access for the physically challenged, and the right to a basic level of health care.

Order

For the market. The market erodes traditional human relations based on arbitrary privilege and hierarchy. By virtue of property rights and civil rights, individuals engage only in transactions of their own choosing. Freedom of choice and a sense of autonomy contribute to personal well-being, and a satisfied citizenry usually implies an orderly society.

The market also fosters order by increasing specialization of labor, so that formerly diverse and separate groups become mutually dependent. When individuals benefit from market transactions, they have an interest in treating each other respectfully. Even nations may be less belligerent when their economic well-being depends on the prosperity of their trading partners.

Finally, the market contributes to order by distributing society's benefits and burdens without visible political authority. Each person's success or failure appears to result from impersonal market forces, so there is no obvious target for resentment or envy. When individuals accept responsibility for their own fate, they are less likely to disrupt society.

Against the market. The dynamism of the market undermines traditional values and social structures. As individuals pursue their private interests, cohesive communities and shared purposes are increasingly displaced by the pursuit of satisfaction through consumption and ownership of commodities. This individualism undermines the self-restraint and virtue essential to social order. The market functions well only within a social context based on respect for ethical norms and individual rights. When self-interested behavior degenerates into unbridled selfishness, social bonds begin to unravel.

Another potential source of disorder in market societies arises from the conflict of interest between owners of productive property and workers dependent on employment for their livelihood. Owners generally seek maximum production from workers at minimum cost, while workers want higher wages and more satisfying working conditions. This conflict may extend beyond the workplace as class resentment and hostility manifest themselves in crime and racial and ethnic unrest.

GOVERNMENT AS A POLITICAL INSTITUTION

As a political institution, government seems well-suited to pursue justice by promoting freedom, equity, and order. However, government also has significant potential to violate these ideals.

Freedom

For government. Government enables citizens to reach goals they would be unable to attain through private action, and therefore contributes to freedom by broadening the range of feasible choices. For example, education, national defense, and security from crime may be better obtained through government financing.

Freedom is more than the absence of external constraints; it also requires a basic level of material well-being and a social environment conducive to developing and practicing a broad range of human capacities. Government may contribute to these conditions of freedom and also restrain powerful individuals and groups from restricting the freedom of others.

By providing an alternative to the market as an arena in which goals can be pursued, government not only increases the choices available to citizens but allows for the development of a broader range of preferences and values. For example, citizens' commitment to racial equality or environmental protection may be strengthened when they observe the authority of government being directed toward those goals. Government serves as a model and teacher, enabling citizens to develop their capacities more fully.

Against government. Few public policies have unanimous support and, therefore, government necessarily infringes on the freedom of some citizens. Taxes, regulations, and laws are considered legitimate restrictions when they are approved by the majority, do not violate individual rights, and are aimed at promoting the public interest. However, since modern societies often lack a clear consensus on the meaning of both individual rights and the public interest, particular government actions may be perceived as violations of freedom. More generally, democratic governments may be coercive to the extent that they enable the will of the majority to be imposed on the minority.

With its monopoly on the legitimate use of force through command over the police and military, government has the potential to severely restrict freedom. Some governments have either revised or abandoned the rule of law to engage in arbitrary arrest, seizure of property, and surveillance. Freedom can also be curtailed without resorting to visible oppression. If factions of society hold undue influence over government, it ceases to represent the public interest and becomes a tool with which powerful groups oppress their fellow citizens.

Equity

For government. Equity requires that people be treated in accordance with their rights. Whereas the market recognizes only property rights in determining the distribution of income, a broader conception of equity includes the recognition of human rights. Property rights entitle owners to market-determined earnings of their resources, while government assigns human rights to secure those individual interests deemed worthy of support, even if they are not backed by individual purchasing power. While equity based on property rights relies solely on the criterion of productivity, human rights may recognize other criteria of equity such as need, dignity, or simply a person's status as a citizen. If human rights entitle individuals to economic resources, only government can protect these rights and secure equity.

In the case of a clearly specified human right such as the right to legal counsel for accused criminals, government's responsibilities are discharged by providing public defenders. However, human rights are often not codified, but rather implied by legislation aimed at alleviating perceived inequities. For example, welfare programs and regulated prices imply that citizens have a right to a decent standard of living, but government has never explicitly enacted such a right. As a result, government's responsibilities in pursuing an equitable distribution of income are ill-defined and subject to ongoing political contestation.

Against government. A competitive market distributes income in accordance with the productivity of resources. When government overrides market distributions, it confronts the problem of formulating an alternative criterion of equity. A democratic government will respond to input from citizens, yet citizens with different conceptions of equity will send conflicting messages to government. Moreover, some citizens may promote their private goals by wrapping their appeals to government in the cloak of equity. For example, tobacco farmers may base their requests for government subsidies on the need for economic stimulus to regions lacking a strong industrial base.

These demands from citizens may degenerate into competition among interest groups seeking to control government for their own benefit. More powerful groups are likely to win this battle, enabling them to use government to oppress less advantaged groups. As a result, government itself may be perceived as a major source of inequity by those who lose income, status, or power as a result of taxes and regulations. In summary, when government supersedes the market's linkage of rewards with productivity, the absence of consensus on alternative criteria of fairness may result in widespread perceptions of inequity.

Order

For government. Government promotes orderly human interaction by defining and enforcing rights and obligations, thereby enabling individuals to form stable expectations of human behavior. Without public knowledge of the law, resolution of conflict would absorb substantial economic resources. Government also fosters order by maintaining society's culture, traditions, and boundaries. As a visible symbol and expression of society's collective identity, a respected government becomes an object of psychological allegiance, facilitating the formation of both individual identity and a sense of shared purpose and trust among citizens.

Government further contributes to order by promoting equality of opportunity. When disparities of income, wealth, and power impede social mobility for less advantaged persons, order is jeopardized by anger, frustration, and alienation. Finally, government secures order by altering incentives to make self-interest more consistent with the public interest. For example, the threat of punishment may discourage disorderly behavior. By controlling crime, government may reduce defensive aggression such as purchasing guns for self-protection.

Against government. Because government can supersede the market's distribution of income, citizens may attempt to use governmental authority to benefit themselves. Moreover, this process often becomes self-reinforcing. As some individuals or groups gain benefits from government, other citizens conclude that money flows to power, and power requires organization. Interest groups proliferate and demands on government intensify. This politicization of the economy may contribute to disorder in two ways. First, productive resources are diverted to the political struggle for control of government, resulting in slower growth and reduced competitiveness. Second, when government becomes a major determinant of individual success in a society lacking consensus about social justice, resentment toward government erodes support for public authority. Citizens perceive government as simply a tool with which some groups maintain privileges at the expense of others. The combination of a sluggish economy and political alienation results in social disorder.

GOVERNMENT AS AN ECONOMIC INSTITUTION

A primary human goal is the quest for security. One strategy for achieving security is individual action aimed at claiming resources for private use; such behavior created the market as a social institution. However, an alternative approach to security is cooperation and purposeful coordination of human activities to increase a group's ability to cope with scarcity and uncertainty. Because collective action can often be more effective than individual action, humans have a strong interest in forming organizations with rules and structures of authority. These organizations range from labor unions to corporations to government. Government is unique in that its laws are applicable to all persons within its jurisdiction and can be enforced through the legitimate use of force. One reason citizens consent to governmental authority is to secure justice, but government also contributes to the economic goals of efficiency, growth, and stability.

Efficiency

For government. Government may improve efficiency by responding to imperfections in the market. For example, lack of information can be remedied by government provision. Concentrations of private power that impede competition can be addressed with antitrust lawsuits, regulation, or public

ownership. When externalities exist, government can redirect resources by
taxing, subsidizing, regulating, or directly financing goods such as national
defense and highways.

Government also promotes efficiency by enhancing the quality and quantity of resources available for production. During recessions, government
may pursue policies to create jobs and increase production. Public education
contributes to a skilled labor force. The stability created by a system of laws
encourages owners of resources to engage their assets in risky ventures. Even
the redistributive activities of government may promote efficiency by revital-
izing human resources and by creating the perception of fairness. Individuals
work together more effectively when they share a sense of community, and
social solidarity is enhanced by an equitable distribution of income.

In addition to improving economic efficiency, government can contribute to a broader social efficiency by pursuing goals incapable of attainment in the market. Citizens may want safe neighborhoods, clean air, and
social justice, but the market responds only to money-backed demand for
profitable commodities. If preferences for noncommodities are also recognized, then efficiency requires government action to reallocate resources.

Against government. Government lacks the internal pressure for efficiency created by competitive market forces. Since public goods are
financed through compulsory taxation, government may provide unsatisfactory services without fear of losing customers. Moreover, bureaucratic
processes are typically slow and inflexible. All these problems are com-
pounded by the self-interest of politicians and bureaucrats whose pursuit
of higher incomes and increased power may subvert efficiency.

Even when politicians have the best of intentions, government may be
insensitive to citizens' preferences communicated through voting. Elections
are held only periodically, and voters must select among candidates offering entire packages of programs. As a result, voters cannot precisely specify which programs they support. The voting process also fails to allow
citizens to express the intensity of their preferences, and, with a system of
majority rule, those citizens who are outvoted will be forced to pay taxes
for programs they do not support. For these reasons, voting may be a less
efficient method for registering preferences than is the process of spending
money in the market.

In addition to its own inefficiency, government may cause inefficiency in
the market by imposing regulations, altering incentives, and redirecting
resources. Government intervention undermines the security of property
rights and reduces the motivation of individuals to make rational choices. In
theory, the buyer of a commodity in the market pays the full cost and enjoys
the full benefit of that commodity, but the costs and benefits of public goods
are spread across the entire population. Since individuals will neither bear the
full cost nor enjoy the full benefit of their political choices, they are less motivated to make decisions based on careful assessments of costs and benefits.

Growth

For government. Growth is contingent on the ability of society to produce more than it consumes and to direct this surplus into productive investment. Government may be able to improve the market's ability to produce a surplus. When custom and tradition keep resources out of productive use, government has the power to pry these resources loose and place them into active production. Furthermore, with its control over taxes, spending, and interest rates, government can steer resources toward capital accumulation. By financing education and research, government can contribute to the long-run growth of the economy. Finally, government reduces uncertainty for private investors by establishing well-defined property rights, a smoothly functioning legal system, and stable market conditions.

Against government. Government taxation and borrowing absorb money that might otherwise have flowed into productive private investment. Regulations may divert resources from their most efficient use and contribute to stagnation. Subsidies and other forms of protective legislation shield firms from competitive pressures to innovate and modernize. Government redistribution of income may undermine incentives to engage in productive activity. Not only is the positive incentive of higher income diminished by taxes and regulations, but the disincentives posed by hunger and deprivation are partially removed by welfare programs and social security. Government efforts to achieve greater equality through income redistribution tend to penalize success and reward failure, potentially diminishing the market's dynamic potential for growth.

Stability

For government. The very presence of government authority increases stability by minimizing conflict and providing security of property. Appropriate government policies encourage "business confidence" that is essential to stability. Even policies opposed by some businesses may be beneficial to the economy. For example, antitrust policies, minimum-wage laws, and progressive taxation can counterbalance the market's tendency to foster concentrations of wealth and power that jeopardize stability. Finally, when recession or inflation occurs, government can respond with appropriate fiscal or monetary policies.

Against government. Government efforts to redirect resources and alter the distribution of income may, by reducing profitability and undermining business confidence, contribute to instability. Government also has the power to create a "political business cycle" as politicians seeking reelection overstimulate the economy in hopes of creating a temporary boom to please voters. Once the election is over, the stimulus is withdrawn and the economy slips into recession. Even when government officials act with the best of intentions, the tools of monetary and fiscal policy may increase instability. By the time bureaucrats and politicians recognize a problem, formulate a response, implement the policy, and wait for results, economic conditions may have changed so that the policy is no longer appropriate. More generally, by seeking to perpetuate prosperity, government may suppress the mechanisms, such as rising interest rates, that allow the market to stabilize itself. When prosperity is artificially prolonged, the subsequent recession may be more severe.

POLITICAL ECONOMY

Analysis of the market and government as political and economic institutions suggests that neither is solely capable of organizing society to secure prosperity and justice. Both institutions are sufficiently flawed to require a balancing of political and economic processes to sustain a healthy society. In a positive sense, each institution serves to complement weaknesses of the other. However, the market and government also generate powerful forces reverberating against each other with potentially damaging consequences.

Since the market and government interact with each other, efforts to analyze them separately will yield only partial, and therefore distorted, understandings of the social system. Politics and economics are simply two facets of the process by which society is organized to achieve both individual and community goals. To study this process, the interdisciplinary approach provided by political economy is essential. Although political economy was abandoned by most social scientists in the nineteenth century, events of the twentieth century have accentuated its relevance. As a result of the Great Depression and two world wars, issues such as growth, distribution, and stability were transformed from economic into political issues. The boundary between public life and private life was redrawn, with politics encompassing an ever-larger realm of human activity. More recently, deterioration of the natural environment and growing concerns about the quality of life have led to renewed conflict and negotiation over the appropriate boundary between public and private spheres. As the domains of politics and economics vie for dominance, the interdisciplinary approach of political economy offers great potential for analyzing and responding to the problems confronting modern societies.

ADDITIONAL READING

Bell, Daniel, and Irving Kristol. *The Crisis in Economic Theory*. New York: Basic Books, 1981.
Boulding, Kenneth. *Towards a New Economics*. Brookfield, VT: Edward Elgar, 1992.

Brittan, Samuel. *Capitalism with a Human Face*. Cambridge: Harvard University Press, 1995.

Dahl, Robert A., and Charles E. Lindblom. *Politics, Economics, and Welfare*. New York: Harper & Row, 1953.

Etzioni, Amitai. *The Moral Dimension: Toward a New Economics*. New York: Free Press, 1988.

Heilbroner, Robert. *Behind the Veil of Economics*. New York: W. W. Norton, 1988.

Hirschman, Albert O. *Rival Views of Market Society*. New York: Viking Press, 1986.

Kuttner, Robert. *Everything For Sale: The Virtues and Limits of Markets*. New York: Alfred A. Knopf, 1997.

Lane, Robert. *The Market Experience*. Cambridge: Cambridge University Press, 1991.

Levine, David P. *Wealth and Freedom: An Introduction to Political Economy*. New York: Cambridge University Press, 1995.

Lindblom, Charles E. *Democracy and Market Systems*. Oslo: Norwegian University Press, 1988.

Lowe, Adolph. *Essays in Political Economics: Public Control in a Democratic Society*. New York: New York University Press, 1987.

Lutz, Mark A., and Kenneth Lux. *Humanistic Economics: The New Challenge*. New York: Bootstrap Press, 1988.

Wolf, Charles, Jr. *Markets or Governments: Choosing Between Imperfect Alternatives*. Cambridge: MIT Press, 1988.

Chapter 2

The History of Political Economy

A study of the history of opinion is a necessary preliminary to
the emancipation of the mind.
John Maynard Keynes

He who knows only his own side of the case knows little of that.
John Stuart Mill

Current political and economic issues cannot be fully understood without
an appreciation of the historical evolution of both institutions and ideas.
Although the history of political economy remains obscure for most citizens, many of its ideas have become part of the collective wisdom of society. Before beginning a survey of political economy, a word of caution is in
order. All history is subject to interpretation, and the history of ideas is particularly controversial. No single interpretation of the history of political
economy commands universal agreement.

ORIGINS OF POLITICAL ECONOMY

The period between the fourteenth and eighteenth centuries witnessed a
"great transformation" in Western Europe as the impact of commerce
gradually eroded the feudal economy of the Middle Ages. The newly

emerging market economy provided opportunities for the expression of individual aspirations and encouraged entrepreneurial behavior that had previously been suppressed by church, state, and the community. Although the church struggled to maintain its control over society by placing limitations on the accumulation and use of property, the growing desire of individuals to free themselves from social constraints led to diminishing popular support for both the church and the feudal state.

Along with changes in production and trade, new ideas were emerging. The Renaissance of the fourteenth century paved the way for the scientific inquiries of Copernicus, Galileo, Bacon, and Newton. Another impetus for change came from the Protestant Reformation initiated by Martin Luther in Germany. By the early eighteenth century, the Age of Reason, or Enlightenment, had arrived, and with it came a rejection of the medieval view of society as a divinely ordered hierarchy in which each person had a proper role and purpose. The new worldview centered around the autonomous individual and the human capacity for reason.

The Enlightenment was most prominent in France, where thinkers such as Voltaire, Diderot, D'Alembert, and Condillac sought to demolish superstition and tradition by subjecting all aspects of human existence to the scrutiny of reason. These philosophers believed that most human problems were attributable to poorly structured institutions and to uncritical acceptance of traditional authority emanating from church and state. They blamed prejudice, intolerance, and emotions for suppressing the human capacity to envision a better society and to act accordingly. The leaders of the Enlightenment were optimistic about the power of reason to clear away the debris of past mistakes, leaving an open path for continual social improvement.

To free reason from the shackles of existing traditions, Enlightenment thinkers demanded the liberation of the individual from all social, political, and religious bonds. Only then could humans choose rationally without the taint of prejudice, loyalty, or superstition, and they would presumably choose to abolish all institutions that could not be justified as serving the enlightened interests of mankind. Leaders of the Enlightenment called for nothing less than a total restructuring of society.

Science rose to prominence during this period because it seemed to offer a method for distinguishing between truth and superstition. By revealing the universal laws that govern nature and society, science would liberate mankind from both material deprivation and social oppression. Although the scientific method was initially applied to the external environment, it soon was turned toward the analysis of human existence, first to understand the physical functioning of the body, and then to investigate the operation of the mind. With advances in the understanding of human behavior, Enlightenment thinkers began to anticipate a science of society. If the laws and regularities of human interaction could be understood, a scientific basis for identifying the ideal set of social institutions would be established.

This emergent science of society came to be known as political economy. The same rational, economizing principles that individuals applied to the pursuit of their private interests would be extended to restructure the entire polity. The actual term "political economy" was introduced in 1616 by a French writer, Antoyne de Montchrétien (1575–1621), in his book *Treatise on Political Economy*. The first known English usage occurred in 1767 with the publication of *Inquiry into the Principles of Political Economy* by Sir James Steuart (1712–1780). These early political economists sought to develop guidelines and offer policy recommendations for government efforts to stimulate commerce. Markets were still relatively undeveloped at the time, so government took on significant responsibilities in opening new areas for trade, offering protection from competition, and providing control over product quality. The ideas and policies developed for this early stage of capitalism came to be known as "mercantilism." Active involvement by government in the economy was thought to be a necessary condition for economic prosperity.

By the late eighteenth century, however, the prevailing attitude toward government changed dramatically. Many manufacturers and merchants perceived government not as a beneficent director of economic activities, but as a major obstacle to the pursuit of wealth. Their hostility toward government was based on changing economic and political conditions. In its early stages of development, a flourishing market economy requires that producers have ready access to resources in the form of easily purchasable commodities. In addition, both producers and consumers must be free to pursue their interests relatively unencumbered by social customs and political authority. Both of these conditions were rapidly materializing in England by the second half of the eighteenth century.

The formation of markets for resources proceeded along three lines. First, the elimination of many single-family farms created a market for cheap and mobile labor. Second, the accumulation of wealth through piracy, looting, and early successes in commerce created a mass of financial capital available for borrowing. Third, the confiscation and subsequent sale of church property and public land that had previously been reserved for common use created a market for land. As for political freedom, the combination of the Magna Carta, the English civil war, and the Glorious Revolution of 1688 greatly diminished the power of the monarch and the aristocracy. With these changes in place, the market became a dynamic engine for the production of wealth, far overshadowing the power of government to dispense privileges and grant protection. The future was clearly discernible; the market would become the dominant institution for organizing society.

The subsequent evolution of political economy over the next two centuries is depicted in Figure 2.1. The remainder of this chapter and the next four chapters provide elucidation of this diagram.

Figure 2.1
The History of Political Economy

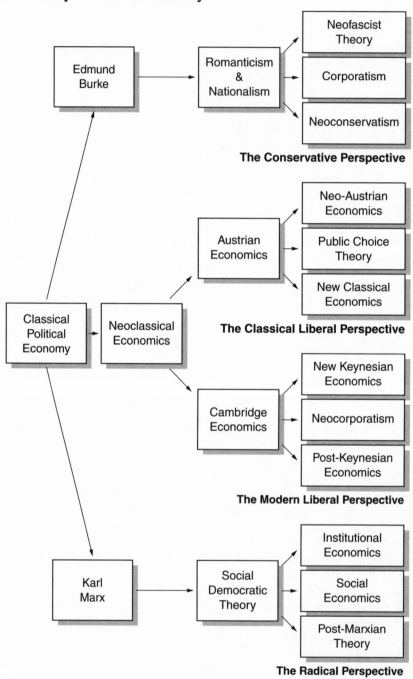

Edmund Burke → Romanticism & Nationalism →

Neofascist Theory

Corporatism

Neoconservatism

The Conservative Perspective

Classical Political Economy → Neoclassical Economics → Austrian Economics →

Neo-Austrian Economics

Public Choice Theory

New Classical Economics

The Classical Liberal Perspective

Cambridge Economics →

New Keynesian Economics

Neocorporatism

Post-Keynesian Economics

The Modern Liberal Perspective

Karl Marx → Social Democratic Theory →

Institutional Economics

Social Economics

Post-Marxian Theory

The Radical Perspective

CLASSICAL POLITICAL ECONOMY

Adam Smith (1723–1790), a Scottish professor of moral philosophy, was fascinated by the market's potential for promoting both individual freedom and material prosperity. Although he was not the first person to advocate laissez-faire policies by government, his book *The Wealth of Nations* (1776) presented the case for free markets with such wisdom that it formed the basis for classical political economy. This school of thought dates roughly from 1776 to the mid-nineteenth century and its proponents include, in addition to Smith, Thomas Malthus (1766–1834), David Ricardo (1772–1823), Nassau Senior (1790–1864), and Jean Baptiste Say (1767–1832).

Classical political economists combined both optimism and pessimism in their visions of a market economy. The optimism centers around the anticipation that the market will generate both increasing wealth and individual freedom without the need for supervision by church or state. In this sense, classical political economy is linked with the Enlightenment, demonstrating that when the shackles of religious and political restrictions are removed, individuals will prosper and society will remain orderly.

Yet beneath this rosy vision lurked impending disaster. Adam Smith repeatedly suggested that the market could not work its magic indefinitely. Malthus and Ricardo were even more pessimistic. With population growing rapidly and the available supply of land relatively fixed, they predicted an inevitable future of subsistence living for the vast majority of the population. Landlords would prosper as they received ever-larger rents due to the increasing demand for land on which to grow food, but capitalists' profits would dwindle as they were forced to pay higher wages so workers could afford to buy increasingly expensive food. Eventually profits would be insufficient to provide capitalists with either the incentive or the means to expand production, and the entire economy would settle into a gloomy "stationary state."

Despite these predictions of widespread poverty and an end to growth, classical political economists remained largely committed to laissez-faire. The future would be grim, but attempts by government to intervene would only worsen the situation because government could control neither the scarcity of land nor the human tendency to overpopulate. The only relief would come from depopulation caused by plagues, famines, and war, or from trade with other countries possessing plentiful land and cheap food.

THE RADICAL EXTENSION

As classical political economy veered toward pessimism, Radical theorists continued to defend the Enlightenment vision of continual progress through the rational reconstruction of society. From the Radical perspective, the classical political economists were failing to carry out the mission of the Enlightenment. Although the power of the state had been challenged and restrained, the power of private property had actually increased due to the elimination of most government restraints. In the spirit of the Enlightenment, Radicals demanded that every aspect of society be subjected to criticism to see whether it could withstand the test of reason. The rights of private property were viewed as no more sacrosanct than the authority of church or state.

Central to the Radical call for a reconstruction of society was a strong commitment to egalitarianism. Until all persons directly participated in the formation of the institutions governing their lives and shared in the benefits derived from those institutions, society would necessarily appear arbitrary and oppressive, and individuals would remain alienated. Radicals condemned private property for breeding selfish interests that conflict with the common good of society. In a private property system, individuals have opposing interests and social cohesion disintegrates as the owners of property oppress those with little or no property. Although each individual is free to choose, oppression arises because inequality of property makes the poor vulnerable to exploitation as the threat of starvation coerces them to work for subsistence wages.

Radicals also condemned private property for alienating individuals from any sense of community or control over their work. Relying on the optimism of the Enlightenment, they concluded that people can join together to collectively direct their social existence. Radicals envisioned a classless society in which free individuals could live in harmony with each other in their work, their communities, and their government. Such a society would be egalitarian and communal, with citizens sharing a broad range of common interests, including a commitment to maintain appropriate conditions for the development and security of every person. Genuine freedom requires access to sufficient resources for well-rounded human development and hence can be secured only when the community as a whole controls productive property.

Examples of early Radical thinkers include William Godwin (1756–1836) in England, Thomas Paine (1737–1809) in America, and the Marquis de Condorcet (1743–1794) in France. These writers were opposed not so much to the principle of private property as to the excessive concentration of ownership that restricted the opportunities and freedom of the majority of the population. In the early 1800s, thinkers such as Robert Owen (1771–1858) of England and Charles Fourier (1772–1837) and Henri de Saint-Simon (1760–1825) of France popularized the idea of eliminating private property. These "utopian socialists" formulated detailed plans for small communities based on shared ownership of property. Owen actually put his ideas into practice, moving to the United States with a group of followers to establish a community in Indiana called New Harmony. Hundreds of other small experiments with communal living occurred during the nineteenth century in both Europe and North America. Growing apprehension over the effects of industrialization and modernization undoubtedly spurred this interest in alternative forms of society. The loss of tradition, the squalor of large cities, and conditions in the early factories persuaded many people that fundamental change was required to improve the quality of human existence.

The influence of Radical thought was heightened immeasurably by Karl Marx (1818–1883), a German philosopher and political economist who constructed an impressive theoretical analysis of capitalism by weaving together classical political economy, the ideas of the German philosopher G. W. F. Hegel (1770–1831), and the communal vision of the utopian socialists. Building on the pessimistic theories of the classical political economists, Marx developed an elaborate theoretical argument that capitalism would eventually crumble and be replaced by a society in which the means of production were communally owned and operated. This new society, Marx claimed, was incubating within capitalism and its birth would coincide with the death of the parent. Thus, unlike the utopian socialists who sought to turn their backs on capitalist society, Marx portrayed capitalism as the essential precondition for a new and better organization of society. In capitalist factories, workers were acquiring the technical knowledge, cooperative skills, and sense of solidarity that would enable them to revolt and establish a communal society.

After Marx's death, his ideas inspired several distinct political traditions. Several theorists, including Georgi Plekhanov (1857–1918) in Russia and Karl Liebknecht (1871–1919) and Karl Kautsky (1854-1938) in Germany upheld Marx's belief in the historical inevitability of communism. However, when a proletarian revolution failed to appear by the early twentieth century, Russian theorists V. I. Lenin (1870–1924) and Leon Trotsky (1879–1940) introduced into Marxism the notion of a "vanguard party" of intellectuals who would lead the workers in the struggle for socialism. This strand of Marxism served as the theoretical basis for the Soviet Union.

In Western Europe and the United States, a different revision of Marx's ideas was formulated by theorists such as Edward Bernstein (1850–1932) in Germany, Sidney and Beatrice Webb (1859–1947 and 1858–1943) in England, Jean Jaurès (1859–1914) in France, and Eugene Debs (1855–1926) and Norman Thomas (1884–1968) in the United States. Acknowledging the rising standard of living enjoyed by workers in capitalist societies, these "social democrats" rejected the Marxian concept of proletarian revolution. Instead, they defended socialism as a more just and efficient economic system whose obvious appeal to the working class would permit an evolutionary transition from capitalism to socialism through the democratic political process. The task of the revisionists was not to foment revolution, but to establish a working-class political party and to educate all citizens about the attractions of socialism.

Another important figure in the historical evolution of Radical thought was the U.S. economist Thorstein Veblen (1857–1929). Veblen rejected much of Marxism as being unscientific and metaphysical, but he remained a trenchant critic of capitalism. His ideas became influential in the Progressive political movement in the United States that sought to reform capitalism by enlarging the role of government in coordinating economic activity.

THE CONSERVATIVE RESPONSE

The progress fostered by the Enlightenment was a mixed blessing. The attack on repressive social institutions broadened the scope for individual initiative and development, resulting in the industrialization and urbanization of western Europe. However, disintegration of the traditional social order created both economic and emotional insecurity for many people. Feudalism had been based on stable, hierarchical social relations, with individual identity derived from one's role within a web of mutual expectations and duties. Such a society may have repressed initiative, but it did provide familiarity and stability within a community. In contrast, the newly emerging industrial society wrenched people out of their accustomed roles. A person might grow up in a rural village, migrate to the nearest city, and seek employment in a factory surrounded by hundreds of other similarly uprooted workers. People no longer felt "at home" in an unfamiliar world of anonymous strangers.

The market's need for readily available resources resulted in most citizens being separated from any viable means of self-sufficiency. Many small farmers, having lost their land, became itinerant workers available for hire. Skilled artisans, who might previously have been members of professional guilds, could not compete against mechanized industry and were forced to seek employment in the factories. Even aristocrats suffered declining power and status as capital replaced land as the primary source of wealth. With these changes, the social bonds maintaining the hierarchical order of feudal society began to disintegrate. People formerly enmeshed in extended families, neighborhoods, churches, and communities now faced the impersonal forces of the market as isolated entities.

The French Revolution of 1789 magnified concerns about a "dark side" of the Enlightenment. The linkage between this conflict and Enlightenment thinking is evidenced by the revolutionaries' call for "liberty, equality, fraternity." The chaos and bloodshed of the revolution cast doubt on the effort to remake society in accordance with human reason. To halt the corrosive impact of the Enlightenment, a renewed defense of traditional society was needed.

Edmund Burke (1729–1797), an Irish member of the British parliament, was among the first to develop a Conservative critique of the Enlightenment. Burke claimed that the Enlightenment effort to fundamentally restructure society was destroying the authority and emotional attachments that unite individuals into communities. Self-interested human reason, he posited, will always resent authority for placing limitations on the scope of individual action. But without authority, all persons suffer as society degenerates into a morass of conflicting desires and passions. Since human reason was not a reliable guide for redesigning society, Burke proposed that the exercise of reason should be confined to efforts by individuals to improve their private lives. The grand schemes of intellectuals and utopians would only disrupt the traditional patterns of human interaction, engendering chaos.

Attempting to develop a defense of established traditions, Burke and subsequent Conservatives looked back to the merits of medieval society. A stable social order must be grounded in traditional institutions such as the church and the patriarchal family. When efforts to reconstruct society destroy traditional institutions, individuals are uprooted from their customary roles in the community. Deprived of a cultural heritage, isolated individuals lose meaning in their lives, become concerned solely with self-gratification, and neglect their duties to others and to society as a whole. From the Conservative perspective, the degeneration of the French Revolution into violent anarchy was attributable to individualism and the pursuit of self-interest. The Revolution foreshadowed an impending collapse of civilization that could be averted only by strengthening traditional values and institutions.

As the Enlightenment was sweeping Great Britain and France, a reaction was brewing in Germany. Having been subjected to military conquest by France and the threat of economic domination by British industry, many Germans expressed disdain toward the cultures of their western neighbors. Fearing the cosmopolitan values and lifestyles spawned by urban industrial society, they were determined to avoid disintegration of their own culture. This reaction to the Enlightenment has been labeled "romanticism." Writers such as Johann Fichte (1762–1814), August von Schlegel (1767–1845), Friedrich von Schelling (1775–1854), and Johann Herder (1744–1803) expressed their opposition to the effects of modernization on Germanic culture. Whereas the Enlightenment stressed the rationality of humans, the importance of science, and the mechanical nature of reality, the German romantics defended the unpredictability and irrationality of humans, the importance of traditional culture in maintaining a cohesive society, and a view of reality that includes spiritual and even mystical elements. Rather than adopting the analytical methods of modern science, the romantics sought to develop their intuition and instincts, their passions and feelings, their sensitivity to beauty, and their sense of harmony with nature. They believed that personal fulfillment could be achieved only within the context of a stable culture based on widely shared values. From their perspective, the Enlightenment view of humans as autonomous, rational, and calculating, merely described the sordid conditions of English culture. The autonomy so highly prized by Enlightenment thinkers was, for the romantics, isolation from the social bonds essential to human happiness.

Even England, the most industrialized country in the world, experienced a flourishing romantic movement. Partly inspired by their German counterparts, British writers such as Samuel Taylor Coleridge (1772–1834), William Wordsworth (1770–1850), and William Blake (1757–1827) expressed the common theme that society had been damaged by modernization and industrialization. Blake referred to the early factories as "dark, satanic mills," and English romantics were generally contemptuous of business and commerce. They sought happiness and fulfillment by turning away from modern society to focus on unspoiled nature and metaphysical contemplation. Ironically, this inward focus on the self would subsequently steer many romantic writers toward support of liberal and radical notions of individual freedom from repressive social institutions. For this reason, romanticism today remains ideologically ambiguous.

A similar ambiguity surrounds the second major thread of nineteenth-century Conservatism. Nationalism originally flourished as an outgrowth of the liberal Enlightenment ideals of popular sovereignty and the rights of man. The idea that a group of people sharing a common language, culture, and heritage could collectively determine their future lay at the root of the French Revolution and many other conflicts of the late eighteenth and early nineteenth centuries. However, the alliance between nationalism and liberalism was short-lived. Whereas liberalism stresses the rights of autonomous individuals, nationalism demands submersion of personal identity in the national group. After the defeat of Napoleon in 1815, a Conservative reaction swept across Europe as governments sought to strengthen their nations against the demands for democracy and individual freedom.

By the mid-nineteenth century, Conservatives in Europe had gained the upper hand in their battle against the forces unleashed by the Enlightenment. The failures of the revolutions of 1848 persuaded Conservatives that the masses could be allowed some participation in politics without destabilizing society. Later in the nineteenth century, Bismarck in Germany and Disraeli in England sought to gain popular support for Conservative governments by establishing rudimentary welfare programs. Government would replace the aristocracy in dispensing charity.

However, an even more important change in Conservatism was the harnessing of nationalist sentiments to promote the goals of stability, order, state power, and economic expansion. Conservatives claimed that a true nation is more than just a collection of individuals sharing the same geographical space; it is based on a common language, common bloodlines, and common culture. This emphasis on cultural purity led Conservative nationalists to oppose free trade. Any nation opening its borders to the free flow of resources, products, and ideas will gradually lose its unique identity, without which, the shared values forming bonds between individuals disintegrate and a nation loses its vitality and power. Only government can effectively oppose the cosmopolitan influences of the international market economy. A strong government enables a nation to be self-determining, free from constraints imposed by other nations and by the forces of the market.

Conservative nationalism is typically linked with cultural and political chauvinism, which explains why racial and ethnic strife, imperialism, and war often accompany nationalist sentiments. The desire for self-determination frequently results in military conquest to expand national borders or spheres of influence against real or imagined foreign threats. Nationalists also find war and imperialism to be useful in diverting public attention away from internal problems and toward the glory and prestige of the nation. Some writers even touted war as a rare opportunity for individuals to transcend the routine of everyday life and display the noble human sentiments of courage, valor, strength, and patriotism. An illustrious example of a nineteenth-century nationalist is the German historian and philosopher Heinrich von Treitschke (1834–1896), whose racist and militarist writings would later provide inspiration for Adolf Hitler (1889–1945) and the Nazi movement.

NEOCLASSICAL ECONOMICS

The rise of Radicalism and Conservatism established alternatives to classical political economy. However, both perspectives met with considerable opposition. Radicalism aroused fears of the confiscation of private property, while many regarded Conservatism as a threat to democracy and modernization. Despite the resistance to Radical and Conservative ideas, the influence of classical political economy waned during the nineteenth century for several reasons. The classical predictions of widespread poverty and slowing growth failed to materialize, raising doubts about the theories underlying those forecasts. Also, Marx's use of classical political economy to attack capitalism caused mainstream political economists to dissociate themselves from Smith and Ricardo. Finally, the combination of an increasingly powerful working class and social problems accompanying industrialization created new demands for government intervention to improve education, old-age security, public health, and occupational safety. In the face of these pressures, the policy of laissez-faire became increasingly unpopular.

With the three dominant perspectives all seemingly flawed, an ideological vacuum was developing. The time was ripe for a new approach to political economy capable of defending both democracy and private property. In 1871, three theorists, writing separately and unknown to one another, simultaneously developed this new theory. Carl Menger (1840–1921) of Austria, W. Stanley Jevons (1835–1882) of England, and Leon Walras (1834–1910) of Switzerland changed the focus of political economy from the classical concern with distribution and growth to a "neoclassical" orientation that dealt solely with the behavior of individual consumers and firms operating in competitive markets.

To emphasize their focus on individual choice, the neoclassical theorists even changed the name of their field of study. Jevons referred to political economy as "the old troublesome double-worded name of our science" and urged his colleagues to replace it with the term "economics." His suggestion gained wide acceptance, and by the beginning of the twentieth century, neoclassical economics had attained dominant status among competing perspectives in political economy. Neoclassical economists sought to construct a theory that matched the scientific rigor of physics. To achieve this goal, they applied mathematics as an analytical method to explain the choices of individual consumers and producers. Under conditions of perfect competition, individuals would engage in mutually beneficial exchanges until they gained the most satisfaction possible from the resources at their command—a situation labeled as efficient by the neoclassical economists. Having demonstrated that free markets result in efficiency, the neoclassical economists largely affirmed the classical prescription of laissez-faire while avoiding the objectionable ideas of class conflict and economic stagnation.

Although early neoclassical economists shared many of the same values and tools of analysis, disagreement among economists in Austria and England gave rise to two separate traditions: Austrian economics and Cambridge economics. Austrian economists were undoubtedly influenced by the political climate in their country during the late nineteenth century. As the Hapsburg empire crumbled, the working class grew increasingly receptive to socialist ideas. In this environment, a group of academic economists in Vienna, including Carl Menger, Friedrich von Wieser (1851–1926), and Eugen von Böhm-Bawerk (1851–1914) sought to demonstrate the appeal of a free-market economy with virtually no government intervention.

In addition to defending the virtues of capitalism, Austrian economists have been harsh critics of Marxism and socialism. Ludwig von Mises (1881–1973) claimed that without the forces of supply and demand operating in a free market, prices could not accurately reflect consumer preferences or the relative scarcity of different resources. Socialist planners, he argued, could not possibly gather enough information about resource availability and consumer preferences to permit calculation of appropriate prices for all products and resources. As a result, shortages and surpluses for different commodities would inevitably plague a socialist economy and inefficiency would be rampant. Only capitalism provides incentive for gathering the information required for efficient choices by allowing individuals to reap the rewards of their own foresight, initiative, and innovation.

In contrast to Austrian economists, Stanley Jevons and subsequent economists at Cambridge University recognized a more positive role for government. Although committed to preserving the freedom of individual choice, their analysis of market failures provided rationales for government intervention to improve the workings of the market. The most prominent of the early Cambridge economists, Alfred Marshall (1842–1924), demonstrated that economic efficiency could be enhanced by taxing those industries in which average costs rose as output expanded and using the revenue to subsidize those industries, such as utilities and transportation, in which average costs fell as they served more customers.

Another Cambridge economist, Arthur C. Pigou (1877–1959), developed the analysis of externalities in which the market fails to allocate resources efficiently because the actions of one person or firm create costs or benefits that are not reflected in market prices. Pigou recommended taxation of those actions creating external costs and subsidies for actions creating external benefits. Since externalities pervade society, the scope for government intervention created by this market failure is potentially quite large.

In 1933, Cambridge economist Joan Robinson (1903–1982) showed that the absence of perfect competition will cause an inefficient allocation of resources and exploitation of workers. She suggested that government could intervene either to promote competition or to directly respond to the problems caused by lack of competition. Three years later, the most significant contribution of Cambridge economics occurred with John Maynard Keynes's (1883–1946) powerful claim that laissez-faire capitalism is inherently prone to depression and unemployment. To remedy this problem, he proposed active government policies to stimulate the market.

MODERN POLITICAL ECONOMY

Within the field of political economy, four broad perspectives currently contend for prominence: Classical Liberalism, Radicalism, Conservatism, and Modern Liberalism. The persistence of these dramatically different viewpoints attests to an irreducible ideological element in political economy. Scientific methods cannot resolve the disputes among alternative perspectives because their differences are ultimately based on commitments to conflicting values. To understand these divisions within political economy, we need to briefly review the historical evolution of ideological labels.

The ideas associated with the Enlightenment have traditionally been called "liberal." Liberalism stands for individual freedom and rights against the arbitrary exercise of power by church, state, and other persons. This commitment to individual freedom and autonomy originally made liberals strongly egalitarian in supporting equal rights for all citizens. In contrast to the hierarchical structure of feudal society, liberals anticipated that the consequence of equal rights would be substantially greater economic equality. As liberals challenged aristocratic privileges, the labels "right" and "left" became part of popular political discourse. In the French National Assembly of 1789, the defenders of aristocratic privilege and hierarchy stood on the right side of the chamber, while the proponents of greater equality and individual freedom stood on the left. As a result, proponents of equality have since been called "leftists," while those who defend hierarchy are called "rightists."

Rightists claim that hierarchical social relations are essential to a good society. Individuals need distinctions of status to differentiate themselves from others. A society lacking sufficient hierarchy will fail to provide incentives for citizens to excel, resulting in a stifling mediocrity and dragging the entire society into economic stagnation, boredom, and apathy. Rightists also defend hierarchy as essential to organize the complex social processes needed to maintain prosperity and order. Just as armies rely on hierarchical chains of command to wage war, other institutions such as corporations, schools, and families also must be hierarchically structured to achieve their objectives.

Leftists, on the other hand, claim that human development flourishes when individuals engage in cooperative, mutually respectful relations that can thrive only when excessive differences in status, power, and wealth are eliminated. According to leftists, a society without substantial equality will distort the development of not only deprived persons, but also those whose privileges undermine their motivation and sense of social responsibility. This suppression of human development, together with the resentment and conflict engendered by sharp class distinctions, will ultimately reduce the efficiency of the economy.

The right/left dichotomy is often treated as synonymous with the conservative/liberal dichotomy. Although this usage of ideological labels may have been appropriate for analyzing political debate in the late eighteenth century, modern discourse has become more complex. In addition to the dispute over hierarchy and equality, both rightists and leftists have developed internal splits over another question: should the private interests of individuals take precedence over the interests of society? Individualists defend the priority of individual interests, while communitarians defend the priority of society's interests.

Individualists claim that a community has no interests other than the aggregation of the individual interests within it. Therefore, the notion of a public interest or common good is a myth; the good community is one that allows individuals to freely pursue their private interests. Individualists are not directly concerned about the well-being of the community because they remain confident that any community securing individual freedom will be made prosperous by the energies and talents of its citizens. For individualists, freedom means the right to pursue one's interests with minimal constraint by society.

In contrast, communitarians view human development as a function of the quality of the social environment and therefore expect the community to provide a supportive and nurturing environment. By themselves, individuals are rather helpless in the face of social forces over which they have no control, but the community as a whole can consciously engage in actions to facilitate the development of individual interests and shape individual character.

Individualists and communitarians have sought to discredit each other through caricature. Communitarians are portrayed as supporting "anthill" or "beehive" societies in which members simply serve their assigned role with no room for individual creativity or expression. Individualists, on the other hand, are accused of advocating an amoral society in which selfish, isolated persons pursue their narrow interests, constrained only by laws and the threat of punishment. Yet communitarians are vigorous defenders of individual dignity, claiming that a nurturing community enables individuals to achieve their full potential. Conversely, individualists value healthy communities but argue that communities are most peaceful and prosperous when individuals are permitted to freely pursue their interests.

The debate between individualists and communitarians has occurred on both the right and left sides of the political spectrum, resulting in four major perspectives within political economy. The differences among these four perspectives are illustrated in Figure 2.2.

In the top-right quadrant, the Classical Liberal perspective is associated with both hierarchy and individualism. Although the earliest forms of liberal thought were highly egalitarian, by the beginning of the nineteenth century, many liberals concluded that the pursuit of individual freedom

Figure 2.2
Value Commitments of Perspectives in Political Economy

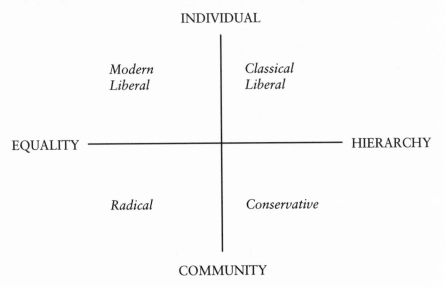

results in hierarchy and that hierarchy is essential for economic prosperity. Classical Liberalism was clearly articulated in the early nineteenth century by classical political economists and was later reinvigorated by neoclassical economists, particularly those of the Austrian school.

In the bottom-right quadrant, the Conservative perspective defends both hierarchy and community. Conservatives from Burke onward have stressed the importance of a harmonious community in molding virtuous persons, but they also view hierarchy as essential to provide leadership by those with superior abilities. A hierarchical community not only establishes the authority and traditions essential for inspiring loyalty and allegiance among citizens, but it also provides the social context within which individuals can successfully find meaning and purpose in their lives.

The bottom-left quadrant shows the Radical perspective combining commitments to both equality and community. Radicals uphold the original egalitarian impulse associated with early liberalism but view this goal as achievable only when the entire community is empowered to collectively establish institutions and allocate resources. Radicals believe that when all citizens participate in constructing society, both personal development and economic prosperity will advance.

Finally, the top-left quadrant illustrates the Modern Liberal perspective's simultaneous commitments to equality and individualism. Like Classical Liberals, Modern Liberals view individual autonomy as essential to guaranteeing both human dignity and a thriving economy; however, they also defend substantial equality as necessary for all persons to develop their capacities fully. Although Modern Liberals recognize potential conflicts between the values of individualism and equality, they remain confident that the two values can reinforce each other when the powers of government and the market are appropriately balanced.

The next four chapters examine each of these contending perspectives separately, seeking to develop an understanding of the value commitments underlying much of the controversy in political economy. This controversy represents more than mere academic debate; the future of mankind is literally at stake. As John Maynard Keynes observed: "The ideas of economists and political philosophers, both when they are right and when they are wrong, are more powerful than is commonly understood. Indeed, the world is ruled by little else."

ADDITIONAL READING

Arblaster, Anthony. *The Rise and Decline of Western Liberalism.* New York: Basil Blackwell, 1984.
Baradat, Leon P. *Political Ideologies: Their Origins and Impact,* 3rd ed. Englewood Cliffs, NJ: Prentice-Hall, 1988.

Cole, Ken, John Cammeron, and Chris Edwards. *Why Economists Disagree: The Political Economy of Economics*. New York: Longman, 1983.

Elliott, John E., and John Cownie, eds. *Competing Philosophies in American Political Economics*. Pacific Palisades, CA: Goodyear, 1975.

Heilbroner, Robert. *The Worldly Philosophers*, 6th ed. New York: Simon & Schuster, 1986.

Hoover, Kenneth. *Ideology and Political Life*. Monterey, CA: Brooks/Cole, 1987.

Polanyi, Karl. *The Great Transformation: The Political and Economic Origins of Our Time*. Boston: Beacon Press, 1944.

Prychitko, David L., ed. *Why Economists Disagree: An Introduction to the Alternative Schools of Thought*. Albany, NY: State University of New York Press, 1998.

Schwarzmantel, John. *The Age of Ideology*. New York: New York University Press, 1988.

Sowell, Thomas. *A Conflict of Visions: Ideological Origins of Political Struggles*. New York: William Morrow, 1987.

Spechler, Martin C. *Perspectives in Economic Thought*. New York: McGraw-Hill, 1990.

Voeglin, Eric. *From Enlightenment to Revolution*. Durham, NC: Duke University Press, 1975.

Ward, Benjamin. *The Ideal Worlds of Economics*. New York: Basic Books, 1979.

Whynes, David K., ed. *What Is Political Economy?* New York: Basil Blackwell, 1984.

PART II

CONTENDING
PERSPECTIVES IN
POLITICAL ECONOMY

Chapter 3

The Classical Liberal
Perspective

Classical Liberalism envisions society as an aggregation of autonomous individuals seeking to pursue their private interests. Ideally, all social interaction should consist of voluntary exchanges among persons, and every individual has the right to be free from the arbitrary exercise of power.

With its focus on individual choice as the primary determinant of social outcomes, Classical Liberalism is ideally suited for expression in the form of economic theory. In fact, the historical development of Classical Liberalism closely aligns with the history of economic thought, starting with classical political economy, continuing with the Austrian branch of neoclassical economics, and culminating in a variety of current bodies of thought including neo-Austrian economics, public choice theory, new classical economics, law and economics, new institutional economics, constitutional economics, libertarianism, supply-side economics, monetarism, and property-rights theory.

ARCHITECTS OF CLASSICAL LIBERALISM

Thomas Hobbes (1588–1679)

English philosopher Thomas Hobbes was one of the first social theorists to adopt the methods of the newly emerging natural sciences for the analysis of human behavior. Influenced by other philosophers such as

Francis Bacon (1561–1626) and René Descartes (1596–1650), Hobbes envisioned the world as a mechanical system operating according to precise laws of nature and devoid of any inherent meaning, purpose, or morality. He sought to uncover the natural laws governing society by analyzing individual behavior. Humans, he claimed, were constantly propelled into motion by the need to satisfy their appetites and desires. Although Hobbes acknowledged nonmaterial desires such as the need for social recognition, he claimed that such desires were best met by the pursuit of wealth. Furthermore, since the universal pursuit of wealth would bring individuals into conflict with one another, humans must become aggressively materialistic to protect themselves from others. In the absence of morality, humans will do whatever gives them pleasure and avoid whatever causes pain. Hobbes concluded that in a "state of nature" prior to government or laws, life would be "solitary, poor, nasty, brutish, and short" because a "war of all against all" would result from the unrestrained pursuit of wealth.

Since violence and death obviously interfere with pleasure, Hobbes reasoned that self-interested persons would voluntarily enter into a "social contract" with others to establish a government with absolute authority to define and protect individual rights. Two points about the social contract are noteworthy. First, it can include only laws that potentially could gain universal consent. Since people would presumably refuse to consent to any law that restrained or harmed them more than other individuals, the government cannot legitimately oppress any particular group or person. Second, since government is created by the people, it must serve the interests of the people. Hobbes opposed the idea of "divine right" as the source of royal power.

The Hobbesian legacy has had a major impact on Classical Liberalism. By starting his analysis with the isolated individual in a state of nature, Hobbes portrayed society and government as secondary and artificial creations. The pursuit of private interests is presumed to be the only purpose of human existence, with politics merely a necessary activity to maintain social order. Hobbes rejected the earlier Aristotelian notion of political activity as the site of human development gained through participation in public life.

Despite Hobbes's strong commitment to individualism, he concluded that government must have absolute authority to establish and enforce laws. So long as the monarch maintained public order, the people could not resist royal authority. The title of Hobbes's major book *Leviathan* (1651) has become synonymous with an authoritarian state. Thus, although Hobbes was a founder of Classical Liberalism, his conclusions about the scope of government authority have been rejected by subsequent Classical Liberals.

John Locke (1632–1704)

John Locke, an English philosopher and physician, followed the Hobbesian method by building his theories on assumptions about individuals in a state of nature. Like Hobbes, Locke assumed the self-interested and acquisitive nature of humans, but he believed that the capacity for reason enabled people to discover "natural laws" that would serve as guides both for restraining the pursuit of self-interest and defining the proper role of government. Whereas Hobbes relied on government to establish and protect property rights because his pessimistic view of humans made the "state of nature" an arena of violence, Locke claimed that property rights existed before government, and therefore government's authority was limited to protecting those natural rights.

In *Two Treatises of Government* (1689), Locke claimed that people's ownership of themselves and their labor is a self-evident truth. When individuals "mix" their labor with a part of nature unclaimed by anyone else, that portion of nature becomes their property. Since this process requires no government action or consent of others, Locke concluded that property rights are natural and therefore no person or government can legitimately violate them.

Locke's writings exhibit the dual commitment of Enlightenment thinkers to freedom and equality. His explanation of the origins of property rights seems to support unlimited freedom to accumulate property and therefore substantial inequality. However, Locke attached two "provisos" to the right to obtain property: property must be used without spoilage or waste, and any claim to property is valid only when "there is enough, and as good left in common for others." Yet, having placed these limits on accumulation, Locke proceeded to remove them. He argued that the use of money permits people to accumulate wealth without spoilage and that the "enough and as good" restriction becomes impractical once all valuable land in a country has been claimed.

Locke's apparent acceptance of unlimited accumulation should be understood within its historical context. At the dawn of the capitalist era, liberal thinkers were confident that individual rights and freedom would result in substantially more equality than had existed under feudal domination. Locke's defense of freedom to accumulate wealth was not insensitive to those who lacked property. He argued that private property benefits all persons in society; poor citizens are better off as wage laborers in a private-property system than if they were living in a society with communal ownership. This shift from defending property as a natural right to defending property for its social benefits is the beginning of a split within Classical Liberalism that ultimately gave birth to a new perspective—Modern Liberalism.

Adam Smith (1723–1790)

Adam Smith, a Scottish professor of moral philosophy, was the first to articulate Classical Liberalism in the form of economic theory rather than the political language of Hobbes and Locke. By Smith's time, political disorder in Great Britain had been largely resolved, and the task at hand was to raise the material standard of living.

In his first major work, *The Theory of Moral Sentiments* (1759), Smith argued that humans are able, through social interaction, to overcome their narrow self-interest and view situations from the perspective of an "impartial spectator." The human capacity for sympathy would restrain aggressive, selfish behavior and create a stable society. Yet Smith was deeply concerned that the emerging market economy unleashed powerful and potentially dangerous motives such as greed, envy, and selfishness. The aggressive pursuit of self-interest threatened to erode the social bonds of sympathy and concern for others. Given these pressures, Smith wondered whether human virtue could withstand the temptations of wealth.

Motivated by these concerns, Smith turned his attention from moral philosophy to political economy. After being introduced to the idea of laissez-faire by a group of French political economists known as the Physiocrats, he concluded that a market society could not only withstand the effects of acquisitive selfishness, but could actually steer this "vice" into productive and socially beneficial channels. Without meaning to do so, self-interested individuals actually promote the good of society by engaging their talents and resources in the most profitable use. By the time he published *The Wealth of Nations* in 1776, Adam Smith had substituted the market for individual conscience as the mechanism for reconciling self-interest with an orderly and prosperous society.

Although Smith is often portrayed as the champion of capitalism, he was not completely optimistic about the market. He found self-interest compatible with the public good only when competition prevailed, and he warned that businessmen would constantly seek to suppress competition and deceive the public to increase profits. Smith also expressed concern about the well-being of workers in a market economy. While he recognized the tremendous efficiency gained by dividing production into separate, routine tasks, he worried that the monotony and mindlessness of factory jobs would render workers "as stupid as it is possible for a human being to become." Finally, Smith set the tone for subsequent classical political economists with his fear that the dynamism and growth of a market society would eventually come to an end as profitable investment opportunities were exhausted.

Whatever qualms he may have expressed about capitalism, Adam Smith's legacy has been his defense of free markets and nonintervention by government. During the seventeenth and eighteenth centuries, mercantilist policies had involved government in taxing commerce, opening new markets in foreign lands, protecting companies from competition, and assuring product quality. Smith believed this meddling interfered with the potential benefits of the market and proposed that government be limited to three functions: law enforcement, printing of money, and provision of certain public goods such as harbors and roads.

Thomas Malthus (1766–1834)

Malthus, a professor of history and political economy at the East India College in England, was most responsible for steering Classical Liberalism away from its earlier predisposition toward the Enlightenment values of optimism, egalitarianism, and faith in reason. In contrast to Enlightenment thinkers, Malthus believed that human misery was caused by nature rather than badly organized institutions. In his book *An Essay on the Principle of Population* (1798), Malthus claimed that population grows at a faster rate than do food supplies because of the limited availability of fertile land. Population growth could be restrained either by "positive checks" such as famines, plagues, and wars, or by "preventive checks" such as delayed marriages and "moral restraint."

Malthus had little hope that humans would be capable of exercising the restraint required to control population growth, so positive checks would be the effective controls on overpopulation. Moreover, Malthus believed that government should not attempt to interfere with the operation of these positive checks. He proposed that raw sewage be permitted to flow in the streets, that insect-infested swamps remain undrained, and that cures for disease be suppressed, thereby allowing nature to carry out the grisly task of limiting population growth.

In addition to rejecting efforts to help the poor, Malthus argued that the privileges and wealth of the upper classes benefitted all of society. He reasoned that workers as a group received insufficient wages to permit them to purchase the vast array of goods being produced by the new factories, so the economy would be plagued by periodic "gluts" of unsold goods unless some members of society could afford to spend large amounts on consumption without adding to production. Idle consumption by the rich was therefore essential to maintain high levels of employment.

Malthus represents a turning point in Classical Liberalism. The Enlightenment attack on aristocratic privilege evolved into a defense of capitalist inequality. Later in the nineteenth century, Malthus's ideas would resurface as "social Darwinism." Relying on the evolutionary theory of Charles Darwin, Herbert Spencer (1820–1903) in England and William Graham Sumner (1840–1910) in America claimed that the human species evolves according to the principle of "survival of the fittest." Any attempts by government to aid the poor would cause deterioration of the human gene pool by allowing unfit members of the human species to survive and reproduce. This biological argument for hierarchy and inequality became a powerful ideological force in Europe and the United States.

Friedrich A. Hayek (1899–1992)

Although born in Austria, Hayek spent most of his adult life in England and America, where he devoted himself to defending laissez-faire capitalism against the challenges posed by Conservatives, Modern Liberals, and Radicals. In *The Road to Serfdom* (1944), Hayek rejected the notion of a middle ground between capitalism and socialism; the concept of a "mixed economy" is untenable. Government intervention disrupts the smooth functioning of a free-market economy, thereby generating the need for additional corrective intervention. This vicious circle by which government-induced problems lead to a larger role for government will eventually push society toward socialism. The only way to halt this process is to resist the initial temptation to improve society through government action.

The movement of Classical Liberalism away from the Enlightenment's optimism and confidence in human reason can be clearly discerned in Hayek's writings. He defended the market not because he believed in the power of individual reason, but rather because of his skepticism about the capacity of the human mind to obtain knowledge. Since each person can have detailed knowledge of only a small portion of society, humans lack sufficient knowledge to plan or direct the entire economy. Hayek explicitly denounced what he called "constructivist rationalism," which seeks to remake society in accordance with more humane and enlightened values.

Hayek praised the market for upholding individual freedom and emphasized its ability to process and transmit vast amounts of information about individual preferences, availability of resources, and technology. Prices reflect the conditions underlying supply and demand, so individuals are able to compensate for their personal lack of knowledge by simply comparing prices. Moreover, through their own particular experience, individuals gain specialized knowledge of niches in the market and may take advantage of any profitable opportunities they discover.

Hayek's distrust of human reason led him to oppose virtually all government activity on the grounds that politicians and bureaucrats cannot know what is best for society. The task of politics should be merely to establish a constitution and set of laws restraining individuals from harming others. Hayek warned that when government is permitted to expand its activities beyond the protection of property rights, it will inevitably become the tool of special interests. Various groups will claim that their interests should be met to promote the public good or to achieve social justice, but these appeals are simply disguised attempts to secure government benefits. The public good is simply the aggregation of the private interests of individuals, and justice is a "mirage" based on the false supposition that some interests are more deserving of fulfillment than others.

Hayek rejected the notion that economics can provide a scientific basis for predicting or attempting to control the future of the economy. Not only is the economy too complex to comprehend, but individual behavior is unpredictable and therefore not amenable to scientific analysis. The most that economics can accomplish is to demonstrate the wisdom of free markets and minimal government. Attempts to use economic theory to guide monetary and fiscal policy will fail.

Hayek also opposed efforts by economists to identify market failures that might warrant government intervention. He claimed that the efficiency of the market in processing information, providing price signals to guide individual choice, and encouraging innovation more than offsets any inefficiency resulting from market failures. Moreover, government does not possess sufficient knowledge to improve the workings of the market. Intervention is likely to cause greater disruption than the market failure.

Robert Nozick (1938–)

A recent restatement of Classical Liberalism has been undertaken by Harvard philosopher Robert Nozick in his book *Anarchy, State, and Utopia* (1974). Nozick argues that the free market will create justice in the distribution of rewards if the following three conditions are met: (1) property must be acquired without theft, fraud, or coercion; (2) transfers of property from one person to another must occur through free exchanges, inheritance, gifts, or charity; and (3) any property holdings failing to meet the first two requirements must be "rectified" through redistribution.

Nozick rejects the notion that justice requires any specific distribution of rewards. On the contrary, if a particular "pattern" of distribution were enforced, then government would have to confiscate and redistribute income earned in the market, thus violating individual liberty. Nozick also dismisses any conception of justice linking reward with individual merit. There are many possible criteria of merit including effort, need, productivity, contribution, social status, or virtue, but society has no way of objectively choosing from among these criteria. Therefore, Nozick argues, any effort to assess individual merit and reward it would be arbitrary.

Nozick instead proposes the following definition of justice: "from each as they choose, to each as they are chosen." Each person's reward should be determined by his or her choices of what to offer in the market and by other people's choices to buy the person's goods or services. Personal income may be justifiably low if an individual chooses not to offer much or if what is offered is not desired by others.

For Nozick, inequality is the result of individual choice. So long as people are free to choose, markets will tend to generate inequality, but this inequality will be fair. In fact, attempts by government to interfere with market distributions are the major cause of injustice. Nozick equates taxation with slavery, claiming that it forces citizens to work for the government. The only legitimate role of government is as a "nightwatch-man" protecting property rights and preserving individual liberty.

In every society, the accumulation of wealth has sometimes involved theft, fraud, or coercion and has therefore violated Nozick's definition of legitimate acquisition of property. If property holdings are illegitimate, Nozick's version of justice requires "rectification" through government redistribution. Nozick acknowledges that his arguments for laissez-faire are undercut by past injustices in the acquisition of property. He even concedes that because current poverty is most likely to be found among the descendants of those who suffered from past injustices, government redistribution might legitimately attempt to make the poorest citizens as well off as possible. In summary, while Nozick defends laissez-faire in principle, his commitment to rectify past injustices leads him to acknowledge the legitimacy of redistributive policies. Most Classical Liberals have been unwilling to accept this particular conclusion.

PRINCIPLES OF CLASSICAL LIBERALISM

The essential features of Classical Liberalism are contained in the definitions it gives to some of the most controversial terms in political economy.

Human Nature. Humans are self-interested and capable of acting autonomously by using their capacity for reason to discover the most efficient means to satisfy their needs and desires.

Society. Society is an aggregation of individuals and has no goals or purposes of its own. The good society permits individuals to pursue their private interests free from arbitrary constraint.

Government. Individuals create government for the purpose of protecting their rights as established by a constitution. Beyond this function, government is best when it governs least.

Morality. No objective method exists for discerning which values are superior to others; therefore, individuals should be free to determine right and wrong based on their personal preferences. The only valid social values are those that all citizens would support. Since nobody wants their property or civil rights to be violated, such violations are wrong and should be illegal.

Freedom. Synonymous with autonomy and independence, freedom is the absence of coercion by government or by other people.

Authority. Legitimate authority arises only through the consent of individuals to relinquish a degree of their autonomy. For example, authority in the workplace may be consented to by employees in exchange for a wage. Authority by government may be consented to by citizens in exchange for protection of their rights to freedom and property.

Equality. Equality means that all citizens have the same opportunity to engage in economic activity and the same civil rights as established by the constitution.

Justice. Justice requires protection of property rights and civil rights established by the constitution and punishment of those who violate the rights of others.

Efficiency. Efficiency is a situation in which no person can be made better off without making someone else worse off. In other words, resources are allocated to those persons most willing and able to pay for them.

CLASSICAL LIBERALISM TODAY

The Great Depression of the 1930s dealt a crushing blow to Classical Liberalism by persuading large numbers of citizens that the free market could not be trusted to organize economic activities. From the Depression to the 1970s, Classical Liberals were conspicuously absent from public discourse, the primary exception being some members of the economics department at the University of Chicago. However, the combination of high inflation, high unemployment, and slow growth during the 1970s set the stage for a resurgence of Classical Liberal thought. Almost overnight, journals, newspapers, and public debates were filled with Classical Liberal proposals for solving the crisis of the modern welfare state. During the past two decades, virtually every country in the West has moved toward reductions in government spending, taxes, regulations, and public ownership. Inflation and unemployment have improved dramatically, and only one recession has occurred in the United States during the past fifteen years. Three of the most prominent schools of thought in contemporary Classical Liberalism are neo-Austrian economics, public choice theory, and new classical economics.

Neo-Austrian Economics

The conquest of Austria by the German army during World War II forced many intellectuals in that country to emigrate. Ludwig von Mises (1881–1973) and Friedrich A. Hayek were the principle carriers of Austrian economics to England and the United States. Although never fully embraced by mainstream economists, Mises and Hayek managed to gain the respect of influential economists such as Lionel Robbins (1898–1984), Fritz Machlup (1881–1973), Oskar Morgenstern (1902–1977), and Gottfried Haberler. More recently, a neo-Austrian school of thought has developed in the United States under the leadership of Israel Kirzner, Murray Rothbard (1926–1995), and Roger Garrison. Neo-Austrian writings are featured in the *Austrian Economics Newsletter*, the *Journal of Libertarian Studies*, *Social Philosophy & Policy*, and *Critical Review*.

Although neo-Austrians are committed to free markets and personal liberty, they reject the neoclassical assumption that individuals possess full information. If full information prevailed, then planners could conceivably replicate the market, and the defense of private property would be weakened.

Neo-Austrians willingly concede that markets are fraught with shortcomings including monopolistic elements, uncertainty, and externalities. Their defense of the market rests not on its ability to allocate resources efficiently at any single point in time, but on its role as an engine for discovering and applying knowledge that will raise standards of living. Individuals occupying unique niches in the market have the best information and the strongest incentive to innovate. No planning agency or bureaucracy can match the dynamism of entrepreneurs in pushing technology forward. In fact, according to neo-Austrians, government intervention will almost always be detrimental because government caters to special-interest groups rather than promoting the public good.

Without the rationality assumptions of neoclassical economics, neo-Austrians rely less on mathematics and more on persuasive argument. In fact, they join with Radicals in rejecting the neoclassical effort to create a scientific economics analogous to physics. Ironically, neo-Austrians conclude that economics is largely a completed project. Having demonstrated the efficiency of markets and the failures of government, neo-Austrian economists have nothing left to do except to continue the effort to persuade other economists, politicians, and the public that laissez-faire is the best policy. The neo-Austrian perspective has influenced mainstream economics through the development of game theory to illuminate situations in which decisions must be made without full information.

Public Choice Theory

In recognition of the growing power of government in capitalist societies, some Classical Liberal theorists have attempted to analyze political decisionmaking by applying the same principles of rational individual choice used to explain the actions of consumers and firms. Rejecting the Modern Liberal view of government as an impartial promoter of the well-being of society, public choice theorists claim that voters, bureaucrats, and politicians behave in the same fashion as do private consumers and producers: they pursue their private interests, seeking maximum utility at minimum cost. Citizens vote for candidates who will deliver the most benefits and the lowest taxes. Bureaucrats seek job security, high wages, professional advancement, and social status while minimizing their work effort. The guiding principle of politicians is vote maximization since they must be reelected to maintain the benefits of public office.

Politics is viewed by public choice theorists as simply economic activity conducted in the public sphere of government instead of the private sphere of the market. This approach to political economy is sometimes called the "Virginia school" because its leading proponents taught at the University of Virginia in the 1960s, moved to Virginia Polytechnic Institute in the 1970s, and finally established a permanent base at George Mason University in the

1980s. The most prominent public choice theorist is James Buchanan, winner of the Nobel Prize in economics in 1986. Other important contributors include Anthony Downs, Gordon Tullock, William Riker, and Richard McKenzie. Buchanan and Tullock founded the Public Choice Society in 1963. Writings from this perspective are featured in the journals *Public Choice, Constitutional Political Economy, The Independent Review,* and *Economics & Politics.*

Public choice theorists uphold the Classical Liberal faith in free markets, but they express concern that democratic politics creates an avenue by which individuals and groups can gain economic benefits while spreading costs among all taxpayers. Because individuals can be expected to pursue their interests by any means available, ending this abuse of democracy requires strict constitutional limits confining government to its appropriate role as protector of property rights.

New Classical Economics

When Keynesian policies faltered in the early 1970s, Classical Liberals were quick to fill the theoretical void. New classical economics describes the modern revival of laissez-faire ideas from the nineteenth century. Some of its leading proponents are Thomas Sargent, Neal Wallace, Robert Lucas, and Robert Barro. Writings by new classical economists can be found in the *Journal of Political Economy* and the *American Economic Review.*

New classical economists focus on the role of expectations in affecting individual behavior. Sargent and Wallace developed the theory of "rational expectations" to demonstrate the fallacy of Keynesian efforts to lower the rate of unemployment. If citizens have rational expectations, their behavior will take into account any anticipated effects of government policy. When government attempts to stimulate the economy, citizens anticipating greater inflation will raise their wage demands, thereby offsetting any tendency for employers to hire more workers. In short, any deliberate effort by government to increase economic activity will be frustrated by the reactions of citizens seeking to defend their income against anticipated inflation. The new classical economists conclude that government cannot lower the level of unemployment and therefore ought to abandon such attempts.

Closely related to new classical economics are two other theoretical approaches: monetarism and supply-side economics. The former, championed by Milton Friedman, seeks to revive the classical idea that the amount of money in the economy affects prices but not the level of employment or output. Monetarists conclude that active monetary policy by the Federal Reserve System can have no positive impact on unemployment and therefore should be abandoned in favor of steady growth of the money supply at a rate sufficient to accommodate increases in real output.

Supply-side economics is so named because it rejects the Keynesian focus on demand management and instead proposes to stimulate the economy through deregulation, tax cuts, and privatization. These policies mesh perfectly with the new classical goal of minimizing the size and role of government.

AN ASSESSMENT OF CLASSICAL LIBERALISM

Classical Liberalism originally provided the ideological ammunition to dislodge the feudal aristocracy from power and to create a society in which individual freedom and aspirations were both permitted and rewarded. By undermining superstition, tradition, and arbitrary power, Classical Liberalism promoted a wider scope for individual expression and cultural diversity. With its insistence on the priority of individual liberty over all other values, Classical Liberalism has served as a bulwark against the abuse of political power. This ideology insists that for individuals to develop and maintain personal identities, an irreducible core of their existence must remain separate from—and even opposed to—larger social processes. Any society that represses the individual desire to formulate and pursue a personal set of goals will lose the human energy unleashed by the pursuit of self-interest. Such energy has been a mainspring of social and economic progress.

However, the changing nature of Western societies poses several challenges to Classical Liberalism's commitment to the market as the primary institution for organizing society. First, industrialization and urbanization have contributed to a proliferation of "externalities" that cause the market to allocate resources inefficiently.

Second, the large-scale production required to take advantage of economies of scale associated with modern technology has proven subversive to effective competition. Without competition, the market contains no mechanism for guiding self-interest into socially useful channels.

Third, the same self-interested behavior motivating individuals and firms to compete in the market also drives them to form groups and seek government protection against the competitive pressures and instability of the market. The resulting politicization of the economy can be reversed only by a government sufficiently powerful to override the groups benefitting from political activity. Thus, Classical Liberals face the paradox that a very powerful government may be necessary to minimize the role of government. The question of whether such a government could be trusted to exercise its power judiciously remains unanswered.

Finally, Classical Liberalism fails to adequately recognize the human desire for community and a sense of common purpose. Individuals want to pursue their private goals and achieve personal success, but they also exhibit commitments to collective goals and the quality of public life. In fact, with rising standards of living in Western societies, "quality of life" issues have become more significant. Concerns about environmental degradation, crime, the spread of AIDS, homelessness, and drug abuse reflect a growing realization that personal income and wealth cannot secure a high-quality lifestyle when public life is deteriorating.

ADDITIONAL READING

Barry, Norman P. *Hayek's Social and Economic Philosophy*. London: Macmillan, 1979.

Boaz, David, ed. *The Libertarian Reader*. New York: The Free Press, 1997.

Boaz, David, and Edward H. Crane, eds. *Market Liberalism: A Paradigm for the 21st Century*. Washington, DC: Cato Institute, 1993.

Brittan, Samuel. *A Restatement of Economic Liberalism*, 2nd ed. London: Macmillan, 1988.

Buchanan, James M. *Post-socialist Political Economy*. Lyme, NH: Edward Elgar, 1997.

Burke, T. Patrick. *Ethical Principles for a Free Market*. New York: Paragon House, 1993.

Conway, David. *Classical Liberalism: The Unvanquished Ideal*. New York: St. Martin's, 1995.

Friedman, Milton. *Capitalism and Freedom*. Chicago: University of Chicago Press, 1962.

Friedman, Milton, and Rose Friedman. *Free to Choose: A Personal Statement*. New York: Harcourt Brace Jovanovich, 1980.

Hendrickson, Mark W., ed. *The Morality of Capitalism*. Irvington-on-Hudson, NY: The Foundation for Economic Education, 1996.

Machan, Tibor. *Capitalism and Individualism*. New York: St. Martin's, 1990.

McKenzie, Richard, and Gordon Tullock. *Modern Political Economy*. New York: McGraw-Hill, 1978.

Rand, Ayn. *Capitalism: The Unknown Ideal*. New York: Signet, 1967.

Roberts, Paul Craig. *The Supply-Side Revolution*. Cambridge: Harvard University Press, 1984.

Rockwell, Llewellyn H., Jr., ed. *The Free Market Reader*. Burlingame, CA: The Ludwig von Mises Institute, 1988.

Rothbard, Murray. *For a New Liberty*. New York: Collier-Macmillan, 1978.

Rowley, Charles K. *Liberty and the State*. Brookfield, VT: Edward Elgar, 1993.

Schotter, Andrew. *Free Market Economics*. New York: St. Martin's, 1985.

Shand, Alexander H. *Free Market Morality: The Political Economy of the Austrian School*. New York: Routledge, 1989.

Stigler, George J., ed. *Chicago Studies in Political Economy*. Chicago: University of Chicago Press, 1988.

Vaughn, Karen I. *Austrian Economics in America*. New York: Cambridge University Press, 1994.

Chapter 4

The Radical Perspective

Although Radical ideas can be traced to antiquity, modern Radicalism was born out of conflict between the democratic aspirations of the Enlightenment and the emerging power of private property rights. Radicals claimed that public control of production was essential to attaining the Enlightenment values of freedom, equality, and justice. During the nineteenth century, as Classical Liberalism became increasingly pessimistic and anti-egalitarian, Radicalism exerted an immense influence among the working class and intellectuals. It raised the possibility of transcending capitalism to achieve a more humane, cooperative society. The specter of socialism was sufficiently threatening to defenders of private property to trigger major revisions in liberal theory and policies. Thus, while Radicalism's direct influence in the United States and Western Europe has been minimal, it has indirectly changed the contours of society by pushing liberalism toward acceptance of the welfare state and government regulation of business.

ARCHITECTS OF RADICALISM

Jean Jacques Rousseau (1712–1778)

Unlike Hobbes's and Locke's portrayal of humans as self-interested creatures who establish government only to protect their individual rights, the

French philosopher Rousseau claimed that humans need to be engaged in a community to develop fully. Without a network of social relations, the individual is isolated, lonely, and helpless. For Rousseau, "our sweetest existence is relative and collective, and our true ego is not completely inside us."

Yet despite his praise of social life, Rousseau was a trenchant critic of existing societies. In *Discourse on the Origin of Inequality* (1775), he blamed unequal holdings of property for destroying the naturally peaceful and cooperative nature of humans. Inequality enabled wealthier individuals to dominate others, and this subordination caused selfish and competitive traits to appear as people sought to protect themselves from the power of the wealthy. Unlike Classical Liberal theorists, who attributed acquisitive materialism to human nature, Rousseau believed that human behavior adapted to social circumstances. Different institutional arrangements would cause evolution in patterns of behavior. Rousseau proposed a reorganization of society to promote greater individual freedom, equality, and a sense of community.

In *On the Social Contract* (1762), Rousseau outlined the details of this reorganization. He advocated popular sovereignty in which all citizens would actively participate in politics. For Rousseau, government by the people meant more than the clashing of individual or group interests. The experience of living in a true democracy would teach citizenship skills, particularly the ability to merge one's personal interests with the public interest. Rousseau called the public interest the *general will* and claimed that it reflected the interests of people in their roles as citizens rather than as private individuals. To assure that the *general will* would prevail, Rousseau proposed the abolition of all groups seeking to promote their own narrow interests at the expense of the well-being of society.

Once the *general will* had been determined, each individual would be morally obliged to obey it. Rousseau suggested that recalcitrant persons who placed their private interests above the good of society should be "forced to be free." This phrase has echoed hauntingly in the twentieth century as totalitarian regimes have banished dissidents to labor camps and mental asylums for "reeducation." However, Rousseau claimed that the opportunity to participate in shaping society's rules and institutions would create the desire to protect and promote the interests of society. Participatory democracy was the key to solving the tension between individual freedom and social order. Individuals could conform to the *general will* and yet still be free if they participated in establishing the institutions by which they were governed. For Rousseau, government was not a threat to individual freedom if it functioned simply as a means by which citizens could realize and pursue their common interests.

To facilitate participatory democracy, Rousseau envisioned small communities in which private interests and the public interest would be harmonized through face-to-face dialog among citizens. Ongoing discussion and debate would create shared values and a sense of solidarity. Rousseau also believed that democracy and freedom required greater equality of property holdings so that no citizen would be completely dependent on others for survival. This equality would be maintained by a progressive income tax, a tax on luxury goods, and government regulation of economic activity.

Although Rousseau was a vehement critic of repressive governments, his legacy has provided support for totalitarianism. By portraying narrow self-interest as immoral and damaging to society, Rousseau created the rationale for extending government control over all aspects of life to assure that private interests do not interfere with the public good. While Rousseau relied on small communities to harmonize private and public interests without coercion, the potential for oppression increases as the size of the community grows. If the community is an entire nation, the opportunities for meaningful political participation are limited, and any proclaimed *general will* is likely to reflect the decisions of a small ruling party. Without political participation, enforcement of the *general will* will be perceived as oppressive by many citizens.

Karl Marx (1818–1883)

Marx, a German political economist, spent most of his adult life in London. After earning a doctorate in philosophy at the University of Berlin, where he was heavily influenced by the ideas of G. W. F. Hegel, Marx discovered socialism by reading the works of the utopian socialists, including Fourier and Saint-Simon. A friendship with Friedrich Engels (1820–1895) established a lifelong working relationship resulting in many coauthored works.

Marx believed that the material conditions of society, specifically the production process, exerted a profound influence on all other dimensions of human existence, including politics, religion, and ideas. Marx's critics have labeled his approach "economic determinism," but he acknowledged mutual interaction among the economy, other social institutions, and human consciousness.

Marx mocked the utopian socialists for their naive belief that small groups of people could simply retreat from capitalist society to form communities based on collective property. Without the benefits of modern technology, the division of labor, and large-scale production, these communities would be doomed to poverty and failure. Marx was convinced that a successful socialism could emerge only out of capitalist society, so he dedicated himself to understanding the inner workings of the capitalist system and the reasons for its ultimate demise.

According to Marx, the accumulation of capital is the driving force shaping all other aspects of the social system. In *Das Kapital* (1867), he analyzed the process by which capital seeks self-expansion through profits.

Because capital accumulation proceeds in a fashion largely independent of the will of any person or of society as a whole, Marx argued that capital, rather than government or citizens, is the actual ruler of society. Capital dictates both public policy and individual behavior. Whereas Classical Liberals defended the autonomy of capital as essential to protecting individual freedom from oppression by government and aristocrats, Marx argued that the power of capital subverted the ability of citizens to shape society in accordance with their democratically determined collective interests. In short, the freedom of capital meant a loss of freedom for people. Competitive pressures forced even the capitalists to adhere to the dictates of capital. They could not pay higher wages or provide safer workplaces without losing their competitive edge. Capitalists were not evil people; the blame for society's problems lay with capital—that "cancerous cell" whose growth would eventually destroy existing society.

Marx's claim that capital accumulation is the primary force shaping capitalist societies seems to imply that machines have a demonic control over human beings. However, Marx used the word "capital" to signify more than just machines and factories; capital is the social relationship between owners and workers. According to Marx, capital creates profits not because machines are productive, but because the dominant power of the owners of capital enables them to pay workers a wage worth less than the products being manufactured. When Marx attributed exploitation and other social problems to "the logic of capital accumulation," he was not blaming machines; instead, he faulted the class structure that gave power to a small minority of the population.

Marx's understanding of capitalism led him to predict that the system would result in a falling rate of profit, increasing centralization of ownership, the elimination of the middle class, and perpetual misery for workers. Yet he also viewed capitalism as laying the groundwork for a future socialist society. In its short lifespan, capitalism had brought about more technological developments and accumulation of productive assets than had occurred in all previous history. Moreover, the experience of working in large factories was causing workers to develop more cooperative attitudes and a greater sense of solidarity. The combination of "class consciousness" and the depressions brought about by falling profits would eventually trigger a proletarian revolution and the establishment of socialism.

Marx anticipated that a proletarian revolution would entail a massive uprising by a vast majority of the population and therefore would be quite democratic. To prevent a counterrevolution and to handle the administration of the new socialist society, a "dictatorship of the proletariat" would be necessary. However, even this dictatorship would be democratic in that it would represent the interests of nearly all citizens and would oppress only ex-capitalists and reactionaries who attempted to resist the will of the people. In a socialist society, productive assets would be subject to public control, and people would be paid according to their productive contribution to society.

After an unspecified number of years, socialism would complete the task of enlarging productive capacity and creating a more cooperative "socialist man." With the advent of communism would come an end to scarcity and a "withering away of the state" since a highly cooperative society would have no need for police, courts, or prisons. Communism would operate according to the slogan: "from each according to his ability, to each according to his needs."

Edward Bernstein (1850–1932)

Because of his political activism, Edward Bernstein was exiled from his native Germany and lived in England from 1880 to 1901. Bernstein formed a strong friendship with Friedrich Engels and became a major figure in Marxist political circles. At the same time, however, Bernstein met Sidney and Beatrice Webb (1859–1947 and 1858–1943), who had founded a Radical group called the Fabian Society. Under the influence of the Fabians, Bernstein concluded that orthodox Marxism had been rendered obsolete by the evolving nature of capitalism. The middle class was growing rather than disappearing, workers' standards of living were rising, ownership was being dispersed through the public sale of corporate stock, and the increasing market power of large corporations was putting an end to cut-throat competition. Bernstein concluded that neither the collapse of capitalism nor a proletarian revolution was inevitable. Instead, socialism could be ushered in gradually and peacefully through the democratic political process because workers outnumbered capitalists. To facilitate this process, political leadership and educational programs were needed to demonstrate to workers that their interests lay with socialism.

In *Evolutionary Socialism* (1899), Bernstein explicitly broke his allegiance to Marxism. He objected to the Hegelian aspects of Marxism that portrayed history as the inevitable movement toward a predetermined endpoint. In addition, Bernstein rejected Marx's claims to have developed a science of society. Socialism, he claimed, would materialize not because "laws of motion" would determine the course of history, but because socialism was a morally superior and hence more appealing system for a large majority of the population.

In place of Hegel, Bernstein relied on the ethics of the German philosopher Immanuel Kant (1724–1804) to argue that capitalism was immoral because it encouraged people to regard one another as means to achieve their own private ends. Socialism, by contrast, would enable people to respect and be compassionate toward others without falling behind in a competitive struggle for dominance. Bernstein's ideas were important in establishing a Radical tradition known as "revisionism," which provided the basis for social democratic political parties in Europe.

Thorstein Veblen (1857–1929)

A distinctly American brand of Radicalism was founded by Thorstein Veblen, a political economist whose caustic critique of corporate capitalism and bourgeois lifestyles influenced American social theory significantly. In his book *The Theory of the Leisure Class* (1899), Veblen contrasted "dynamic" aspects of society such as science, the use of tools, and the "instinct for workmanship," with "static" aspects such as superstition, ritual, and habit. Veblen praised modern technology for undermining old traditions and myths, but argued that capitalist production, with its focus on profits, tended to thwart the potential dynamism of technology.

Although capitalism was once a progressive force in vanquishing feudal customs and authority, it spawned a new privileged class. This "leisure class" had little direct involvement in production but lived in splendor on income derived from the ownership of property. Veblen argued that the leisure class interfered with the efficiency of capitalism by serving as role models for the rest of society. The extravagant lifestyles of the rich set a standard to which all other classes aspired. Unable to afford genuine luxury, the middle and lower classes attempted to emulate the leisure class by engaging in "conspicuous consumption." Since the motivation behind conspicuous consumption is to relieve the insecurity and sense of inferiority created by the existence of a leisure class, Veblen concluded that abolishing this class would conserve resources and make everyone happier.

Another problem created by the leisure class is erosion of the "instinct for workmanship." While capitalism depends on the work ethic, Veblen argued that the frivolous lifestyle of the leisure class creates frustration and resentment throughout society. Seeking to emulate the leisure class, people develop an aversion to work and seek shortcuts to success. Even businesses are prone to this syndrome. Rather than encouraging innovation and the production of high-quality products, corporations try to manipulate the market and the consumer in pursuit of short-term profits. Veblen coined the term "planned obsolescence" to describe the manufacture of products that quickly deteriorate, forcing consumers to replace them often.

Veblen believed that modern technology made large corporations and concentrations of business power inevitable. Returning to an earlier era of competitive capitalism was not a feasible option, so he proposed that control of corporations be delegated to engineers and scientists who, by virtue of their training and temperament, focus on efficiency and quality. By relying on "technocrats" to restore dynamism to modern societies, Veblen steered a path between capitalism and Marxian socialism. While convinced of the waste and inefficiency of modern capitalism, he was also critical of Marx and had no confidence in government expropriation of the means of production. He anticipated that scientists and engineers would operate businesses in the public interest without the bureaucracy and concentration of power entailed by government ownership.

Veblen left a dual legacy. First, his ideas served as inspiration for the American populist movement with its mistrust of corporations, government, and the rich. In the 1920s and 1930s, the Progressives and even the Democratic Party were influenced by Veblen as they attempted to clean up government and end business corruption. Second, in the realm of theory, Veblen was the intellectual inspiration for a tradition within political economy known as "institutional economics."

V. I. Lenin (1870–1924)

Vladimir Ilyich Ulyanov, Russian theorist and activist who adopted the name "Lenin," led the first successful socialist revolution in 1917. An extremely forceful personality and skilled debater, Lenin almost single-handedly refashioned Marxism to address the particular situation of Russia in the early twentieth century. Because Marx had said very little about conducting a revolution or about the nature of postrevolutionary society, Lenin faced a formidable task.

Marx had envisioned socialism as arising from the misery and alienation of workers in the most advanced capitalist countries. Moreover, given Marx's predictions of centralized business power and a vanishing middle class, the workers would constitute a vast majority of the population so that a proletarian revolution would be spontaneous, widely supported, and democratic. In contrast, Lenin was faced with a backward country ruled by an autocratic tsar and lacking a large industrial working class. In *What Is To Be Done?* (1902), Lenin proposed that a "vanguard party" of dedicated intellectuals take responsibility for initiating the revolution and providing leadership for the masses. He also urged Radicals to resist the temptation to join reform movements that would accomplish only minor changes in the status quo; a genuine revolution was the only solution to Russia's backwardness.

In *Imperialism, The Highest Stage of Capitalism* (1916), Lenin developed another theoretical argument favoring the possibility of revolution in Russia. He claimed that capitalism had evolved from its earlier competitive phase into a monopoly phase that required corporations to move beyond national boundaries in their quest for cheap resources and markets for their products. Imperialism had three major consequences. First, it generated higher profits, thereby permitting capitalists to pay higher wages to their workers in the industrialized countries of Western Europe and North America. Lenin concluded that workers in these countries had unwittingly become incorporated into the exploiting class because they were benefitting from the profits extracted from their fellow workers in the less-developed countries. As an "aristocracy of labor," workers in the industrialized countries could no longer be expected to provide the impetus for a socialist revolution. Second, increasing oppression of the less-developed countries would fuel revolutionary anger outside the core of the global capitalist economy. Lenin argued that Russia, as the most backward of the European nations, was the "weakest link" in the capitalist chain and therefore would be the first to break. Finally, imperialism would lead to war between the advanced capitalist nations as they struggled for control of global resources and markets. Lenin viewed World War I as an imperialist conflict and was confident that the capitalist countries would so devastate each other that socialism would quickly spread from Russia throughout Europe.

Lenin left an ambiguous legacy. His insistence on the role of a vanguard party in leading the revolution has given the Leninist tradition a permanent antidemocratic imprint. Leninism is associated with a mistrust of the masses and the consequent need for authoritarian leadership. Lenin is accused of establishing a brutal, paranoid style of governing that set the stage for later atrocities committed by Stalin. However, defenders of Lenin point out that he called for decentralization of power as soon as the revolution had succeeded and that he abandoned this policy only when the threat of counterrevolution and economic collapse endangered the new socialist society. When the crisis passed in 1921, he again initiated decentralization with the New Economic Policy. Had Lenin not died in 1924, the Soviet Union might have taken a dramatically different course than it did under Stalin.

Jürgen Habermas (1929–)

Habermas is a German social theorist whose prolific writings during the past thirty years have had a major impact on Radical thought. Like many Radicals, Habermas was deeply disillusioned by Stalinism and the authoritarian nature of the Soviet Union. Rather than dismissing Soviet practices as an aberration from true Marxism, he has attempted to construct a new Radicalism more explicitly sensitive to concerns about individual freedom.

In *Knowledge and Human Interests* (1968), Habermas argues that humans have three distinct types of interests: an interest in controlling nature, an interest in improved communication with others, and an interest in eliminating oppressive social structures. He indicts capitalism for promoting the interest in control at the expense of the interests in communication and liberation. The profit motive constantly drives firms to increase the technical efficiency of their production; this pressure spreads throughout society as education, social interaction, family life, and recreation become merely rational means to achieve the end of greater wealth. Instead of earning money to live a more expressive and fulfilling life, people learn to structure their lives to increase their earning potential.

In a more recent book, *Communication and the Evolution of Society* (1979), Habermas relies on the notion of "communicative ethics" to develop a critique of both capitalist and authoritarian socialist societies. If humans do indeed have an interest in improved communication, then they will seek to remove any structures of domination in society that interfere with sincere and meaningful dialog. Habermas defines an "ideal speech situation" as one in which neither party to a conversation has power over the other. The outcome of the dialog will be determined by the quality of the ideas being exchanged, not by the relative power of the participants. He claims that hierarchical power relations in capitalism and authoritarian socialism block the human interest in communication.

Habermas perceives the major challenge to capitalism coming not from workers demanding a more equal distribution of income, but rather from the social movements that have coalesced around such issues as environmental protection, women's liberation, and nuclear disarmament. The very success of capitalism in raising standards of living frees individuals to focus on improving the quality of their lives. The major obstacle to this goal, according to Habermas, is the dominance of profit-making and technical rationality over the human interests in expressive communication and liberation.

PRINCIPLES OF RADICALISM

The following definitions capture many of the essential features of the Radical perspective.

Human Nature. Humans have certain biological needs and a capacity for reason, but their social and natural environments significantly affect their consciousness and behavior. The social context provided by language, traditions, values, and modes of interaction is so essential to human development that individuals cannot fully realize their talents and capacities except in association with other persons.

Society. Society is more than just a collection of individuals. Society is a living organism into which individuals enter at birth and leave at death. Because society precedes the individual, it has interests apart from—and potentially conflicting with—any particular individual's desires. A good society encourages the fullest possible range of personal development and social relations based on mutual respect.

Government. Government properly serves as the representative of the collective interests of citizens. Government permits citizens to do for themselves collectively what they cannot accomplish as individuals.

Morality. Although Marxists have traditionally rejected the notion of a Radical ethic, non-Marxist Radicals find a basis for morality in the human need for social relationships based on mutual respect. An individual action or a social system is immoral if it treats people as objects and demeans their humanity.

Freedom. Freedom is the ability to fully develop one's human capacities. Freedom can be achieved only in the context of a nurturing community based on cooperation and participation.

Authority. With the possible exception of revolutionary leadership, authority is legitimate only when democratically established, based on widespread participation, and publicly accountable.

Equality. Equality means not just equal opportunity, but also substantial equality of result. To achieve equality may require taxation or even confiscation of property income along with governmental efforts to assist disadvantaged persons.

Justice. Justice means that rewards are distributed in accordance with those rights established by the democratic political process. Citizens should have rights to those conditions essential to human development such as material necessities and health care. Justice also includes the impartial administration of the law.

Efficiency. Efficiency means that society's resources are used in a way that maximizes the attainment of society's goals including such intangible goals as justice, solidarity, and human development.

RADICALISM TODAY

The brutality of Stalinism during the 1930s and 1940s was a major blow to the credibility of Radical ideas. After World War II, the anticommunism of the McCarthy era effectively suppressed Radical voices in America until the 1960s. However, with the emergence of mass political movements for civil rights, student power, women's liberation, environmental protection and an end to the war in Vietnam, the Radical perspective enjoyed a renaissance. Three of the most important contemporary Radical schools of thought are institutional economics, social economics, and post-Marxian theory.

Institutional Economics

Institutional economics arose out of Thorstein Veblen's scathing criticism of both Marxism and neoclassical economics. Veblen found the neoclassical portrayal of autonomous individuals rationally pursuing maximum utility to be as implausible as the Hegelian dialectics underlying Marxism. He proposed to analyze the economy as an evolving process embedded in an institutional framework including the legal system, political system, educational system, family life, work, customs, and ethics. Because the entire array of institutions allocates society's resources and distributes income, to study the market in abstraction would be a pointless and misleading exercise.

Veblen's approach was indebted to two major intellectual influences. Pragmatism, a philosophical perspective developed by John Dewey

(1859–1952), William James (1842–1910), and Charles Sanders Peirce (1839–1914), evaluated moral principles and scientific beliefs according to their usefulness in solving practical problems. The "historical school" of political economy, developed in Germany in the mid-nineteenth century by Wilhelm Roscher (1817–1894) and Gustav Schmoller (1838–1917), emphasized the evolutionary nature of economic systems and the importance of constructing economic theory on a solid base of data gathered through empirical research. One of Veblen's teachers, Richard T. Ely (1854–1893), did graduate work in Germany during the 1870s and was largely responsible for introducing the ideas of the historical school to American economists. Ely was the principal founder of the American Economic Association, the leading professional organization of economists.

Prior to World War II, a strong case can be made that institutionalism was the dominant approach to economics in the United States. In 1920, institutional economist Wesley C. Mitchell (1874–1948) established the National Bureau for Economic Research, which is today the leading private organization for gathering statistical data on the U.S. economy. During the 1930s, many of the economists advising Franklin Roosevelt in fashioning the New Deal were institutionalists. At the University of Wisconsin, John R. Commons (1862–1945) created a flourishing center of institutional research; Clarence Ayres (1891–1972) later did the same at the University of Texas.

Despite these successes, institutionalism lost its prominence after World War II. Its decline can be traced to three factors. First, the rise of McCarthyism and the Cold War created a political climate that was hostile to any ideas suggesting major restructuring of capitalist institutions. Second, the apparent success and acceptance of Keynesian economics eased many doubts about the viability of capitalism and undermined proposals for radical change. Third, the publication of Paul Samuelson's *Foundations of Economic Analysis* in 1949 marked the full-fledged mathematization of economic theory. Institutionalism is less suited for expression in mathematical form because it analyzes customary patterns of group behavior rather than the rational behavior of individuals. The institutional approach has been described as "storytelling," relying on a narrative style to convey understanding of economic processes. As economists gained increasing influence in government policymaking, the more "scientific" mathematical methods of neoclassical economics successfully dominated the less rigorous institutional approach.

Institutionalists criticize the neoclassical assumptions of rational consumers and perfect competition for disguising the power relations and inefficiency of real-world capitalism. They devote much of their research to issues such as economic development and industrial organization, where the perfectly competitive neoclassical model is least appropriate. Institutionalists have been reluctant to specify their visions of the proper balance between market and government, but underlying their approach is an emphasis on the Radical values of equality and community.

Among the prominent contemporary institutionalists are Daniel Fusfeld, Marc Tool, Douglas Dowd, Ron Stanfield, and William Dugger. Institutionalist writings are presented in the *Journal of Economic Issues.*

Social Economics

The roots of social economics lie in nineteenth-century continental European economic thought. German and French political economists exhibited much greater skepticism toward free markets than did their British counterparts. They were particularly concerned about the effects of markets on culture and the spiritual well-being of citizens. In 1931, Pope Pius XI issued an encyclical criticizing markets for undermining the moral basis of society. In 1941, the Catholic Economic Association (CEA) was founded in the United States as part of an effort to engage Christian ethics and economic theory. In 1970, the CEA changed its name to the Association for Social Economics and opened membership to non-Catholics.

Social economics also has secular roots. In 1936, John Maurice Clark (1884–1963), an ex-president of the American Economic Association, published *Preface to Social Economics,* in which he urged the inclusion of values and ethics in economic reasoning. Over the past half-century, social economics has been closely linked with institutional economics as many of the same theorists identify with both schools of thought. Prominent contemporary social economists include Amitai Etzioni, Warren Samuels, and Stephen Worland. The major journals in which writings from this tradition can be found are the *Review of Social Economy* and the *Forum for Social Economics.*

Like institutional economists, social economists have devoted much of their effort to criticizing neoclassical economics and constructing alternative methods for analyzing economic activity. Social economics is touted as offering a more integrated, holistic, evolutionary approach incorporating social, cultural, and political factors into its understanding of economic affairs. The ethical vision of social economists points toward greater equality, decentralization, and accountability of power, and the priority of human development over profit.

Post-Marxian Theory

During the nineteenth and early twentieth centuries, Marxism was hardly visible in the United States due to rising standards of living and government repression of Radical organizations. Even when the Great Depression triggered a resurgence of Radicalism, little of it was explicitly

Marxist. By the 1950s, Marxian economics in the United States was confined primarily to the works of two theorists—Paul Sweezy, the editor of *Monthly Review*, and Paul Baran (1909–1964), a professor of economics at Stanford University.

However, the 1960s witnessed a renewal of the Marxist tradition. Under the umbrella of the Union for Radical Political Economics (URPE), Marxism gained recognition as a legitimate field of scholarly research. However, few Marxists in the United States or Europe aligned themselves with the Soviet version of socialism as consisting of centralized planning, public ownership of all means of production, and an authoritarian government. Western Marxists sought to develop new critiques of capitalism that would eventually lead to decentralized, democratic, and participatory forms of socialism. Within this "post-Marxian" tradition, a variety of approaches have flourished. Some theorists, including Howard Sherman, Duncan Foley, and David Laibman, have retained traditional Marxian concepts such as the labor theory of value and the falling rate of profit. Writings from this perspective can be found in journals such as *Marxism Today*, *Science & Society*, and the *Review of Radical Political Economics*.

A second post-Marxian approach rejects most of Marx's theoretical categories, claiming that changes in capitalism have rendered Marx's original analysis obsolete. Marx himself is criticized for being insufficiently sensitive to issues of individuality, race, gender, and pluralism. Indeed, theorists from this perspective are so intent on preserving individual rights and enlarging the scope of freedom and democracy that they might be labeled "post-liberals" rather than post-Marxians. Among the most prominent theorists representing this approach are Herbert Gintis, David Gordon (1944–1996), Samuel Bowles, Richard Edwards, and Thomas Weisskopf. This perspective is represented in journals such as *Politics & Society*, *Socialist Review*, *Radical America*, and *New Left Review*.

A third version of post-Marxism is called analytical Marxism. Theorists such as John Roemer, Jon Elster, and Adam Przeworski have adopted the techniques of neoclassical economics, including game theory and mathematical modeling, to demonstrate Marxian concepts such as exploitation and class conflict. Finally, other post-Marxian theorists, including Richard Wolff, Stephen Resnick, and Jack Amariglio, have sought to revitalize Marxian analysis by introducing concepts from contemporary philosophy including poststructuralism and postmodernism. Their writings are presented in the journal *Rethinking Marxism*.

Post-Marxian visions of socialism do not preclude the possibility of considerable private ownership of property and reliance on markets. To prevent abuses of government power, post-Marxians emphasize the necessity of participatory democracy; elected officials and bureaucrats should be publicly accountable for their actions, and citizens should be actively involved in the political process. Another bulwark against tyranny is democratization of the workplace, giving workers extensive control over the production process. With these institutional safeguards, post-Marxians are confident that tensions between individual freedom and social order can be minimized.

AN ASSESSMENT OF RADICALISM

Radicalism grew out of the industrialization process of Western Europe. A new class appeared, lacking access to productive property and, therefore, having no means of support except selling labor for wages. As capitalism undermined the self-sufficiency of rural areas, farmers flocked to the cities, only to find squalor, disease, horrendous working conditions, and subsistence wages. These conditions contrasted so sharply with the bright future anticipated by Enlightenment thinkers that attention turned toward private wealth as the last bastion of privilege and unaccountable power. Some workers and intellectuals began to demand the abolition of private ownership of large-scale means of production.

Radical demands for greater equality have been partially realized through the welfare state. By threatening to confiscate property, Radicals forced the wealthy to make concessions. For example, the extension of civil and human rights in democratic societies has given workers greater protection against the power of employers. Government support for labor unions and a minimum wage partially insulates workers from competitive market forces.

The perennial appeal of Radicalism is the vision of human liberation. Radicalism shares the hope fundamental to nearly all religions—the coming of a new age when people will live together in universal peace and prosperity. Marxism has been called a religion for those who have lost faith in God. Radicalism also holds out a more secular appeal with its promise of giving people control over their lives and destiny by restructuring social institutions. For those who feel oppressed by slave owners, feudal lords, or capitalist bosses, this opportunity for self-determination through cooperation has been a powerful magnet.

With its emphasis on the social dimension of human existence, Radicalism is attuned to Western religious and ethical beliefs that have traditionally condemned selfishness. Even if the pursuit of self-interest promotes economic prosperity, theorists have perennially been concerned with its potential for undermining individual virtue and distorting human relations. By appealing to the human capacities for cooperation and compassion, Radicalism stakes out the moral highground in its confrontation with liberal individualism.

Despite these strengths, the Radical perspective is currently in considerable disarray. Radicalism has been badly tarnished by the behavior of governments purportedly following Marxist principles. The bleak and oppressive conditions in countries that have tried socialism provide powerful testimony against Radical proposals. In fact, with only a few exceptions, every country in which socialism occurred is currently moving rapidly toward capitalism, introducing private property, competition, profitability, and decentralized authority as solutions to the failures of a centrally planned economy.

Radicals initially anticipated that changes in Russia and Eastern Europe signaled not a rejection of socialism in favor of capitalism, but a victory of democracy over totalitarianism. With dictatorial regimes removed from power, they hoped that citizens might establish the first genuine forms of democratic socialism. However, these visions are fading as industrial assets in Russia and Eastern Europe are rapidly accumulating in the hands of small numbers of powerful individuals. Radicals now foresee a phase of "robber capitalism" resembling the United States economy in the late nineteenth century and express concern that reactionary nationalism may develop as citizens express their disillusionment with capitalism.

Even before communism began to crumble, many Radicals were rethinking their principles in light of disappointment with existing socialist societies. Radicals now acknowledge that some of the problems traditionally blamed on capitalism may be inherent in any form of social organization. For example, the problem of motivating productive activity does not disappear with the advent of socialism, nor does the problem of scarcity of resources and making choices between alternative uses of those resources. Not all conflicts in society are class conflicts, and therefore not all conflicts will disappear with the elimination of classes. Moreover, problems of individual loneliness, alienation, and frustration do not vanish along with capitalism. If conflict will persist in any future society, then Marx's vision of communism as a society in which neither market nor government mediates conflict should be rejected. Government serves not only to represent the collective interests of society, but also to resolve the conflicting interests of individuals and groups within society. Furthermore, given the inherent problems of relying on government to mediate all conflict, the market may be essential to socialist society as an arena in which the private interests of individuals find expression and fulfillment.

The flaw with any pure form of Radicalism is neglect of the private sphere within which individuals formulate life-plans and pursue interests. While humans may have significantly greater capacities for sympathy and cooperation than have yet been exhibited, an irreducible core of each person must remain self-interested. To completely merge one's identity with a larger group would mean the loss of any identity distinct from the group. Without individual aspirations to motivate action, no society can retain its vitality.

Stated differently, while free individuals might collectively choose to establish a more egalitarian and cooperative society, they cannot be expected to permit society to determine their destiny. In addition to their social selves, humans have private lives, and liberty must mean something other than conformance to the will of society. The compatibility between individual liberty and social solidarity is limited by the fact that individuals remain separate entities distinct from the society in which they live.

ADDITIONAL READING

Attewell, Paul. *Radical Political Economy Since the Sixties*. New Brunswick, NJ: Rutgers University Press, 1984.

Bowles, Samuel, and Richard Edwards, eds. *Radical Political Economy*. Brookfield, VT: Edward Elgar, 1989.

Burkitt, Brian. *Radical Political Economy*. New York: New York University Press, 1984.

Coughlin, Richard M., ed. *Morality, Rationality, and Efficiency: New Perspectives on Socio-Economics*, Armonk, NY: M. E. Sharpe, 1991.

Dugger, William M., ed. *Radical Institutionalism*. Westport, CT: Greenwood, 1989.

Edwards, Richard C., Michael Reich, and Thomas E. Weisskopf. *The Capitalist System*, 3rd ed. Englewood Cliffs, NJ: Prentice-Hall, 1985.

Foldvary, Fred E., ed. *Beyond Neo-classical Economics*. Brookfield, VT: Edward Elgar, 1996.

Heilbroner, Robert. *Marxism: For and Against*. New York: W. W. Norton, 1980.

———. *The Nature and Logic of Capitalism*. New York: W. W. Norton, 1985.

Lippit, Victor D., ed. *Radical Political Economy: Explorations in Alternative Economic Analysis*. Armonk, NY: M. E. Sharpe, 1996.

Mosely, Fred. *Heterodox Economic Theories: True or False*. Brookfield, VT: Edward Elgar, 1995.

Roberts, Bruce, and Sue Finer, eds. *Radical Economics*. Boston: Kluwer, 1992.

Sawyer, Malcolm C. *The Challenge of Radical Political Economy: An Introduction to Alternatives to Neo-Classical Economics*. Savage, MD: Barnes & Noble, 1989.

Sayer, Andrew R. *Radical Political Economy: A Critique*. Cambridge: Blackwell, 1995.

Sherman, Howard J. *Foundations of Radical Political Economy*. Armonk, NY: M. E. Sharpe, 1987.

Stanfield, J. Ron. *Economics, Power and Culture: Essays in the Development of Radical Institutionalism*. New York: St. Martin's, 1995.

Wolff, Richard D., and Stephen A. Resnick. *Economics: Marxian versus Neo-classical*. Baltimore: Johns Hopkins University Press, 1987.

Chapter 5

The Conservative
Perspective

At the outset of this chapter, a word of caution about ideological labels is needed. In the nineteenth century, "conservative" referred to ideas and theorists defending hierarchy and community against the perceived threats posed by capitalist individualism and democracy. At that time, Conservatism was a backward-looking reaction to the disintegration of traditional society caused by industrialization and mass political movements in Europe. In the United States, nineteenth-century Conservatism was primarily a southern phenomenon oriented toward defense of traditional ways of life based on the plantation system and slavery.

By the beginning of the twentieth century, however, Conservatives concluded that the working class was not a mob intent on attacking all privilege and could be persuaded to support Conservative ideals. As Classical Liberalism collapsed in Europe in the 1920s and in the United States a decade later, a rightist coalition emerged with Classical Liberals affirming Conservative ideals of nationalism and tradition while Conservatives yielded to the Classical Liberal priorities of free markets and individual liberty. Modern Liberals hastened this ideological realignment by attaching the label "conservative" to Classical Liberals so that Modern Liberalism could lay claim to the tradition of freedom and democracy.

The marriage of Classical Liberalism and Conservatism after World War II was advantageous to both groups. Most Conservatives were anxious to rid themselves of the taint of fascism and to embrace capitalism and democracy as bulwarks against totalitarianism from both the left and the right. Classical Liberals, sensing that the tides of history were shifting against them, viewed Conservatives as their most obvious allies in resisting communism and defending the unfettered rights of private property. This rightist coalition was institutionalized in 1946 with the establishment of the Foundation for Economic Education, which assembled U.S. corporate sponsors to fund research and publish papers and books defending liberty and property. The following year, Friedrich Hayek organized the Mont Pelerin Society, named after the Swiss town where the first conference was held, to provide a supportive organization for intellectuals seeking to reverse the trend toward government power. Although Hayek, Milton Friedman, and other Classical Liberal members insisted they were not Conservatives, they made little effort to dispute the Modern Liberal claim to the liberal tradition.

Starting in 1955, William F. Buckley Jr.'s *National Review* magazine actively promoted the fusion of Conservative and Classical Liberal perspectives. Conservatives would swallow their fear of the market and yield to laissez-faire economic policies, while Classical Liberals would accept the role of government in policing internal dissent and challenging communism around the world. Since the 1950s, the political spectrum has been effectively reduced to three camps: conservatives (including Conservatives and Classical Liberals), liberals (meaning Modern Liberals), and Radicals.

Despite the fact that ideological defenses of free markets and individual liberty are now labeled "conservative," this text continues to use the nineteenth-century meaning of that label. Although this unconventional usage may pose minor difficulties in translating current political discourse into the framework developed in this book, the insights gained through maintaining the distinction between Conservatism and Classical Liberal are substantial. When Classical Liberalism is called "conservatism," genuine Conservatism tends to be forgotten or ignored. Also, the goal of understanding the historical roots of modern debates is better achieved by continuity over time in the meaning of ideological labels. Finally, the alliance between Classical Liberalism and Conservatism appears to be disintegrating in the absence of a global communist threat. The nineteenth-century distinction between the two ideologies may become increasingly relevant in assessing the political debates of the twenty-first century.

ARCHITECTS OF CONSERVATISM

Edmund Burke (1729–1797)

Burke, a member of the British parliament and a distinguished orator, was a reform-minded Whig who opposed royal authority and supported the American quest for independence. He was not opposed to change in principle, but the bloodshed and anarchy of the French Revolution persuaded him that a vigorous defense of traditional society was needed to prevent revolutionary sentiments from spreading throughout Europe.

In *Reflections on the Revolution in France* (1790), Burke blamed the Revolution on the ideals of the Enlightenment. The revolutionary goal of total social change is doomed to failure because society is not a mechanism that can be taken apart and then restructured. Society is a fragile organism; its institutions are not products of rational human design, but have evolved over the ages to suit the unique features of particular peoples and countries. Values and beliefs should not be changed abruptly because they represent the "collective wisdom of the ages." Burke even defended prejudice as a force steering people toward traditional behavior without the need to think about what is right.

According to Burke, humans are neither autonomous nor rational. They are passionate beings who need the institutions, customs, and rules provided by society to control their desires and form personal identities. He viewed isolated individuals, ruled by their passions, as incapable of achieving the fulfillment that comes from virtuous living within an orderly community. Fearing that traditional values of respect, duty, and patriotism had been vanquished by selfish materialism, Burke declared: "The age of chivalry is gone. That of sophisters, economists, and calculators has succeeded, and the glory of Europe is extinguished forever."

Claiming that individuals need moral guidance and authority, Burke proposed a national church and an aristocratic government. He distrusted democracy, arguing that the common person had neither the time nor inclination to acquire sufficient knowledge to vote wisely. Democracy would only turn the political process into a battle between competing private interests. Aristocrats, he believed, were ideally suited to govern because their wealth and leisure freed them from the scramble for personal gain, thereby enabling them to impartially promote the public interest.

Burke supported private property and a market economy, but he claimed that self-interest must be restrained by moral considerations. He urged businessmen to behave in an honorable and chivalrous manner by placing their duties to society above their quest for maximum profit. Burke wanted economic activity to remain relatively free from government intervention, but he also believed that freedom requires structures of authority to restrain the passions of individuals. He envisioned a society in which authority would be so embedded in traditional hierarchical structures that it would be largely invisible.

Thomas Carlyle (1795–1881)

Carlyle, a British social critic and historian, was a major figure in the Conservative reaction to industrialization. He feared that commercial society was destroying the emotional bonds and sense of duty that made civilization possible. In particular, Carlyle scorned classical political economy, calling it "the dismal science" and "pig philosophy" because it portrayed society as an arena in which pleasure-seeking individuals struggle against each other to get ahead.

Carlyle believed in the necessity of a hierarchical society governed by charismatic leaders who could generate consensus among different groups. Yet he was not simply a defender of the status quo. He blamed the British aristocracy for neglecting its duty to govern wisely as it was swept up in the capitalist pursuit of pleasure and profit. In *On Heroes and Hero-Worship* (1841), he claimed that certain individuals are born leaders and should be permitted to rise to positions of power. Unlike Burke, Carlyle admired Robespierre and other leaders of the French Revolution for seizing the opportunity to regenerate a stagnant society.

However, Carlyle was no democrat; he viewed rule by the masses as a tragedy stemming from the aristocracy's failure to govern wisely. Democracy spawns a clamor of competing interests, each lacking a vision of the public good. His preferred model of society was revealed by his admiration of Prussia and its military spirit. The ideal society would have no political campaigns or elections. The wisest and most capable individuals would simply be promoted to positions of authority as is done in an army. A hierarchical and authoritarian society promotes order, discipline, cohesion, and a sense of purpose. Such societies become great nations and citizens prosper both materially and spiritually.

In addition to his rejection of democracy, Carlyle condemned liberal notions of freedom. If freedom means that individuals have no duties restraining them, then the free pursuit of desires will lead to anarchy and the destruction of society. Genuine freedom can be achieved only in the context of a society based on shared values and common goals. Carlyle feared that capitalism was undermining freedom and order by replacing the traditional hierarchy based on virtue and wisdom with a new hierarchy based on wealth. Traditional hierarchy had been a stabilizing force because each class recognized its duties and functions; the aristocracy would govern wisely, while the rest of the population labored and lived in peace. However, because capitalism promotes competition among self-interested individuals, the resulting hierarchy of wealth does not carry with it any sense of social obligation. Those who succeed feel no duty to wield their power for the social good, and those who fail have little respect for or allegiance to society and its leaders.

To dampen the effects of capitalism, Carlyle proposed that political leaders should take responsibility for the moral and spiritual regeneration of society through a government-sponsored national church. In addition, government could provide public assistance programs, regulation of business, and efforts to reform social relations within factories. While granting that "despotism is essential in most enterprises," Carlyle suggested that hierarchical authority would be more effective if people had an emotional attachment to their place of work, and this could be achieved by giving workers a voice in the decisionmaking process. This suggestion illustrates a recurring tendency in Conservative thought to propose quasi-socialist solutions to the problems of capitalist society. Conservatives share common ground with Radicals in viewing an active community life as the antidote to the destructive forces of competitive individualism.

Vilfredo Pareto (1848–1923)

An Italian economist and sociologist who spent most of his career at the University of Lausanne in Switzerland, Pareto's fame derives primarily from his book *Manual of Political Economy* (1906) in which he argued that competitive markets and free trade result in an efficient allocation of resources. His definition of efficiency, now referred to as "Pareto optimality," was a situation in which no reallocation can make one person better off without making another person worse off.

Despite his arguments for the economic advantages of free markets, Pareto's Conservatism, exhibited in *The Mind and Society* (1916), led him to claim that all societies are naturally and inevitably controlled by elites. He even developed a mathematical formula, known as "Pareto's law," showing the degree of inequality that is natural for any society. In addition to defending a natural hierarchy, Pareto argued that power passes back and forth between two fundamentally different elite groups. He used the label "foxes" to describe cunning, flexible, risk-taking elites. Foxes are likely to be innovative capitalists who thrive in a dynamic social environment. Lions, on the other hand, are resistant to change and willing to use force to defend the status quo. Lions are found in the aristocracy and in that portion of the capitalist class that has made its fortune and now lives on property income.

When foxes control the government, society is dynamic and markets are relatively free, but foxes will not exert the force necessary to maintain an orderly society. In particular, the openness of a fox-controlled government permits non-elites, such as workers and farmers, to gain greater political power. In response to political instability, lions will overthrow the fox government in a "circulation of elites." Lions will use whatever force necessary to restore order. They are likely to suppress free trade and to restrict democracy, but these actions protect property and profits from the dangers of egalitarian social reforms.

Pareto believed that both foxes and lions are essential to society. Foxes sustain economic prosperity but fail to resist disorder, while lions defend private property but are likely to cause the economy to stagnate under their heavy-handed tactics. When Benito Mussolini and the Italian fascists took power in 1921, they honored Pareto as an intellectual founder and, indeed, the fascists were a classic example of a "lion" government. However, the fascists ignored Pareto's prediction that lions would eventually be overthrown.

Joseph Schumpeter (1883–1950)

An Austrian native, Schumpeter studied under Wieser and Böhm-Bawerk at the University of Vienna. Although he is sometimes linked with the Classical Liberalism of the Austrian school, he constructed a unique analysis of capitalism that places him within the Conservative perspective. After immigrating to the United States in 1931 to escape Nazism, Schumpeter taught for several decades at Harvard. Along with Keynes, he is widely regarded as one of the most eminent economists of the twentieth century.

In *The Theory of Economic Development* (1911), Schumpeter outlined his vision of capitalism. The driving force behind the system is the entrepreneur who, through continual innovation, creates profitable investment opportunities and thereby sustains economic growth. However, the essential role of the entrepreneur is also the weak point of capitalism. In *Capitalism, Socialism and Democracy* (1942), Schumpeter praised successful entrepreneurs for creating huge enterprises with sufficient resources to fund research and innovation. He had no doubt that corporate capitalism was far superior to the free-market competition of earlier periods. However, with the bureaucratization of innovation and administration, the entrepreneurial function was becoming increasingly obsolete. Ironically, the success of capitalism in promoting efficiency was simultaneously destroying the very source of its own dynamism.

Another trend highlighted by Schumpeter was the democratizing of the political process. With special interests vying against each other to gain political power, Schumpeter believed that politicians seeking reelection would increasingly pander to narrow interests. A democratic government's tendency to experiment with reform and intervention would gradually undermine the traditional values and hierarchical social structures essential to maintaining the public's sense of patriotism, loyalty, and morality. Without these traditional sentiments to buffer a market economy, the disintegrating effects of competition and rational self-interest would cause the entire system to self-destruct.

As an example of the dangerous consequences of rational self-interest, Schumpeter claimed that capitalism threatens the nuclear family because fewer people will choose to marry or have children once they calculate the actual costs and benefits. The prosperity created by capitalism gives rise to a class of intellectuals who, frustrated by their failure to achieve the status and wealth of successful entrepreneurs, seek to turn public opinion against big business and private property. The relative power of intellectuals is heightened by the growing passivity of capitalists who, having withdrawn from active participation in production, lose their strong emotional attachment to private property. As absentee owners, the capitalists lack the character or energy to resist their enemies.

Convinced that socialism would replace capitalism, Schumpeter tried to envision a socialism that would be acceptable to Conservatives. He conceded that capitalism was already largely socialized because the dynamic entrepreneur had been replaced by bureaucratic administrators. If socialism simply meant that government bureaucrats would replace corporate bureaucrats, there would be little impact on efficiency, and government would gain greater control over the destructive tendencies of the market. With government and business working together to maintain a stable, hierarchical society, socialism could be compatible with Conservative goals. However, the key to Conservative socialism is government's ability to administer the economy without being influenced by popular pressures and the demands of special-interest groups. To insulate government, Schumpeter opposed active and widespread participation by citizens in the political process. As long as the political realm remained sealed from democratic pressures, government administration of the economy might be better suited than capitalism to sustaining Conservative values of stability, order, and hierarchy.

Leo Strauss (1899–1973)

Leo Strauss, a political philosopher at the University of Chicago for many years, devoted himself to resolving what he called "the crisis of modernity"—the corrosive effects of the Enlightenment legacy of individualism, ethical relativism, and faith in technology. In *Natural Right and History* (1953), he contrasted two conceptions of natural right. In Greek and early Christian society, natural right was based on a morality existing independently of individual desires. Humans had a moral duty to seek the good, and the purpose of politics was to cultivate virtue among citizens.

By contrast, early liberal theorists such as Hobbes and Locke used the notion of natural right to refer to the rights of autonomous individuals to pursue their self-interest without arbitrary restraint. This liberal version of natural right unlinked the earlier connection between rights and corresponding moral duties. Although Hobbes and Locke may have contributed to the toppling of the aristocratic power structure, they opened a Pandora's box of social disruptions. According to Strauss, when moral issues are relegated to individual choice, society will lack standards of excellence, truth, justice, and beauty. By making individual autonomy the primary social value, liberalism transforms society into a mass of rootless individuals pursuing their private passions, undermines the moral framework essential to nurturing civic virtue, and thereby condemns humans to alienation, anomie, narcissism, decadence, and nihilism.

The impact of democracy on modern society disturbed Strauss as well. Democracy permits people lacking in virtue and wisdom to become the rulers of society. Democratic governments are controlled by the short-sighted demands of citizens. Strauss worried that citizens in democratic societies are so preoccupied with private pleasures that they lack the courage and conviction to respond to broad social issues.

Another aspect of the "crisis of modernity" is the tendency of science and technology to push aside morality. Liberal societies seek to resolve problems by gaining greater technical mastery over nature to better satisfy human desires. However, Strauss believed that the most fundamental problems facing modern societies are moral problems caused by the rejection of standards of right and wrong. The social sciences such as economics and political science cannot comprehend or respond to moral decline because their pretense of value-neutrality and emphasis on quantitative technique blind them to moral issues. In Strauss's words, social scientists are "fiddling while Rome burns."

Strauss wanted government to be more than a neutral referee; it should act as a moral force in society by purposefully sustaining such values as patriotism, respect, and a sense of duty. Despite his qualms about democracy, Strauss remained sensitive to the dangers of totalitarianism. While his ideal form of government would entail rule by society's wisest and most virtuous leaders, he acknowledged that such a government was unlikely to appear in modern societies. Eventually, he accepted democracy, proposing only that popular participation in government be limited so that leaders would not be subjected to the pressures of popular demands.

Michael Oakeshott (1901–1990)

A professor of political science at the London School of Economics, Michael Oakeshott sought to make Conservatism appealing to the modern mind. Rejecting any reliance on religion or natural law, he simply claimed that existing customs and institutions, having slowly evolved in response to the accumulated wisdom of many generations, are superior to experiments in social reform.

In *Rationalism in Politics* (1962), Oakeshott blamed the expansion of government intervention on the rationalistic mentality that is the legacy of Enlightenment figures such as Descartes and Bacon. He criticized rationalism for seeking to impose an abstract, theoretical ideal on society to make it more fair and efficient. Rationalism is an unreliable guide because human reason can never fully comprehend the complexity of society and is usually critical of traditional authority, custom, prejudice, and habit. Therefore, government efforts to rationalize society will inevitably disrupt the institutions guiding individual lives. Moreover, this breakdown of traditional institutions leads to additional government intervention as individualism breeds envy, jealously, and resentment, which cause citizens to demand greater security and equality.

Oakeshott valued tradition not only because it has withstood the test of time, but also because it makes social restraints on individual choice seem natural and therefore largely invisible. Without tradition to guide the impulses of citizens toward socially useful goals, individuals resent any limitations on the gratification of their desires. In the absence of tradition, social conflicts cannot be resolved in a manner that is acceptable to opposing parties.

Despite his strong defense of tradition and authority, Oakeshott supported considerable individual freedom because he believed that humans form their personal identity by internalizing the culture in which they live. As a result of this socialization process, the range of choices that individuals actually make will usually be compatible with an orderly society. What Oakeshott opposed was the freedom of citizens to act collectively through government to restructure their society. In *On Human Conduct* (1975), he argued that society is not an "enterprise" with concrete goals such as full employment, the elimination of poverty, or social justice; instead, society is a "moral association" having no concrete goals but existing merely to provide a stable environment within which individuals discover meaning, purpose, and a personal identity as they pursue their private goals.

According to Oakeshott, government should not be involved in economic affairs, and economic interests should not be permitted to influence government. If politics is permitted to degenerate into an arena of clashing private interests, then government, lacking a rational basis for resolving conflicting desires, will inevitably become coercive and arbitrary. Government should remain peripheral to the economy, acting merely to protect property and enforce the law. Oakeshott's commitment to laissez-faire was not motivated by concerns about the inefficiency of government intervention. Rather, he believed that government intervention disrupts the process by which traditional institutions make individual freedom compatible with social order.

PRINCIPLES OF CONSERVATISM

The essential tenets of Conservatism are summarized in the following definitions:

Human Nature. Humans are driven by strong passions that can be directed toward either evil or good. The human capacity for reason is limited, with some persons having greater rational powers than others. The manner in which instincts and desires are molded into a unique personality is a function of the roles played and associations formed with others. In fact, humans cannot develop as persons without the bonds of social organization.

Society. Society is an organic structure based on a natural hierarchical order. The quality of society is a fundamental determinant of the interests and behavior of individuals. The good society sustains a stable hierarchy of social relations that enables individuals to discover a unique role and identity for themselves. Without hierarchy, all persons become homogeneous and the formation of individual personality is blocked.

Government. The purpose of government is to maintain the natural order of society. During periods of social stability, government can simply uphold tradition and preserve existing institutions by serving as a visible symbol of the unity of the nation and by creating a moral climate conducive to the development of virtuous citizens. Government should not only enforce laws protecting property rights, but should actively nurture those institutions such as the family and neighborhood that provide a social context within which individuals develop.

Morality. Morality exists independently of individual opinions of right and wrong, and therefore moral persons must give higher priority to the pursuit of virtue than to the satisfaction of personal desires. Individual reason is an unreliable guide to morality because reason alone is not sufficiently powerful to override human passions. Only the emotional attachments and prejudices that arise from living within a stable and supportive community can guide humans toward virtue. Moral values include civility, loyalty, patriotism, chivalry, obedience, courage, faithfulness, deference to authority, graciousness, and honor.

Freedom. Freedom exists when individuals are subject neither to arbitrary power nor their own passions. Freedom does not mean license to do whatever the individual desires. Since isolated individuals cannot gain control of their passions, freedom requires the authority, traditions, and order provided by a stable community.

Authority. Authority is legitimate when it resides with persons who fill traditional roles of leadership in society and who have knowledge of truth and virtue. Authority is essential for maintaining order and tradition in any social organization from the family to the nation.

Equality. People are equal only in their formal status as citizens of the community. This equality requires an impartial administration of justice in the protection of their rights and punishment of their crimes.

Justice. Justice is fulfilled when order is maintained and the law is administered impartially.

Efficiency. Efficiency means that society functions smoothly in achieving not only material production, but also in attaining nonmaterial goals such as the maintenance of order, culture, cohesive communities, and individual virtue.

CONSERVATISM TODAY

Conservatism's inability to gain widespread popularity in the United States has been attributed to the country's revolutionary origins, to the absence of a feudal aristocracy, and to the emphasis on freedom of individual choice. During the nineteenth and early twentieth centuries, American Conservatism was found almost exclusively in the South, where the plantation system and slavery were ideally suited for an ideology that emphasized the importance of hierarchical community.

However, Conservatism was revitalized by the devastation wrought by World War I and the Great Depression. These events served to undermine the faith in reason and progress that had characterized Western societies since the Enlightenment. As skeptics toward reason and science, Conservatives often expressed their ideas in poetry and literature. T. S. Eliot (1888–1965) and Ezra Pound (1885–1972) claimed that societies committed to individualism and technological progress were increasingly characterized by mindless conformity, cultural degeneracy, and a loss of purpose. They blamed both capitalism and democracy for degrading human spirituality and creativity. Capitalism's mass production breeds mediocrity, moral decay, and insipid consumerism. Citizens of a "mass society" lose the capacity for independent thought and seek only passive forms of entertainment that make no demands on their intellectual or artistic capacities.

Conservatives have largely ignored neoclassical economic theory, claiming that it reflects the worst aspects of modern society—the alienation of the individual from social bonds and community values, the focus on material gratification of sensual appetites, and the elevation of profitmaking and efficiency as the guiding values for society. Economics, according to Conservatives, serves to justify acquisitive and selfish behavior, thereby undermining the cohesiveness and stability of society. The ethic of utility-maximization legitimizes a materialistic lifestyle in which the consumption of commodities is the primary source of pleasure.

However, in contrast to traditional economic theory, political economy can accommodate a vision of society as a community bearing responsibility for the quality of life of its citizens. Conservative writers who find economic matters too important to be left to liberal economists, are now devoting considerable attention to political economy. Conservative political economy currently appears in a variety of forms including neo-fascist theory, corporatism, and neoconservatism.

Neo-fascist Theory

As liberalism and democracy gained ascendancy in the West, Conservatives could no longer simply defend the status quo. They needed a strategy for restoring the ideals that had been vanquished by a century of industrialization and modernization. As practiced in Germany and Italy during the 1930s and 1940s, traditional fascism relied on a charismatic leader to mobilize society, renew national and racial unity, and conduct violence and war against threats to the nation.

The roots of fascism lie in the romantic and nationalist beliefs that Western civilization has been in a state of moral and cultural decline ever since the Enlightenment unleashed the corrosive forces of individualism, rationalism, atheism, and materialism. As traditional values, institutions, and communities are destroyed, humans become alienated, culture degenerates, and society slowly crumbles.

Although World War II was fought to defeat fascism, considerable evidence appears today of "neo-fascist" sentiments in both Europe and the United States. During the 1980s, groups such as the Order, Aryan Nations, White Aryan Resistance, and the Posse Comitatus proliferated. The economic prosperity of the 1990s has undermined the growth of such organizations, but numerous unofficial state militias have formed and young "skinheads" give Nazi salutes and desecrate Jewish synagogues and cemeteries. Neo-fascism appeals to subordinate groups experiencing alienation and a sense of powerlessness. It promises to restore both economic prosperity and national or racial pride.

Neo-fascism condemns liberals for making individual freedom the supreme value, thereby denigrating the importance of community. Liberalism breeds an abstract, universal mentality that mocks parochial, local, or even national values as narrow and prejudiced and therefore inappropriate for society as a whole. Only abstract values, such as freedom and tolerance, are acceptable to liberalism. However, these values fail to reinforce people's emotional commitments to particular ethnic, racial, or national communities. Liberalism wants to replace the parochial community with "the brotherhood of man," but a global community remains merely an abstraction and cannot meet the emotional needs of humans for a sense of belonging and attachment. If humans attempt to identify with all mankind, they end up identifying with nothing concrete and become alienated.

The linkage of liberal ideas with the quest for a global community explains why neo-fascists regard communism and "one-world government" as the logical culmination of liberalism and democracy. Communists exploit the human need for community by promising a new society based on equality and collective ownership of the means of production. But communism suppresses the human need for private property and for membership in a specific community based on race, ethnicity, or nationality. Only neo-fascism can speak to these needs while simultaneously combating the torpor and decadence generated by liberal democracy. Neo-fascism, therefore, represents a battle against both communism and capitalism. It relies on racism and nationalism to promote community while preserving private property in recognition of the human need for emotional attachments to particular objects and places.

Corporatism

Corporatism proposes to reduce conflict and resentment in society by establishing organizations for each particular occupation or industry. These groups would provide individuals with communities in which to overcome the isolation and alienation of modern society. The various organizations would be integrated into a cooperative framework, with government serving as the ultimate authority and mediator. By consolidating individual interests into large groups, corporatists intend to place decisionmaking in the hands of group leaders who can resolve conflicts without resorting to strikes or other forms of civil unrest.

Like fascism, corporatism has roots in romanticism and nationalism, but it also grew out of the Roman Catholic church's vision of creating new communities to replace those destroyed by industrialization and urbanization. Early corporatist thinkers hoped that organizing capitalist society into groups would reduce class conflict and social unrest. By the twentieth century, corporatism was gaining increasing favor among capitalists as a solution to "cut-throat competition" in which all businesses were hurt. The success of business–government cooperation during World War I persuaded many industrialists that corporatism was the wave of the future. Indeed, corporatism was the basis for the National Industrial Recovery Act (NIRA) of 1933, which was designed to combat the Great Depression by giving labor the right to collectively bargain and by permitting corporations to cooperate with one another in establishing plans for production and pricing.

Ironically, had the Supreme Court not declared the NIRA unconstitutional in 1935, the United States would have embarked on a course bearing similarities to the institutional framework of Nazi Germany. After the NIRA was abolished, collective bargaining was reestablished through the Wagner Act of 1935. Not until the late 1930s, when the United States began preparing for war, did the Depression fade in response to the stimulus of government spending. After World War II, corporatism was largely discredited in the United States due to its similarity to fascism. However, some business leaders continue to be attracted by the prospect of a coordinated economy with no strikes and stable profits. During the economic turmoil of the 1970s, corporatist proposals were formulated by David Rockefeller's Trilateral Commission, Henry Ford's Initiative Committee on Economic Planning, and by the editors of *Business Week* magazine. Since the Reagan years, corporatism has been largely dormant as business leaders are generally satisfied with the performance of the economy.

With its emphasis on groups and a sense of community, corporatism also holds some appeal for those on the political left. The nineteenth-century concepts of guild socialism and social democracy had links to corporatist ideals. However, whereas Conservative corporatism (also called authoritarian corporatism or state corporatism) preserves hierarchy and stability by enforcing a consensus reached by leaders of large groups, leftist corporatism (also called liberal corporatism, social corporatism, or neocorporatism) encourages democratic participation and the inclusion of all group interests as a means of promoting greater equality. The economies of Sweden and Austria are the best examples of neocorporatism.

Neoconservatism

A relatively new variant of Conservatism was formulated during the 1970s and 1980s by writers including Irving Kristol, Nathan Glazer, Michael Novak, Peter Berger, Norman Podhoretz, Robert Nisbet, Seymour Martin Lipset, and George Will. Neoconservative ideas can be found in journals such as *The Public Interest* and *Commentary*. Many of the neoconservatives were Radicals during their youth, but were pushed toward Conservatism by their disgust with the student counterculture of the 1960s, their dissatisfaction with the conciliatory nature of U.S. foreign policy, and their disillusionment with the welfare state as a solution to poverty and crime.

Neoconservatives present themselves as not much different from Classical Liberals in their support for democracy, markets, and individual liberty. However, while neoconservatives may appreciate the market's vitality and efficiency, they also fear its potential for undermining traditional values and culture. The market stimulates and unleashes individual desires for sensual gratification that conflict with the respect for authority, the work ethic, and the sense of moral responsibility required for an orderly society. Also, neoconservatives reject the ethical relativism of Classical Liberalism, claiming that some values and lifestyles are better than others. Finally, while neoconservatives oppose many current government programs, they do defend a significant role for government in sustaining a social climate conducive to individual moral development and social cohesion.

Neoconservatives claim that an "adversary culture" or "new class" composed of professors, journalists, entertainers, social workers, health-care professionals, and government bureaucrats has effectively captured control of public opinion by virtue of its visibility and influence on the media. These groups are assumed to be significantly more liberal than the general population, and they use their power to build support for government spending on social programs from which they directly benefit as providers of health, education, and other human services.

Neoconservatives support a capitalist economy, constitutional democracy, and government efforts to cultivate civic virtue by nurturing traditional institutions such as the nuclear family, religion, and the local community. They share the fear of traditional Conservatives that unbridled capitalism undermines the social bonds holding individuals together in community, leaving them isolated and prone to cynicism and nihilism.

AN ASSESSMENT OF CONSERVATISM

Conservatism has evolved over the past two centuries not so much because of changes in its fundamental principles, but rather because of the evolving nature of the problems confronting modern societies. Early Conservatives blamed social disintegration and rootlessness on industrialization and opposed both liberal democracy and laissez-faire capitalism. By the end of the nineteenth century, however, a greater threat loomed on the horizon as socialism became an influential political ideal soon to materialize in Russia. The prospect of socialism gaining a foothold in Western nations caused Conservatives to suppress their concerns about capitalism. After witnessing socialism in Russia and fascism in Germany and Italy, most Conservatives conceded that capitalist democracy was the least evil of all feasible systems. Since World War II, Conservatism has been wedded to Classical Liberalism as the two formed a unified opposition to most forms of government intervention.

However, Conservatives continue to believe that social order ultimately rests on tradition and authority, and the market, with its emphasis on social mobility and "getting ahead," undermines both. Conservatives are respectful of government for its role as the visible representation of social unity, while Classical Liberals often express contempt for government. Conservatives also believe that social order requires some repression of desires either by the individual's own commitment to virtue, by the social conditioning provided by community values and institutions, or, ultimately, by the threat of punishment from government. A capitalist market economy, on the other hand, fosters an ethic legitimizing the unbridled pursuit of pleasure. Conservatives seek to maintain the integrity of national cultures, while the market breeds cosmopolitan attitudes and lifestyles. Finally, Conservatives uphold a morality based on objective values, but the market makes the individual consumer the sole arbiter of values. This tension between the market and Conservative ideals explains why Conservatives and Classical Liberals, despite their common interest in protecting private property and hierarchy, will never be entirely compatible. With the dissolution of communism as a major threat to Western nations, the alliance between Conservatives and Classical Liberals can be expected to loosen, and the two perspectives will once again clash over their fundamentally different views of the market and government.

The Conservative critique of modern society highlights some of the failures of capitalist democracies. High-material standards of living are accompanied by individual alienation, declining civic virtue, and diminished legitimacy of public institutions. Conservatives point to the prevalence of anti-social behavior and the number of young people who reject mainstream culture as evidence of an increasingly difficult struggle to find meaning and purpose in an amoral, commercialized society. The fact that many Conservative themes such as loss of meaning, alienation, and spiritual emptiness are also found in Radical critiques of capitalism illustrates the commitment shared by both perspectives to a strong and vibrant community life.

However, two major obstacles confront any significant renewal of Conservative influence. First, Conservatism resists the two major trends in modern civilization: egalitarianism and individualism. These societal values, deeply embedded in Western culture, will assure widespread resistance to any proposals for strengthening hierarchical authority. Only an economic collapse or the threat of impending social chaos would open political space for the reassertion of authority.

Second, Conservatives have, for the most part, been unable to offer concrete proposals for generating cultural renewal without resorting to racism or national chauvinism. These values conflict with another powerful ideal in modern life: the brotherhood of mankind. At a time when barriers between East and West are crumbling and global economic integration is proceeding, appeals to parochial values and local culture seem antiquated. Yet this difficulty may point the way for the future of Conservatism. Rather than seeking to shape national or global policy, Conservatives might effectively pursue their ideals by focusing on family, neighborhood, and community revitalization.

ADDITIONAL READING

Allison, Lincoln. *Right Principles: A Conservative Philosophy of Politics*. Oxford: Basil Blackwell, 1984.

Buckley, William F., ed. *Conservative Thought in the Twentieth Century*. New York: Bobbs-Merrill, 1970.

Drury, Shadia B. *Leo Strauss and the American Right*. New York: St. Martin's, 1997.

Holmes, Stephen. *The Anatomy of Antiliberalism*. Cambridge: Harvard University Press, 1993.

Kirk, Russell. *The Conservative Mind: From Burke to Eliot*. Washington, DC: Henry Regnery, 1995.

Kristol, Irving. *Neoconservatism: The Autobiography of an Ideal*. New York: The Free Press, 1995.

Lakoff, George. *Moral Politics: What Conservatives Know That Liberals Don't*. Chicago: University of Chicago Press, 1996.

Muller, Jerry Z., ed. *Conservatism*. Princeton: Princeton University Press, 1997.

Nash, George. *The Conservative Intellectual Movement in the U.S. since 1945.* New York: Basic Books, 1979.

Nisbet, Robert. *Conservatism: Dream and Reality.* Minneapolis: University of Minnesota Press, 1986.

O'Sullivan, Noel. *Conservatism.* New York: St. Martin's, 1976.

Rossiter, Clinton. *Conservatism in America*, 2nd ed. Cambridge: Harvard University Press, 1982.

Scruton, Roger. *Conservative Texts: An Anthology.* New York: St. Martin's, 1991.

Steinfels, Peter. *The Neoconservatives: The Men Who Are Changing America's Politics.* New York: Simon & Schuster, 1979.

White, R. J., ed. *The Conservative Tradition.* New York: New York University Press, 1957.

Chapter 6

The Modern Liberal Perspective

The roots of Modern Liberalism lie deep in the tradition of Classical Liberalism. Although early Classical Liberal theorists such as John Locke and Adam Smith expressed reservations about the wisdom of sole reliance on the market to organize society, their commitment to individual liberty and private property precluded any significant action by government. With the emergence of Radical and Conservative challenges to capitalism, however, came a growing perception that laissez-faire policies were incapable of generating widespread political support. In response to this problem, Modern Liberalism emerged as a combination of appealing elements from the existing ideological perspectives. This eclectic and hybrid nature contributed greatly to its flexibility and resilience. As a result, Modern Liberals dominated for much of the twentieth century as they sought to promote social justice while preserving both private property and democracy.

ARCHITECTS OF MODERN LIBERALISM

Jeremy Bentham (1748–1832)

The critique of Classical Liberalism began with efforts to discredit the Lockean notions of natural law and natural rights. English philosopher and legal theorist Jeremy Bentham argued that Classical Liberal theorists used the term "natural" simply to defend their own particular vision of the good society. Bentham sought instead to develop a scientific basis for social theory. He based his theories on a system of ethics known as utilitarianism. In *An Introduction to the Principles of Morals and Legislation* (1789), he claimed that pain and pleasure were the sole determinants of human behavior and the sole criteria of right and wrong. For an individual or for society as a whole, the best course of action is that which maximizes pleasure and minimizes pain. Although Bentham acknowledged the impossibility of measuring the pleasures of different persons and precisely calculating the social consequences of a particular policy, he suggested that politicians should proceed as if such calculations could be made. Only then would political decisions be based on an objective assessment of their consequences.

To understand Bentham's motive for replacing natural law with utilitarianism, we must focus on the changing political environment of late eighteenth-century England. Classical Liberals had relied on the doctrines of natural law and natural rights to support their arguments against the arbitrary power of church and state. As that battle was being won, however, a new struggle between workers and owners of property began to develop. With the grounds of political conflict shifting, the doctrine of natural rights became unacceptable to defenders of private property for two reasons. First, Radicals such as Tom Paine had used the concept of natural rights to defend workers' rights to participate in the political process. Among property owners, the prospect of extending the vote to workers raised fears of "mob rule" and a "tyranny of the majority" that might eventually result in confiscation of property. Second, the doctrine of natural rights offered such firm protection for property that it precluded government reforms aimed at ameliorating the conflict between workers and property owners. If property rights were absolutely inviolable, then government could not legitimately tax, regulate, or redistribute property. In short, natural rights served to protect the status quo.

In contrast to the doctrine of natural rights, utilitarianism provided a flexible and pragmatic basis for government intervention. Any reform resulting in favorable consequences for society as a whole was considered legitimate. Bentham claimed that rights were established by society's laws, not by the laws of nature. With new laws, government could legitimately create or eliminate certain property rights as long as the laws served the public interest. Cutting all ties to natural law and natural rights enabled Modern Liberalism to assure a wide latitude for government action.

On the controversial issue of whether government should engage in redistribution of income and wealth, Bentham equivocated. On one hand, utilitarianism provides a strong argument in favor of redistribution. The law of diminishing marginal utility suggests that rich people get less pleasure from a dollar than do poor people, and therefore society's total utility can be increased by taking money from the rich and giving it to the poor. Bentham stated that "the more nearly the actual proportion [of wealth] approaches equality, the greater will be the total mass of happiness." On the other hand, Bentham feared that redistribution would undermine the security of property rights and reduce incentives, thereby contributing to stagnation of the economy. He concluded that "when security and equality are in opposition, there should be no hesitation: equality should give way." Thus, while Bentham opened the door for extensive government activity, he tended to support laissez-faire policies in economic affairs. His proposals for reform were largely confined to the judiciary and penal systems, education, and the electoral process.

John Stuart Mill (1806–1873)

John Stuart Mill was one of the major intellectual figures of the nineteenth century. His father, James Mill, was also a prominent economist and, along with Jeremy Bentham, he decided to use his son as an experiment in rearing the ideal human being. The young boy was taught Greek and calculus before he was ten and authored scholarly books while still a teenager. However, this rigorous intellectual training left John Stuart Mill emotionally unfulfilled and, as a young man, he began reading the romantic writings of Coleridge and Carlyle to explore the nonintellectual side of life. From that point on, Mill's work reflects an effort to steer a middle course between the calculating rationality of Bentham's utilitarianism and the romantic themes of spiritual introspection and emotional expression.

Mill affirmed the utilitarian guideline for organizing society in a manner that produces the greatest amount of pleasure. However, in contrast to Bentham, Mill introduced the idea of qualitative differences in pleasures. He believed that the pleasures associated with intellectual and artistic expression were superior to the pleasures of ownership or consumption. In his words, it is "better to be Socrates dissatisfied than a fool satisfied." Mill based his arguments for the superiority of certain types of pleasure on Aristotle's claim that the ultimate purpose of human life is to develop and exercise those capacities unique to the human species. For both Aristotle and Mill, these capacities include the ability to reason and to act consciously. Other activities such as eating, drinking, and procreating are functions common to all animals and therefore cannot be sources of ultimate human fulfillment.

This notion of a hierarchy of pleasures represents a challenge to the ethical relativism of Classical Liberalism. Modern Liberals had a basis for making judgments concerning the lifestyles that society ought to promote and hence a rationale for government intervention. However, Mill himself generally opposed legislative efforts to cultivate individual virtue. In *On Liberty* (1859), he argued that government should interfere with individual freedom only to prevent citizens from harming one another. Despite this dictum, Mill did support three specific forms of intervention: public funding for education, government encouragement of birth control, and an inheritance tax to offset the tendency for property holdings to become concentrated.

Mill's efforts to synthesize the best of Classical Liberal, Conservative, and Radical ideas set the tone for the subsequent development of Modern Liberalism. Mill championed the cause of individual liberty and yet valued the role of "superior minds" in providing guidance and leadership for the rest of society. He supported universal suffrage, but only with the provision that educated citizens would have multiple votes so that their impact on the political process would be greater. In *Principles of Political Economy* (1848), Mill emphasized the importance of secure property rights in fostering economic prosperity, yet he also favored experiments with cooperatives in hopes that they might eventually lead to a decentralized form of socialism.

Mill believed that both capitalism and democracy, while flawed, served essential functions. Capitalism facilitated the accumulation of wealth that would free humans from the drudgery of menial labor and permit them to focus on the higher pleasures of intellectual and artistic expression. Full democracy, by permitting all citizens to participate in society's collective decisionmaking, would give citizens a sense of self-worth and dignity that would, in turn, arouse their desire for more fulfilling lifestyles. Mill acknowledged that social change would take time, but government could hasten the process by providing public education and by promoting greater social equality.

Thomas Hill Green (1836–1882)

T. H. Green, an Oxford philosopher, sought to strike a balance between the individualism of Classical Liberalism and the romantic notion of organic community that had stimulated both Conservative and Radical thought. Green was concerned that Classical Liberalism, with its emphasis on protection of property rights and laissez-faire, would not appeal to workers. The English Reform Bill of 1867 extended suffrage rights to a broad spectrum of the working class, and if these new voters were to be peacefully integrated into the political process, government action to improve their living conditions would be necessary.

Green supported many of the tenets of Classical Liberalism, including individual freedom, property rights, individual initiative, and self-reliance. However, he redefined certain principles to challenge the commitment to laissez-faire. Whereas Classical Liberals viewed humans as rationally pursuing maximum pleasure, Green claimed that humans do not seek pleasure directly, but rather strive to fulfill images of the kind of person they want to be. In *Lectures on the Principles of Political Obligation* (1879), he argued that because these self-images are formed in a social environment, they reflect the shared values of a particular culture. Thus individuals will possess a moral sensibility encompassing certain duties and obligations to others.

Green also revised the meaning of freedom. Whereas Classical Liberals focused exclusively on the absence of external constraint, Green defined freedom in a positive sense as the ability to develop a lifeplan and to pursue it effectively. Positive freedom requires that individuals possess adequate economic resources to carry out a lifeplan, so workers living on subsistence wages may need government assistance to achieve freedom.

Finally, Green revised the basis of property rights. Classical Liberals claimed a natural right to whatever holdings are acquired without violating the legal rights of others. In contrast, Green claimed that property rights depend on society's recognition of their usefulness in promoting the public interest. In other words, rather than accepting the Classical Liberal view that the public interest is synonymous with the protection of property rights, Green argued that the public interest has an independent status prior to, and determinative of, property rights.

Although Green accepted the concept of private property in principle, he criticized the existing degree of inequality in property holdings. Excessive inequality interfered with the freedom of many workers who did not possess adequate resources to effectively pursue a lifeplan. Since lack of freedom is contrary to the public interest, the existing concentration of wealth was unacceptable. In determining the proper extent of government efforts to redistribute wealth, Green proposed that property rights should be judged for their contribution to positive freedom. Property that enables individuals to carry out a lifeplan contributes to initiative, self-reliance, and innovation and thus deserves society's protection. However, property that merely confers privilege and power over other persons is advantageous only to the individual property owner and conflicts with the public interest. Such property rights may be legitimately limited by government.

Green condoned government intervention only to assure that each citizen has positive freedom. By releasing the initiative and energy that is suppressed by poverty, government can create a dynamic economy in which every citizen has dignity and a decent standard of living.

Alfred Marshall (1842–1924)

An economics professor at Cambridge University in England, Alfred Marshall developed much of the microeconomic theory that is taught in undergraduate courses today. Although Stanley Jevons was the first to suggest substituting the word "economics" for "political economy," the title of Marshall's textbook, *Principles of Economics* (1890), confirmed that the change in labels had been accomplished. By rejecting the term "political economy," Marshall did not intend to exclude political or ethical considerations from public debate. Prior to becoming an economist, he studied ethics and was familiar with the writings of Hegel and Kant. Marshall was deeply concerned about the plight of the poor and believed that economics could provide guidance in public efforts to improve the quality of human existence. He was motivated to adopt the term "economics" instead of "political economy" by his desire to create a more scientific understanding of society. Limiting the scope of analysis to "that part of individual and social action which is most closely connected with the attainment and with the use of the material requisites of well-being," Marshall anticipated a narrower focus on measurable phenomena that could be expressed in mathematical form. However, this definition meant that Marshall acknowledged the existence of noneconomic dimensions of life and noneconomic values that might also affect government policymaking.

For many of Marshall's successors at Cambridge, the distinction between economics and political economy allowed economics to share the objectivity and rigor of the physical sciences, while political economy incorporated ethical considerations and permitted consideration of both economic and noneconomic goals. In sharp contrast, the Classical Liberalism of the Austrian school portrayed economics as covering the allocation of scarce resources to any goal, thereby making economics the "science of rational choice" and denying the existence of noneconomic values.

Marshall was not a strong advocate of government intervention. In fact, he was quite cautious about any proposals that would restrict economic freedom or violate property rights, claiming that freedom and security of property were essential to stimulate innovation, entrepreneurship, and economic growth. As a first line of attack against the problems of poverty and human suffering, Marshall hoped that individual citizens and businesses would engage in "economic chivalry" through public service and charitable contributions. However, he did recognize certain failings of the market economy, including unequal power in labor–management relations, the presence of negative externalities such as pollution, and the inability of the market to provide public goods such as universal education. His receptiveness to some government intervention is exemplified by his claim that "the human will, guided by careful thought, can so modify circumstances as to [improve] the economic, as well as the moral, well-being of the masses of people."

John Maynard Keynes (1883–1946)

As an economist from Cambridge University, John Maynard Keynes was fully aware of the various flaws in the market uncovered by Marshall and Pigou. However, his condemnation of laissez-faire capitalism went far beyond previous criticisms. He blamed the "economic anarchy" of free markets for causing high unemployment and excessive inequality in the distribution of income.

In *The General Theory of Employment, Interest, and Money* (1936), Keynes attributed recessions to inadequate spending. This claim challenged the traditional wisdom of most economists who assumed that the main obstacle to growth was a lack of saving. Keynes argued that saving is beneficial only if the money is channeled back into the economy through borrowing and investment. When investors become pessimistic about the future, they hesitate to commit money to new projects. This reluctance to invest triggers a "multiplier effect" as the economy slows, workers are laid off, and businesses close.

Prior to Keynes, most economists believed that recessions were self-correcting; they regarded any slowdown in the economy as a temporary aberration requiring no government remedies. Keynes, on the other hand, pointed to the Great Depression as evidence that the economy could sink into seemingly permanent stagnation. To the economists who argued that the economy would bounce back in the long run, Keynes replied: "In the long run we are all dead." The cure for recession was increased government spending to supplement inadequate spending by consumers and businesses. Moreover, this government spending would be more effective when financed by borrowing rather than taxes, since taxes tend to depress private spending. In calling for "deficit spending," Keynes challenged the wisdom of generations of economists committed to balanced government budgets.

The Keynesian explanation of recessions also served to justify government efforts to redistribute income. Since low-income families spend a larger percentage of any additional income than do high-income families, government can increase total private spending by taxing the rich and giving to the poor. Whereas Bentham and Mill had been fearful that redistribution would adversely affect incentives and capital accumulation, Keynes argued that greater equality was essential to promoting full employment and growth. This commitment to a more equal distribution of income explains why Keynesianism justifies government support for labor unions in their quest for higher wages.

Keynes attempted, without much success, to persuade Franklin Roosevelt to experiment with the new economics. However, World War II forced the Western nations to engage in massive deficit spending, and the results seemed to confirm the Keynesian message. Factories quickly reopened, people went back to work, and the economy was operating at full employment within a short time. This success persuaded many economists and policymakers to change their view of the proper role of government. In 1946, the U.S. Congress passed the Employment Act, committing government to pursue all practical means to maintain full employment.

John Rawls (1921–)

John Rawls is a Harvard philosopher whose book *A Theory of Justice* (1971) touched off an intensive reexamination of the ethical foundations of political economy. Rawls was responding to an emerging dilemma within Modern Liberalism. Although Modern Liberals had successfully challenged the inviolability of property rights and the supremacy of the free market, they lacked criteria for determining which property rights should be restrained and how much redistribution should occur. Without a theory of the public interest or a theory of justice, Modern Liberal governments operated without principles, making them vulnerable to the pressures of special-interest groups. The political process was in danger of degenerating into a free-for-all in which more aggressive and powerful groups gain benefits from government at the expense of less powerful groups.

Faced with this dilemma, Rawls sought to determine theoretically the particular distribution of wealth that would be viewed as fair by all members of society. He claimed that the human tendency to give priority to self-interest impedes any effort to achieve consensus on questions of justice. This problem can be avoided theoretically, however, by conceiving a situation in which individuals formulate principles of justice without any knowledge of their own particular interests. If several people want to divide a cake fairly, the person cutting the cake chooses his portion last to assure that self-interest will not affect the size of the slices.

In a hypothetical situation in which people are ignorant of their own particular interests, Rawls argues that two principles of justice would be formulated. First, each person would be granted the same basic liberties; and second, wealth would be redistributed so as to maximize the well-being of the poorest members of society. The second principle is more controversial, but Rawls claims that people truly ignorant of their own position in society would choose to protect the poorest group since they might be a member of that group. Rawls does not condemn self-interest; he simply argues that people can be objective in formulating principles of justice only when they ignore the interests attached to their particular role in society.

Maximizing the well-being of the poorest groups in society will probably not require perfect equality. Rawls recognizes the role of inequality in providing incentives and fostering capital accumulation that ultimately benefits everyone. However, redistribution of wealth should proceed until any further transfers so dampen incentives and growth that the poor would be harmed. Rawls does not claim to know at what point redistribution should be halted, and it is possible that some nations may already be at or beyond the optimal degree of equality.

At first glance, Rawls's image of people suspending awareness of their own economic status seems highly implausible. However, he supports his theory by claiming that humans progress through stages of moral development. In the highest stage, actions are based on universal principles rather than narrow self-interest. If the Rawlsian concept of justice would indeed be chosen by truly moral persons, then government redistribution could be justified despite protests by those adversely affected. Rawls anticipates that the experience of living in a fair society will minimize such protests as individuals develop a moral sensibility enabling them to value justice above their own material gains.

Rawls is the first Modern Liberal to offer a criterion of distributive justice. If accepted, the Rawlsian principles would put an end to many of the political struggles that have threatened to destroy the cohesiveness of modern societies. However, despite the widespread attention given to Rawls's ideas, his theory of justice has not been widely embraced by Modern Liberals because it potentially mandates massive redistribution of wealth.

PRINCIPLES OF MODERN LIBERALISM

Because of its synthetic nature, Modern Liberalism is not easily expressed in concise terms. However, the following definitions convey the essential character of this perspective.

Human Nature. Humans are capable of rational choice, but their social environment significantly shapes their goals. To develop fully, humans need social relations based on mutual respect, and this need creates moral sentiments that restrain pure selfishness except in situations where deprivation creates pathological behavior.

Society. Society is an aggregation of individuals with both private and collective interests. To fulfill both sets of interests, the institutions of markets and government are essential to society.

Government. The purpose of government is to impartially protect rights and to serve as a means by which citizens can collectively pursue goals that they cannot attain as individuals. However, these goals must promote the public interest; government should not favor any particular conception of the good society.

Morality. For the most part, values are subjective and therefore relative. However, certain values should appeal to all rational persons, thus forming the basis for an objective morality. Values considered to be universally valid include respect for the rights and dignity of all persons, concern for the environment, and respect for the autonomy of other nations. More controversial values include rights to occupational safety, health care, and old-age income security.

Authority. Legitimate authority exists when power is exercised in the public interest. However, since Modern Liberalism offers no clear definition of the public interest, the distinction between legitimate and illegitimate authority is subject to interpretation. Modern Liberalism lacks a coherent theory of political obligation that specifies the condition under which citizens have a duty to obey laws.

Freedom. Freedom has two meanings. In a negative sense, freedom is the absence of coercion or constraints imposed by other people or by government. In a positive sense, freedom is the ability to effectively pursue one's goals. These two freedoms may conflict with each other when the negative freedom of some persons poses an obstacle to the positive freedom of others.

Equality. "Equality of opportunity" and "equality under the law" are two important components of social equality. However, both are jeopardized by inequality of wealth and income, so greater "equality of result" is essential to achieving social equality.

Justice. Justice is achieved when both human rights and property rights are upheld. When these rights conflict, society, acting through government, must find a balance that best serves the public interest.

Efficiency. Efficiency means maximizing the value of goods and services produced. However, efficiency is only one criterion of a good society and may be superseded by considerations of freedom, equality, or justice.

MODERN LIBERALISM TODAY

World War II forced a dramatic expansion of the economic role of governments in most nations. The success of the war effort largely dispelled whatever doubts had lingered about the power of government to stimulate the economy. Economies that had been languishing in depression for a decade suddenly sprang to life, providing full employment and astonishing levels of output. When the war ended, there was no guarantee that depression would not return, and most governments took strong measures to guarantee continued prosperity. With Radicalism and Conservatism seemingly discredited by the horrors of Stalinist Russia and Nazi Germany and with Classical Liberalism blamed for the Great Depression, a consensus formed around Modern Liberalism that would dominate Western politics for the next three decades. Currently, Modern Liberal ideas appear in various forms including new Keynesian economics, neocorporatism, and post-Keynesian economics.

New Keynesian Economics

Despite the Keynesian revolution of the 1930s and 1940s, most U.S. Keynesian economists, led by Paul Samuelson, affirmed the complementarity of Keynesian macroeconomics and neoclassical microeconomics. The former offered an understanding of the economy as a whole, while the latter was useful in explaining the behavior of individual consumers and firms. Samuelson proposed a "neoclassical synthesis" in which both doctrines would coexist peacefully.

By the 1960s, the neoclassical synthesis had become so influential that economists were formally installed at the highest levels of government power. In addition to Samuelson, the leading economists of that period included Robert Solow, Walter Heller (1915–1987), James Tobin, Gardner Ackley, and Arthur Okun (1928–1980). Operating as members of or consultants to the President's Council of Economic Advisors, they popularized the notion of "fine-tuning," in which fiscal and monetary policy would be used to adjust the level of aggregate spending until a full-employment, noninflationary economy was achieved. The proponents of the neoclassical synthesis largely opposed government intervention in the internal functioning of the economy. Using a mechanical analogy, fiscal and monetary policy can be viewed as the accelerator of an automobile. Changing speed requires no tinkering with the engine, but merely pressing or easing of the accelerator.

The economic turmoil of the 1970s and 1980s seriously discredited the neoclassical synthesis. Some Modern Liberals defected to Classical Liberalism and others to Radicalism. However, many sought to construct a "new Keynesian" economics responsive to the criticisms being launched by new classical economists. Whereas Keynes relied on macro variables such as consumption, saving, and investment to demonstrate the inherent instability of the market, the new Keynesians seek to explain the macro economy by analyzing its micro foundations. Like neoclassical economists, they assume that individuals and firms rationally seek to maximize utility or profit. The macro performance of the economy is viewed as the aggregated micro behavior of individuals and firms.

However, new Keynesians part ways with new classical economists in explaining unemployment, recession, and inflation. While new classicals attribute instability to government intervention, new Keynesians blame imperfections in markets such as lack of information, monopoly elements, and resource immobility. The policy implications of new Keynesian economics differ from both Keynesian and new classical economics. Unlike traditional Keynesianism, new Keynesians have little confidence in monetary and fiscal policy to boost or stabilize aggregate demand. In contrast to new classical economists, new Keynesians call for active government policies to remedy the structural imperfections preventing markets from operating efficiently. Examples of such policies include dissemination of employment information through computerized job networks, government funds for training and certifying young and unemployed workers, and portable pensions and benefits to increase labor mobility.

Prominent new Keynesians include Lawrence Summers, Alan Blinder, and Joseph Stiglitz, all of whom have been appointed to high offices in government and hold professorships at prestigious universities. New Keynesian ideas are disseminated in the *Journal of Economic Perspectives*.

Neocorporatism

Although corporatism has a Conservative lineage, the Scandinavian countries and Austria practice a Modern Liberal version of corporatism emphasizing social equality and democratic participation. This "neocorporatism" was proposed in the United States during the 1980s under the label of industrial policy. Government would provide leadership in fostering cooperation among corporations, labor unions, and other powerful interest groups. The logic behind neocorporatism is that the modern economy is so dominated by interest groups that laissez-faire policies simply permit more powerful groups to prey on unorganized entities such as small businesses, farmers, non-unionized workers, and the poor. Breaking up the clusters of power is deemed both politically infeasible and inefficient, so the only alternative is government coordination of conflicting interests in an effort to promote stability and prosperity.

In addition to mediating conflict, government would reduce uncertainty by providing guidelines for economic development. Government would also become more active in stimulating the economy through funding for education, transportation, job training, and research and development. Neocorporatists favor government aid to industries with significant potential for growth. Strategic trade policy, including subsidies and tariffs, might be used to propel selected industries to international dominance. Underlying these proposals is the belief that government must have a coherent vision of the future and take steps to realize that vision if the economy is to be competitive in the global market.

Leading proponents of neocorporatism in the United States include Lester Thurow, Robert Kuttner, and ex-Secretary of Labor Robert Reich. Neocorporatism has failed to gain widespread acceptance because the proposals for enlarging government's authority run counter to the political tides of the late twentieth century. When the idea of industrial policy was first presented in the 1980s, the Japanese and European economies were held up as shining examples of what neocorporatism could achieve. Today, with European unemployment exceeding ten percent and Japan in a lengthy recession, critics of neocorporatism can turn the tables, using Europe and Japan as arguments against government coordination of the economy.

Post-Keynesian Economics

The declining prestige of Keynesian economics in the 1970s was symptomatic of the general disarray afflicting Modern Liberalism. Some economists sought to rescue Keynesian ideas by arguing that American economists such as Paul Samuelson had misinterpreted Keynes's ideas. Early figures in post-Keynesian economics include Joan Robinson, a colleague of Keynes at Cambridge University, and Michal Kalecki (1899–1970), a Polish economist who independently arrived at many of the same ideas as Keynes. Other important early contributors include Piero Sraffa (1898–1983), Maurice Dobb (1900–1976), and Nicholas Kaldor (1908–1986). In the United States, post-Keynesian economics was advanced by Sidney Weintraub (1914–1983), Alfred Eichner (1937–1988), and Hyman Minsky (1919–1996). Contemporary post-Keynesians include Paul Davidson, Geoff Harcourt, Victoria Chick, and John Eatwell. Post-Keynesian writings are featured in the *Journal of Post Keynesian Economics*, the *Cambridge Journal of Economics*, and the *Review of Political Economy*.

Keynes called for two major reforms: government action to regulate aggregate spending and government control or "socialization" of investment. United States policymakers adopted the first reform but ignored the second because it requires more extensive government management of the economy. Yet without control over investment, post-Keynesians believe that government cannot maintain both price stability and low unemployment for extended periods.

Post-Keynesians attribute the failure of "demand management" to the increasing concentration of production in the advanced capitalist economies. In the absence of effective competition, firms possess "market power" and utilize "mark-up pricing" by simply adding a desired profit margin to their costs to determine the price of their product. In this context, governmental efforts to control inflation are stymied. When government cuts spending or tightens the money supply, businesses simply lay off workers and reduce output rather than lower their prices. The result is stagflation—simultaneous inflation and unemployment.

From the post-Keynesian perspective, stagflation can be resolved by government efforts to control wages and prices, to become directly involved in directing investment to particular industries, and perhaps to operate such key industries as energy and communications. Post-Keynesians believe that the free-market economy is not only prone to stagflation, but cannot generate the growth in productivity required to remain competitive in international markets.

AN ASSESSMENT OF MODERN LIBERALISM

Modern Liberalism was the dominant ideology in Western nations from the end of World War II until the early-1970s. Its appeal stemmed not only from the success of Keynesian economics in maintaining prosperity during that period, but also from the postwar revulsion toward any pure form of ideology. Modern Liberalism offered a flexible and pragmatic approach well-suited to the public's increasingly nondogmatic attitude toward social and political issues.

The declining influence of Modern Liberalism in recent years can be explained by three factors. First, the emergence of stagflation in the early 1970s rendered impotent the Keynesian tools of demand management. The economy could not be simultaneously stimulated to reduce unemployment and slowed to control inflation. Moreover, stagflation meant that Modern Liberal efforts to promote disadvantaged groups came increasingly at the expense of other citizens. Economist Lester Thurow coined the term "zero-sum society" to describe a no-growth economy in which one group's gain is another group's loss. In a zero-sum society, redistributive policies are likely to create resentment and anger, thereby eroding public support for Modern Liberalism.

Second, Modern Liberalism's emphasis on universal values such as justice and human rights often conflicts with citizens' attachments to particular values and cultures. On issues ranging from welfare to criminal justice, Modern Liberalism is widely perceived as defending abstract rights while remaining insensitive to the wishes and interests of particular individuals or groups. For this reason, critics blame Modern Liberalism for a decline of moral standards and disintegration of traditional culture.

Finally, the flexibility of Modern Liberalism has created problems. Because it encompasses values taken from conflicting ideologies, Modern Liberalism lacks a clear and coherent vision of the public interest and therefore possesses no firm criteria by which to assess the performance of either the market or government. The Modern Liberal commitment to individualism means that individual preferences must be the ultimate source of social values, yet Modern Liberalism is also committed to greater equality, even if this goal requires manipulation of the market economy by government. Once the beneficence of the market has been questioned, some criterion of justice or the public interest is essential to give coherence to government activities. Modern Liberal economists have relied on the concept of economic efficiency as the criterion for government intervention; government should improve the efficiency of the market by correcting certain failures, thereby promoting the well-being of society. However, developments in economic theory have demonstrated that efficiency is not synonymous with maximum social welfare, leaving Modern Liberals without clear guidelines for policymaking.

In attempting to resolve this dilemma, Modern Liberals face a choice. They can simply accept the absence of a theory of justice, leaving both the market and government without firm moral legitimacy, or they can formulate specific principles of justice to clearly define the public interest. To choose the latter route, however, would commit Modern Liberals to government action aimed at bringing society into conformance with the principles of justice. Most Modern Liberals remain too firmly committed to the notions of ethical relativism, pluralism, diversity, and tolerance to support any precise definition of justice that would legitimize such a powerful role for government.

Despite these difficulties, Modern Liberalism is likely to remain a powerful ideology. For those who find Conservatism, Classical Liberalism, and Radicalism to be unacceptable, the synthetic and compromising nature of Modern Liberalism will continue to hold appeal. Proponents of Modern Liberalism offer no ultimate resolution of the conflicts between human rights and property rights, between freedom and equality, or between individualism and community, claiming that these tensions between opposing ideals are essential features of human existence.

ADDITIONAL READING

Anderson, Walter Truett, ed. *Rethinking Liberalism*. New York: Avon, 1983.

Arestis, Philip, and Thanes Skouras, eds. *Post-Keynesian Economic Theory*. Armonk, NY: M. E. Sharpe, 1985.

Eichner, Alfred, ed. *A Guide to Post-Keynesian Economics*. White Plains, NY: M. E. Sharpe, 1979.

Gutman, Amy. *Liberal Equality*. New York: Cambridge University Press, 1980.

Kuttner, Robert. *The End of Laissez-Faire: National Purpose and the Global Economy After the Cold War*. New York: Alfred Knopf, 1991.

MacLean, Douglas, and Claudia Mills, eds. *Liberalism Reconsidered*. Totowa, NJ: Rowman & Allanheld, 1983.

Reich, Robert B. *The Resurgent Liberal*. New York: Times Books, 1989.

Rosenblum, Nancy L., ed. *Liberalism and the Moral Life*. Cambridge, MA: Harvard University Press, 1989.

Rothenberg, Randall. *The Neoliberals*. New York: Simon & Schuster, 1984.

Shapiro, Ian. *The Evolution of Rights in Liberal Theory*. Cambridge: Cambridge University Press, 1986.

Spitz, David. *The Real World of Liberalism*. Chicago: University of Chicago Press, 1982.

PART III

CONTEMPORARY
ISSUES IN POLITICAL
ECONOMY

Chapter 7

Government and
the Market

During the first half of the twentieth century, the combination of two world wars and the Great Depression served as a catalyst for expanding the role of government. Public reaction was generally favorable up to the 1960s. However, the political and economic upheavals of the past three decades have fostered a pervasive cynicism and hostility toward government. Politicians now frequently campaign for office as "outsiders" promising to repair the damage caused by previous policies. Public apathy is reflected in low voter turnouts and a relative lack of interest in political affairs.

In this chapter, we confront some of the basic questions about democracy and capitalism: What is government's proper role in a market economy? What aspects of modern society prevent government from serving its proper role and what changes in the economy and society might remedy political shortcomings? Different answers to these questions come from each of the four ideological perspectives.

THE CLASSICAL LIBERAL PERSPECTIVE

The Proper Role of Government

The Classical Liberal view of government is succinctly expressed by Thomas Jefferson's famous dictum: "that government is best which governs least." The defense of a laissez-faire policy derives from the view that government represents a social contract among rational, self-interested persons who would agree only to policies promoting their own interests. As a result, government should be prohibited from engaging in any activities conferring benefits upon some citizens at the expense of others. The proper role of government is reduced to that of a "referee" or "night-watchman," enforcing laws protecting private property and the civil rights shared by all citizens.

Virtually all Classical Liberals accept government's role in establishing and enforcing a system of laws to protect individual rights. Beyond that function, consensus has been difficult to achieve. Adam Smith proposed that government should print and regulate the money supply, provide certain "public goods" such as national defense, harbors, and roads, and levy taxes to finance its functions. However, other Classical Liberals, particularly those who are inclined toward libertarianism or even anarchism, argue that these activities are both unnecessary and counterproductive. Friedrich Hayek claimed that a government monopoly on the printing of currency leads to excessive creation of money and a consequent devaluation of its worth. He proposed a system in which several private firms would be commissioned to issue different currencies. Competition to promote the use of each currency would provide a strong incentive for each firm to limit printing because citizens would be attracted to a currency that maintains its value over time.

Classical Liberals also challenge the argument that provision of public goods establishes a rationale for government action. They argue that most of the goods and services currently provided by government could be supplied by private firms. In fact, government provision of goods and services may explain why the private sector has not entered these markets. For example, the availability of public education reduces demand for private schools, expectations of social security benefits reduce private saving for retirement, and the existence of welfare programs diminishes contributions to private charities.

Even the authority of government to tax is controversial among Classical Liberals. At the time of the American Revolution, representative democracy was envisioned as the best method for keeping taxes low. If elected representatives approved a tax, then citizens had implicitly consented to be taxed. If large numbers of citizens opposed the tax, they could vote for different representatives in the next election. However, the growth of government power has led many Classical Liberals to describe taxation as looting, plunder, or theft, in which citizens are deprived of their legitimate earnings by the coercive power of government.

Classical Liberals challenge the very concept of "market failure," arguing that many so-called failures actually result from government intervention and would not occur if government were restricted to its proper role. For example, the market power of large corporations is attributed to government-imposed barriers to competition such as regulations and tariffs on foreign goods. The power of labor unions is based on legislation protecting the right to organize and bargain collectively. Similarly, the instability of the market is blamed on government's efforts to manipulate the level of economic activity with monetary and fiscal policy.

Even if the market contains imperfections, Classical Liberals argue that government action to correct these flaws is likely to make matters worse.[1] Since government lacks the specific information known by private decisionmakers, policies designed to correct market failures will inevitably be misguided and lead to unintended consequences. Classical Liberals use the term "government failure" to describe a variety of processes by which government action reduces the efficiency of the market. In addition to disrupting efficiency, government intervention violates individual freedom. Citizens are the best judges of their own well-being and should be able to express their choices freely in the market.

To ensure that government is restricted to its proper role, Classical Liberals insist on the necessity of a constitution to establish the scope of government authority.[2] Classical Liberals not only distrust politicians, they believe that voters will pressure government to expand its functions unless a constitution forbids such expansion. Any government that is free to exercise its power, or any democracy in which all laws and rights are subject to the whims of the majority, will inevitably oppress individual liberty. The U.S. Constitution places some constraints on government by separating power among the executive, legislative, and judicial branches, and by establishing certain rights of citizenship. However, Classical Liberals would like to prohibit any governmental action not specifically condoned by the Constitution.

The Actual Role of Government

From the Classical Liberal perspective, government in modern societies neither promotes the public interest nor serves as benevolent guardian protecting the property and rights of all citizens. Just the opposite is true; government is a predatory oppressor, extorting money from citizens and limiting their freedom. Moreover, government is the primary tool by which powerful groups secure their privileges and oppress their fellow citizens. At best, government is an inefficient bureaucracy, squandering resources while providing services that, for the most part, are either unnecessary or could have been produced in the private sector at lower cost.

The Classical Liberal analysis of government is called "public choice theory." Pioneered during the 1960s by Anthony Downs, James Buchanan, and Gordon Tullock, this body of ideas reflects the application of neoclassical economic analysis to the political process.[3] The theory assumes that the self-interested, maximizing behavior attributed to individuals in the market applies as well to political activity. Unless constitutional constraints on the boundaries of political choice are strictly maintained, the pressures created by individuals and groups seeking to advance their self-interest via the political process will result in continual growth of government and a corresponding threat to both liberty and efficiency. Public choice theorists do not blame individuals and groups for utilizing whatever means are available to attain their goals; rather, they blame the judiciary branch of government, particularly the Supreme Court, for failing to adhere to the "original intent" of the framers of the Constitution to minimize the role of government. From the Classical Liberal perspective, the proliferation of new laws, regulations, and public policies in recent decades goes far beyond constitutional limitations on government activity.

Public choice theory focuses on three aspects of the political process: the behavior of interest groups, the behavior of politicians and bureaucrats, and the behavior of voters.

Behavior of interest groups. Public choice theorists use the term "rent-seeking" to describe efforts by individuals or groups to increase their income by using the regulatory power of government.[4] In economic theory, "rent" is broadly defined as income accruing to a factor of production in excess of what that factor could earn in its best alternative use in a competitive market. Rent arises when the supply of a particular resource is limited so that a higher price does not elicit an increase in the quantity of the resource supplied. An example of economic rent is the high salaries earned by professional athletes because of their rare physical skills.

Businesses and individuals seek rent when they use the power of government to artificially restrict the supply or increase the demand for the resources they own. Economist George Stigler (1911–1991) claimed that much government regulation is initiated by businesses seeking protection from competition. If this is true, then regulations are likely to serve the interests of the affected industries rather than the general public. Government agencies with responsibility for regulation have been "captured" by the very industries they are intended to regulate.[5]

Regulations benefit business when they mandate the purchase of a particular product or reduce competition by blocking entry into an industry. For example, licensing in occupations such as medicine and dentistry limits entry and therefore protects the income of those already in that occupation. Government protection of certain rights for labor unions promotes the interests of union members. Zoning laws protect property values in particular neighborhoods. By increasing the cost of doing business, regulations may actually benefit large corporations by driving marginal firms out of an industry and discouraging the entry of new firms.

The expansion of rent-seeking behavior undermines the performance of modern economies. First, government is confronted with ever-increasing demands for benefits as people look to the political process for economic benefits that should be attainable only through market activity. Second, the high tax rates required to meet the demands of rent-seekers discourage productive activity and thus reduce the tax base from which government derives its revenue. Third, tax avoidance and evasion become pervasive as citizens try to protect themselves against the power of government to seize their income for the benefit of special-interest groups. Fourth, the growing perception that lobbying and political organizing are more rewarding than market activity causes a diversion of resources away from production and a resulting erosion of efficiency in the private sector. The combination of more government spending and a declining tax base has created the massive deficits in the government's budget.[6]

To explain why interest groups proliferate in a democratic political system not firmly constrained by a constitution, public choice theorists argue that the benefits of any particular government program are often concentrated on a small segment of the population while the costs are dispersed among all taxpayers. This imbalance gives interest groups a strong incentive to organize and lobby in favor of particular programs, while taxpayers are less motivated to resist since the cost to the individual citizen of any single program is usually quite small.

Behavior of bureaucrats and politicians. The expansion of government's role is also attributed to the self-interest of government employees. Bureaucrats become "empire builders" since a larger agency offers greater opportunities for career advancement, more funding, more recognition, and more power. After a bureaucratic agency reaches a certain size, it can essentially perpetuate itself by creating a large constituency of employees, clients, and other beneficiaries who will resist any efforts to reduce funding.[7]

As for elected politicians, public choice theory portrays them as "political entrepreneurs" who have entered politics anticipating high rewards in terms of money and power. To explain why legislation benefitting only a narrow-interest group is often approved, public choice theorists claim that politicians have learned the art of "logrolling," forming coalitions in which they agree to vote for the favored legislation of other politicians in return for the promise of reciprocal support. As a result, many bills are passed that would not otherwise gain a majority vote and government continues to expand.

Politicians are also portrayed as suffering from "rational myopia." Because their primary goal is reelection, politicians focus only on the current impact of public policy while ignoring long-term consequences. This mindset contributes to budget deficits as politicians seeking reelection are anxious to provide the immediate benefits associated with government spending while shifting the costs onto future generations.

Behavior of voters. By interpreting political behavior as purely self-interested, public choice theorists encounter difficulty in explaining why people bother to vote. Voting requires time and effort, yet individuals realize that their single votes will, in all likelihood, have no impact on the outcome of any election. Therefore, the rational person, after comparing the costs and benefits of a trip to the voting booth, would seemingly choose not to vote. Similarly, citizens can be expected to remain "rationally ignorant" about politics.[8] Becoming an informed citizen takes time and effort, and since this knowledge is unlikely to benefit the individual in terms of influencing the outcome of an election, voters seem to have no incentive to acquire sufficient knowledge to vote wisely.

These arguments lead public choice theorists to worry about the outcomes of democratic elections. The people willing to incur the costs of becoming informed and voting are likely to be those who have a strong interest in some particular issue or program, creating a bias in favor of government expansion. Other concerns about democracy include the claim that voting is an imprecise method for registering individual preferences since elections are infrequent, citizens are not permitted to vote separately on each policy, and citizens have little discretion over the quantity or quality of public goods. Indeed, public choice theorists argue that government will normally provide too many public goods since a majority of voters can force the minority to share the burden of financing any particular public good. In summary, public choice theorists fear that democracy breeds interest groups seeking to manipulate government for private purposes.[9]

Proposals for Political Reform

Since Classical Liberals attribute most government problems to a failure of the judiciary branch to abide by the original intent of the framers of the Constitution, their most basic proposal entails the appointment of Supreme Court justices who will declare unconstitutional the vast array of government programs that currently regulate economic activity and redistribute income. Unless constitutional constraints on the role of government are enforced by the judiciary, the self-interested behavior found in the market will spill over into the political arena where mechanisms for resolving opposing interests are much less reliable. Classical Liberals fear that if the political process degenerates into a competitive struggle for material benefits, government may be forced to increase its power to successfully dominate the various interest groups in society. This "new Leviathan" might be successful in maintaining order, but it would curtail individual freedom.

If Supreme Court justices are unable or unwilling to tighten the reins on government, some Classical Liberals suggest amending the Constitution to define more explicitly the limitations on governmental authority. Examples of proposed amendments include requirements that the government balance its budget every year, that all appropriations of public funds be subject to a two-thirds voting rule to make coalition-formation more difficult, that the Federal Reserve Board maintain a fixed rate of monetary growth, that the progressive income tax be replaced with a flat-rate tax, and that government spending be limited to no more than twenty-five percent of the Gross Domestic Product (GDP).

Classical Liberals also support deregulation of business and "privatization" of much of the activity now undertaken by government. Recent experiments with privatization include the use of private jails, private courts and judges, private education, and private police forces. Those government programs dealing with income maintenance and social security could be privatized by initiating mandatory private pensions or insurance policies to protect citizens against the loss of income that may accompany unemployment, illness, disability, or old age.[10]

Another Classical Liberal approach to government reform has been developed under the label "law and economics." Led by Richard Posner and Richard Epstein, both associated with the University of Chicago law school, law and economics applies neoclassical economic analysis to the legal system. According to Posner and Epstein, the overriding purpose of law should be to promote economic efficiency and maximize the creation of wealth. High on their list of proposed changes is tort reform to reduce the penalties paid by corporations found guilty of negligent behavior. Large payments to plaintiffs transfer money away from corporations that could have used it more productively. Posner and Epstein also claim that many government regulations and taxes violate the Constitution and should therefore be declared illegal. To facilitate the elimination of laws restricting business activity, they propose that government be required to compensate businesses for any costs imposed by regulations. Similarly, the redistributive function of government could be abolished by revising tax laws to assure that each citizen pays no taxes in excess of the value of government services and benefits received.[11]

In general, Classical Liberals favor all policies that result in a reduced role for government. Several state governments have experimented with so-called "sunset laws" that require new legislative approval each year for every governmental program. The reasoning behind such laws is that legislators will vote more responsibly if their actions are subject to frequent public scrutiny. Another Classical Liberal strategy is to cut off the "lifeblood" of government by reducing taxes. Given the difficulty in persuading politicians to reduce popular spending programs, some Classical Liberals conclude that tax cuts are more effective at shrinking the size of the government.

The potential danger of tax cuts is that deficits may swell due to dwindling tax revenue and continued spending. Those Classical Liberals calling themselves "supply-siders" have sought to allay fears of rising deficits by arguing that reduced tax rates will stimulate economic activity sufficiently to generate even greater tax revenue. Milton Friedman, on the other hand, claims that the budget deficit cannot be lowered by increasing tax revenue because government will always spend any additional revenue. He favors direct cuts in spending as the most effective way to reduce the role of government.

THE RADICAL PERSPECTIVE

The Proper Role of Government

To analyze the Radical view of government requires a distinction between Marxian and non-Marxian forms of Radicalism. From the traditional Marxian perspective, the very notion of a "proper" role for government is meaningless. Marxists argue that government reflects the conditions of production in any given society and that changing conditions will lead to new roles for government. In a capitalist society, government primarily serves the interests of the bourgeoisie by facilitating the accumulation of capital. In socialism, government administers production in the interests of society as a whole. Marx labeled socialist government a "dictatorship of the proletariat," although he felt confident it would be more reflective of the will of the people than capitalist democracy because no single class could manipulate government for its own narrow purposes.

The functions of a socialist government include solidifying socialism by suppressing bourgeois efforts to restore capitalism, promoting material prosperity by planning and coordinating the economy, and promoting unity among citizens. Marxists anticipate a transformation from the bourgeois focus on wealth and consumption to the public-spiritedness of a new "socialist man."

According to traditional Marxism, socialism will eventually evolve into communism in which there will be a "withering away of the state." Communism will be characterized by material abundance and social cooperation, so most laws, regulations, police, courts, and prisons will no longer be necessary. Government's role will consist of "the administration of things" as it coordinates production.

Turning to non-Marxian forms of Radicalism, we find certain functions that government ought to perform in any society. The proper role of government is to serve as representative of the collective interests of all citizens. Government should be fully accountable to the public for its actions, and this ideal can be achieved only when most or all citizens actively participate in the political process. Government in a capitalist society falls short of the democratic ideal because unequal class power distorts politics in favor of the owners of capital. Capitalism's inability to provide genuine democracy provides one of the chief arguments in favor of socialism. Only by ending or restraining the power of capitalists can society establish a government that truly serves the public interest rather than powerful private interests.

The Actual Role of Government

Radicals engage in an ongoing debate about the functions of government in a capitalist society. This debate involves three distinct theories of the state.

Instrumentalism. In *The Communist Manifesto*, Marx claimed that "the executive of the modern state is but a committee for managing the common affairs of the whole bourgeoisie." This perspective treats government as an instrument used by the ruling class to promote its own interests.[12] For example, foreign policy is oriented toward opening markets and assuring the availability of cheap resources from around the world. Immigration policy assures an inflow of cheap foreign labor to hold down wages. Import quotas and tariffs protect businesses from foreign competition. Government regulations eliminate smaller competitors and smooth fluctuations in prices and profits. Ironically, the Radical instrumentalist view resembles the Classical Liberal claim that government in modern society has become the tool of powerful interest groups.

Instrumentalists believe that government supports businesses by socializing costs and privatizing benefits. For example, infrastructure such as transportation and communication systems, waste disposal, education, and crime prevention is essential to business, but government provision means that taxpayers bear the cost of maintaining such services. Another socialization of costs is the tax deductibility of business expenses such as meals, entertainment, and depreciation of capital. To privatize benefits, government leaves actual production of most public goods to the private sector. For example, supplying military weapons and equipment to government yields profits for many corporations. Private firms have gained access to the most profitable components of mail delivery, leaving the post office with the less lucrative service of carrying letters. Various public services, ranging from incarceration of prisoners to custodial services for public buildings, are increasingly provided by private firms.

In summary, instrumentalism portrays government's actual role as serving the interests of the capitalist class. Capitalists exert control over government through the selection of political candidates and the formation of public policy through funding of "think tanks," lobbying efforts, and political campaigns. Any apparent benefits accruing to the middle and lower classes represent token gestures designed to maintain order and stability. Since the capitalist class uses government to protect its own interests while other classes are left to fend for themselves in the market, Radicals claim that modern societies operate on the principle of "socialism for the rich, capitalism for the poor."

Structuralism. Structuralist theorists agree with the instrumentalist view that government functions primarily to serve the interests of the capitalist class, but they claim that this role is dictated by the structure of the economy rather than direct control by the ruling class.[13] Different industries have conflicting interests, so they cannot exert uniform control over government. However, government can still promote the general process of capital accumulation. Structuralist theorists use phrases such as "structural imperatives," "the dictates of accumulation," "systemic constraints," or "laws of motion" to describe the forces emanating from the economy that largely determine the scope and content of government policy.

The impact of structural imperatives on public policy is transmitted through two channels. First, because prosperity in a capitalist economy hinges on healthy rates of capital accumulation, citizens tend to identify their own interests with those of capitalists. For example, employees of a steel mill may oppose regulations to limit air pollution because they fear that reduced profitability for the mill may cost them their jobs. Second, the threat of a "capital strike" poses a continual constraint on public policy. Government actions that undermine profitability may discourage capitalists from investing in the domestic economy. To avoid the recession that would surely follow a strike by capitalists, government must maintain "business confidence" by creating conditions conducive to high profits and continuing investment.

The content of government policy will change in response to evolving economic conditions. In the seventeenth and eighteenth centuries, the interventionist policies associated with mercantilism were appropriate for reducing risk and expanding markets. Once the capitalist economy was established, laissez-faire policies removed the remnants of feudal and mercantilist strictures on production and exchange. By the late nineteenth century, the transition to monopoly capitalism required that government protect businesses against the perils of cut-throat competition. Government codified and enforced business ethics, passed antitrust laws, and initiated quality controls on various products. The Great Depression of the 1930s mandated a vastly enlarged role for government in providing sufficient liquidity and spending to maintain profitability and accumulation. These goals were accomplished by establishing high levels of military spending, by consciously pursuing expansionary monetary and fiscal policies, and by equalizing income through progressive taxation, labor unions, and welfare programs. These latter policies also function to maintain social order by assuaging the anger of low-income families. Most recently, the development of supply-side constraints on accumulation has led to tax cuts, deregulation, and privatization.

Class struggle theory. A third Radical theory of the state portrays politics as an arena in which conflicting class interests vie with one another for dominance. Government is a "contested instrument," potentially able to serve either bourgeois or proletarian interests depending on the balance of class power at any given time.[14] Thus government in capitalist society will seek to promote not only accumulation, but also legitimation of the system of private ownership.[15] Accumulation is essential for economic prosperity, but the viability of capitalism also requires that a broad spectrum of the population perceive the system as legitimate. Government efforts to promote legitimation may conflict with the narrow interests of capitalists in maximizing profits in the short run. For example, welfare programs, minimum-wage laws, and protection of the environment are likely to reduce profits for some businesses, but without such policies, social unrest might threaten the entire capitalist system.

Proposals for Political Reform

Radicals who adhere to either instrumentalist or structuralist theories of government tend to be pessimistic about the prospects for political reform within capitalism. Whether government is controlled by the ruling class or by the structural imperatives of the economy, policies that directly advance the interests of workers are unlikely except during periodic crises in capitalism when the very survival of the system is at stake.

However, the class struggle theory in which government is viewed as a "contested instrument" raises the possibility that working-class efforts to influence and even gain control of government may be effective. A well-organized working class can achieve political victories aimed at challenging capitalist control of the economy. Reform-minded Radicals concede that the capitalist class will strongly resist these challenges, but they are optimistic that a combination of legal reforms, government policies, and perhaps compensation for lost property rights may soften the opposition.

When opposing class interests are sufficiently balanced that government can neither impose austerity measures to restore profitability nor grant more favorable conditions to workers, the solution will likely be some form of corporatism to break the political stalemate. While corporatism has appeared in both Conservative and Modern Liberal versions, the overriding theme has been stronger government action to forge a consensus on the distribution of society's benefits and burdens.

If, as happened in Germany and Italy in the 1920s, large numbers of citizens conclude that foreigners, minorities, cultural change, and liberal individualism are responsible for the nation's economic woes, then Conservative corporatism is likely to be the outcome. However, the more likely event is that corporatism will appear in its Modern Liberal form as an effort by government to promote cooperation, increased productivity, industrial peace, and improved conditions for the working class. Yet Radicals warn that Modern Liberal corporatism is still committed to preserving capitalism and the privileges of private property and may therefore take on fascist overtones. This "friendly fascism" will appear benign and committed to the public interest, but the "iron fist in the velvet glove" will be used when necessary to enforce austerity measures, silence political dissent, and restore conditions for rapid capital accumulation. Only socialism can combine genuine popular democracy with economic prosperity.[16]

Some Radicals propose to facilitate the transition from capitalism to socialism by amending the Constitution. In addition to the protection of civil rights, Radicals want the Constitution to define and protect economic rights such as jobs with a livable wage, a clean environment, occupational safety, and health care. Other Radicals warn that tampering with the Constitution might open doors to Conservative efforts to curtail existing civil rights such as free speech.

In light of the collapse of Soviet-style socialism, many Radicals have abandoned the goal of complete nationalization of the means of production. Instead, they propose to make authority in both the private sector and government open to popular input and democratically accountable. This vision of "participatory democracy" entails decentralization of authority throughout society, increased worker and community control of industry, and direct citizen involvement in government.[17] The economy would have a mixture of publicly and privately owned property, reliance on both the market and government to allocate resources, and sufficient inequality in wealth and income to provide incentives for production.

THE CONSERVATIVE PERSPECTIVE

The Proper Role of Government

Conservatives want a government powerful enough to suppress the aggression of any particular person or group, but, in an orderly and stable society, they envision little need for the exercise of government authority. While Classical Liberals oppose government because of its potential for restricting individual freedom and causing inefficiency, Conservatives believe that the greatest evil of government is its tendency to undermine hierarchy, authority, and virtue by destroying individual responsibility and the "intermediate institutions" of society such as family, church, and neighborhood, which serve as buffers against both market forces and government power. Government is most dangerous when dominated by either technocrats seeking to impose rational policies for social improvement or by the masses who lack sufficient wisdom to govern well.

The ideal Conservative government would be administered by highly experienced and talented individuals motivated neither by self-interest nor by a strong desire to use government as an instrument for social change. The proper role of government consists primarily of maintaining a moral and cultural climate conducive to the development of stable communities and well-adjusted individuals. In a healthy society in which hierarchical authority pervades all institutions, government would be required to do very little. Hierarchical communities remain largely self-governing because they generate the dispositions conducive to social order and the maintenance of tradition.

The informal relations between dominant and subordinate persons, arising spontaneously out of acknowledged differences in ability, provide the basis for habitual deference to authority and socially responsible behavior. Loyalty to friends, duty to family, piety toward church, patriotism toward country, and, in general, respect for authority are the true bonds that unite society and regulate individual behavior. When social relations are naturally self-regulating, little need arises for political intervention in the form of laws and public policy. Communities will spontaneously develop systems of rules to promote order, which need not be perceived as restraints on individual freedom since they arise from the moral beliefs of community members.

During the nineteenth century, a dominant theme of Conservatism was suspicion of, if not hostility toward, democracy. Conservatives believed that the masses could not vote wisely and would be motivated by envy and resentment to confiscate the property of the rich. Democracy would bring a "tyranny of the majority" and "rule by the mob." Alexis de Tocqueville (1805–1859), a Frenchman who traveled through America in 1836, feared that democracy would encourage political leaders to pursue egalitarian policies in hopes of winning votes.[18] Two Italian social theorists, Vilfredo Pareto and Gaetano Mosca (1858–1941), were also skeptical about democracy, claiming that hierarchy is the only type of social structure in accordance with the natural differences in human nature.[19] Politicians claiming to be democrats were merely disguising their ambition for power.

Early in the twentieth century, Conservative writers developed theories of mass behavior, arguing that the dislocations caused by industrialization had uprooted people from the traditional constraints of stable communities and created a working class prone to irrational and violent behavior.[20] However, after witnessing fascism and communism during the 1920s and 1930s, most Conservatives accepted democracy as the least evil political system. To make democracy less threatening to the preservation of hierarchical authority, Conservatives imposed restrictions on participation in the political process. The economist Joseph Schumpeter, for example, portrayed democracy as simply a struggle among elites to gain votes. Popular participation in politics should be limited to periodic elections to choose which elites would govern.[21]

The Actual Role of Government

Conservatives link the deterioration of government with the industrialization and modernization accompanying the rise of capitalism. In a capitalist society, wealth and liberty replace virtue and order as primary values. An oligarchy based on ownership of capital supersedes the traditional aristocracy. The polarization of classes causes conflict in the relations between rich and poor. Demagogues arise to exploit the resentment of the poor and to persecute the rich. Moreover, the trend toward urbanization and geographic mobility undermines the stability of traditional communities and the legitimacy of traditional authority.[22] As market forces wrench individuals from their customary social contexts, family, community, and religion lose much of their significance in people's lives. The market fosters a critical and skeptical attitude because it offers only impersonal social relations lacking the sense of belonging and attachment found in traditional communities.

As society is destabilized by the market, government responds with programs intended to protect individuals. Yet efforts by government to provide welfare, employment, housing, and health care actually erode the viability of local communities and other intermediate institutions. The authority of parents, clergy, and local officials is replaced by social workers, job counselors, bureaucrats, and technical experts. A self-perpetuating cycle arises whereby social disintegration leads to more government intervention, which leads to further social disintegration.

As traditional communities are undermined, isolated individuals lose the virtues of civility, deference to authority, and self-restraint. Lacking a sense of connectedness with others or with past traditions to give meaning to their lives, they focus on immediate gratification. Ironically, the extreme individualism resulting from the erosion of authority paves the way for totalitarianism in the form of fascism and communism. When individuals refuse to recognize authority in their families, workplaces, and communities, government must become sufficiently powerful to prevent the pursuit of individual self-interest from degenerating into chaos. Citizens may even welcome totalitarianism as a solution to social decay.[23]

Proposals for Political Reform

From the Conservative perspective, the powerful forces unleashed by capitalism and democracy constantly push modern societies in the direction of increased governmental power and a corresponding diminution of the role of intermediate institutions. Believing that this drift toward totalitarianism is caused by individual demands for unconditional freedom and unlimited pleasure, Conservatives would restrain popular demands and insulate government from democratic pressures. For example, Conservative corporatists propose an alliance between business and government to ease the dislocations created by the market and to reduce uncertainty and risk for business.[24] To supplement the intermediate institutions damaged by capitalism and democracy, corporatists propose occupational groupings that provide workers with a sense of belonging and restrain worker demands for higher wages and increased benefits. Social groups would be hierarchical, with demands from below being filtered and amended by officials at every level of the hierarchy. Government would be effectively insulated from what the Trilateral Commission called an "excess of democracy" because popular demands would never be channeled directly to government.[25] Corporatism attempts to harness the dynamism of capitalism while minimizing its disruptive aspects.

For many Conservatives, however, corporatist proposals are dangerous insofar as they open the door for abuse of government power. These Conservatives attempt instead to reinvigorate society's intermediate institutions to restore the traditional constraints on individual behavior found in close-knit communities. For example, Conservatives have proposed a decentralization of governmental authority to increase the responsibilities and status of local officials. Decentralization also would permit states and local communities to develop policies best suited to their own particular situations.

Conservative writer George Will proposes that government should actively mold the "manners and morals" of citizens.[26] Government should be more than a neutral referee in the struggle among self-interested individuals. It also bears responsibility for creating proper sentiments, opinions, and behavior. Government must be a tutor as well as a servant to "help persons want what they ought to want." George Will rejects the liberal effort to keep morality out of public life. A government that fails to promote values will foster citizens devoid of patriotism, loyalty, or any sense of obligation. In Will's words, "a completely and permanently open mind will be an empty mind." Another Conservative, Robert Nisbet, suggests that a society without hierarchical authority leaves man "free in all his solitary misery."[27]

Not only should government create a sense of unity and common vision among citizens, it should directly nurture intermediate institutions. For example, tax breaks might be granted to families in which a parent remains at home to raise children; to parents who send their children to private schools; or to employers who contribute to community activities. Some Conservatives even support a modified version of the welfare state that would encourage stable families, self-reliance, and local initiative. Instead of giving welfare checks directly to needy people, the money might be given to churches that reach out to the poor and draw them into a supportive group where community contact and mentoring can guide them toward employment.

Because Conservatives believe in objective values, they favor efforts by government to discourage "immoral" activities such as the sale of pornography, gambling, drug abuse, and prostitution. They favor greater censorship of material presented in the media, particularly if children might view it. Finally, Conservatives want government to become more involved in the process by which traditional values are transmitted to the next generation. To accomplish this goal, they propose that public schools place increased emphasis on teaching values such as patriotism, duty, honor, hard work, and self-discipline.

THE MODERN LIBERAL PERSPECTIVE

The Proper Role of Government

Modern Liberals have been the chief proponents of the dramatic expansion of government during the past century. From their perspective, a mixed economy, combining capitalism and an active democratic government, offers a middle path between the disruptive forces of unbridled capitalism and the totalitarianism of fascism or communism. Modern Liberals want to utilize the dynamic potential of capitalism for creating wealth while relying on government to maintain security and fairness for all citizens.

Modern Liberal economists have developed sophisticated theoretical arguments to reveal flaws in the operation of the market that reduce its potential for achieving society's goals. These "market failures" fall into six broad categories: lack of perfect competition, externalities, public goods, instability, inequity, and socially undesirable outcomes.[28]

1. *Lack of perfect competition.* Markets will fail to achieve economic efficiency if the conditions of perfect competition are violated. Economists define perfect competition as a situation in which many buyers and sellers of a homogeneous product interact with one another, resources are perfectly mobile, and all agents possess full knowledge of all information relevant to making rational decisions. Rarely is any one of these assumptions met, let alone all of them simultaneously. Thus actual markets will normally fail to achieve efficiency. Possible examples of government remedies for imperfect competition include publicizing knowledge when information is lacking and subsidizing relocation when resources are immobile.

Competition is also reduced by what economists call "economies of scale." These occur when the cost of producing a unit of output decreases as the size of the firm increases. The typical effect of economies of scale is that smaller firms, operating with higher unit costs, cannot compete with their larger rivals, eventually leading to oligopoly and possibly even monopoly. To remedy this tendency for competition to eliminate itself, Modern Liberals propose either antitrust laws to block corporate mergers and acquisitions or, in the case of "natural monopolies" such as utilities, regulation by a public agency.

The growth of the consumer electronics and computer industries has raised new concerns about the viability of competition in unregulated markets. Modern Liberals claim that products such as electronic equipment and computer software are susceptible to monopolization by the first producer to attain dominance in the industry. That company's technology becomes the industry standard, and various complementary products are designed by firms in other industries to be compatible with the standard. With virtually the entire market committed to a particular standard, competitors have little chance of successfully challenging the dominant firm, and monopoly power is secured. This phenomenon requires even stricter scrutiny of industry structures, vigorous enforcement of existing antitrust laws, and perhaps even the passage of new laws.

2. *Externalities.* An externality arises when a market transaction results in benefits or damages to "third parties" not directly involved in the transaction. Externalities arise because of missing markets; parties are unable to negotiate certain exchanges due to high transaction costs of gathering information, specifying contracts, and monitoring compliance. Because the market registers only the private costs and benefits of a good or activity, the market will produce less than the optimal amount of products with positive externalities and more than the optimal amount of products with negative externalities. One solution to this problem is to tax those products creating negative externalities and to subsidize products generating positive externalities. Alternatively, prohibitions may be placed on activities with negative externalities such as under-age drinking, and participation may be required for activities with positive externalities such as education.

3. *Public goods.* An extreme case of a positive externality arises when nearly every person in society would benefit from a good or service but, because the benefits are external to the market, consumers cannot be charged and no private firm can profitably produce the good. These "public goods"—such as national defense, highways, and police protection—have two characteristics: they are nonexclusive, meaning that nonpayers cannot be excluded from enjoying the benefits, and they are nonrival in the sense that one person's enjoyment of the benefits does not diminish the availability of the good for others. Public goods are not produced by the private sector because of the problem posed by "free riders." Knowing they cannot be excluded from the benefits, individuals have no incentive to pay for the good and will instead take a free ride.

Since public goods will not be produced through the market, government must finance them with tax revenues. Modern Liberals generally believe that government provides inadequate amounts of public goods, as reflected in the deteriorating condition of many parks, schools, roads, and bridges. The exception to this claim is national defense. Modern Liberals charge that corporate lobbying by the defense industry has resulted in too much spending on the military. As the threat of foreign aggression recedes, Modern Liberals are confident that national security can be maintained with much smaller defense budgets and that the "peace dividend" can be used for social programs.

4. *Instability.* The Great Depression persuaded Modern Liberals that a market economy is inherently prone to cycles of boom and bust and that government intervention in the form of fiscal and monetary policy tends to

decrease this instability. By softening recessions, government promotes a more efficient allocation of resources and a higher rate of long-term growth.

5. *Inequity.* The market-determined distribution of income is only as fair as the distribution of "initial assets" held by individuals as they enter the market. Modern Liberals view the current ownership of wealth as so unequal that it violates any reasonable standard of fairness. Although attempts to redistribute income may impede efficiency by distorting incentives, most Modern Liberals value justice sufficiently to accept small losses of efficiency. They also claim that redistribution may actually enhance efficiency by increasing spending on goods and services, by contributing to the development of labor resources and citizenship skills of the poor, and by satisfying the desire of most citizens to end hunger and suffering in an affluent society. The desired redistribution can be accomplished through transfer payments and progressive taxation.

6. *Socially undesirable outcomes.* In certain instances, the market will generate results widely regarded as violating the values of a society. While Modern Liberals defend individual autonomy and choice, they also support some government efforts to encourage or discourage certain behaviors and values. In the case of drug laws or bans on smoking in public areas, the intervention may be justified in terms of correcting an externality, but an alternative justification is that society simply wants to discourage these activities. Also, government may designate certain "merit goods" such as food, clothing, and shelter that every citizen should have regardless of ability to pay.[29] Programs such as affirmative action and comparable worth, designed to redress past discrimination, are based on notions of fairness that Modern Liberals believe to be morally correct despite lack of support from many citizens. In this case, Modern Liberals claim that government can legitimately educate and change the preferences of citizens rather than simply respond to existing desires. Paternalistic action by government also may be justified in cases where citizens do not act rationally due to "cognitive dissonance."[30] For example, young people may not save for their retirement because doing so means acknowledging the unpleasant fact of their own mortality. The social security system forces people to put money into a government fund for public pensions.

Modern Liberals envision government as staffed by highly trained professionals who formulate and administer rational policies using scientific techniques such as cost–benefit analysis and environmental impact statements.[31] Modern Liberals fully expect government to grow as society matures because rising incomes tend to increase the demand for public goods such as crime prevention, public safety, and a cleaner environment. The expansion of government budgets is also attributable to the fact that government provides mostly labor-intensive services. In recent decades, labor costs have risen faster than capital costs, and technological progress in services has not matched progress in manufacturing goods.[32]

The Actual Role of Government

The concentration of wealth and power in the industrialized nations poses a challenge to the Modern Liberal view of government as a benevolent administrator and impartial defender of the public interest. Increasingly, government is subjected to the demands of large, well-organized interest groups. In recognition of the changing political landscape, political scientists such as Robert Dahl, David Easton, and David Truman have revised the Modern Liberal theory of the state by introducing the notion of interest-group pluralism.[33] While acknowledging that groups have replaced individuals as the primary actors in politics, pluralists seek to preserve the image of democratic government as representative of the interests of society as a whole.

Pluralist theorists treat political power as separate from economic power, arguing that political power is widely dispersed among a variety of interest groups. Corporations, labor unions, environmentalists, senior citizens, and other groups attempt to influence legislation, with the resulting government policies reflecting the balance of these competing interests. The most controversial aspect of pluralism is the claim that groups wield influence in direct proportion to the size of their membership. Critics argue that pluralists overlook the effect of concentrated wealth in giving some groups significantly greater impact on the political process.

While the doctrine of interest-group pluralism reflects the changing nature of politics in industrialized countries, it has consequences reaching far beyond the realm of academic theory. By encouraging competition among interest groups, pluralism effectively legitimizes the transformation of politics into a battle between conflicting interests with no common ground on which to reach consensus. The worst fears of Conservatives and Classical Liberals have been realized as politics has degenerated into a Hobbesian "war of all against all." The result has been a rapid expansion of government programs aimed at satisfying various interest groups, large budget deficits, and a widespread loss of public confidence in government.

Unlike Conservatives and Classical Liberals, Modern Liberals have been reluctant to rely on constitutional constraints to guide public policy. In the early twentieth century, Modern Liberal jurists such as Oliver Wendell Holmes, Jr. (1841–1935), Louis Brandeis (1856–1941), and Roscoe Pound (1870–1964) initiated a loose interpretation of the Constitution to permit an expanding role for government. Furthermore, Modern Liberals have been largely unwilling to resolve political conflict by appealing to a well-defined vision of the public interest or the good society. To do so would jeopardize their commitment to individual autonomy and freedom of private choice. By the 1970s, Modern Liberals had reached an impasse; they were unable to restrain the political disorder unleashed by opening government to the intense pressures of interest groups.[34]

Conservatives, Classical Liberals, and Radicals all agree that Modern Liberalism's difficulties stem from attempting to combine a capitalist economy with government efforts to achieve a more egalitarian society, thereby subverting the virtues of each. Government suppresses the disciplining restraints of the competitive market, and the market undermines the power of government to achieve its egalitarian goals. Conservatives would go further to argue that an active government combined with a relatively free market undermines the cultural and moral constraints on the pursuit of private interests, thus diminishing the organizing capacity of both government and market. Without cultural, moral, economic, or political discipline, society is left adrift in a sea of conflicting interests.

Proposals for Political Reform

As a result of these dilemmas, Modern Liberals have been forced to reassess their political agenda. Although a consensus has not yet been reached, the following three strands of Modern Liberal reform policies have emerged in recent years:

1. *Neoliberalism.* This body of ideas would move Modern Liberalism closer to Classical Liberalism by reducing the role of government in economic affairs.[35] Instead of focusing on equity and the redistribution of income, government would concentrate on efficiency and growth. Neoliberals argue that equity cannot be achieved unless the economy is thriving, and past efforts to achieve equity through transfer payments and regulations have actually impeded the dynamism of the market. Neoliberals largely accept the Classical Liberal argument that government has become a tool of special interests, so that policies intended to promote equity often simply cater to interest groups. Therefore, reducing or eliminating many facets of government activity may actually benefit less advantaged groups in society.

2. *Neocorporatism.* Modern Liberal economists Lester Thurow and Robert Reich have popularized the notion of using the power of government to actively promote both social justice and economic growth.[36] The vision of a vigorous government working hand-in-hand with corporations, labor unions, and other interest groups to coordinate economic activity is reminiscent of the corporatism proposed by Conservatives in the early twentieth century. However, Conservative corporatism is intended to preserve political stability by channeling dissent and conflict through organized channels

of hierarchy. In contrast, neocorporatism seeks cooperation between groups for the purpose of increasing participation and equality. For example, representatives of unions and local communities might be given seats on the boards of directors of corporations. In addition to promoting equality, however, neocorporatism would stimulate investment and productivity to enhance the competitiveness of the economy. Advocates of neocorporatism have admired the Japanese Ministry of International Trade and Industry (MITI) as an example of government targeting investment funds to specific industries, facilitating international trade, and closing down industries that are no longer competitive.[37]

3. *Democratic planning.* Some Modern Liberals have moved closer to the Radical perspective, expressing skepticism that neocorporatism can restrain corporate dominance over government. They note that business and government have been working together since the early twentieth century, and business has been largely successful in using government to advance its own interests.[38] Economist John Kenneth Galbraith and political scientist Robert Dahl propose greater government control over business and increased democratization of government and the economy.[39] Galbraith supports nationalization of key industries such as energy and communications and increased public control over investment decisions in other sectors of the economy. To assure that this expanded authority of government is democratically accountable, planning advocates propose fundamental revisions in the political system, including greater public financing of political campaigns, stricter rules on lobbying and outside income for politicians, and voter registration drives to increase participation in elections.

NOTES

1. See Tyler Cowen, ed., *The Theory of Market Failure: A Critical Examination*, Fairfax, VA: George Mason University Press, 1988.
2. Classical Liberal arguments for a constitution as the basis for viable democracy are found in Friedrich A. Hayek, *The Constitution of Liberty*, Chicago: University of Chicago Press, 1960; James M. Buchanan and Gordon Tullock, *Calculus of Consent: The Logical Foundations of Constitutional Democracy*, Ann Arbor: University of Michigan Press, 1965; James M. Buchanan, *Constitutional Economics*, Cambridge, MA: Blackwell, 1991; Dwight R. Lee and Richard McKenzie, *Regulating Government: A Preface to Constitutional Economics*, Lexington, MA: Lexington Books, 1987; and Gerald W. Scully, *Constitutional Economics: The Framework for Economic Growth and Social Progress*, Washington, DC: The Heritage Foundation, 1991.
3. Major works in public choice theory include Anthony Downs, *An Economic Theory of Democracy*, New York: Harper & Row, 1957; James M. Buchanan and Robert D. Tollison, *Theory of Public Choice: Political Applications of Economics*,

Ann Arbor: University of Michigan Press, 1972; Gordon Tullock, *Private Wants, Public Means*, New York: Basic Books, 1970; Mancur Olson, *The Logic of Collective Action: Public Goals and the Theory of Groups*, Cambridge, MA: Harvard University Press, 1965; and Charles K. Rowley, ed., *Public Choice Theory*, Brookfield, VT: Edward Elgar, 1993. For critiques of public choice theory, see Lars Udehn, *The Limits of Public Choice*, New York: Routledge, 1996; Donald P. Green and Ian Shapiro, *Pathologies of Rational Choice Theory*, New Haven: Yale University Press, 1994; Kristen R. Monroe, ed., *The Economic Approach to Politics: A Critical Reassessment of the Theory of Rational Action*, New York: HarperCollins, 1991; and Jeffrey Friedman, ed., *The Rational Choice Controversy*, New Haven, CT: Yale University Press, 1996.

4. On the theory of rent-seeking, see David C. Colander, ed., *Neoclassical Political Economy: The Analysis of Rent-seeking and DUP Activities*, Cambridge, MA: Ballinger, 1984. See also Robert D. Tollison and Roger D. Congleton, eds., *The Economic Analysis of Rent-Seeking*, Brookfield, VT: Edward Elgar, 1995; Charles K. Rowley, Robert D. Tollison, and Gordon Tullock, *The Political Economy of Rent-Seeking*, Boston: Martinus Nijhoff, 1988; and Gordon Tullock, *Rent Seeking*, Brookfield, VT: Edward Elgar, 1993.

5. See George J. Stigler, "The Theory of Economic Regulation," *Bell Journal of Economics & Management Science* 2, no. 1 (Spring 1971): 3–21. For additional analysis of the politics of regulation, see Barry Mitnick, *The Political Economy of Regulation*, New York: Columbia University Press, 1980; James Q. Wilson, ed., *The Politics of Regulation*, New York: Basic Books, 1980; and Kenneth J. Meier, *Regulation: Politics, Bureaucracy and Economics*, New York: St. Martin's Press, 1985.

6. The Classical Liberal explanation of budget deficits is elaborated in James M. Buchanan and Richard M. Wagner, *Democracy in Deficit: The Political Legacy of Lord Keynes*, New York: Academic Press, 1977; Phillip Cagan, ed., *The Economy in Deficit*, Washington, DC: American Enterprise Institute, 1985; James M. Buchanan, Charles K. Rowley, and Robert D. Tollison, eds., *Deficits*, New York: Basil Blackwell, 1987; and Joseph White and Aaron Wildavsky, *The Deficit and the Public Interest*, Berkeley, CA: University of California Press, 1989.

7. The functioning of bureaucracy is examined in Anthony Downs, *Inside Bureaucracy*, Boston: Little, Brown, 1967; Aaron Wildavsky, *The Politics of the Budgetary Process*, 4th ed., Boston: Little, Brown, 1984; William A. Niskanen, *Bureaucracy and Public Economics*, Brookfield, VT: Edward Elgar, 1994; William C. Mitchell and Randy T. Simmons, *Beyond Politics: Markets, Welfare and the Failure of Bureaucracy*, Boulder, CO: Westview Press, 1994; and James P. Pinkerton, *What Comes Next: The End of Big Government—and the New Paradigm Ahead*, New York: Hyperion, 1995.

8. See Anthony Downs, *An Economic Theory of Democracy*, New York: Harper and Row, 1957.

9. For Classical Liberal analyses of the problems associated with democracy, see Samuel Brittan, *The Economic Consequences of Democracy*, London: Temple Smith, 1977. See also Dan Usher, *The Economic Prerequisite to Democracy*, New York: Columbia University Press, 1981.

10. Privatization is discussed in Richard Hula, ed., *Market Based Public Policy*, New York: Macmillan, 1987; Edward H. Crane and David Boaz, *An American*

Vision: Policies for the '90s, Washington, DC: Cato Institute, 1988; John D. Donahue, *The Privatization Decision: Public Ends, Private Means*, New York: Basic Books, 1989; Michael E. Beesley, *Privatization, Regulation and Deregulation*, New York: Routledge, 1992; Dexter Whitfield, *The Welfare State: Privatization, Deregulation, Commercialization of Public Services*, Boulder, CO: Westview Press, 1992; Fred E. Foldvary, *Public Goods and Private Communities: The Market Provision of Social Services*, Brookfield, VT: Edward Elgar, 1994; Stephen Edgell, Sandin Walklate, and Gareth Williams, *Debating the Future of the Public Sphere: Transforming the Public and Private Domains in Free Market Societies*, Brookfield, VT: Avebury, 1995; Elizabeth I. Bailey and Janet Rothenberg Pack, eds., *The Political Economy of Privatization and Deregulation*, Brookfield, VT: Edward Elgar, 1995; and Philip Morgan, ed., *Privatization and the Welfare State: Implications for Consumers and the Workforce*, Brookfield, VT: Dartmouth Publishing Company, 1995.

11. See Richard A. Posner, *The Economics of Justice*, Cambridge, MA: Harvard University Press, 1981; Richard A. Posner, *Overcoming Law*, Cambridge, MA: Harvard University Press, 1995; and Richard Epstein, *Simple Rules for a Complex World*, Cambridge, MA: Harvard University Press, 1995.

12. Instrumentalist interpretations of government are found in C. Wright Mills, *The Power Elite*, New York: Oxford University Press, 1956; G. William Domhoff, *State Autonomy or Class Dominance*, New York: Aldine de Gruyter, 1996; and G. William Domhoff, *The Power Elite and the State*, New York: Aldine de Gruyter, 1990.

13. For a structuralist interpretation of government, see Nicos Poulantzas, *Political Power and Social Classes*, London: New Left Books, 1975.

14. The Radical view of the state as a "contested instrument" is presented in Bob Jessop, *The Capitalist State*, New York: New York University Press, 1982; Ralph Miliband, *The State in Capitalist Society*, New York: Basic Books, 1969; and Ian Gough, *The Political Economy of the Welfare State*, London: Macmillan, 1979.

15. See James O'Connor, *The Fiscal Crisis of the State*, New York: St. Martin's, 1973.

16. See Bertram Gross, *Friendly Fascism: The New Face of Power in America*, New York: M. Evans, 1980.

17. See Benjamin R. Barber, *Strong Democracy*, Berkeley: University of California Press, 1984; Philip Green, *Retrieving Democracy: In Search of Civic Equality*, Totowa, NJ: Rowman & Allanheld, 1985; Carol Could, *Rethinking Democracy: Freedom and Social Cooperation in Politics, Economics and Society*, New York: Cambridge University Press, 1988; Jane J. Mansbridge, *Beyond Adversarial Democracy*, New York: Basic Books, 1980; and Peter Bachrach and Aryeh Botwinick, *Power and Empowerment: A Radical Theory of Participatory Democracy*, Philadelphia: Temple University Press, 1992; Paul Hirst, *Associational Democracy: New Forms of Economic and Social Governance*, Cambridge, UK: Polity, 1994; Chantal Mouffe, ed., *Dimensions of Radical Democracy: Pluralism, Citizenship, Community*, London: Verso, 1992; C. Douglas Lummis, *Radical Democracy*, Ithaca, NY: Cornell University Press, 1996; and David Copp, Jean Hampton, and John Roemer, eds., *The Idea of Democracy*, Cambridge, UK: Cambridge University Press, 1993.

18. Alexis de Tocqueville, *Democracy in America*, edited by J. P. Mayer and M. Lerner, New York: Harper & Row, 1966.

19. The origins of modern elite theory are found in Vilfredo Pareto, *Sociological Writings*, edited by S. E. Finer, New York: Praeger, 1966; and Gaetano Mosca, *The Ruling Class*, edited by A. Livingston, New York: McGraw-Hill, 1939.

20. See José Ortega y Gasset, *The Revolt of the Masses* [1932], Notre Dame, IN: University of Notre Dame Press, 1985.

21. Joseph Schumpeter, *Capitalism, Socialism and Democracy*, New York: Harper & Brothers, 1950.

22. See Robert A. Nisbet, *The Twilight of Authority*, New York: Oxford University Press, 1975.

23. See Jacob Talmon, *The Origins of Totalitarian Democracy*, New York: Praeger, 1960. See also Lionel Trilling, *The Liberal Imagination*, New York: Viking Press, 1950.

24. Recent works on corporatism include Colin Crouch, ed., *State and Economy in Contemporary Capitalism*, New York: St. Martin's 1979; Philippe Schmitter and Gerhard Lehmbruch, eds., *Trends Toward Corporatist Intermediation*, Beverly Hills, CA: Sage, 1979; James M. Simmie, *Power, Property, and Corporatism*, London: Macmillan, 1982; Peter J. Williamson, *Varieties of Corporatism*, New York: Cambridge University Press, 1986; Wyn Grant, ed., *The Political Economy of Corporatism*, New York: St. Martin's, 1985; Louis Galambos and Joseph Pratt, *The Rise of the Corporate Commonwealth*, New York: Basic Books, 1989; and Martin J. Sklar, *The Corporate Reconstruction of American Capitalism*, New York: Cambridge University Press, 1988.

25. See Michael Crozier, Samuel P. Huntington, and Joji Watanuki, eds., *The Crisis of Democracy*, New York: New York University Press, 1975.

26. George Will, *Statecraft As Soulcraft*, New York: Simon & Schuster, 1983.

27. Robert A. Nisbet, *Community and Power*, New York: Oxford University Press, 1962.

28. The classic article on market failure is F. M. Bator, "The Anatomy of Market Failure," *Quarterly Journal of Economics* 72, no. 288 (1958): 351–79.

29. The concept of merit goods was introduced in Richard A. Musgrave, *The Theory of Public Finance*, New York: McGraw-Hill, 1959.

30. This argument is developed in G. A. Akerlof and W. T. Dickens, "The Economic Consequences of Cognitive Dissonance," *American Economic Review* 72, no. 3 (June 1982): 307–19.

31. For a Modern Liberal critique of the concept of government failure, see Donald A. Wittman, *The Myth of Democratic Failure: Why Political Institutions are Efficient*, Chicago: University of Chicago Press, 1995.

32. See Harold G. Vatter and John F. Walker, *The Inevitability of Government Growth*, New York: Columbia University Press, 1990. See also John F. Walker and Harold G. Vatter, *The Rise of Big Government in the United States*, Armonk, NY: M. E. Sharpe, 1997.

33. See Robert A. Dahl, *Pluralist Democracy in the United States*, Chicago: Rand McNally, 1967; David Easton, *The Political System*, New York: Alfred A. Knopf, 1981; and David Truman, *The Governing Process*, New York: Alfred A. Knopf, 1951.

34. See Robert A. Dahl, *Dilemmas of Pluralist Democracy*, New Haven, CT: Yale University Press, 1982. See also Theodore Lowi, *The End of Liberalism: The Second Republic of the U.S.*, 2nd ed., New York: W. W. Norton, 1979.

35. For an overview of neoliberalism, see Randall Rothenberg, *The Neoliberals: Creating the New American Politics*, New York: Simon & Schuster, 1984. Important works include Mickey Kaus, *The End of Equality*, New York: Basic Books, 1995; and Paul Krugman, *The Age of Diminished Expectations*, 3rd ed., Cambridge, MA: MIT Press, 1997.

36. Lester Thurow, *The Zero-Sum Society*, New York: Basic Books, 1980; Lester Thurow, *The Zero-Sum Solution: Building a World-Class American Economy*, New York: Simon & Schuster, 1985; Lester Thurow, *The Future of Capitalism: How Today's Economic Forces Shape Tomorrow's World*, New York: W. Morrow & Co., 1996; Robert B. Reich, *The Next American Frontier*, New York: Times Books, 1983; Robert B. Reich, *Tales of A New America*, New York: Times Books, 1987; Robert B. Reich, *The Resurgent Liberal*, New York: Times Books, 1989; Robert B. Reich, *The Work of Nations: Preparing Ourselves for 21st Century Capitalism*, New York: Vintage Books, 1992.

37. For Classical Liberal critiques of industrial policy, see Richard B. McKenzie, *Competing Visions: The Political Conflict Over America's Economic Future*, Washington, DC: Cato Institute, 1985; and Chalmers Johnson, ed., *The Industrial Policy Debate*, San Francisco: Institute for Contemporary Studies Press, 1984.

38. For critical accounts of the history of business and government cooperation in the United States, see Gabriel Kolko, *The Triumph of Conservatism: A Reinterpretation of American History, 1900–1916*, New York: Free Press, 1963; James Weinstein, *The Corporate Ideal in the Liberal State 1900–1918*, Boston: Beacon Press, 1969; Donald Stabile, *Prophets of Order: Class, Technocracy, and Socialism in America*, Boston: South End Press, 1985; and R. Jeffrey Lustig, *Corporate Liberalism: The Origins of Modern American Political Theory 1880–1920*, Berkeley: University of California Press, 1982.

39. John Kenneth Galbraith, *Economics and the Public Purpose*, Boston: Houghton Mifflin, 1973; and Robert A. Dahl, *Democracy, Liberty, and Equality*, New York: Oxford University Press, 1986.

ADDITIONAL READING

Bowles, Samuel, and Herbert Gintis. *Democracy and Capitalism*. New York: Basic Books, 1986.

Brittan, Samuel. *The Role and Limits of Government*. Minneapolis: University of Minnesota Press, 1983.

Buchanan, James M. *The Limits of Liberty: Between Anarchy and Leviathan*. Chicago: University of Chicago Press, 1975.

Carnoy, Martin. *The State and Political Theory*. Princeton, NJ: Princeton University Press, 1984.

Clarke, Simon. *Keynesianism, Monetarism, and the Crisis of the State*. Brookfield, VT: Edward Elgar, 1988.

Cohen, Jeffrey E. *Politics and Economic Policy in the United States*. Boston: Houghton Mifflin, 1997.

David, Wilfred L. *Political Economy of Economic Policy*. New York: Praeger, 1988.

Dolbeare, Kenneth. *Democracy at Risk: The Politics of Economic Renewal*. Chatham, NJ: Chatham House, 1984.

Dugger, William M., and William T. Waller, Jr., eds., *The Stratified State: Radical Institutionalist Theories of Participation and Duality.* Armonk, NY: M. E. Sharpe, 1992.

Duncan, Graeme, ed. *Democracy and the Capitalist State.* New York: Cambridge University Press, 1989.

Esping-Anderson, Gosta. *Politics Against Markets.* Princeton, NJ: Princeton University Press, 1985.

Ferguson, Thomas, and Joel Rogers, eds. *The Political Economy.* Armonk, NY: M. E. Sharpe, 1984.

Freeman, John R. *Democracy and Markets: The Politics of Mixed Economies.* Ithaca, NY: Cornell University Press.

Glazer, Nathan. *The Limits of Social Policy.* Cambridge, MA: Harvard University Press, 1988.

Greenberg, Edward S. *Capitalism and the American Political Ideal.* Armonk, NY: M. E. Sharpe, 1985.

Hibbs, Douglas A. *The American Political Economy.* Cambridge, MA: Harvard University Press, 1987.

Jordon, Bill. *The State: Authority and Autonomy.* New York: Basil Blackwell, 1985.

Kristol, Irving. *On the Democratic Ideal in America.* New York: Harper & Row, 1972.

Levinson, Marc. *Beyond Free Markets: The Revival of Activist Economics.* Lexington, MA: Lexington Books, 1988.

Mills, Edwin S. *The Burden of Government.* Stanford: Hoover Institution Press, 1986.

Nell, Edward. *Prosperity and Public Spending.* New York: Unwin & Hyman, 1988.

Peretz, Paul, ed. *The Politics of American Economic Policy Making.* Armonk, NY: M. E. Sharpe, 1987.

Stiglitz, Joseph. *The Role of the State.* Oxford: Basil Blackwell, 1989.

Stone, Alan, and E. J. Harpham, eds. *The Political Economy of Public Policy.* Beverly Hills, CA: Sage, 1982.

Suleiman, Ezra N., and John Waterbury, eds. *The Political Economy of Public Sector Reform and Privatization.* Boulder, CO: Westview Press, 1990.

Chapter 8

Inflation and Unemployment

Macroeconomic instability, also known as the business cycle, has plagued Western nations since the beginning of industrialization. Inflationary periods lead to economic and political dislocations that jeopardize prosperity and social order. Recessions impose severe hardship in terms of unemployment, crime, and a plethora of unmet human needs. To protect themselves against the insecurity caused by economic instability, individuals, unions, corporations, and government have sought to suppress the forces of market competition and, in so doing, have transformed the institutional structure of modern societies.

Although the relative prosperity of the decades following World War II persuaded some economists that the business cycle had been conquered, the turmoil of recent decades has demonstrated the elusive nature of economic stability. Contemporary political economists are locked in profound debates concerning the underlying causes of instability and the merits of alternative policies for combating inflation and unemployment.

THE CLASSICAL LIBERAL PERSPECTIVE

Explanations of Instability

Classical Liberals assume that a competitive market economy contains built-in stabilizing mechanisms. This viewpoint was originally articulated in the early nineteenth century by a French economist, Jean Baptiste Say (1767–1832). His theory, known as Say's Law, states that supply creates its own demand. Production of output generates an identical amount of income. Any portion of income not spent on consumer goods and services will be spent on capital goods because interest rates adjust until the amount of saving is matched by an equal amount of borrowing for investment purposes. Say's Law does not imply that every commodity is guaranteed to sell, but it assures that the total amount of spending on consumption and investment will, ignoring government and international trade, match the value of output. That some goods remain unsold is merely a temporary phenomenon as production shifts to more desired goods. Furthermore, market incentives are ideally suited to facilitate the rapid movement of resources into more profitable lines of production. These transitions normally occur so smoothly that the economy as a whole experiences little or no disruption. Any employment will be "frictional" or "structural" as workers move from declining to expanding industries and occupations.

Classical Liberals of the nineteenth century were so certain of the inherent stability of a market economy that they attributed the actual ups and downs of the economy to external forces. For example, W. Stanley Jevons (1835–1882) claimed that sunspots affected agriculture and thereby caused the entire economy to slump. Other economists attributed business cycles to periodic discoveries of gold, waves of emigration from Europe to the United States, or wars. These explanations of instability remained dominant until the Great Depression when the apparent failure of the market resulted in a loss of status for Classical Liberalism lasting for the next forty years.

The Classical Liberal resistance to Keynesian macro theory came primarily from Austrian economists such as Ludwig von Mises and Friedrich A. Hayek who insisted that government mismanagement of the money supply caused business cycles. According to the Austrians, central banks such as the Federal Reserve drive interest rates artificially low by issuing too much money. Low interest rates result in too much borrowing and spending which, in turn, cause inflation. Eventually, the central bank must tighten the money supply, driving interest rates upward and causing a recession as the economy falls back to a sustainable rate of growth. Since the Austrians believed that overstimulation of the economy by the central bank creates the conditions leading to recession, they viewed the Keynesian remedy of more government spending as worsening the problem.[1]

Another Classical Liberal economist who fought against the Keynesian revolution was Milton Friedman of the University of Chicago. Friedman claims that the Depression was caused by the Federal Reserve System and trade protectionism. The Federal Reserve Act of 1913 established the Federal Reserve System, a central bank in control of the money supply.

During the 1920s, the U.S. economy experienced deflation and high interest rates as the Fed kept a tight grip on the money supply. By 1929, these conditions finally spoiled the optimism fueling speculation in the stock market. The ensuing crash triggered an economic downturn that might have been short-lived had Congress not passed the Smoot–Hawley Act of 1930, imposing high tariffs on imported goods. When other countries retaliated with similar tariffs, international trade collapsed and a full-blown depression followed. From Friedman's perspective, these instances of government intervention, first the Fed's inept handling of the money supply and later the Smoot–Hawley tariffs, prevented the natural equilibrating forces of the market from quickly restoring prosperity.[2]

The Austrian economists and Friedman gained little attention until the Western economies encountered serious difficulties in the 1970s. The inability of Keynesian policies to cope with simultaneous inflation and recession opened the door for a resurgence of Classical Liberalism. Under the labels of supply-side economics, monetarism, and new classical economics, Classical Liberal political economy returned to center-stage nearly as quickly as it had exited in the 1930s. These theories purport to demonstrate that government causes both inflation and unemployment. However, some disagreement remains over the connection between government and instability.

Supply-side economics, as popularized by Arthur Laffer, Jack Kemp, and Jude Wanniski, blames inflation and unemployment on the rising costs associated with government regulations, taxes, and the inefficiency of government programs.[3] Rising costs of production lead to reduced output and employment as well as higher prices.

Monetarist economists, led by Milton Friedman, focus on the Federal Reserve System as the cause of instability.[4] By assuming that the economy naturally operates at or near full employment and that the velocity of money is fairly constant, monetarists conclude that any increase in the money supply exceeding the real growth rate of the economy will cause inflation. This "demand-pull" inflation results from "too many dollars chasing too few goods."

New classical economists such as Robert Lucas, Thomas Sargent, Neil Wallace, and Robert Barro propose a slightly different version of government's role in destabilizing the economy.[5] They argue that individuals quickly learn from experience to anticipate the effects of government action. These "rational expectations" enable individuals to effectively block government efforts to stimulate the economy. For example, if the Fed increases the money supply, workers may demand higher wages in anticipation of higher prices, and businesses, anticipating higher costs, will raise prices to maintain their profits. New classical economists conclude that a monetary stimulus causes only inflation, without any lasting impact on the level of employment or output.

All Classical Liberals view deficit spending by government as a primary cause of inflation. Besides adding to aggregate demand and pulling prices upward, deficits force the government to compete with the private sector to borrow money. As government bonds are sold in credit markets, bond prices drop and interest rates rise. Higher interest rates "crowd out" borrowing for private investment, ultimately leading to slower growth rates in productivity and output.

Government also causes unemployment by interfering with the market's efficient allocation of resources. Minimum-wage laws, federal protection of labor unions, and regulations all discourage businesses from hiring more employees, while welfare programs cause some people to shun work. Classical Liberals believe a "natural rate of unemployment" is attributable to the combined interventions and market rigidities imposed by government. Government also indirectly contributes to unemployment by causing inflation. Once inflation begins, it feeds on itself. An "inflationary psychology" causes individuals to spend rather than save and to use their market power to raise prices. Also, inflation impairs the market's capacity to allocate resources efficiently, thereby reducing output and contributing to further price increases. Unchecked inflation will eventually cause the economy to collapse into depression, as happened in Germany in the 1920s. Thus government must intervene to intentionally engineer a recession by applying the monetary and fiscal brakes. Again, unemployment results from government's futile efforts to stimulate the economy beyond its productive capacity.

While supply-side, monetarist, and new classical economists blame government for initiating inflation and unemployment, they offer little explanation for such irresponsible policies. Another body of ideas called public choice theory fills this gap. The actions of government are attributed to the self-interest of politicians, bureaucrats, and voters. Since voters are attracted by government benefits but not by taxes, politicians provide more benefits and lower taxes. Deficit spending financed by government borrowing places the burden of present benefits onto future generations not yet able to vote. Similarly, increasing the money supply may create the illusion of prosperity because voters focus on the short-run stimulus to employment and income despite the eventual erosion of these gains by inflation.

Classical Liberals also believe that politicians cause economic instability in their quest for reelection. During the year or so prior to an election, government policies are manipulated to stimulate the economy so that citizens will be content when they enter the voting booth. After the election, the economy must be slowed to counteract inflationary pressures resulting from the stimulation. Classical Liberals call this process the "political business cycle" and argue that it constitutes a significant component of the economic instability of Western nations.[6]

Finally, economist Mancur Olson (1932–1998) claimed that government's past success in preventing recessions contributed to the solidification of rent-seeking coalitions and interest groups that obstruct the efficiency and flexibility of the market. Without the periodic discipline of recessions forcing firms and workers to renew their commitments to efficiency, the economy is gradually shackled by "social rigidities" consisting of interest groups with power to suppress competition. Once these groups capture the authority of government to advance their interests, the vitality of the market is drained and economic decline is inevitable.[7]

Stabilization Policies

The guiding principle behind Classical Liberal stabilization policies is the belief in the inherent stability of a market economy free from the restraints of government intervention. Once the barriers to profitability, saving, and investment are removed by lowering taxes, reducing regulations, stabilizing the money supply, and eliminating the budget deficit, the market economy will naturally generate noninflationary growth. Classical Liberals also view inflation as a more serious problem than unemployment since inflationary pressures disrupt the market and are ultimately responsible for subsequent recessions. They discount the severity of unemployment, arguing that official statistics overstate the problem since many people considered unemployed by the government actually work in the "underground economy."

Despite a consensus among Classical Liberals that the size of government must be reduced to stabilize the economy, they disagree on the strategies for accomplishing this goal. Some Classical Liberals want the Fed to maintain a fixed rate of money growth equal to the two to three percent long-run trend in real growth of the economy. They propose increased independence of the Fed from political influence by Congress and the President or even an amendment to the Constitution requiring a fixed rate of monetary expansion.[8]

Friedrich Hayek developed the idea of ending the Fed's monopoly on money creation by allowing several privately-issued currencies to circulate. Since the public would gravitate toward currencies that maintain their value, competitive pressures would force each issuer to limit the amount of money created.[9] Another Classical Liberal strategy to restrain the growth of money calls for a return to the gold standard. Money creation would be limited by the size of a nation's official holdings of gold.

Classical Liberals also favor deregulation and privatization as methods for reducing the scope of governmental activity. These policies would reduce government spending, lower business costs, encourage more competition, and improve efficiency. Classical Liberals argue that most of the activities currently performed by government originated from the pressures of special-interest groups, including the various bureaucracies that administer government programs. A vast array of government programs can be eliminated or transferred to the private sector without damaging the public interest.

Most Classical Liberals call for cuts in government spending to reduce the size of government and stabilize the economy. The unprecedented expansion of federal budget deficits during the 1980s and early 1990s heightened concerns about government spending. Some Classical Liberals favor an amendment to the Constitution requiring a balanced budget or establishing a ceiling for government spending as a percentage of GDP. Other Classical Liberals, particularly supply-side economists, favor lower tax rates instead, arguing that the incentive of higher after-tax earnings will lead to increased productive activity and therefore a broader tax base. With more to tax, government revenues may actually increase despite lower tax rates. In short, supply-siders claim that we can "grow our way out of the deficit."

However, not all Classical Liberals accept supply-side theories. While relishing the idea that tax reductions serve to cut off the "lifeblood" of government, Milton Friedman argues that insufficient tax revenue has not restrained government spending in the past. Friedman doubts that lower tax rates can actually lead to increased tax revenue; instead, tax cuts may simply result in larger deficits unless matched by similar or greater reductions in government spending.

Classical Liberals challenge the notion of a trade-off between inflation and unemployment; they insist that only unanticipated inflation reduces unemployment. As soon as people become accustomed to any particular rate of inflation, the economy returns to the "natural rate" of unemployment, which can be lowered only by restoring competition to the market through institutional reforms such as breaking up unions, deregulation, and elimination of the welfare state.

When recessions occur, Classical Liberals oppose government efforts to alleviate the hardship associated with unemployment and bankruptcy. They believe that recessions restore discipline and efficiency to the economy. If government cushions the impact, the market's self-correcting mechanisms are thwarted. Conversely, if government resists the political pressures to intervene, recessions will be short-lived and the economy will resume stable growth.

THE RADICAL PERSPECTIVE

Explanations of Instability

Radicals believe that instability is an unavoidable condition of a capitalist economy, but they offer a variety of different and sometimes conflicting explanations for the business cycle.[10] Radical "crisis theory" views inflation as a manifestation of the struggle between opposing classes to enlarge their respective shares of income. Recessions and unemployment, on the other hand, serve two purposes. They discipline the labor force by enlarging the "reserve army of the unemployed," thereby creating insecurity among all workers. Also, recessions eliminate the excess productive capacity caused by overly optimistic investments during the preceding boom period. Once a recession lowers the costs of labor and capital, another expansion can begin.

In 1925, the Soviet economist Nikolai Kondratiev (1892–1938) observed that capitalism experiences long-term cycles lasting fifty to sixty years. For each cycle, unique conditions contribute to expansion and specific obstacles eventually impede capital accumulation, leading to recession. After a period of stagnation, the impediments are resolved, clearing the way for further accumulation. However, another recession inevitably follows; the successful resolution of one set of impediments creates conditions posing new and different obstacles.[11]

Kondratiev described a sixty-year cycle, dating from the 1780s to the 1840s, in which the invention of labor-saving technology such as the steam engine fueled expansion. However, this technology caused political resistance by both workers who feared the factories and aristocrats seeking to preserve their power and status. Political and social conflict interfered with capital accumulation until the advocates of laissez-faire triumphed and capitalism entered its next phase of expansion.

A fifty-year cycle lasting from the 1840s to the 1890s was based on further development of labor-saving technology and the success of laissez-faire policies in abolishing the remnants of feudal and mercantilist restrictions on production and trade. By the 1870s, corporations had established capital-intensive production processes requiring huge, uninterrupted flows of revenue to remain profitable. However, cut-throat competition and the growing militancy of labor unions prevented firms from generating adequate profit, and the economy entered a prolonged stagnation until 1896. This era illustrates what Radicals call the falling rate of profit. As production becomes more capital-intensive, the rate of profit tends to fall because businesses have less labor to exploit in proportion to the amount of capital being used.

The problem of inadequate profits in the late nineteenth century was eventually resolved. Large corporations successfully monopolized their industries, gaining greater control over product prices and resource costs. In addition, imperialism opened new markets and provided cheaper raw materials. Until World War I, capitalism thrived under these conditions. However, the very success of monopolization and imperialism in bolstering profits eventually resulted in such concentrated wealth and income that the economy began to suffer from inadequate spending or "underconsumption."[12] Because wealthy individuals often save substantial portions of their income, increasing concentration of income meant that saving was rising more rapidly than business investment, resulting in inadequate demand for products and eventual cutbacks in production. Radicals attribute the Great Depression to underconsumption.

The solution to the Depression was a vastly enlarged role for government in the form of military spending, the welfare state, government regulation, and collective bargaining for unions. By the 1970s, however, these solutions for underconsumption had become obstacles to healthy rates of capital accumulation. In this respect, Radicals concur with Classical Liberals in viewing government intervention as a factor in economic stagnation.[13] Although welfare programs increase aggregate demand by placing money in the hands of people likely to spend it, welfare also results in what Radicals call "decommodification of labor." Welfare establishes a "social wage" received by workers even if they are unemployed, so labor is no longer a commodity whose value is determined by supply and demand. A capitalist economy cannot function well once labor has been decommodified; most jobs are so alienating that people will avoid work if government provides a social wage as an alternative.

Government involvement in the economy also leads to the "politicization of accumulation." This phenomenon results from the success of workers in using the democratic political process to secure rights such as occupational health and safety, collective bargaining, nondiscrimination, and protection against arbitrary layoffs. These rights diminish the prerogatives of capitalists and may pose barriers to profitability and accumulation. While Radicals strongly support workers' rights, they claim that capitalism will falter when the power of workers threatens to override the power of capitalists.

Once the economy has been politicized, the allocation of resources no longer appears natural and inevitable, and the distribution of income becomes subject to bitter struggles between interest groups. Capitalism is revealed as a system of power rather than a natural mechanism for accommodating individual preferences. As government and the economic system lose legitimacy in the eyes of citizens, the political battle to gain control of government undermines the accumulation process.[14]

The Keynesian solution to instability poses yet another problem for capitalism. The prosperity accomplished through Keynesian policies during the 1960s effectively suppressed the discipline of the market. Corporations became more powerful and resistant to competitive forces. Organized labor secured market power through collective bargaining and the threat of strikes. The economy grew increasingly segmented, dividing into a "primary sector" consisting of large corporations and unionized workers, and a "secondary sector" composed of small businesses and unorganized workers. The firms and unions in the primary sector remain relatively insulated from competitive pressures and therefore possess the power to raise prices and wages. This phenomenon gives modern capitalism a built-in inflationary tendency controllable only by maintaining slack in the economy through unemployment and slow growth.

The increased power of labor unions forms the basis for another Radical explanation of the business cycle—the "profit squeeze" theory.[15] During periods of expansion, unemployment declines and workers demand and receive higher wages. As the expansion continues, rising wage costs squeeze corporate profits, causing government to intentionally slow the economy as a means of disciplining workers and restraining wage demands. This Radical version of the "political business cycle" views government as using monetary and fiscal policy to assist businesses in holding down labor costs by periodically cooling the economy.[16]

Radicals view the federal budget deficit as a significant problem, but they do not blame politicians or voters. The "fiscal crisis of the state" simply manifests deeper structural problems in contemporary capitalism.[17] To bolster corporate profits, government initiates vast spending programs aimed at both stimulating demand and socializing many business costs. At the same time, corporate taxes are kept low to reduce business costs even further. The net effect of increased spending and insufficient taxes is a budget deficit. Radicals attribute recent reductions in the size of the deficit to cyclical prosperity. However, another recession will eventually trigger renewed expansion of the deficit.

Radicals argue that the demise of Keynesianism was sealed by the globalization of the economy. When national economies were relatively autonomous, policies designed to stimulate growth through government programs aimed at raising wages and aggregate demand were relatively effective. However, in a global economy, these same policies create perverse effects. Higher wages lead to higher business costs and reduced ability to export. The combination of higher wages and government regulations encourages "capital flight" as businesses relocate to countries with lower cost structures. Finally, the earlier success of Keynesianism in assuring adequate demand, stable profits, and economic growth undermines the pressure on businesses to innovate. With only modest gains in productivity, countries relying on Keynesian policies fall behind in international competition. Under these conditions, even the supporters of Keynesianism have begun to search for different solutions.

Stabilization Policies

According to Radicals, the traditional policy of slowing the economy to stop inflation is no longer viable.[18] Personal, corporate, government, and international debt is so immense that any significant downturn in the economy could trigger a chain-reaction of bankruptcies, leading to economic disaster. Also, in a segmented or dual economy, the secondary sector serves as a buffer for the primary sector. A recession that devastates small-business owners, farmers, and unorganized workers may have little impact in quelling the inflationary pressures emanating from corporations and unions in the primary sector. Finally, rights won through political struggles by workers, minorities, women, and other groups have tilted the balance of class power, creating political gridlock in Western economies. When no class or group has sufficient power to impose its agenda on society, government policy drifts aimlessly.

Radicals attribute the relative health of the U.S. economy during the 1990s to several factors. First, the effects of "Reaganomics" during the 1980s in eroding union power, cutting taxes, and deregulating businesses have substantially reduced business costs and increased profits, thereby restoring business confidence.[19] Second, the increasing globalization of trade has reduced business costs for labor and raw materials and slowed inflation by undermining market power. Third, huge budget deficits have provided a Keynesian stimulus to aggregate demand.

However, Radicals caution that these favorable conditions may impede future growth. The same policies that restored profitability have also produced a growing gap between rich and poor, a condition that preceded the Great Depression. Globalization also has negative consequences. Free trade with low-wage nations may pull down U.S. wages, further exacerbating income inequality. Some Radicals foresee the next major downturn being triggered by deflation as falling wages and commodity prices lead to competitive price cuts for manufactured goods. Corporations and nations struggling for market share in the global economy will be forced to accept lower profits which, in turn, will depress investment and growth. The last experience with deflation occurred during the Great Depression, when governments were finally able to revive their nations' economies with spending on World War II. However, now that domestic competition has been superseded by global competition, national governments have lost the ability to control their economies, and no international governing body exists with sufficient authority to pull the world market out of a deflationary spiral.[20]

From the Radical perspective, the ultimate solution to instability is a greater degree of public control and/or ownership of the major means of production. As steps toward achieving this goal, Radicals propose various combinations of the following policies.

1. *Partial Nationalization.* Government control of key industries such as energy, communications, transportation, and banking might take the form of buyouts of private shareholders, with existing management retaining its role. Alternatively, government might install its own managerial bureaucracy to administer public industries.

2. *Economic Planning.* Planning could consist of government forecasts or guideposts designed to aid private decisionmakers, or it might entail mandatory directives to industries and firms. To the extent that private

production remains a significant part of a socialist economy, government should have some control over the allocation of credit, the location of new businesses, and the mobility of existing businesses.[21]

3. *Democratization.* Radicals believe that government in a genuine socialist society should represent the public interest and be fully accountable to citizens. In both the political and economic spheres, Radicals call for decentralization of power and popular input into decisionmaking. Businesses should be democratized by establishing worker participation in decisionmaking or even direct ownership of productive assets. Radicals believe that democratized firms can improve efficiency through reduced waste and enhanced productivity.[22]

4. *Greater Equality.* A more equal distribution of wealth and income would improve stability by maintaining sufficient consumption spending and by reducing the dependency of the economy on the psychological moods of wealthy investors. This goal can be achieved by taxes on property income and policies to secure employment at good wages for all able-bodied citizens. Radicals also favor a guaranteed minimum standard of living for those persons unable to participate in the labor force.

Radicals acknowledge that these policies will not be enacted as long as government is controlled by the capitalist class. Therefore, the immediate strategy to deal with inflation and unemployment is to organize a broad-based political party representing the interests of all workers. Radicals are confident that a socialist political movement encompassing a large majority of the population can generate public policies leading to a stable and prosperous economy.

THE CONSERVATIVE PERSPECTIVE

Explanations of Instability

With the notable exception of Joseph Schumpeter, Conservatives have not offered economic theories to explain instability. Schumpeter attributed business cycles to waves of technological innovation periodically sweeping through the economy.[23] For example, the development of both the railroad and automobile industries required huge investments that stimulated economic growth. Schumpeter claimed that innovation tended to occur in spurts during periods of tranquility and optimism. Eventually, however, the ideas of the original "innovator" are copied by legions of less competent "imitators" who saturate the market and reduce profitability. As pessimism sets in, innovations dry up, investment is reduced, and the economy slumps. Schumpeter viewed recessions as unavoidable and useful; they served as "rubbish disposal" by forcing the liquidation of excess capacity and closure of inefficient firms. Renewed innovation would eventually initiate a new round of expansion and prosperity.

For most Conservative theorists, the explanation of instability encompasses a broader analysis than that offered by standard economic theory. Conservatives believe that markets function well only in the context of a society based on traditional values and hierarchical authority. Even in this setting, however, the market fosters self-interest, materialism, and moral relativism, all of which threaten hierarchical authority and thus stability.

This linkage between markets and instability has a long history dating to the origins of capitalism. The industrial revolution established not only new methods of production, but also new attitudes and lifestyles that disrupted the traditional patterns of feudal society. People became more mobile and calculating in their behavior, and new tastes and expectations developed. As capitalists gained power, traditional sources of authority such as the church, the state, and local elites declined in significance. Individuals began to view themselves as independent entities capable of defining and pursuing their own interests. The ensuing diversity of values and lifestyles undermined the stability and order of communities.

With the social fabric disintegrating, self-interested individuals became skeptical of the authority of aristocrats and capitalists alike, and bitter conflict over individual rights and rewards ensued. To gain advantage in this conflict, individuals formed interest groups such as labor unions, professional associations, and manufacturing groups. On one hand, Conservatives applaud the formation of groups to shelter individuals from the impersonal forces of the market and to promote a sense of identity, belonging, and purpose. But to function smoothly, these groups must operate within the context of a broad social consensus that restrains self-interest to preserve a stable and orderly society. Because this condition has not been met in modern societies, Conservatives argue that individuals exploit their group membership to gain more income for less work. In summary, while Conservatives welcome occupational groups as a means to sustain individual virtue and high productivity, the actual role of interest groups in modern societies is simply to advance the material interests of their members by protecting them from the disciplining forces of competition.

The market power of interest groups enables them to raise prices above competitive levels. The resulting inflation is perhaps more damaging for its social and psychological effects than for its direct influence on the economy. Inflation breeds insecurity and anxiety by creating uncertainty and by revaluing the worth of assets. Conflict between inflation's winners and losers contributes to social disorder. The virtues of hard work, thrift, and planning for the future are discredited as debtors and spenders are rewarded for their profligacy. The work ethic is undermined as individuals increasingly look for ways to profit from inflation through speculative activities.

Interest groups also place demands on government to provide benefits while resisting additional taxes. As a result, government spends more than it taxes, budget deficits grow, and government borrowing absorbs private savings that should be funding private investment. Inflation and sluggish growth inevitably result.

In addition to fostering the emergence of interest groups, the market also contributes to instability by eroding traditional values and culture. The Great Depression was preceded by a decade of cultural transformation including changing roles for women, the loss of millions of single-family farms, and new forms of music, art, and literature that challenged traditional tastes. From the Conservative perspective, the Depression was linked to greed, speculation, and cultural disintegration. Conservatives lament the fact that Western nations responded to the Depression with the liberal welfare state rather than a government–business alliance to restore hierarchical authority and stability. The welfare state effectively destroyed the dynamism of modern societies by fostering laziness, dependency, and a vast government bureaucracy. As the role of government grew, it undermined the broad array of "intermediate institutions" such as family, church, and neighborhood that provide individuals with identity and self-discipline. For Conservatives, the problem of economic instability is simply one more symptom of the cultural transformations that have produced women's liberation, the decline of religion, high divorce rates, lack of discipline in schools, and deterioration of the work ethic.[24]

While Conservatives implicate government as contributing to economic instability, the root causes lie much deeper. Government is controlled by citizens who have been transformed into isolated pleasure-seekers by the disruptive forces of industrialization and modernization. The inability of government to balance its budget mirrors the modern insistence on immediate gratification. Citizens and corporations focus more intently on short-term gains for themselves rather than the long-term health of society.

Stabilization Policies

Because Conservatives believe that economic problems such as inflation and unemployment reflect the erosion of traditional values and institutions, any viable solution must address issues seemingly unrelated to economics. Conservatives believe that economic stability can be improved by policies such as allowing prayer in public schools, banning pornography, and restoring authority in the family, the workplace, and the school. Efforts to directly confront economic problems, such as price controls or government job creation, simply place more power in the hands of government and further erode local communities.

However, some Conservatives envision a positive role for government in stabilizing the economy. Proposals for corporatism entail increased government involvement in coordinating and even planning economic activity.[25] For example, during the 1970s, Henry Ford II established the Initiative Committee for Economic Planning to explore strategies for cooperation among government, business, and labor in developing broad goals for the future of the economy. Similarly, in 1971, David Rockefeller organized the Trilateral Commission consisting of 180 members from North America, Western Europe, and Eastern Asia.[26] Although the membership of the commission was diverse, the general thrust of its publications favored a government–business coalition to restore economic prosperity. The Conservative nature of the Trilateral Commission was reflected in its concern that government be insulated from the political pressures of interest groups. Condemning what they called an "excess of democracy," the Trilateralists proposed greater autonomy for the executive branch of government in initiating public policy. They even suggested that the President's term of office be lengthened from four to eight years.

Corporatism was presented to the American public by the editors of *Business Week* magazine in a special issue in 1981.[27] Claiming that the most pressing problems confronting the U.S. economy were insufficient saving and a consequent shortage of capital, the editors warned that Americans would have to make sacrifices in their standards of living so that more resources could be directed toward investment and capital accumulation. Corporatism seeks to secure these sacrifices by reducing popular input into the democratic political process and promoting harmonious relations among labor, business, and government, thus minimizing adversarial and confrontational demands for higher wages and more benefits.

The most extreme Conservative proposal for stabilizing the economy is fascism, which controls inflation and unemployment by eliminating labor unions, freezing prices, planning the economy, suspending democracy and civil rights, and using whatever force is necessary to ensure high levels of production. The German and Italian economies experienced remarkable recoveries during the 1930s under fascism.

THE MODERN LIBERAL PERSPECTIVE

Explanations of Instability

A distinctly Modern Liberal explanation of instability first appeared during the 1930s when John Maynard Keynes challenged the laissez-faire policies of Classical Liberalism by suggesting that the level of investment would fluctuate in response to business sentiments concerning future profitability.[28] Widespread pessimism would cause investment to fall, despite availability of funds and low interest rates, and declining investment would result in a multiplied drop in national income.

Implicit in Keynes's theory is the Modern Liberal belief that increasing concentration of business power during the half century prior to the Depression enabled corporations to divert a larger share of national income to wealthy shareholders. Since wealthy families often save a considerable portion of their income, this increasing inequality caused total spending to lag behind production. Lacking sufficient demand for their products, corporations reduced investment and laid off workers, contributing to further declines in income and spending. The economy fell into an "underemployment equilibrium" with the prospect of permanent depression.

American Keynesians argued that business cycles could be managed by the appropriate combination of monetary and fiscal policy to adjust aggregate demand and restore investors' confidence. As a recession looms, government should increase its spending and/or reduce taxes. Conversely, the beginning of an inflationary boom should be met with cuts in government spending and/or tax increases. Government policymakers should be able to "fine-tune" the economy and maintain stable growth indefinitely. The first real test of Keynesian theory came with preparations for World War II. As governments around the world initiated massive spending on weapons and manpower, the Depression quickly faded. Within six months after the bombing of Pearl Harbor, the unemployment rate in the United States fell to virtually zero.

Keynesian policies attracted Modern Liberals because, in addition to stabilizing the economy, they promoted greater equality. If inadequate spending was the cause of recessions, then money should be placed in the hands of those people most likely to spend it—the poor. By attacking the Classical Liberal argument that growth and efficiency require significant inequality so that wealthy people can save and provide funds for investment, Keynesianism provided Modern Liberalism with an economic theory appealing to a broad spectrum of middle- and lower-class voters. Even many wealthy voters finally agreed that Keynesian policies produced growth and were therefore good for business.

Once World War II ended, Modern Liberals sought to maintain much of the wartime planning apparatus that had steered the economy to unprecedented levels of output. However, the political opposition of Classical Liberals and Conservatives was sufficiently powerful to force the dismantling of most wartime government agencies. Modern Liberals won a minor victory with the passage of the 1946 Employment Act, which established the President's Council of Economic Advisors and committed the federal government to pursuing all practical methods to maintain high levels of employment. In practice, the Employment Act had little impact on government policy. Fortunately for the Modern Liberal agenda, the Cold War with the Soviet Union quickly provided a new rationale for large-scale military spending that would sustain economic growth and high levels of employment.

Confidence in Keynesian economics peaked in the mid-1960s as a combination of tax cuts and increases in government spending resulted in full employment and prosperity. However, by the end of that decade, both inflation and unemployment were rising, and Modern Liberals were hard-pressed to offer explanations. Traditional Keynesian policy is capable of handling either unemployment or inflation but helpless when confronted with both simultaneously.

While some Modern Liberal economists insist that the turmoil of the 1970s was a temporary disruption caused by "external shocks" such as OPEC price hikes, currency devaluations, natural disasters, changing demographics, and global realignments of power, post-Keynesian economists conclude that the increasing concentration of wealth and power since World War II has rendered Keynesian "demand management" obsolete.[29] Traditional Keynesian policies remained effective until the 1970s because the economy was sufficiently competitive and unified to suppress inflation with moderate levels of unemployment. However, as large corporations and labor unions began to exercise their market power to raise prices even during periods of slack demand, a new, more insidious, "cost-push" inflation appeared.[30] If government reduced aggregate demand through monetary and fiscal policies, powerful corporations simply laid off workers and cut back production rather than lowering their prices. The resulting recession would bankrupt many small businesses and lead to further concentration of power. On the other hand, if government prevented recession by increasing aggregate demand, corporations and labor unions took advantage of the stimulus by initiating additional wage and price increases.

These corporate and union efforts to secure higher profits and wages have established a strong inflationary tendency in the economy. Yet because the upward pressure on prices is caused by the power of suppliers rather than by excess demand, restrictive fiscal and monetary policy no longer restrain inflation without causing rising levels of unemployment. Conversely, unemployment cannot be reduced simply by stimulating aggregate demand because a portion of the labor force is barred from work by structural rigidities such as racial and sexual discrimination and the dual labor market.

Stabilization Policies

Modern Liberals acknowledge that supply-side factors now bear much of the responsibility for inflation and unemployment, but they reject the policy agenda of supply-side economics. Tax cuts and deregulation may reduce business costs, but Modern Liberals doubt that the resulting increases in profits will be directed toward new investment. Corporations prefer to acquire additional assets through mergers and acquisitions rather than investing in new capital and creating additional jobs. According to Modern Liberals, tax cuts for corporations and wealthy individuals are not only unfair but lead to larger deficits, more government borrowing, and higher interest rates.

Modern Liberals also reject monetarist proposals for tight monetary policy. The resulting high interest rates are most injurious to small businesses and capital-intensive industries such as farming. Since these sectors are not the primary source of rising prices, tight money will be ineffective in combating inflation. More generally, Modern Liberals reject all proposals to fight inflation by slowing the pace of the economy. The large corporations and labor unions that initiate wage and price increases possess sufficient market power to weather a slowdown in the economy without rolling back prices. Furthermore, the people who suffer the most during recession—minorities, women, immigrants, unorganized workers, and small businesses—are not responsible for inflation. Therefore, slowing the economy to control inflation is not only ineffective but also unfair.

Given the obsolescence of monetary and fiscal policy, some Modern Liberals propose a fundamentally different type of intervention consisting of more direct government involvement in the private sector. Lester Thurow of MIT and Robert Reich of Harvard are two of the leading advocates of "industrial policy" for combating sluggish growth and inflationary pressures.[31] Government would consciously exert greater control over the direction and composition of economic activity through a variety of methods. Frequently mentioned components of Modern Liberal stabilization policy include:

1. *Cuts in military spending.* Modern Liberals argue that the United States has implicitly had an industrial policy since World War II, and that policy has stimulated the defense industry at the expense of more socially useful industries. Although Modern Liberals were strong advocates of military spending during the 1950s and 1960s, they now believe that military spending contributes to inflation and unemployment by diverting resources and manpower away from industries in which the United States must advance to remain competitive in international markets. In the absence of any significant external threats to U.S. national security, Modern Liberals believe that large reductions in military spending are both feasible and desirable.

2. *Incomes policy.* Some Modern Liberals propose that government should establish wage and price guidelines to dampen inflation. Seeking to avoid the mandatory nature of price controls, economists Sidney Weintraub and Henry Wallich (1914–1988) proposed a "tax-based incomes policy" (TIP) to impose tax penalties on those businesses raising

wages or prices in excess of government guidelines. Businesses holding wage and price increases below the guidelines would receive tax rebates from the government. A similar proposal by economist Abba Lerner (1903–1982), labeled "market anti-inflation plan"(MAP), would require firms to bid for government licenses to increase their prices and wages faster than the average rate of growth in productivity.

3. *Consumption tax.* Acknowledging the problem posed by low rates of saving and huge federal budget deficits, some Modern Liberals propose a tax on consumption in the form of a national sales tax or a value-added tax (VAT). While income taxes tend to discourage productive activity, a consumption tax would discourage spending and encourage saving. The regressivity normally associated with a sales tax could be minimized by giving all families a tax deduction equal to the value of standard necessities or by refunding taxes paid by low-income families.

4. *Incentives for saving.* In addition to a consumption tax, Modern Liberals seek to increase the incentives to save, particularly among low-income families, by exempting a specified amount of interest income from taxation or by making saving tax deductible.

5. *Mild protectionism.* As the U.S. economy experiences wrenching transitions due to foreign competition, Modern Liberals want to provide firms with sufficient time to adjust to new market conditions. Protectionism in the form of temporary quotas or tariffs on imports would allow U.S. firms to make changes without losing markets.

6. *Greater equality.* Noting the parallels between the concentration of wealth that occurred in the 1920s and the 1990s, Modern Liberals claim that dispersion of wealth is essential to a healthy economy. They propose higher income-tax rates on wealthy families, higher estate taxes, greater funding for programs benefitting low-income families, and a commitment to full employment.

7. *Investment in people.* In an age of increasing technological sophistication, a highly trained labor force is essential in staying competitive. Yet corporations are reluctant to provide training in general skills because of the potential loss of workers to other employers. From the corporation's viewpoint, replacing existing employees with more highly skilled workers may make sense. However, for society as a whole, the costs of layoffs in terms of community dislocations, crime, welfare, and family distress make retraining of current employees the more efficient option.[32] Modern Liberals propose to upgrade the quality of the labor force with increased funding for public education, tax credits for educational expenses, closer

links between academic and vocational studies, and tax breaks or subsidies to corporations for retraining employees.

8. *Credit allocation.* Some Modern Liberals want government to increase its involvement in making low-interest loans or subsidies to particular industries and regions. Critics have charged that the stock market, not government, is best suited to determine which industries are likely to be "winners" and which will be "losers." In response, Modern Liberals propose that government should provide matching loans or grants to firms and industries attracting private capital. The selection of "winners" is left to the private sector, with government adding its support to growth industries.

9. *Deficit reduction.* Although Keynesian economics condones deficit spending, the immense size of deficits during the 1980s and early 1990s persuaded most Modern Liberals that deficits now absorb savings that could otherwise be used for private investment and impose an immense burden on future generations to pay interest on the national debt. An exception is economist Robert Eisner who argues that a significant portion of government spending represents investments in both human and physical capital. Since these investments will yield benefits for future generations, the current generation should not be expected to pay the full cost. Eisner claims that the size of the deficit is less important than the composition of government spending. The more government spends on human and physical capital, the less worrisome is the deficit.[33]

10. *Neocorporatism.* Some Modern Liberals envision a "new social contract" in which government would coordinate the interaction of major interest groups and all parties would agree to act in a socially responsible manner. Labor unions would be less aggressive in their wage demands if they believed that corporations would exercise similar restraint in raising the prices of consumer goods. Conversely, corporations would feel less compelled to raise prices if they could be assured that wage costs would remain relatively stable. One proposal for increasing cooperation is to place representatives of government, unions, consumers, and local communities on the boards of directors of corporations. Because each of these groups is ultimately affected by the corporation, they become "stakeholders" with a strong interest in assuring that corporate decisions are socially responsible.

In summary, Modern Liberals are relatively optimistic that the U.S. economy can perform admirably in the coming decades if the right government policies are adopted. Adding to this optimism is their belief that certain favorable trends are apparent. The aging of the U.S. population should increase savings, and global competition has resulted in greater efficiency and productivity for U.S. businesses.[34] The opening of trade and investment opportunities around the world also holds promise for renewed growth and prosperity. The Keynesian dream of conquering the business cycle may yet become reality.

NOTES

1. See Friedrich A. Hayek, *Unemployment and Monetary Policy: Government as Generator of the "Business Cycle,"* Washington, DC: Cato Institute, 1979.

2. Milton Friedman and Anna J. Schwartz, *A Monetary History of the United States 1867–1960*, Princeton, NJ: Princeton University Press, 1963. For other Classical Liberal interpretations of the Great Depression, see Lionel Robbins, *The Great Depression*, London: Macmillan, 1934; Murray Rothbard, *America's Great Depression*, Kansas City, KS: Sheed & Ward, 1975; and Thomas E. Hall and J. David Ferguson, *The Great Depression*, Ann Arbor: University of Michigan Press, 1998.

3. Key works in supply-side economics include Jack Kemp, *An American Renaissance: A Strategy for the 80s*, New York: Harper & Row, 1979; Victor A. Canto, Marc A. Miles, and Arthur B. Laffer, *Foundations of Supply-side Economics: Theory and Evidence*, New York: Academic Press, 1983; Paul Craig Roberts, *The Supply-Side Revolution: An Insider's Account of Policymaking in Washington*, Cambridge, MA: Harvard University Press, 1984; and Jude Wanniski, *The Way the World Works*, New York: Basic Books, 1978.

4. See George Macesich, *The Politics of Monetarism: Its Historical and Institutional Development*, Totowa, NJ: Rowman & Allanheld, 1984; G. R. Steele, *Monetarism and the Demise of Keynesian Economics*, New York: St. Martin's Press, 1989; and Thomas Mayer, *Monetarism and Macroeconomic Policy*, Brookfield, VT: Edward Elgar Publishers, 1990.

5. See G. K. Shaw, *Rational Expectations: An Elementary Exposition*, New York: St. Martin's, 1984; and Jerome Stein, *Monetarist, Keynesian and New Classical Economics*, Oxford: Basil Blackwell, 1982.

6. See Thomas D. Willett, ed., *Political Business Cycles: The Political Economy of Money, Inflation, and Unemployment*, Durham, NC: Duke University Press, 1988; and Alberto Alesina and Nouriel Roubini, *Political Cycles and the Macroeconomy*, Cambridge, MA: MIT Press, 1998.

7. Mancur Olson, *The Rise and Decline of Nations: Economic Growth, Stagflation, and Social Rigidities*, New Haven, CT: Yale University Press, 1982.

8. See H. G. Brennen and James M. Buchanan, *Monopoly in Money and Inflation: The Case for a Constitution to Discipline Government*, London: Institute of Economic Affairs, 1981.

9. See Friedrich A. Hayek, *Denationalization of Money*, London: Institute of Economic Affairs, 1976. For a more recent treatment of this subject, see Lawrence H. White, *Competition and Currency*, New York: New York University Press, 1989.

10. Radical interpretations of inflation and unemployment are presented in James O'Connor, *Accumulation Crisis*, New York: Basil Blackwell, 1984; Michael

Bernstein and David Adler, eds., *Understanding American Economic Decline*, New York: Cambridge University Press, 1994; David Kotz, Terence McDonough, and Michael Reich, eds., *Social Structures of Accumulation: The Political Economy of Growth and Crisis*, Cambridge: Cambridge University Press, 1994; and Kenneth Hoover and Raymond Plant, *Conservative Capitalism in Britain and the United States: A Critical Appraisal*, New York: Routledge, 1989.

11. For a summary of the Radical view of the historical evolution of business cycles, see Chapter 3 of Erik Olin Wright, *Class, Crisis, and the State*, London: New Left Books, 1978.

12. The theory of underconsumption is fully elaborated in Paul Baran and Paul Sweezy, *Monopoly Capital: An Essay on the American Economic and Social Order*, New York: Monthly Review Press, 1966.

13. See Samuel Bowles, David M. Gordon, and Thomas E. Weisskopf, *After the Wasteland: A Democratic Economics for the Year 2000*. New York: M. E. Sharpe, 1990.

14. Problems surrounding legitimacy are analyzed in William Connolly, ed., *Legitimacy and the State*, New York: New York University Press, 1984, and Jürgen Habermas, *Legitimation Crisis*, Boston: Beacon Press, 1975.

15. See Howard Sherman, *Stagflation: A Radical Theory of Unemployment and Inflation*, New York: Harper & Row, 1976.

16. See Michal Kalecki, "Political Aspects of Full Employment," *Political Quarterly* 14, no. 4 (1943): 322–30. For a more recent account, see Raford Boddy and James Crotty, "Class Conflict and Macro Policy: The Political Business Cycle," *Review of Radical Political Economics* 7, (Spring 1975): 1–19.

17. See James O'Connor, *The Fiscal Crisis of the State*, New York: St. Martin's, 1973. See also Robert L. Heilbroner and Peter Bernstein, *The Debt and the Deficit: False Alarms, Real Possibilities*, New York: W. W. Norton, 1989.

18. Radical critiques of the economic policies of the 1980s are presented in Frank Ackerman, *Reaganomics: Rhetoric vs. Reality*, Boston: South End Press, 1982; Stephen Rousseas, *The Political Economy of Reaganomics: A Critique*, Armonk, NY: M. E. Sharpe, 1982; Robert Lekachman, *Greed Is Not Enough: Reaganomics*, New York: Pantheon, 1982; and Charles K. Wilbur and Kenneth P. Jameson, *Beyond Reaganomics*, University of Notre Dame Press, 1990.

19. See Stephen A. Marglin and Juliet B. Schor, eds., *The Golden Age of Capitalism: Reinterpreting the Postwar Experience*, Oxford: Clarendon Press, 1990.

20. See Robert Heilbroner, *21st Century Capitalism*, New York: W. W. Norton, 1993.

21. Proposals for controls on capital mobility are presented in Barry Bluestone and Bennett Harrison, *The Deindustrialization of America*, New York: Basic Books, 1982. See also Bennett Harrison and Barry Bluestone, *The Great U-Turn: Corporate Restructuring and the Polarizing of America*, New York: Basic Books, 1988. A Classical Liberal response to the Radical proposal for controls on capital is presented in Richard B. McKenzie, *Fugitive Industry: The Economics and Politics of Deindustrialization*, San Francisco: Pacific Institute, 1984.

22. See Samuel Bowles and Herbert Gintis, "Efficient Redistribution: New Rules for Markets, States, and Communities," *Politics & Society* 24:4, December, 1996, 307–342.

23. Joseph Schumpeter, *The Theory of Economic Development*, 3rd ed., Cambridge, MA: Harvard University Press, 1951. See also Joseph Schumpeter, *Business Cycles*, New York: McGraw-Hill, 1939.

24. See George Gilder, *Wealth and Poverty*, New York: Basic Books, 1981.

25. Descriptions of corporatism are presented in Gerhard Lehmbruch and Phillippe Schmitter, eds., *Patterns of Corporatist Policy-making*, Beverly Hills, CA: Sage, 1982; and Louis Galambos and Joseph Pratt, *The Rise of the Corporate Commonwealth*, New York: Basic Books, 1989.

26. See Michael Crozier, Samuel P. Huntington, and Joji Watanuki, eds., *The Crisis of Democracy*, New York: New York University Press, 1975. For a Radical critique of the Trilateral Commission, see Holly Sklar, ed., *Trilateralism: The Trilateral Commission and Elite Planning for World Management*, Boston: South End Press, 1980.

27. The material in *Business Week* magazine was subsequently published in book form. See Seymour Zucker and The Business Week Team, *The Reindustrialization of America*, Boston: Houghton Mifflin, 1982.

28. John Maynard Keynes, *The General Theory of Employment, Interest, and Money*, New York: Harcourt, Brace & World, 1964.

29. See Alfred Eichner, ed., *A Guide to Post-Keynesian Economics*, White Plains, NY: M. E. Sharpe, 1979; Philip Arestis and Thanes Skouras, eds., *Post-Keynesian Economic Theory*, Armonk, NY: M. E. Sharpe, 1985; Paul Davidson, *Controversies In Post-Keynesian Economics*, Brookfield, VT: Edward Elgar, 1991; John Pheby, ed., *New Directions in Post-Keynesian Economics*, Brookfield, VT: Edward Elgar, 1989; and Philip Arestis and Victoria Chick, *Recent Developments in Post-Keynesian Economics*, Brookfield, VT: Edward Elgar, 1992.

30. On the emergence of market power, see Wallace C. Peterson, ed., *Market Power and the Economy*, Boston: Kluwer Academic Publishers, 1988; John Munkirs, *The Transformation of American Capitalism*, Armonk, NY: M. E. Sharpe, 1985; and William Dugger, *Corporate Hegemony*, Westport, CT: Greenwood Press, 1989.

31. See Ira C. Magaziner and Robert B. Reich, *Minding America's Business: The Decline and Rise of the American Economy*, New York: Harcourt Brace Jovanovich, 1982; Robert B. Reich, *The Work of Nations: Preparing Ourselves for 21st Century Capitalism*, New York: Vintage Books, 1992; Lester Thurow, *The Zero-Sum Solution*, New York: Basic Books, 1984; and Lester Thurow, *The Future Of Capitalism: How Today's Economic Forces Shape Tomorrow's World*, New York: W. Morrow & Co., 1996.

32. See Thomas S. Moore, *The Disposable Work Force*, New York: Aldine de Gruyter, 1996.

33. Robert Eisner, *The Great Deficit Scares: The Federal Budget, Trade, and Social Security*, Washington, DC: Brookings Institution, 1997.

34. See John Rutledge and Deborah Allen, *Rust to Riches: The Coming of the Second Industrial Revolution*, New York: Harper & Row, 1989.

ADDITIONAL READING

Adams, Gerald F., and Lawrence R. Klein, eds. *Industrial Politics for Growth and Competitiveness: An Economic Perspective.* Lexington, MA: D. C. Heath, 1983.

Arestis, Philip, and Mike Marshall, eds. *The Political Economy of Full Employment.* Brookfield, VT: Edward Elgar, 1995.

Clarke, Simon. *Keynesianism, Monetarism and the Crisis of the State.* Brookfield, VT: Edward Elgar, 1988.

Epstein, Gerald A., and Herbert M. Gintis, eds. *Macroeconomic Policy After The Conservative Era.* New York: Cambridge University Press, 1995.

Heilbroner, Robert L. *Beyond Boom and Crash.* New York: W. W. Norton, 1978.

Higgs, Robert. *Crisis and Leviathan: Critical Issues in the Emergence of the Mixed Economy.* New York: Oxford University Press, 1986.

Hillier, Brian. *Macroeconomics: Models, Debates and Development.* New York: Basil Blackwell, 1986.

Hirsch, Fred, and John H. Goldthorpe, eds. *The Political Economy of Inflation.* Cambridge, MA: Harvard University Press, 1978.

Lindberg, Leon N., and Charles S. Maier, eds. *The Politics of Inflation and Economic Stagnation.* Washington, DC: Brookings Institution, 1985.

Offe, Claus. *Disorganized Capitalism.* Cambridge: MIT Press, 1985.

Peterson, Wallace C. *The Silent Depression.* New York: W. W. Norton, 1994.

Rowthorn, Bob. *Capitalism, Conflict and Inflation: Essays in Political Economy.* London: Lawrence and Wishart, 1980.

Shafer, Todd, and Jeff Faux. *Reclaiming Prosperity: A Blueprint for Progressive Economic Reform.* Armonk, NY: M. E. Sharpe, 1996.

Sherman, Howard J., and Gary R. Evans. *Macroeconomics: Keynesian, Monetarist and Marxist Views.* New York: Harper & Row, 1984.

Weidenbaum, Murray. *Rendezvous with Reality: The American Economy After Reagan.* New York: Basic Books, 1988.

Weintraub, Sidney. *Capitalism's Inflation and Unemployment Crisis: Beyond Monetarism and Keynesianism.* Reading, MA: Addison-Wesley, 1978.

Wilson, Thomas. *Inflation, Unemployment, and the Market.* Oxford: Oxford University Press, 1984.

Chapter 9

Poverty and Inequality

The persistence of poverty amidst affluence is one of the most troubling aspects of modern societies. Even in the nineteenth century, the concentration of wealth and power led to public hostility toward big business, paving the way for increased regulation of the economy. In the early twentieth century, Congress legislated progressive income and inheritance taxes. After the Great Depression, even stronger efforts were made to address the problems of poverty and inequality. Yet despite the growth of the welfare state, no significant change in the distribution of income has been accomplished. In fact, during the last two decades, income inequality increased significantly both within and among countries.[1] This chapter addresses some of the central questions concerning poverty and inequality. What causes inequality? How much inequality is healthy for the economy? Should government seek to change the distribution of wealth and income?

THE CLASSICAL LIBERAL PERSPECTIVE

Explanations of Inequality

Classical Liberals offer the following explanations of inequality:

1. *Individual productivity.* In the late nineteenth century, American economist John Bates Clark (1847–1938) developed the "marginal productivity theory" of income distribution to demonstrate that a perfectly competitive market rewards each factor of production in accordance with its contribution to output.[2] Employers will use and pay for factors of production as long as the value of the marginal product is greater than the cost. The law of diminishing returns assures a declining marginal product for every factor, so there is a specific level of utilization of both labor and capital at which remuneration is equal to the value of the marginal product. Employers maximize profit when they operate at this level, causing income to be distributed according to the quantity and quality of the factors of production made available by each person.

Building on Clark's marginal productivity theory, neoclassical economists have developed the concept of "human capital" to describe the talents and knowledge possessed by individuals.[3] Human capital enhances the value of labor, thereby increasing the potential income of the owner. As long as markets remain perfectly competitive, the rate of return to human capital will be identical for all persons. Any difference would cause a shift of labor away from occupations with lower rates of return and toward occupations with higher rates of return. When all such shifts have been accomplished, the rate of return to human capital equalizes throughout the economy. Any inequality of income is explained by the fact that some people possess more valuable human capital or other resources than other people do.

2. *Individual preferences.* Although Classical Liberals acknowledge that differences in abilities and preferences may be genetically determined, they prefer to emphasize individuals' freedom to shape their own destiny. Adam Smith, for example, doubted that innate abilities accounted for the differences between "a philosopher and a common street porter." Avoiding arguments based on genetically determined traits, Classical Liberals focus on the role of individual choice in determining the distribution of income. Even if people's abilities are similar, they achieve different degrees of success by choosing to develop and use those abilities. People who invest in themselves through education and training will increase their earning capacity, while those who prefer leisure will fall behind.

From this perspective, even poverty becomes a matter of individual choice. Some people place such high value on leisure and current pleasure that they are unwilling to make sacrifices or plan for the future. In the terminology of neoclassical economists, these people have a "short time-horizon," making them unwilling to delay gratification and thus unable to accumulate savings or invest in human capital.[4] Poverty may simply be the result of choices by people who value leisure more than the material rewards of work. In summary, Classical Liberals portray inequality as arising largely from individual choice—both the choices of individuals to acquire and supply productive resources and the choices of individuals to demand the resources possessed by others. In the words of philosopher Robert Nozick, the market operates according to the distributive rule: "from each as he chooses, to each as he is chosen."

3. *Technology.* Classical Liberals attribute much of the current gap between rich and poor to changing technology. For example, the computer revolution has created intense demand for people with advanced technical knowledge while eliminating many routine jobs. As a result, salaries for professional and technical employees have been rising while less-skilled workers experience wage stagnation. Technology also concentrates the rewards of certain occupations among fewer people. In fields such as music, film, sports, and publishing, the development of global communications systems tends to create a single world market in which only a few superstars succeed. Before radio and television, every city had local talents who prospered by practicing their craft. Now, with mass media connecting all corners of the globe, a handful of actors, athletes, writers, and musicians earn millions of dollars each year while the rest gain little public attention. The same trend is observable in other industries such as computer software, banking, and retail sales. This "winner-take-all" economy is the result of technological change.[5]

4. *Government intervention.* Classical Liberals acknowledge that markets are never perfectly competitive. If information is lacking or resources are immobile, the distribution of income is partially a matter of being in the right place at the right time. Also, concentrations of market power may cause greater inequality by restricting entry into desirable industries and occupations. However, Classical Liberals view many market imperfections as symptoms of government interference. For example, minimum-wage laws discourage the hiring of unskilled workers, while welfare programs erode self-reliance, initiative, and family unity. Government enables interest groups to restrict competition and block the advancement of less privileged groups. Classical Liberals claim that market power could not survive the pressures of potential competition without legal protection and favorable treatment from government. Therefore, they ultimately blame government for inequality arising from lack of competition.

Arguments for Inequality

During the transition from feudalism to capitalism, Classical Liberals stood in the forefront of efforts to demolish privilege and hierarchy. The Enlightenment offered a vision of society in which distinctions of class, race, creed, or nationality would not affect social mobility. Enlightenment thinkers defended the basic natural equality of all persons and assumed that the destruction of traditional customs and institutions would result in much greater equality in income and wealth. However, this strong egalitarianism was most evident among French thinkers. English social theorists, in contrast, expressed doubts about the natural equality of persons. John Locke, for example, suggested that workers had less capacity for rational thought.[6] The early Classical Liberals were unwilling to allow people without property to vote. Thus, despite its roots in the egalitarian spirit of the Enlightenment, Classical Liberalism began to justify inequality at an early stage in its evolution.[7] The Classical Liberal defense of inequality is based on the following arguments:

1. *Freedom.* According to Classical Liberals, if individuals are free to choose, inequality will inevitably arise among persons with different abilities and different preferences for work, saving, and risk-taking. Inequality is inextricably linked with freedom, and efforts to suppress natural inequality require expansion of governmental power and a corresponding reduction of freedom. Government would have to restrict what Robert Nozick calls "capitalist acts between consenting adults" or redistribute the income that results from free contracting and exchange. In either case, individual freedom has been curtailed.

Milton Friedman argues that inequality provides a bulwark against government repression. The accumulation of wealth in private hands creates "foci of power" throughout society that offset the political power of government and contribute to a freer society. For example, ideas or innovations unpopular with the government can still gain financial support when some individuals have substantial wealth at their disposal.

2. *Justice.* Classical Liberals view inequality resulting from competitive market transactions as fair and just.[8] Some individuals receive more money than others, but they may also have incurred substantial costs in terms of advanced education, stress, and sacrificed leisure. Neoclassical economists use the term "compensating wage differentials" to describe the greater rewards for jobs with higher training costs, greater levels of responsibility, and greater risk of failure. If one considers all the advantages and disadvantages of different occupations, individuals are more equal in their well-being than their relative wage levels would indicate.

Echoing J. B. Clark's marginal productivity theory, Milton Friedman claims that a market society is fair because each person is rewarded "according to what he and the instruments he owns produces." However, Friedrich Hayek claimed that ethical arguments about the justice of the market are futile because chance, in both the randomness of genetic endowment and the discovery of profitable opportunities, plays such a large role in determining individual success.[9] Moreover, reliance on the marginal productivity theory to demonstrate the justice of markets assumes a "productivity ethic" that views rewards in accordance with productive contribution as morally correct. While productivity would probably be high on any list of criteria of justice, alternative criteria such as individual needs or rights do exist, and society has no objective method for choosing among competing criteria of justice. For these reasons, Hayek made no claim for the fairness of markets, focusing instead on their capacity to protect individual freedom and promote economic efficiency.

Another problem with Classical Liberal efforts to claim fairness for rewards based on productivity is that the marginal product of any factor of production depends on both the supply of and demand for that factor. Since the pattern of ownership of economic resources affects supply and demand, the distribution of income is dependent on the distribution of wealth. Those who own wealth in the form of land, physical capital, or human abilities derive income from that wealth by making it available for the production of valued commodities. Yet without a prior justification of the distribution of wealth, the marginal productivity theory offers no moral defense of the distribution of income. If, as Robert Nozick acknowledges, coercion and theft have affected past accumulations of wealth, then the market-determined distribution of income cannot be fair since it reflects these past injustices.[10]

3. *Efficiency.* Classical Liberals rely on three distinct arguments to link inequality with efficiency. First, inequality establishes powerful incentives for productive behavior. The knowledge that effort, risk-taking, and innovation can result in material gains and upward social mobility serves to motivate human activity. Opportunities to "get ahead" and the visible presence of luxurious lifestyles stimulate desires and unleash human energy. Adam Smith referred to this admiration of wealth as a "deception which rouses and keeps in continual motion the industry of mankind."

Second, inequality generates saving from which investment is financed. Only relatively wealthy people can be expected to save substantial portions of their income, so attempts to reduce inequality will lower saving and investment, cause a decline in economic growth, and eventually harm both rich and poor. Classical Liberals reject the Keynesian concern that too much saving harms the economy, claiming that more saving will simply increase the supply of funds available for lending, drive down interest rates, and stimulate more borrowing and investment.

Finally, economic efficiency is enhanced by a complex division of labor which, in turn, requires a hierarchical chain of command to effectively coordinate production within the firm. Inequality of wealth and income inevitably results from hierarchy.

Responses to Poverty

Early Classical Liberal theorists such as Thomas Malthus claimed that poverty was the unfortunate consequence of the human propensity to over-populate a world with limited fertile soil. Malthus urged that poverty be ignored because any efforts to assist the poor would only encourage additional population growth and further misery. Although some Classical Liberals favored private charity as a solution to poverty, they warned that any assistance should be minimal so as to retain incentives to work. Welfare not only rewards irresponsible behavior, it demoralizes all citizens by breaking the link between effort and reward.

By the 1960s, however, the dramatic expansion of government's role in the economy persuaded some Classical Liberals to adopt a more activist stance toward poverty. Since they viewed government as a major cause of poverty, they could no longer attribute poverty solely to the choices of poor persons. These Classical Liberals acknowledged a public responsibility to aid citizens damaged by misguided government policies. The most notable proposal, often associated with Milton Friedman, is a negative income tax. This policy would establish a break-even level of income; any person earning more would pay taxes, and any person earning less would receive money from the government. With a negative income tax, each citizen would be assured of receiving at least a specified minimum income. Friedman claims that such a program redistributes income most efficiently. All other welfare programs could be abolished, and the money could go directly to needy recipients. Paperwork and bureaucracy would be reduced since determining the level of a family's benefits would require only a tax form. The negative income tax also would promote the dignity and self-esteem of recipients by eliminating trips to the welfare office and giving them control over their purchases. Finally, a negative income tax would eliminate differences in levels of support among states, thereby ending the phenomenon of the "welfare magnet" in which states or cities with more generous welfare programs attract additional clients.

Although the Nixon administration seriously considered the negative income tax, its popularity has declined in recent years. Most Classical Liberals now favor economic growth as the optimal solution to poverty. Using the slogan "a rising tide lifts all boats," they claim that policies to increase the rate of investment and stimulate growth are the only reliable methods to reduce poverty. Growth increases the incentives for productive behavior by offering greater opportunities for individual advancement. Classical Liberals prefer growth to welfare because they believe that welfare programs actually create poverty by fostering dependency, causing the breakup of families, and encouraging teen pregnancy. Less government aid would motivate low-income people to become more self-reliant and to develop the initiative to lift themselves out of poverty.[11]

Some Classical Liberals acknowledge that eliminating welfare is not a politically viable option and instead seek to discourage applications for welfare and motivate current recipients to find work by making eligibility requirements more stringent. Proposals include requiring recipients to be married, enrolled in educational or vocational training programs, or engaged in public jobs such as sweeping sidewalks and cleaning parks. The rationale behind these proposals is that participation in welfare programs should change individual behavior toward increased self-reliance, responsibility, and ambition.

THE RADICAL PERSPECTIVE

Explanations of Inequality

Radicals claim that income derived from the ownership of property often represents exploitation and creates conflict within society. Therefore, while Radicals condone unequal rewards for different types of labor, they condemn most property income in societies with highly unequal ownership of the means of production. They believe that concentrated private ownership creates oppression of the working class by the owning class. This oppression begins in the production process, where employees have little control over their work, and ultimately affects all social institutions including the family, schools, and government.

According to Radicals, poverty and inequality persist in capitalism because they function to promote profitability and capital accumulation.[12] In explaining inequality, Radicals rely on four broad arguments.

1. *Primitive accumulation.* The unequal pattern of ownership in capitalism reflects a historical struggle for wealth and status, with the victors gaining power and dominance over the rest of the population. The history of class struggle encompasses not only the exploitation of industrial workers, but also slavery and the expropriation of land occupied by native Americans. Radicals view the concentration of property ownership as a prerequisite for the development of capitalism. In Europe, between the sixteenth and eighteenth centuries, the process of "primitive accumulation" accomplished the initial concentration of wealth required for large-scale investment and production. In addition to piracy, plunder, and looting, a major component of primitive accumulation was the "enclosure movement" in England that resulted in the eviction of many small farmers so that land could be used for grazing sheep to supply wool for the emerging textile industry.

Once wealth was sufficiently concentrated, capitalists could establish profitable enterprises. However, this profit arose because capitalists controlled access to the means of production. Most citizens, stripped of any alternative means of support, had no choice but to enter the factories. Faced with plentiful supplies of labor, capitalists paid only subsistence wages and reaped the surplus produced by workers.

2. *The reserve army.* Marx called unemployed workers a "reserve army" that functions to keep employed workers in a constant state of insecurity. The reserve army disciplines workers to accept low wages and maintain high productivity. If a period of rapid growth and job creation depletes the reserve army, wages begin to rise and employers gradually replace workers with labor-saving machinery. The resulting layoffs replenish the reserve army and renew downward pressure on wages. The reserve army also serves as a buffer to absorb the shocks and dislocations of economic change. As firms expand and contract, they can change the size of their labor force without disturbing permanent employees. The notion of a reserve army offers a rebuttal to the Classical Liberal claim that the development of technology increases labor productivity and results in higher wages. If the supply of labor increases along with labor productivity, wages may stay constant or even fall. Government strategies to increase the supply of labor include lax enforcement of immigration laws, free-trade policies, and cuts in welfare benefits.

3. *The law of uneven development.* Radicals believe that both internal and external economies cause concentrations of capital in particular areas and leave other areas underdeveloped. Internal economies, often called economies of scale, occur when large-scale production results in lower average costs. Internal economies may drive smaller firms out of business, causing further concentration of capital. In contrast, external economies arise when the operation of one firm provides benefits for other firms. External economies explain why some areas experience sudden bursts of growth; once development has passed a certain threshold, the presence of local infrastructure, suppliers, and subsidiary industries reduces business costs and new firms are attracted to the area. The law of uneven development demonstrates that poverty and inequality may reflect regional patterns of capital accumulation rather than the abilities and preferences of individuals.

4. *Dual labor markets.* Radicals claim that labor markets in modern capitalist economies are divided into a "primary" sector, consisting of workers with appropriate credentials and personal attributes who compete for high-paying corporate positions, and a "secondary" sector, consisting of workers lacking credentials and personal attributes who compete for

jobs with smaller firms offering lower wages and less fulfilling work environments.[13] While barriers such as racial and sexual discrimination reinforce dual labor markets, Radicals argue that the fundamental cause of labor market segmentation is the difference in "market power" between large, monopolistic firms and small, competitive firms. Workers in the primary sector earn a higher rate of return on their human capital than do workers in the secondary sector because large corporations can pay higher wages while still maintaining a satisfactory rate of profit.

From the Radical perspective, dual labor markets benefit capitalists by maintaining labor force stability. The skilled employees in the primary sector are offered attractive wages and working conditions to secure their allegiance and dedication. Less desirable employees can then be hired for menial jobs at low wages. With little mobility between the two labor markets, workers in the primary sector receive wages in excess of the competitive level, while workers in the secondary sector receive lower wages than if the entire labor market were unified. Workers in the secondary sector are, in effect, subsidizing the high wages of workers in the primary sector.

Dual labor markets also maintain divisions and disharmony among workers, thereby undermining their bargaining power. By pitting lower-paid workers against higher-paid workers, capitalists "divide and conquer" the labor force. Radicals deny that low wages in the secondary sector are caused by low levels of human capital and productivity among workers, claiming instead that workers' behaviors and attitudes are largely conditioned by their wage level and work experience. Those who have endured low wages and unpleasant working conditions may develop a record of low productivity, absenteeism, and frequent job turnover. In contrast, primary sector workers tend to be highly dependable and committed to their firm because they are paid well and enjoy job security and pleasant working conditions. In summary, Radicals argue that attributing low wages to low levels of human capital puts the cart before the horse; low wages and meager job prospects cause low levels of productivity among workers in the secondary sector.

Arguments for Equality

Radicals embrace the Enlightenment claim that "all men are created equal." For Radicals, this statement does not mean that individuals have identical abilities, but rather that humans are, by virtue of being citizens, entitled to participate in political and economic decisionmaking and to enjoy a standard of living sufficient to fully develop their personal abilities.[14] Three arguments underlie this strong commitment to equality.

1. *Efficiency*. Radicals believe that economic efficiency is promoted by greater equality. While inequality may be functional in maintaining

profitability within capitalism, it ultimately reduces society's well-being. By keeping a portion of the population subordinate, inequality wastes much human talent and energy. Poverty not only prevents some people from gaining the resources to develop their capacities, but lowers their self-esteem and motivation to excel. At the other end of the social hierarchy, the rich may squander their personal abilities in lifestyles of leisure and frivolous consumption. Even technological development may be slowed by an incompatibility between hierarchical social structures and those technologies dependent on cooperative, group-oriented work relations.

2. *Social order.* A society with extensive poverty and inequality will be forced to devote substantial resources to repress citizens' anger and frustration resulting from deprivation and hopelessness. Police protection, courts and prisons, and elaborate insurance and security measures become necessary in a class-divided society. Extreme concentrations of wealth also lead to displays of affluence and contemptuous attitudes toward the poor, fostering tension and social conflict. The pursuit of wealth and status spurred by sharp inequalities will result in deterioration of the restraints on self-aggrandizement. The tendency to overstep the bounds of legal and ethical behavior erodes basic values and leads to social disorder.

3. *Human rights.* Radicals support equality because they believe oppression and suffering diminish the dignity of all persons. Marx labeled humans as "species beings" united by common interests that overshadow their individual differences. He condemned capitalism for alienating people from their social existence and causing them, instead, to focus on the pursuit of private, material gain. Radicals believe that every person deserves a decent standard of living.

To summarize, Radicals object not to differences in income, but to the division of society into an owning class whose income derives primarily from capital, and a working class whose major source of income is wages for labor. If classes were eliminated, Radicals would accept inequality that reflected different contributions by individuals to society. In fact, Marx strenuously argued against equality in socialism, claiming that justice would be fulfilled when society's tasks and rewards were allocated according to the dictum: "from each according to his abilities, to each according to his contribution." Even Marx's vision of communism upheld unequal distribution based on people's different needs.

Responses to Poverty

Because poverty and inequality are functionally necessary to capitalism, Radicals doubt the viability of redistributive policies that stop short of a

major restructuring of the economy. In fact, they claim that many governmental efforts aimed at helping the poor actually perpetuate inequality. The
social programs associated with the modern welfare state often function to
pacify low-income people and prevent social disorder. The major expan-
sions in the role of the welfare state occurred during periods when widespread discontent threatened to overturn the existing power structure.
Capitalist welfare programs are not designed to reduce poverty and unemployment, since depletion of the reserve army would increase the bargaining power of workers. Radicals conclude that the primary purpose of
welfare programs is to maintain a pool of cheap labor and control over a
potentially rebellious lower class.[15]

In the past, Radicals were likely to favor a guaranteed minimum income
as a means of assuring that the basic needs of all citizens were met.[16]
However, the growing public disillusion with welfare has raised doubts
about the political viability of income transfers to able-bodied persons. The
notion of an entitlement or right to a decent standard of living has fostered
antagonism toward the poor resembling the resentment against wealthy
aristocrats in previous centuries. In an ironic twist, the poor are viewed by
many as the new privileged elite who have the luxury of living without
working. The Classical Liberal linkage between productive contribution
and reward is deeply embedded in modern ethics and is even mirrored in
Marx's insistence that reward correspond to labor. For these reasons,
Radicals tend to focus more on full employment and public provision of
basic necessities such as health care and transportation. Full employment
might be achieved either through government incentives to private employers or reliance on government as the employer of last resort. Also, appropriate fiscal and monetary policies might be used to push the economy
toward high levels of employment.

A recent Radical proposal for reducing inequality is called "asset-based
redistribution." Samuel Bowles and Herbert Gintis argue that giving all citizens ownership rights to assets such as workplaces and residences would
result in increased productivity and efficiency as individuals assume the
rights and responsibilities of property ownership. Admittedly, some individuals would use their property more wisely than others, but Bowles and
Gintis believe that the resulting inequality would be substantially less than
in most existing societies where the bulk of assets are owned by a small
minority of the population. This proposal reflects a growing disenchant-
ment among Radicals with the traditional vision of socialism as consisting
of public ownership of property and central planning of production.
According to Bowles and Gintis, the socialist goal of a more egalitarian
society is achievable through a market economy in which an equitable pattern of property ownership has been established and government provides
various regulations and insurance programs as buffers against the vagaries
of the market.[17]

THE CONSERVATIVE PERSPECTIVE

Explanations of Inequality

Conservatives offer the following explanations of inequality.

1. *Innate differences in ability.* Conservatism arose in opposition to the Enlightenment belief in the basic equality of all people. Conservatives emphasize innate differences in individual abilities, claiming that people naturally seek to occupy those social roles compatible with their strengths and weaknesses. For example, the Italian economist and sociologist Vilfredo Pareto attributed inequality to different psychological characteristics of individuals. Some people are forceful and bold, others are clever and innovative, and still others are passive and dull.[18] Pareto concluded that these universal and fixed traits of human nature dictate hierarchical social relations and a relatively constant degree of inequality in every society. In recent years, the Conservative appeal to innate differences in individual abilities has been most prominently articulated by William Shockley, Arthur Jensen, Richard Herrnstein (1930–1994), and Charles Murray.[19]

2. *Functionality of hierarchy.* Talcott Parsons (1902–1979), one of the most eminent American sociologists, sought to understand social institutions by analyzing their purpose or function in promoting the well-being of society. During the 1940s, two of Parsons's students, Kingsley Davis (1908–1997) and Wilbert Moore, proposed that inequality of wealth, power, and status is "functional" in achieving society's goals of increased production and social order.[20] Every society requires that individuals adopt values, goals, and patterns of behavior conducive to social order. Without clear lines of authority and hierarchical social relations, this socialization process breaks down, individuals lose their sense of personal identity, and apathy and hedonism become pervasive. Hierarchy also establishes authority in the workplace to permit effective coordination of production. Hierarchy minimizes conflict by establishing rights and duties attached to particular social roles, enabling individuals to form reasonable expectations of others. Finally, the incentives provided by hierarchy and inequality are essential to recruit talented persons to fill the most important and difficult roles in society. Without substantial differences in financial remuneration and social status, few people would accept positions requiring substantial effort and sacrifice to acquire skills and knowledge.

Since hierarchy and inequality are functional to achieving society's goals, they will arise even if personal abilities are quite similar. If individuals with exceptional ability don't actually exist, then society will invent them; some persons will, perhaps arbitrarily, be designated as leaders and authority figures. In such circumstances, a high income doesn't necessarily reflect the personal attributes of the recipient, but it attests to society's need to legitimize leadership roles by attaching money, status, and prestige to them.

3. *Capitalism*. During the nineteenth century, Conservatives expressed contempt for the profit-seeking activities of businessmen and worried that the dynamism of the market would upset the natural order of society. By mobilizing resources and focusing attention on money-making and consumption, capitalism pulls people out of their traditional social networks and transforms them into autonomous and calculating maximizers of utility. These isolated individuals seek immediate gratification rather than engaging in long-term, constructive efforts to build meaningful lives through education, marriage, work, and involvement in the community. Thus, the narrow pursuit of pleasure actually contributes to poverty and misery.

During the early stages of capitalism, Conservatives frequently clashed with Classical Liberals by advocating political control to curb the excesses of capitalism. Although Conservatives are now generally hostile toward government, they still fear that unregulated markets will disrupt the natural hierarchy and jeopardize stability and order.[21] Of particular concern is free trade between countries. Some Conservatives claim that competition with low-wage countries is pulling down wages and destroying industries in the United States and western Europe.

4. *Government*. Conservatives vacillate about the effect of government on society. During the early nineteenth century, they looked to wise political leaders to restrain market competition. Government also bore responsibility for fostering a social and cultural environment conducive to individual virtue and self-restraint. However, with the extension of democracy in the late nineteenth century, Conservatives feared that politicians would engage in expedient efforts to woo voters with short-term benefits and that government would become an instrument used by various factions to advance narrow interests. After witnessing the Russian Revolution, fascism in Europe, and the New Deal in the United States, many Conservatives concluded that government poses a greater danger to society than does capitalism. When the masses (or tyrants claiming to represent the masses) hold the reins of governmental authority, subversion of the natural order is inevitable. New inequalities of wealth and status will be forged by interest groups using government as their weapon.

5. *Culture*. Conservatives argue that culture is a key determinant of individual behavior and that some cultures generate more poverty than others. From the perspective of many Conservatives, non-Eurocentric cultures are viewed as promoting idleness, irresponsibility, and a focus on immediate pleasure. These values conflict with the behaviors required for success in a capitalist economy and, therefore, people from these cultures are disproportionately poor.[22]

Arguments for Inequality

The Conservative case for inequality includes the following arguments:

1. *Cultural diversity*. Inequality in wealth and social status encourages a variety of talents and cultures. Excessive equality would create a uniform and homogeneous society lacking varieties of tastes and lifestyles that make life interesting. Without concentrated wealth, cultural institutions such as art museums, opera, and symphony orchestras might disappear.[23]

2. *Preservation of intermediate institutions*. Conservatives value those intermediate institutions such as family, church, and neighborhood that shelter the individual from the isolation of a market economy and the power of government. Intermediate institutions socialize the individual and provide a sense of security, belonging, and identity. Since these institutions are based on the hierarchical authority of parents, ministers, and local officials, the preservation of inequality is essential. When government, in its pursuit of equality, takes responsibility for individual security, the intermediate institutions lose much of their purpose and consequently begin to wither.[24]

3. *Prevention of totalitarianism*. According to Conservatives, inequality is hardly noticed when it appears natural and inevitable. However, when egalitarian policies raise the prospect of increased income for the lower classes, people become increasingly dissatisfied with their present status and envious of those who have more. A flood of "rising expectations" overwhelms any actual benefits received from government. Therefore, rather than reducing resentment and class antagonisms, egalitarian policies raise the public's awareness of and irritation with any remaining social distinctions. Because humans innately need to distinguish themselves from others, the leveling of social status will impede the search for meaning and purpose. The pursuit of equality not only undermines authority and traditional values, it causes the disintegration of individual personalities as manifested in apathy and malaise throughout society. Ultimately, the combination of apathetic citizens and social disorder will open the door to totalitarianism and the loss of individual freedom.

4. *Preservation of elites*. The incentives provided by inequality of income and social status are essential to motivate talented people to contribute to the well-being of society. Without adequate incentives, elite individuals will not share their talents and knowledge. These elites provide essential governing and managerial skills, but they also serve as visible role models. Standards of conduct and ethics are transmitted throughout society by the behavior of natural leaders in government, business, the church, and the community.

5. *Restraining democracy.* In addition to favoring inequality of wealth and social status, Conservatives support inequality in political participation. If the masses fully participate in the political process, politicians will pander to resentment and envy with confiscatory taxation of property income, deficit spending, and excessive money creation. Such policies will satisfy voters in the short run but ultimately lead to economic ruin and moral decay.

Responses to Poverty

Conservative proposals for dealing with poverty include the following policies:

1. *Eugenics.* Conservatives who adhere to genetic interpretations of inequality have proposed selective forms of population control such as sterilization of impoverished persons. They would reduce poverty by preventing the birth of children with deficient genetic endowments. Such thinking was not uncommon during the early twentieth century when an active "eugenics" movement appeared, culminating in Nazi efforts in Germany to breed a super-race. More recently, American physicist William Shockley became so concerned about deterioration of the human gene pool that he established a sperm bank for Nobel prize winners.

2. *Tracking.* Some Conservatives propose a more rigorous system of tracking in public schools to steer children toward appropriate adult roles. Tracking improves the match between individuals and the social roles they occupy and functions to lower the expectations of those who will occupy the bottom rungs of the socioeconomic ladder. Conservatives believe that poverty in affluent societies is more a matter of perception than actual material deprivation. If individuals recognize their limited possibilities at an early age, less anger and resentment and, consequently, less crime and social disorder will occur.

3. *Mild welfare.* Neoconservatives such as Irving Kristol and George Will accept the need for government involvement in enlarging opportunities for the poor. Claiming that defects in both the market and governmental policy have disrupted the natural order of society, neoconservatives acknowledge that poverty is not always the fault of the poor and that private charity is inadequate. Since poverty contributes to crime and class hostility, neoconservatives justify some welfare programs as enabling the poor to retain their virtue and self-respect so they eventually will be integrated into mainstream society.

Neoconservatives struggle to devise poverty programs that foster virtue and social order without destabilizing the intermediate institutions of family, church, and neighborhood. While government is an obvious source of funds and leadership for making social improvements, neoconservatives remain skeptical of "social engineering" and "top-down" programs. Therefore, if government is to help solve poverty, neoconservatives urge that programs be designed to restore the functioning of intermediate institutions.[25] Once family, church, and neighborhood regain their significance, individuals will once again make long-term commitments and lead productive lives. Some Conservatives support changes in tax laws to encourage the formation and maintenance of families, "workfare" to provide welfare recipients with job experience and self-respect, and community-based programs that respond to the unique situations of different clients.[26] With the restoration of healthy communities, many individuals unable to support themselves due to disabilities can be cared for by families, neighbors, or churches. Conservatives anticipate that well-designed poverty programs will eventually eliminate much of the need for intervention by government.

THE MODERN LIBERAL PERSPECTIVE

Explanations of Inequality

Modern Liberals seek to promote greater equality while protecting individual freedom and private property. The following explanations of inequality can be found in the writings of Modern Liberal theorists.

1. *Imperfect competition.* Because the market never meets all the conditions for perfect competition, the distribution of income will be unfair even by the standards of neoclassical economic theory.[27] To the extent that monopolies and oligopolies exist, that information is lacking, that resources are immobile, and that competing products are not homogeneous, the marginal productivity criterion for distribution will be violated. In other words, those individuals and groups with market power, better information, and more mobile resources will "exploit" less advantaged groups.[28] Imperfect competition also means that the market will fail to adjust instantaneously to changes in technology, resource availability, or consumer preferences. While gradual adjustments occur, some individuals will lose income and others will profit enormously from the temporary disequilibrium. For example, the development of computer technology has displaced thousands of bookkeepers while making Bill Gates the wealthiest person in the world.

2. *Past injustice.* Even if perfect competition did exist, the highly unequal ownership of capital and land would create excessive inequality in the distribution of income. Modern Liberals criticize the prevailing distribution of property by tracing it back to the forcible seizure of land and

wealth prior to the strict enforcement of property rights and contracts. Even after property rights became legally protected, much wealth was gained through unethical and illegal tactics. The present distribution of wealth and income reflects the fact that members of previous generations were dispossessed by slavery, by expropriation of land, and by exploitation in the labor market. The market perpetuates these past injustices by recognizing all property rights regardless of their origin.

3. *Cycle of poverty.* Children who grow up in disadvantaged families often fail to develop the personal attributes required for success in the market. During the 1950s, Modern Liberals appealed to the notion of a "culture of poverty" to describe the transmission from one generation to the next of certain psychological and behavioral characteristics commonly associated with poverty. For example, apathy, poor work habits, an inability to focus on long-term goals, and a lack of social skills were attributed to environmental causes. By the 1970s, however, many Modern Liberals viewed the "culture of poverty" explanation as placing the blame for poverty on the values and lifestyles of the poor. Instead, they developed a "situational" theory of poverty, portraying the behavior of the poor as a pragmatic response to circumstances. Tendencies to avoid marriage, education, or saving derive from a lack of money.

4. *Discrimination.* The market permits the expression of all preferences backed by money, even if those preferences include bigotry. When prejudice is combined with market power due to concentrated wealth, discrimination can flourish. Those individuals whose race, gender, ethnic background, age, or appearance does not match societal norms for people in better-paid positions may encounter difficulty in achieving economic success.

5. *Inadequate educational system.* Modern Liberals believe that public education is underfunded and offers unequal qualities of education to children of different classes and races. As a result, some people enter the labor force lacking basic skills required for success in the modern economy.

Arguments for Equality

Unlike Radicals, Modern Liberals are confident that substantially greater equality can be achieved within the confines of capitalism. To justify redistribution, they have developed a wide variety of arguments in favor of increased equality.

1. *Maximization of utility.* The utilitarian philosophy developed by Jeremy Bentham and John Stuart Mill in the mid-nineteenth century provided the first Modern Liberal argument for greater equality. If individuals

possess equal capacities for pleasure, then, according to the law of diminishing marginal utility, a rich person gets less satisfaction from a dollar than does a poor person. Redistributing money from rich to poor increases total satisfaction because the loss of utility by the rich would be less than the gain in utility experienced by the poor. Bentham and Mill did not push for redistribution, however, fearing that property owners would feel insecure and stop investing.

2. *Freedom*. Later in the nineteenth century, Thomas Hill Green argued that freedom requires access to certain basic necessities such as food, clothing, shelter, education, and health care. Society can promote freedom by establishing a set of "human rights" or "citizenship rights" including not only civil rights such as freedom of speech, but also economic rights to a job, a basic standard of living, and other essentials to lead a dignified human existence. To the extent that the market fails to recognize human rights, government should supplement the market.

3. *Growth*. During the 1930s, John Maynard Keynes added another powerful argument for pursuing greater equality. Claiming that poor people are more likely than rich people to spend any additional income they receive, Keynes proposed that a redistribution of income from rich to poor would increase total spending which would, in turn, create more jobs and raise output. The appeal of the Keynesian argument is that everyone benefits from greater equality. Even the rich, who will likely pay higher taxes to finance redistribution, benefit from a growing economy.

4. *Political stability*. Keynes also argued that greater equality was essential to preserve popular support for capitalism and democracy. He believed that both fascism and communism had been fueled by widespread anger and resentment over excessive inequality, poverty, and unemployment.

5. *Maximization of social welfare*. Welfare economics is the branch of economics that analyzes the conditions under which society's well-being would be maximized. Whereas earlier economists such as Jevons assumed that free markets yielded maximum welfare, the discovery of market failures such as externalities and public goods provided strong arguments for government intervention. By the 1930s, economists such as Abram Bergson, John Hicks (1904–1989), Nicholas Kaldor, and Abba Lerner had uncovered a more serious problem with markets. They demonstrated that even a perfectly competitive market with no market failures cannot be expected to produce maximum social welfare. While the market may yield an efficient allocation of resources, efficiency means only that individuals have gained maximum utility from the "initial endowment" of assets with which they enter into market exchanges. However, a different distribution

of these assets might result in greater social welfare. Welfare economists reached the dramatic conclusion that markets will maximize social welfare only if an optimal distribution of assets has first been established.

Welfare economists don't claim to know this optimal distribution, but they place responsibility for establishing it with government. This theoretical development gives government priority over the market in promoting society's well-being and, therefore, represents a direct challenge to the Classical Liberal faith in the capacity of the market to promote both justice and prosperity. Welfare economics represents the logical culmination of utilitarianism. If society's goal is the maximization of utility or welfare, then only those property rights contributing to that goal can be defended. Although Modern Liberals aren't specific about which property rights are legitimate, they often presume that redistribution in favor of the poor would improve society's well-being.

6. *Efficiency*. To the extent that social solidarity exists in society, more affluent citizens will experience pangs of anxiety and perhaps guilt over the presence of poverty in their midst. Due to this emotional discomfort, not to mention fear of crime and civil disorder, wealthy people might actually be willing to sacrifice some of their income to reduce poverty. Yet as individuals, they can have no significant impact on poverty and therefore have little incentive to contribute to charity. This dilemma reveals that the distribution of income has the characteristics of a "public good." Many citizens might desire a more equal distribution of income, but they remain "free riders," hoping to benefit from someone else's efforts to reduce poverty. Economists Harold Hochman and James Rodgers have demonstrated that if the distribution of income is a public good, then the market is unlikely to yield an efficient allocation of resources.[29] In this case, some government efforts to redistribute income can be justified purely on the grounds of improved efficiency, because some people can be made better off without necessarily making others worse off.

The technical efficiency of the economy might also be enhanced by greater equality. With less poverty, fewer resources would be diverted to crime control, welfare programs, drug abuse, property insurance, and health care. Conversely, less extreme concentrations of wealth would mean fewer resources for conspicuous consumption and waste. To support this argument, Modern Liberals note that international comparisons reveal little correlation between inequality and economic growth. Countries such as Japan and Germany have more equal distributions of income and yet have experienced periods of rapid economic growth.

7. *Justice*. Because excessive inequality of property easily translates into unequal power and social status, any society that values equal opportunity for every individual to compete fairly should also favor greater equality of

wealth and income. Without justice and social solidarity, citizens are likely to experience despair, insecurity, envy, and hostility. Too much inequality challenges the legitimacy of property holdings because rewards no longer appear to correspond to individual effort and ability. People with large property holdings often appear to be richly rewarded for leading lives of leisure. The aspirations of the poor decline as they perceive the market to be merely a power struggle in which those who already own property always win.

The most recent case for a link between equality and justice comes from philosopher John Rawls, who claims that even a distribution of income in accordance with personal ability would not be fair because ability is affected by randomly distributed genetic endowments. According to Rawls, justice requires that income and wealth be distributed in a manner that maximizes the well-being of the poorest members of society. In other words, rich people are entitled to their wealth only if it contributes to capital accumulation, job creation, and rising standards of living for the poor. Greater equality should be pursued until any further redistribution would so damage incentives and capital accumulation that the poor would actually be harmed.

Despite a strong commitment to greater equality, Modern Liberals, with the exception of Rawls, have been reluctant to specify an optimal distribution. In fact, many Modern Liberals remain skeptical and cautious about redistributive efforts. Bentham and Mill opposed significant redistribution, fearing that property owners would feel threatened and would cease to engage their assets in productive ventures. Modern Liberal economists have also expressed concern that, beyond a certain level, equality is incompatible with economic efficiency.[30] Efforts to promote too much equality will dampen the incentives for work and investment by both those from whom money is taken and those to whom money is given. With lowered incentives, the level of economic activity will decline due to inefficiency. This "big tradeoff" between equality and efficiency has been the primary reason for caution about any significant redistribution.

Responses to Poverty

Modern Liberalism currently stands at a historic watershed in its approach to poverty. In the past, the market was condemned for permitting and even exacerbating poverty, and government programs to redistribute wealth and income were favored. The progressive income tax, the inheritance tax, welfare programs, labor unions, agricultural price supports, rent controls, minimum-wage laws, and social security were all intended to reduce poverty and inequality. Modern Liberal economists acknowledged that regulated prices caused inefficiency, but they argued that such policies were more politically feasible than outright redistribution of income. For example, the public would be more likely to favor milk price supports than direct cash transfers to dairy farmers. However, by the 1960s, the results of previous government efforts were so disappointing that Lyndon Johnson launched a "War on Poverty" consisting of various welfare programs and civil-rights laws. Unfortunately, the rising costs of the Vietnam war and the onset of stagflation in the early 1970s effectively ended Modern Liberal hopes for a quick solution to poverty.

In redesigning poverty programs, Modern Liberals have had to confront two related constraints. First, concerns about budget deficits make any significant expansion of funds to combat poverty unlikely. Second, the current political climate is characterized by widespread resentment and insensitivity toward the poor.[31] Recognizing the unpopularity of traditional welfare programs, Modern Liberals now urge that public policy be reoriented from dealing directly with the victims of poverty to challenging the market forces and government policies causing poverty.[32] The variety of Modern Liberal proposals currently being considered include:

1. Means-tested benefits to restrict government benefits to only those persons falling below a designated level of income or wealth. This strategy could be implemented with social security, student loans, farm subsidies, and Medicare.
2. Tax incentives for employers who hire and train people previously unemployed or receiving public assistance.
3. "Workfare" programs that require welfare recipients to engage in public jobs—such as cleaning parks or sweeping sidewalks—in exchange for aid. While such programs are intended to maintain self-esteem and provide experience with the daily routine of working, some Modern Liberals are critical, claiming that the menial jobs provided by workfare teach no employable skills.
4. Federally funded day-care centers and training programs to provide parents and young workers with increased opportunities to enter the labor force.
5. Affirmative action programs to promote the hiring of women and minorities, as well as comparable worth programs to secure pay equity.
6. Busing programs to establish racial balance throughout school districts to provide all children with an opportunity for equal education.
7. Labor market policies to train unemployed workers, improve the flow of information between employers and job seekers, and assist workers with job-search procedures and interviewing techniques.
8. Industrial policy to involve government in coordinating the allocation of resources by targeting credit toward specific industries and generally attempting to increase the efficiency and fairness of the economy.
9. The dispersion of profit and stock-ownership through profit-sharing schemes and employee stock-ownership plans (ESOPs).[33]

10. A high minimum wage. Modern Liberals claim that raising the minimum wage will provide employers with increased incentives to improve labor productivity by upgrading the skills of the workforce. They also claim that a higher minimum wage can actually increase employment by increasing worker satisfaction and effort.[34]

NOTES

1. For recent analyses of income and wealth distribution in the United States, see Edward N. Wolff, *Top Heavy: A Study of the Increasing Inequality of Wealth in America*, New York: Twentieth Century Fund Press, 1995; Anthony B. Atkinson, Lee Rainwater, and Timothy M. Smeeding, *Income Distribution in OECD Countries*, Paris: OECD, 1995; Jeffrey H. Bergstrand, *et al.*, eds., *The Changing Distribution of Income in an Open U.S. Economy*, New York: North-Holland, 1994; Denny Braun, *The Rich Get Richer: The Rise of Income Inequality in the United States and the World*, Chicago: Nelson-Hall, 1991; and Sheldon Danziger and Peter Gottschalk, *Uneven Tides: Rising Inequality in America*, New York: Russell Sage, 1992.

2. See John Bates Clark, *The Distribution of Wealth*, New York: Macmillan, 1899. For an introduction to and critique of the marginal productivity theory of distribution, see David Schweickart, *Against Capitalism*, New York: Cambridge University Press, 1993.

3. Human capital theory is described in detail in Gary Becker, *Human Capital*, 2nd ed., New York: National Bureau of Economic Research, 1975. For a Radical critique, see Samuel Bowles and Herbert Gintis, "The Problem with Human Capital Theory, A Marxian Critique," *American Economic Review* 65, no. 2 (May 1975): 74–82.

4. The concept of a short time-horizon is utilized in Edward C. Banfield, *The Unheavenly City: The Nature and Future of Our Urban Crisis*, Boston: Little, Brown, 1968.

5. See Robert H. Frank and Philip J. Cook, *The Winner-take-all Society*, New York: Free Press, 1995. The authors of this book do not condone the growing inequality attributable to technology, and propose public policies to address the problem.

6. For a detailed analysis of Locke's argument for differences in rationality between the classes, see C. B. Macpherson, *The Political Theory of Possessive Individualism*, Oxford: Clarendon, 1962.

7. The evolution of the concept of equality in Classical Liberal thought is presented in Amy Gutman, *Liberal Equality*, New York: Cambridge University Press, 1980. See also Ian Shapiro, *The Evolution of Rights in Liberal Theory*, New York: Cambridge University Press, 1986.

8. For a Classical Liberal treatment of the issue of fairness and markets, see Richard B. McKenzie, *The Fairness of Markets*, Lexington, MA: D. C. Heath, 1987. See also Gordon Tullock, *Economics of Income Redistribution*, Boston: Kluwer-Nijhoff, 1983.

9. Hayek's critique of justice is developed in *The Mirage of Social Justice*, Vol. 2, of *Law, Legislation, and Liberty*, London: Routledge & Kegan Paul, 1982.

10. Robert Nozick, *Anarchy, State, and Utopia*, New York: Basic Books, 1974.

11. See Charles Murray, *Losing Ground: American Social Policy 1950–1980*, New York: Basic Books, 1984.

12. For a fuller account of the functionality of poverty, see Herbert Gans, "The Positive Functions of Poverty," *American Journal of Sociology* 78, no. 2 (1972): 275–89. See also Charles Sackrey, *The Political Economy of Urban Poverty*, New York: W. W. Norton, 1973.

13. Radical analysis of dual labor markets is presented in David M. Gordon, Richard C. Edwards, and Michael Reich, *Segmented Work, Divided Workers*, New York: Cambridge University Press, 1982; Richard C. Edwards, David M. Gordon, and Michael Reich, eds., *Labor Market Segmentation*, Lexington, MA: D. C. Heath, 1975; and David M. Gordon, *Theories of Poverty and Unemployment: Orthodox, Radical and Dual Labor Market Perspectives*, Lexington, MA: D. C. Heath, 1972.

14. See R. H. Tawney, *Equality*, London: George Allen and Unwin, 1931.

15. See Francis Fox Piven and Richard Cloward, *Regulating the Poor*, New York: Pantheon, 1971.

16. Arguments for a guaranteed annual income are presented in Michael L. Murray, ". . .*And Economic Justice for All": Welfare Reform for the 21st Century*, Armonk, NY: M. E. Sharpe, 1997.

17. Samuel Bowles and Herbert Gintis, "Efficient Redistribution: New Rules for Markets, States, and Communities," *Politics & Society*, Vol. 24, No. 4, December, 1996.

18. Vilfredo Pareto, *The Mind and Society: A Treatise of General Sociology*, New York: Dover, 1935.

19. See Arthur R. Jensen, "How Much Can We Boost IQ and Scholastic Achievement?," *Harvard Educational Review* 39, no. 1 (Winter 1969): 1–123; Richard Herrnstein, *IQ and the Meritocracy*, Boston: Little, Brown, 1973; and Richard J. Herrnstein and Charles Murray, *The Bell Curve: Intelligence and Class Structure in American Life*, New York: Free Press, 1994. Excellent surveys of the debate over intelligence are presented in Daniel Seligman, *A Question of Intelligence: The IQ Debate in America*, New York: Carol Publishing Group, 1992; and Russell Jacoby and Naomi Glauberman, *The Bell Curve Debate: History, Documents, Opinions*, New York: Times Books, 1995.

20. Kingsley Davis and Wilbert Moore, "Some Principles of Stratification," *American Sociological Review* 10 (April 1945): 242–49. For a fuller treatment of the functional nature of hierarchy and inequality, see Talcott Parsons, *The Social System*, Glencoe, IL: Free Press, 1951.

21. See Kevin Phillips, *The Politics of Rich and Poor: Wealth and the American Electorate in the Reagan Aftermath*, New York: Harper Collins, 1990.

22. These arguments are developed in Lawrence Mead, *The New Politics of Poverty*, New York: Basic Books, 1992.

23. See Bertrand de Jouvenel, *The Ethics of Redistribution* (1951), Indianapolis: Liberty Press, 1990; and William A. Henry III, *In Defense of Elitism*, New York: Doubleday, 1994.

24. The erosion of community in modern society is detailed in Robert A. Nisbet, *The Quest for Community: A Study in the Ethics of Order and Freedom*, New York: Oxford University Press, 1953.

25. On the importance of intermediate institutions in poverty programs, see Peter L. Berger and Richard J. Neuhaus, *To Empower People: The Role of Mediating Structures in Public Policy*, 2nd ed., Washington, DC: American Enterprise Institute, 1996; Michael Novak, ed., *Democracy and Mediating Structures: A Theological Inquiry*, Washington, DC: American Enterprise Institute, 1980; and Michael Novak, *The Catholic Ethic and the Spirit of Capitalism*, New York: Free Press, 1993.

26. For a fuller account of Conservative policies for reducing poverty, see Stuart Butler and Anna Kondratas, *Out of the Poverty Trap: A Conservative Strategy for Welfare Reform*, New York: Free Press, 1987.

27. For a Modern Liberal critique of the inability of labor markets in modern capitalist economies to sustain full employment and create fairness, see Lester Thurow, *Generating Inequality: Mechanisms of Distribution in the U.S. Economy*, New York: Basic Books, 1975.

28. The neoclassical theory of exploitation is developed in chapters 25 and 26 of Joan Robinson, *The Economics of Imperfect Competition*, London: Macmillan, 1933.

29. Harold M. Hochman and James D. Rodgers, "Pareto Optimal Redistribution," *American Economic Review* 59, no. 4 (1969): 542–57.

30. See Arthur M. Okun, *Equality and Efficiency: The Big Trade-off*, Washington, DC: Brookings Institution, 1975.

31. Lester Thurow, *The Zero-Sum Society: Distribution and the Possibilities for Economic Change*, New York: Basic Books, 1980.

32. A summary of Modern Liberal policies for combatting poverty and inequality is presented in Herbert Gans, *More Equality*, New York: Vintage Books, 1974. For more recent assessments of the accomplishments and failures of poverty programs, see Sheldon Danziger and Daniel H. Weinberg, eds., *Fighting Poverty: What Works and What Doesn't*, Cambridge, MA: Harvard University Press, 1986; and Sheldon Danziger, Gary D. Sandefur, and Daniel H. Weinberg, eds., *Confronting Poverty: Prescriptions for Change*, Cambridge: Harvard University Press, 1994.

33. See Martin L. Weitzman, *The Share Economy: Conquering Stagflation*, Cambridge, MA: Harvard University Press, 1984; Louis O. Kelso and Patricia Hetter Kelso, *Democracy and Economic Power: Extending the ESOP Revolution*, Cambridge, MA: Ballinger, 1986; and Glenville Jenkins and Michael Poole, *The Impact of Economic Democracy: Profit Sharing and Employee Sharing Schemes*, New York: Routledge, 1990.

34. See David Card and Alan B. Krueger, *Myth and Measurement: The New Economics of the Minimum Wage*. Princeton, NJ: Princeton University Press, 1995.

ADDITIONAL READING

Atkinson, A. B. *The Economics of Inequality*. Oxford: Clarendon, 1983.

Baker, John. *Arguing for Equality*. New York: Verso, 1987.

Bonner, John. *Economic Efficiency and Social Justice*. Brookfield, VT: Edward Elgar, 1995.

Brown, Henry Phelps. *Egalitarianism and the Generation of Inequality*. Oxford: Clarendon, 1988.

Combee, Jerry, and Edgar Norton. *Economic Justice in Perspective: A Book of Readings*. Englewood Cliffs, NJ: Prentice Hall, 1991.

Dovring, Folke. *Inequality: The Political Economy of Income Distribution*. New York: Praeger, 1991.

Edsall, Thomas. *The New Politics of Inequality: How Political Power Shapes Economic Policy*. New York: W. W. Norton, 1984.

Green, Phillip. *The Pursuit of Inequality*. New York: Pantheon, 1981.

Hochschild, Jennifer. *What's Fair: American Beliefs about Distributive Justice*. Cambridge, MA: Harvard University Press, 1981.

Jencks, Christopher, and Paul Peterson, eds. *The Urban Underclass*. Washington, DC: Brookings Institute, 1991.

Kelso, William A. *Poverty and the Underclass*. New York: New York University Press, 1994.

Kuttner, Robert. *The Economic Illusion: False Choices Between Prosperity and Social Justice*. Boston: Houghton-Mifflin, 1984.

Nelson, Joel I. *Post-Industrial Capitalism: Exploring Economic Inequality in America*. Thousand Oaks, CA: Sage Publications, 1995.

Phillips, Derek. *Equality, Justice, and Rectification*. London: Academic Press, 1979.

Pierson, Christopher. *The New Political Economy of Welfare*. State College, PA: Pennsylvania State University Press, 1991.

Ratcliff, Richard E., Melvin L. Oliver, and Thomas M. Shapiro. *The Politics of Wealth and Inequality*. Greenwich, CT: JAI Press, 1995.

Sen, Amartya. *On Economic Inequality*. New York: Oxford University Press, 1997.

Sunstein, Cass R. *Free Markets and Social Justice*. New York: Oxford University Press, 1997.

Temkin, Larry S. *Inequality*. Oxford: Oxford University Press, 1993.

Wadden, Alex. *The Politics of Social Welfare*. Brookfield, VT: Edward Elgar, 1997.

Winfield, Richard Dien. *The Just Economy*. New York: Routledge, 1988.

Zajac, Edward E. *Political Economy of Fairness*. Cambridge: MIT Press, 1995.

Chapter 10

Labor and Industry

Work occupies a central role in the lives of most people, and the nature of work affects nearly all dimensions of human existence. Political economists have long debated the question of how best to organize society's productive activities. How should labor be divided, industries organized, and authority delegated? Is the market of government better suited to arrange work that is efficient, yet satisfying for the people involved? In this chapter, we shall investigate sharply contrasting interpretations of the role of work in human life, the structure of authority in production, and the effect of labor unions on the economy.

THE CLASSICAL LIBERAL PERSPECTIVE

The Nature of Work

The early stages of the development of Classical Liberalism corresponded with the rise of the factory system and large-scale production. Formerly independent farmers and craftsmen turned to wage-labor for their livelihoods. The early Classical Liberal theorists assumed that workers disliked the monotony and submissiveness of factory work. Adam Smith worried that industrial jobs would cause workers to become "as stupid and ignorant as it is possible for a human creature to become."[1] To assure that workers would enter the factories, Classical Liberals sought to abolish all forms of public welfare and increase the penalties for vagrancy and theft.

Although Classical Liberals no longer believe that work is inherently harmful, they do assume that most people would prefer not to work. The incentive of monetary rewards is the primary enticement into the labor force. Individuals choose to work because the anticipated utility of their earnings exceeds the costs in terms of sacrificed leisure and the unpleasantness of work. Individuals decide when, where, and how much to work by assessing the relative benefits and sacrifices associated with different jobs and choosing the type of work offering the greatest net advantage.[2]

Although a few talented individuals will be able to support themselves through personally fulfilling work, Classical Liberals assume that most people view work as a "disutility." A job is merely a means to earn money so that leisure time can be enjoyed more fully. Unstimulating work may actually be appealing to those seeking to support themselves with the least possible use of mental and physical energies. If some people want fulfilling work, Classical Liberals defend the market as the best guarantee that such preferences can be met. For example, artists may devote themselves to their crafts if they are willing to accept a lower standard of living. People who value a more personalized work environment may seek employment in small businesses, with awareness that they may sacrifice higher wages and greater job security. The market allows people to balance their desire for satisfying work against the value of higher wages.

Explanations of Hierarchy

Classical Liberals claim that existing institutional arrangements have proven their worth by surviving in a competitive market. The history of market-oriented societies consists of a continual elimination of inefficient institutions as superior practices evolve over time. Applying this logic to the structure of authority within the workplace, Classical Liberals conclude that competition forces firms to adopt the most efficient organization of work. If owners or managers adopt an inefficient structure of authority, they will be penalized by the market as the firm experiences higher costs and reduced profits.

Early in the twentieth century, management theorists such as Frederick W. Taylor (1856–1915) and Frank Gilbreth (1868–1924) initiated "time-and-motion studies" to reduce skilled jobs to simple, routine motions quickly mastered by any worker.[3] Taylor's "scientific management" was based on the Classical Liberal view of work as intrinsically unpleasant. Workers are motivated solely by financial incentives. Taylor assumed that workers derive little satisfaction from their jobs and therefore would not object to routinization. Scientific management would actually relieve workers from all responsibilities for planning and coordinating the production process. Workers would simply engage in repetitive physical motions. This more efficient division of labor also permitted management to monitor work performance more effectively by establishing quantity, quality, and time standards for each specific task.

In arguing that the market dictates an efficient organization of the firm, Classical Liberals encounter an apparent contradiction. While defending individual choice coordinated by the market as the best institutional arrangement for achieving efficiency, Classical Liberals recognize the obvious efficiency of large corporations in which thousands of people are "governed" by hierarchical, centralized authority. The success of the modern corporation seems to indicate that efficiency can be enhanced by suppressing individual choice and market forces over a significant range of the production process.

To resolve this contradiction, Classical Liberal economists have formulated "new institutional economics" and "property rights theory" to demonstrate that corporate hierarchies and other seemingly nonmarket institutions are efficient and arise from the rational choices of self-interested individuals.[4] Both of these theoretical approaches view society as a market in which individuals engage in mutually beneficial exchanges. If the benefits of an exchange are not immediately realized, both parties will seek to negotiate a contract specifying future rights and obligations. Yet contracting is often made difficult by the presence of "transaction costs." Economists define a transaction cost as any cost not directly related to the production of a commodity. Examples of transaction costs include the expense of gathering information and specifying and enforcing contracts.

In the case of labor contracts, employers are often unwilling to fully specify the obligations of both labor and management in a contract. Their reluctance stems from imperfect information about the potential productivity of workers as well as a desire for flexibility in assigning tasks. According to Classical Liberal economists, a hierarchical "governance structure" within the firm solves these difficulties in labor contracting by establishing a pyramid of command through which employers may assign tasks and monitor work performance. Hierarchy permits corporations to economize on transaction costs that would result from drawing up a fully specified contract with each worker. The corporation will expand hierarchical control as long as the benefits gained by reducing transaction costs and increasing output exceed the cost of additional supervision.

New institutional economics also offers an explanation for differences in governance structures affecting white-collar and blue-collar workers. Because employers assume manual labor is unpleasant and unfulfilling, they conclude that workers will "shirk" their duties unless faced with the prospect of detection and penalties. Therefore, rigid hierarchies and overt authority prevail in industries such as mining and manufacturing. White-collar workers, on the other hand, are more likely to resent close supervision, and they perform tasks that are more difficult to monitor. Also, white-collar workers often acquire skills on the job, so firing a worker and training a replacement is costly. In such circumstances, direct supervision may be less efficient than instilling in workers a sense of dedication to the job and loyalty to the firm. This strategy is accomplished by establishing promotion ladders and pay raises unrelated to productivity. Higher salaries can be economical if they sufficiently reduce the need for supervision.

Classical liberals argue that a cooperative or egalitarian system whereby workers monitor one another and share in the benefits of increased productivity is infeasible. With so many people sharing the benefits, the amount received by any single worker would be insufficient to provide an incentive for monitoring co-workers. Only when the benefits of enhanced efficiency accrue to a small number of owners and supervisory personnel will incentive be adequate to elicit effective management of the firm.

According to Classical Liberals, hierarchy within the firm is entirely consistent with workers' freedom. If hierarchy is efficient, and efficiency is essential to the long-term viability of the firm, then even employees of worker-owned firms would appoint or hire supervisory personnel and encourage effective supervision by granting them the benefits accruing from increased productivity. Thus, the structure of authority is independent of who owns the firm. In the words of economist Paul Samuelson, "it makes no difference whether capital hires labor or the other way around."[5]

In a capitalist economy, workers may seek employment in a less hierarchical firm if they so desire. However, the large number of workers in traditionally-structured jobs suggests that they value high wages more than satisfying work. If people wanted more egalitarian work, they would seek employment at lower wages with firms offering less structured environments. Employers should willingly dismantle hierarchy in exchange for lower wages as long as reduced wage costs offset any loss of productivity. If employers resist change, groups of workers could obtain loans to start their own firms. If egalitarian work relations are truly more efficient, these worker-owned firms would gradually drive capitalist firms out of business. However, the virtual absence of large worker-controlled firms in capitalist societies persuades Classical Liberals that hierarchy is the most efficient form of work organization.[6]

The Role of Unions

Classical Liberals oppose labor unions, viewing them as groups seeking to promote their own interests by suppressing competition in labor markets. To the extent that unions are successful in their goal of raising wages, they cause the following problems:

1. Higher wages cause employers to substitute capital for labor, resulting in loss of jobs.

2. Employers whose production processes are necessarily labor-intensive and who operate in competitive markets will experience lower profits, forcing them either to relocate or shut down. In either case, the region or nation in which unions are strong will suffer loss of industry.
3. Employers with sufficient market power to pass on increased wage costs in the form of higher prices will be able to avoid falling profits, but consumers will bear the burden of a rising cost of living.
4. By forcing consumers to pay higher prices for union-produced goods, labor unions divert demand from nonunion industries. Firms in those industries will be forced to either cut wages or reduce production and lay off workers. Therefore, the gains made by unionized workers come largely at the expense of other workers.
5. To the extent that union demands for higher wages cause inflation, government will be forced to implement contractionary fiscal and monetary policies resulting in unemployment.

In addition to raising wages, unions also lower productivity. Union demands for seniority and job security protect workers from the disciplining forces of market competition. Unions also practice "featherbedding"; they retain jobs that have been rendered obsolete by changing technology. As unions usurp managerial authority, they interfere with efficient production. Finally, by focusing on the conflicting interests of labor and management, unions contribute to animosity and resentment. Classical Liberals insist that both management and workers share a common interest in high profits so that firms can expand, create new jobs, and pay higher wages in the future.

Historically, mass unionization did not succeed until unions were exempted from antitrust laws and protected by favorable legislation. Thus, some Classical Liberals propose the application of existing antitrust laws to unions and the passage of "right to work" laws abolishing the mandatory hiring of union workers in particular firms. Another proposal to reduce union power is to place legal restrictions on the right to strike.

THE RADICAL PERSPECTIVE

The Nature of Work

Radicals believe that work can be one of the most valuable aspects of human existence. The active engagement of one's physical and mental capacities in purposeful activity designed to change the external world is intrinsically fulfilling. Work provides a context for becoming fully human through the exercise and development of abilities, the formation of meaningful social relations, and the transformation of ideas into material form. The products of work represent material expressions of the self. By viewing and appreciating the fruits of their labor, workers attain greater self-awareness.

In contrast to this positive account of work's potentiality, Radicals depict most work in capitalist societies as degrading and alienating.[7] Profit-driven employers divide work into mere repetitive motions requiring little skill, thought, or creativity. Hence, workers have few opportunities to develop new abilities. In addition, capitalist bosses monitor the work process, suppressing workers' sense of autonomy and dignity. Finally, since capitalists own the output of businesses, workers are denied the gratification that comes from viewing their products as extensions of themselves. As a result, jobs in a capitalist economy offer little personal satisfaction to the worker.

Radicals condemn capitalism because it permits one group of people—the capitalists—to control the organization of work and the products of other people's labor. Work cannot provide an outlet for self-expression and creativity when workers simply perform motions to carry out the capitalists' plans. Marx portrayed work in capitalism as so alienating that people actually lose essential aspects of their humanity. Never having experienced fulfilling jobs, workers center their lives around biological functions such as eating, drinking, and procreating rather than developing their uniquely human capacities for creative thought and expression. Modern Radicals have extended this argument to claim that alienated workers will encounter difficulty in finding fulfillment during their leisure time.[8] Dissatisfaction with work permeates nonworking hours and results in problems such as divorce, drug abuse, and family violence. Workers who endure boring jobs will inevitably be frustrated with the overall quality of their lives.

Yet if work is so oppressive, why is there so little active resistance to capitalist control of production? Radicals explain that most people have no access to alternative means of production and therefore are at the mercy of capitalists. Moreover, workers are subject to psychological distortions called "false consciousness." Because capitalists treat workers as factors of production rather than as human beings, workers develop corresponding low self-esteem and come to believe that they deserve their powerless position in society. Workers also may exhibit what psychologists call a "hostage syndrome." Case studies demonstrate that hostages tend to identify with and develop sympathy for their captors. Since the captor has complete power, the captor's viewpoint dominates that of the hostage. Workers, who are essentially captive to the power of capital, may cease to resist their plight and actually seek approval from their employers as a means of self-validation.

Although Radicals condemn the alienating nature of work in capitalism, they express ambivalence about the nature of work in a socialist or communist society. Marx envisioned a future society without authority or a division of labor in which a person could "hunt in the morning, fish in the afternoon, rear cattle in the evening, [and] criticize after dinner."[9] Yet Marx also rejected utopian socialists who envisioned communities without divisions of labor and modern technology. In his most explicit writings on this point, Marx predicted that industrial labor would be unfulfilling even in a communist society. To maximize freedom and human satisfaction, he favored technological advances to shorten the workday, leaving people with as much free time as possible for personal development.[10] This strategy is echoed in the works of Radical theorists such as Herbert Marcuse (1898–1979) and André Gorz.[11]

In contrast to the Marxian view, significant numbers of Radicals today insist that industrial labor can be made fulfilling by establishing worker control over the production process.[12] Workers would actively participate in the conception, implementation, and execution of all phases of production. Worker control does not preclude delegating authority to democratically elected managers accountable to workers. Workers would retain sufficient power to assure that the work experience fosters personal development.

Explanations of Hierarchy

Radical explanations of hierarchy are based on Marx's distinction between labor-power and labor. Labor-power is the ability to work; it is the commodity sold by workers to capitalists in exchange for wages. In contrast, labor is the actual productive activity of workers. The purchase of labor-power by capitalists does not guarantee that a specific amount of labor will be performed, so capitalists confront the ongoing task of extracting as much labor as possible from their employees. Workers, knowing that capitalists reap most of the benefits of increased productivity, have little incentive to exert themselves. Faced with this resistance, capitalists establish hierarchical structures of control to increase the amount of labor performed.

Hierarchy also serves to reduce wage costs. Gradations of authority create social distance and artificial barriers among workers occupying different strata within the firm. By creating competition between workers for promotions, capitalist employers fragment the workforce into antagonistic groups, ensuring the maintenance of control over workers and suppressing wage costs.

Although capitalists establish hierarchical control to secure high productivity and low wages, Radicals argue that hierarchy actually reduces efficiency. The inefficiency of hierarchy manifests itself in unmotivated workers, extra layers of supervisory personnel, increased conflict within the workplace, and an inability to utilize technology relying on a cooperative and knowledgeable workforce. Understanding this argument requires a brief excursion into the Radical interpretation of labor history and changes in the organization of work.[13]

According to Radicals, early capitalists introduced labor-saving technology to improve labor productivity and to reduce their reliance on skilled artisans and craftworkers who, because they fully understood the production process, could potentially leave and start their own competing firms. Breaking down skilled work into numerous routine tasks enabled capitalists to reduce the majority of jobs to physical motions requiring no particular skill. As the increasingly limited tasks of workers narrowed their understanding of the business, capitalists gained a monopoly over knowledge of the production process and were able to exercise arbitrary control over the organization and pace of work. As an added benefit for capitalists, wages were held down by the virtually limitless supply of unskilled labor.

However, this strategy of "deskilling" the labor force created a new set of problems. The increasing homogeneity of workers led to an awareness of their common interest in organizing to defend themselves. In response, capitalists launched a new strategy of intentionally stratifying or segmenting the labor force. Hierarchical distinctions based on race, sex, level of education, and credentials were utilized to "divide and conquer" the labor force. For white-collar workers, hierarchical control was gradually bureaucratized in order to minimize the arbitrary exercise of power so offensive to professionals.

Radicals claim that technology and the internal structure of the firm have been influenced more by capitalist concerns about maintaining control over the labor force than by concerns about efficiency. Capitalists are only indirectly concerned about efficiency to the extent that it coincides with profit maximization. While Classical Liberals argue that competitive market forces make the capitalists' interest in maximizing profit synonymous with society's interest in efficiency, Radicals claim that profit-maximization and efficiency will normally diverge. Although hierarchy may be advantageous to the capitalist, it is inefficient and therefore contrary to the public interest.[14]

The debate between Radicals and Classical Liberals on the efficiency of the capitalist firm has been difficult to resolve. First, empirical testing of the efficiency of different forms of work organization is likely to be inconclusive; no two firms are identical in every respect except for hierarchical versus egalitarian structures of work. Second, efficiency ultimately hinges on the motivation of workers. Classical Liberals, who believe that most work is dissatisfying, anticipate that workers will "shirk" unless placed within a hierarchical structure of command and supervision. In contrast, Radicals believe that humans want and need to perform meaningful work and that the implementation of more egalitarian and participatory forms of work would unleash the repressed talents and energies of workers who presently merely endure their jobs. These conflicting beliefs cannot be scientifically proven or disproven because human motivation results from historical, cultural, and economic factors that vary over time and between societies.

The third difficulty in resolving this debate lies in disagreement over the meaning of efficiency. Classical Liberals define efficiency in production as cost-minimization and therefore feel confident that the same competitive market forces driving firms to minimize costs will simultaneously enforce efficiency. Radicals, by contrast, define efficiency as input-minimization; a business is efficient if it produces a particular good with the fewest economic resources. Competition may enforce cost-minimization relative to other capitalist firms, but Radicals argue that capitalist firms actually use more resources than would similar worker-controlled firms relying on more egalitarian methods of production.

To demonstrate the inefficiency of capitalism, Radicals point out that firms can potentially increase output without a corresponding increase in cost by hiring additional supervisory personnel to extract greater amounts of labor from workers. Although this achievement appears to be efficient in terms of cost-minimization, the additional supervisors raise the amount of labor being used to produce a particular product. Costs do not rise because employees are working harder without an increase in pay. Radicals conclude that hierarchy is inefficient because it fails to minimize the hours of labor used to produce society's output.

Even if hierarchy failed to minimize costs, Radicals believe that capitalists would maintain authoritarian structures to secure profitability. The Classical Liberal argument that competitive forces will subvert any inefficient hierarchy rests on the assumption that at least one capitalist will initiate the process by converting to an egalitarian organization of work. However, the maverick capitalist would simply succeed in demonstrating the superiority of worker control, thereby hastening the demise of capitalism. Capitalists realize that even if worker control increases productivity and profits, it will foster new forms of employee relations and consciousness threatening to capitalist ownership. Radicals conclude that capitalists will suppress egalitarian structures of work even if they are more efficient.

Classical Liberal economists respond to the foregoing argument by pointing out that if worker control were efficient, then groups of workers would obtain loans either to start their own businesses or to buy out their employers. Radicals, in turn, suggest two major obstacles to the establishment of worker-owned firms. First, banks and other lending institutions generally require significant collateral on large loans, effectively barring groups of workers from obtaining the financing to start or buy out businesses. Second, the alienating nature of most jobs in capitalism has conditioned workers to doubt their own entrepreneurial and organizational abilities. In spite of these obstacles, Radicals remain confident that the superiority of worker control will eventually prove itself, although the transition will require struggles for political power both within the firm and throughout society.

The Role of Unions

Radicals claim that unions have evolved from their original purpose of challenging capitalist power to actually serving the interests of capitalists by assuring predictable labor costs so long-term investment decisions can be made. In return for union cooperation, capitalists grant substantial wage increases, knowing that higher costs can be passed on to consumers through higher prices. Radicals use the term "embourgeoisement" to describe the process by which portions of the working class have managed to secure for themselves a comfortable standard of living while ignoring the plight of women, minorities, and nonunionized workers.

However, Radicals do not blame workers for the actions of labor unions. As the U.S. labor movement developed in the late nineteenth century, both moderate and Radical factions competed for dominance. Those farsighted capitalists who recognized the inevitability of unionization took measures to assure victory for the moderates. The American Federation of Labor came to prominence partly because of support from capitalists who viewed it as a lesser evil than the more militant Knights of Labor and International Workers of the World. By backing the moderates, capitalists undermined demands for greater control of the workplace and steered workers toward "bread-and-butter" issues such as higher wages and better working conditions.

Despite these criticisms, Radicals support labor unions as essential to organizing the working class. As the industrialized sectors of the economy deteriorate, Radicals predict that unions will become increasingly politicized. Union demands will extend beyond wage increases to issues involving participation and control. As unionized workers suffer the effects of industrial decline, they will become more interested in broadening their membership by actively organizing minorities, women, government employees, professional workers, and even members of the armed services. Eventually, Radicals hope, unions will evolve from special-interest groups to become representatives of the broad interests of the entire working class.

THE CONSERVATIVE PERSPECTIVE

The Nature of Work

Conservatives exhibit conflicting attitudes toward work. Some religious Conservatives appeal to the notion of "original sin" to argue that work is mankind's punishment for defying God's will and therefore is necessarily unpleasant. Freud's conception of work as repression of pleasure reinforced this view.[15] However, most Conservatives find work honorable and fulfilling when it accords with a "natural order" in which a social hierarchy meshes with the varying natural abilities of different individuals. In a society uncorrupted by rampant individualism and materialism, citizens will accept occupations appropriate to their abilities and social status. Even the most menial tasks offer opportunities for personal satisfaction because all jobs contribute to the effective functioning of society.

The "natural order" is also based on a strong sense of community. Conservatives believe that people develop their talents and find purpose in their lives only in the context of closely knit social structures such as families, churches, and neighborhoods. By offering an opportunity to participate in community life, work enables individuals to achieve personal identity and self-esteem. Conservatives blame the aversion to work in modern societies on industrialization and the accompanying emphasis on egalitarianism, material wealth, and social mobility. As individuals focus on income and status, work loses its intrinsic worth and becomes merely a means to an end. Because the pursuit of wealth has no limits, even successful people may be dissatisfied with their standard of living. The competition for status leads to conflict, hostility, and personal insecurity. This discontent erodes the traditional bonds essential to social order and stability.

Most Conservatives want to restore the intrinsic value of work without sacrificing the prosperity made possible by industrialization. Proposals for accomplishing this goal include the formation of occupational groups to provide workers with a sense of belonging and community, restrictions on free trade to protect workers from global market forces, and strengthening of families, churches, and neighborhoods so that workers can approach their jobs well-sustained by their nonworking lives. Some Conservatives also anticipate that advancing technology will eliminate much of the routine drudgery in society. Sociologist Daniel Bell envisions a "post-industrial society" in which all citizens will have opportunities for stimulating work as well as increased leisure.[16] With the end of material deprivation and insecurity, Conservatives anticipate a fading of the competitive struggle for wealth and renewed interest in community life.

Explanations of Hierarchy

Conservatives believe that hierarchical structures of authority are essential within businesses and throughout society. They offer the following explanations for the emergence and persistence of hierarchy.[17]

1. *Utilization of differences in ability.* Humans are innately endowed with a wide range of temperaments, motivations, and strengths. To function smoothly, society's production processes must be structured to provide appropriate roles for these differing abilities. Conservatives believe that leadership skills, including wisdom, virtue, and charisma, exist in only a

minority of the population, and therefore most individuals must be motivated by top-down authority.

2. *Smooth social interaction.* Humans have psychological needs for hierarchical social structures. Authority is essential to human relations because it provides predictability and stability. Without a clear chain of command, individuals become confused about their rights and duties. Human interaction can degenerate into mass deference in which everyone looks to someone else for leadership. Alternatively, social relations may become a struggle for dominance, with each person refusing to acknowledge the authority of anyone else. In a well-organized hierarchy, leaders know the extent of their authority and subordinates know their responsibilities. Humans need the external standards provided by social structures to guide their actions and define the boundaries of proper conduct.

3. *Role models.* Hierarchy places elites in visible positions where they serve as role models. Human development depends on social mimicry, so all people benefit from prominent displays of talent and virtue by those at the top of the social hierarchy.

4. *Identity formation.* Humans need clear distinctions in social status to enable them to define themselves and their purposes according to their position in the social hierarchy. If everyone has the same status and is treated equally, people will be unable to form unique images of themselves.

The Conservative support for hierarchy does not necessarily extend to all forms of stratification found in modern societies. Conservatives condemn hierarchy when it represents a deviation from the "natural order." The massive dislocations wrought by industrialization and liberalism have generated both illegitimate concentrations of power and a loss of integrity, pride, and skill among workers. By unleashing the acquisitive instinct and making the pursuit of pleasure the paramount value, liberalism has bolstered the belief that work is inherently unpleasant. Aversion to work, in turn, forces employers to routinize tasks so that work performance can be more effectively monitored. As jobs become more routine, workers find fulfillment even more elusive and their distaste for work increases.

To escape this cycle, some Conservatives have proposed experiments with worker participation and cooperation to restore the "natural order." Early Conservatives such as Thomas Carlyle shared with Radicals a strong opposition to capitalist production and its rigid division of labor. They perceived that the anonymity of urban, industrial society threatened traditional authority and community. However, unlike Radicals, Conservatives favor worker participation only insofar as increased cooperation will generate a new sense of respect for management. The degree of hierarchy should be sufficient to make use of different individual abilities yet not so great as to diminish workers' pride and motivation.

The Role of Unions

Conservatives are critical of labor unions for disrupting the natural hierarchy of authority by usurping the prerogatives of owners and their appointed managers.[18] However, Conservatives do not oppose the formation of occupational groupings.[19] Indeed, one of the recurring Conservative critiques of modern society focuses on fragmentation and individualism. Industrialization erodes community life, leaving anonymous individuals with few social bonds. Labor unions, like other "intermediate institutions" such as the family and the church, can integrate individuals into social networks, thereby fostering a sense of loyalty and belonging.

The unions envisioned by Conservatives would not function as special-interest groups seeking maximum income and benefits for their members. Instead, unions should join with neighborhood associations, businesses, and government to promote a unified vision of society's goals and the desire to cooperate and make sacrifices to achieve those goals. The labor union should also function as a social group, providing a community in which personal development is enhanced and members are socialized to accept traditional values.

THE MODERN LIBERAL PERSPECTIVE

The Nature of Work

In the nineteenth century, Modern Liberals largely accepted the Classical Liberal view that work is unpleasant and that monetary incentives and the threat of discipline are necessary to stimulate production. However, this view changed dramatically during the twentieth century. Modern Liberals now claim that technology has created conditions in which most menial tasks can be performed by machines so that jobs can be sources of personal satisfaction and fulfillment.

The rising standard of living brought about by technological progress has permitted most citizens in industrialized nations to meet their physiological needs easily. Increasingly, people seek personal development through exercising their human capacities to the fullest. Social psychologist Abraham Maslow (1908–1970) described this historical transformation in terms of a "hierarchy of needs."[20] Once basic needs for nourishment and safety are met, humans shift their energies to fulfilling higher needs such as love, self-esteem, high-quality social relations, and, ultimately, "self-actualization," or the achievement of one's full potential. For Maslow, meaningful work that stimulates workers to engage their capacities is essential for self-actualization.

Explanations of Hierarchy

Modern Liberals note that F. W. Taylor's principles of "scientific management" were developed during a time when widespread poverty caused many workers to view their jobs primarily as a means of providing food and shelter for their families. However, as standards of living rose, workers began to resist routinization and tight supervision, creating difficulties for businesses relying on the techniques of scientific management. As a result, a new "human relations" approach to management was popularized during the 1920s by Elton Mayo (1880–1949) and extended during the 1940s by Kurt Lewin (1890–1947).[21] These theorists reflected the Modern Liberal belief that people want to work if their jobs offer intrinsic satisfaction. The key to eliciting high productivity from workers is to organize production to satisfy the needs of workers for respect, autonomy, a sense of belonging, and the opportunity to advance. Given a positive environment, workers will cooperate with management in achieving the firm's goals.

When people view work as an opportunity for personal development, wages become only one factor among many determining employee satisfaction. The social needs of employees for companionship, for the respect and approval of colleagues, and for self-direction can be met by reorganizing work to enlarge the range of tasks performed by each individual, to reduce close supervision, and to encourage participation in decisionmaking. Reliance on employee initiative is advantageous to the firm because it eliminates layers of supervisory personnel and results in more satisfied and productive employees.

Modern Liberals conclude that "enlightened management" can reduce hierarchy and "humanize" the workplace without necessarily sacrificing profitability. Workers become more productive when they feel trusted and valued; building trust requires that managers relinquish tight control of the production process. Paradoxically, by empowering workers, management will actually become more effective. The "synergy" of ideas emanating from teams of workers will increase the wealth of the firm. However, humanization of work does have limits. Economist Kenneth Arrow claims that under conditions of uncertainty and imperfect information, some hierarchy is essential to economic efficiency.[22] Even highly motivated workers require clear lines of authority for processing information and communicating decisions. Hierarchy gives workers knowledge of the location of authority and responsibility.

Despite these limitations on worker control, many Modern Liberals believe that greater equality and participation in the workplace are possible. The present need for hierarchical authority derives in part from poverty and discrimination that have left many workers inadequately prepared for self-directed work. The "human relations" approach to management is typically confined to large corporations whose employees are highly educated and well paid. Smaller firms often must rely on employees whose social background and lack of satisfying work experience makes hierarchical authority essential. Modern Liberals conclude that hierarchy can be reduced by attacking the poverty and discrimination that prevent many employees from developing work skills.

A second Modern Liberal rationale for greater humanization of work entails challenging efficiency and profitability as sole determinants of the organization of work. Efficiency is only one standard by which to assess the performance of the economy. Other values such as liberty, justice, and human development may conflict with efficiency, and some sacrifice of efficiency may be warranted if the overall quality of human existence can be enhanced. One strategy for overriding efficiency is to establish certain human rights essential to society. Since the market responds only to property rights, the protection of human rights typically requires various forms of government intervention such as occupational health and safety laws, minimum-wage laws, and anti-discrimination laws. By redirecting market forces, government can create a society that emphasizes the personal development of workers as well as the accumulation of capital. Modern Liberals are willing to sacrifice some efficiency in the pursuit of other social goals, but they are also optimistic that workplace humanization may pay off in terms of increased productivity and profitability.[23]

The Role of Unions

Traditionally, Modern Liberals have supported labor unions as a necessary balance to the concentration of business power. Prior to unionization, businesses could easily hire workers at low wages and fire them at will. Bosses held arbitrary power over workers who were rendered defenseless by fierce competition for jobs. Modern Liberals anticipated that labor unions would provide "countervailing power" for workers in their negotiations with corporations over wages and working conditions.[24]

The Modern Liberal defense of labor unions received a tremendous boost from Keynesian economics. Keynes viewed insufficient spending as the cause of depression and unemployment. Higher wages for workers would benefit the economy by establishing additional purchasing power so that businesses could sell their products. From the Keynesian perspective, labor unions' strength in forcing a more equal distribution of income benefits the entire economy.

In supporting unions, Modern Liberals claim that unions benefit all workers because even nonunionized firms are motivated to pay close attention to union wages to maintain employee morale and to discourage the spread of unions. In addition, unions support a higher minimum wage for all workers to reduce the incentive for employers to substitute nonunion labor in jobs presently held by union members.[25] Unions also lobby for government efforts to create jobs because unemployment provides employers with cheap sources of labor and reduces the bargaining power of unions. Finally, in response to the Classical Liberal charge that unions cause inflation, Modern Liberals argue that corporate efforts to raise profits are the primary cause of "cost-push" inflation. Real wages in the United States have been stagnant since the 1970s, so union demands for higher wages are typically an effort to catch up to rising costs of living initiated by corporate price increases.

As international competition has become a growing concern in recent years, some Modern Liberals have tempered their support for labor unions. The Keynesian advocacy of high wages has been challenged by the increasing mobility of resources and products throughout the global economy. Competitive pressures from abroad force corporations to negotiate more aggressively with unions, sometimes to the point of demanding concessions of previous gains. Modern Liberals now expect unions to be prudent and responsible in their wage demands and to cooperate with management in the adoption of labor-saving technology.

Despite these concerns, Modern Liberals continue to defend unions as essential to the economic security of workers. This security consists of more than high wages; workers have rights to fringe benefits, safe working conditions, and protection against arbitrary power. Because the market does not recognize these human rights, they would remain unprotected without labor unions and government regulation.

NOTES

1. Adam Smith, *The Wealth of Nations*, London: Dent, 1910, vol. 2: 265.

2. For a rigorous presentation of the neoclassical view of work, see Ugo Pagano, *Work and Welfare in Economic Theory*, New York: Basil Blackwell, 1985.

3. Two major works on scientific management are Frederick W. Taylor, *The Principles of Scientific Management*, 1911, New York: W. W. Norton, 1967; and Frank Gilbreth, *Motion Study*, 1911, Easton, PA: Hive, 1972.

4. The pioneering work in "new institutional economics" is Ronald H. Coase, "The Nature of the Firm," *Economica*, 4, (November 1937): 386–405. More recent works include Armen Alchian and Harold Demsetz, "Production, Information Costs, and Economic Organization," *American Economic Review* 62 (December 1972): 777–95; and Oliver E. Williamson, "The Economics of Organizations: The Transaction Approach," *American Journal of Sociology* 87, no. 3 (1981): 548–77. All three of these articles, along with other seminal works in the theory of the organization of the firm, are included in Louis Putterman, ed., *The Economic Nature of the Firm: A Reader*, New York: Cambridge University Press, 1986. See also Richard N. Langlois, ed., *Economics as a Process: Essays in the New Institutional Economics*, New York: Cambridge University Press, 1986; and Oliver E. Williamson, *The Economic Institutions of Capitalism*, New York: Free Press, 1985; Jack J. Vromen, *Economic Evolution: An Enquiry Into The Foundations of New Institutional Economics*, New York: Routledge, 1995; and Oliver E. Williamson, *The Mechanisms of Governance*, New York: Oxford University Press, 1996.

5. Paul Samuelson, "Wage and Interest: A Modern Discussion of the Marxian Theory of Discrimination," *Bell Journal of Economics* 10 (Autumn 1979): 695–705.

6. A Classical Liberal critique of worker participation is presented in Friedrich A. Hayek, *Studies in Philosophy, Politics and Economics*, New York: Simon & Schuster, 1967, chapter 22.

7. For more detail on the Radical view of alienation, see Bertell Ollman, *Alienation: Marx's Conception of Man in Capitalist Society*, New York: Cambridge University Press, 1971. See also Richard Schacht, *The Future of Alienation*, Urbana, IL: University of Illinois Press, 1994; and Andrew Oldenquist and Menachem Rosner, *Alienation, Community, and Work*, New York: Greenwood Press, 1991.

8. The effect of the work experience on leisure time is described and documented in Robert Blauner, *Alienation and Freedom: The Factory Worker and His Industry*, Chicago: University of Chicago Press, 1964; Georges Friedman, *Anatomy of Work*, Glencoe, IL: Free Press, 1961; and Martin Meisner, "The Long Arm of the Job: A Study of Work and Leisure," *Industrial Relations* 10 (October 1971): 239–60.

9. Karl Marx and Friedrich Engels, *The German Ideology*, New York: International Publishers, 1947.

10. See Karl Marx, *Capital*, Vol. 3, New York: International Publishers, 1961, 799–800.

11. Herbert Marcuse, *Eros and Civilization*, Boston: Beacon Press, 1966; Andr Gorz, *Paths to Paradise: On the Liberation from Work*, London: Pluto Press, 1985; and André Gorz, *Critique of Economic Reason*, London: Verso, 1989.

12. The literature on worker control includes Robert A. Dahl, *A Preface to Economic Democracy*, Berkeley: University of California Press, 1985; Edward Greenberg, *Workplace Democracy: The Political Effect of Participation*, Ithaca, NY: Cornell University Press, 1987; Martin Carnoy and Derek Shearer, *Economic Democracy: The Challenge of the 1980s*, White Plains, NY: M. E. Sharpe, 1980; Ronald M. Mason, *Participatory and Workplace Democracy: A Theoretical Development in Critique of Liberalism*, Carbondale, IL: Southern Illinois University Press, 1982; David P. Ellerman, *Property and Contract in Economics: A Case For Economic Democracy*, Cambridge, MA: Blackwell, 1992; Donald A. R. George, *Economic Democracy: The Political Economy of Self-Management and Participation*, Basingstoke: Macmillan, 1993; and Robin Archer, *Economic Democracy: The Politics of Feasible Socialism*, New York: Oxford University Press, 1995.

13. See Stephen Marglin, "What Do Bosses Do: The Origins and Functions of Hierarchy in Capitalist Production," *Review of Radical Political Economics* 6 (Spring 1974): 60–112; Stanley Aronowitz, *False Promises: The Shaping of American Working-Class Consciousness*, New York: McGraw-Hill, 1973; Harry Braverman, *Labor and Monopoly Capital: The Degradation of Work in the Twentieth Century*, New York: Monthly Review Press, 1974; Richard C. Edwards, *Contested Terrain: The Transformation of the Workplace in the Twentieth Century*, New York: Basic Books, 1979; Michael Burawoy, *Manufacturing Consent: Changes in the Labor Process under Monopoly Capitalism*, Chicago: University of Chicago Press, 1979; and William Lazonick, *Business Organization and the Myth of the Market Economy*, Cambridge: Cambridge University Press, 1991.

14. These claims are developed in Samuel Bowles and Herbert Gintis, "Contested Exchange: New Microfoundations for the Political Economy of Capitalism," *Politics & Society* 18, no. 2 (June 1990): 165–222; Samuel Bowles and Herbert Gintis, "The Revenge of Homo Economicus: Contested Exchange and the Revival of Political Economy," *Journal of Economic Perspectives,* 7:1 (Winter 1993): 83–102; and Samuel Bowles, Herbert Gintis, and Bo Gustafsson, eds., *Markets and Democracy: Participation, Accountability and Efficiency,* New York: Cambridge University Press, 1993.

15. Sigmund Freud, *Civilization and Its Discontents,* translated by James Strachey, New York: W. W. Norton, 1961.

16. See Daniel Bell, *The Coming of Post-Industrial Society: A Venture in Social Forecasting,* New York: Basic Books, 1973.

17. The role of hierarchy in society was a central theme of sociologist Talcott Parsons. For an accessible account of Parson's ideas, see Robert J. Holton and Bryan S. Turner, *Talcott Parsons on Economy and Society,* New York: Routledge, 1989.

18. See Seymour Martin Lipset, ed., *Unions in Transition,* San Francisco: Institute for Contemporary Studies Press, 1986.

19. See Emile Durkheim, *The Division of Labor in Society,* New York: Free Press, 1933.

20. Abraham H. Maslow, *Motivation and Personality,* 3rd ed., New York: Harper & Row, 1987.

21. Elton Mayo, *The Human Problems of an Industrial Civilization,* New York: Macmillan, 1933; and Kurt Lewin, *Resolving Social Conflicts,* New York: Harper & Row, 1948.

22. Kenneth J. Arrow, *The Limits of Organization,* New York: W. W. Norton, 1974.

23. On methods for increasing worker participation, see William G. Ouchi, *Theory Z: How American Business Can Meet the Japanese Challenge,* New York: Avon, 1982; and Donald L. Dewar, *The Quality Circle Guide to Participation Management,* Englewood Cliffs, NJ: Prentice-Hall, 1980.

24. See John Kenneth Galbraith, *The New Industrial State,* Boston: Houghton Mifflin, 1967.

25. See Richard B. Freeman and James L. Medoff, *What Do Unions Do?,* New York: Basic Books, 1988.

ADDITIONAL READING

Aoki, Masahiko, Bo Gustafsson, and Oliver Williamson, eds. *The Firm as a Nexus of Treaties.* New York: Russell Sage, 1990.

Burawoy, Michael. *The Politics of Production.* London: Verso, 1985.

Farkas, George, and Paula England, eds. *Industries, Firms, and Jobs: Sociological and Economic Approaches.* New York: Plenum Press, 1988.

Gordon, David M., Richard Edwards and Michael Reich. *Segmented Work, Divided Workers: The Historical Transformation of Labor in the United States.* New York: Cambridge University Press, 1982.

Habermesh, Daniel S., and Albert Rees. *The Economics of Work and Pay,* 4th ed. New York: Harper & Row, 1988.

Harrison, Bennett. *Lean and Mean: Why Large Corporations Will Continue to Dominate the Global Economy.* New York, Guilford Publications, 1997.

Kalleberg, Arne L., and Ivar Berg. *Work and Industry: Structures, Markets, and Processes.* New York: Plenum, 1987.

Kochan, Thomas A., Harry C. Katz, and Robert B. McKersie. *The Transformation of American Industrial Relations.* New York: Basic Books, 1986.

Marshall, Ray. *Unheard Voices: Labor and Economic Policy in a Competitive World.* New York: Basic Books, 1987.

Mishel, Lawrence and Paula B. Voos, eds. *Unions and Economic Competitiveness.* Armonk, NY: M. E. Sharpe, 1992.

Noble, David. *America By Design: Science, Technology, and the Rise of Corporate Capitalism.* New York: Alfred A. Knopf, 1977.

Pahl, R. E., ed. *On Work: Historical, Comparative and Theoretical Approaches.* New York: Basil Blackwell, 1988.

Piore, Michael J., and Charles F. Sabel. *The Second Industrial Divide: Possibilities for Prosperity.* New York: Basic Books, 1984.

Pitelis, Christos, ed. *Transaction Costs, Markets and Hierarchies.* Cambridge, MA: Blackwell, 1993.

Sabel, Charles F. *Work and Politics: The Division of Labor in Industry.* New York: Cambridge University Press, 1982.

Turner, Lowell. *Democracy at Work, Changing World Markets and the Future of Labor Unions.* Ithaca, NY: Cornell University Press, 1991.

Witte, John F. *Democracy, Authority, and Alienation in Work.* Chicago: University of Chicago Press, 1980.

Zieger, Robert H. *American Workers, American Unions,* 2nd ed. Baltimore: Johns Hopkins University Press, 1994.

Chapter 11

Minorities and Discrimination

Political economists disagree on the definition of discrimination. Should discrimination encompass only those hiring and promotion decisions in which equally productive people are paid unequal wages, or should the concept of discrimination be broadened to include the cultural and institutional forces affecting both employees and employers prior to labor-market activities? The broader conception of discrimination is more difficult to assess because family backgrounds, quality of schools, neighborhood environments, and societal attitudes toward minority groups must be considered. Even the narrow conception of discrimination requires a method for measuring individual productivity. Economists typically rely on number of years in school as a proxy for productivity, with discrimination assessed by comparing the relation between average adult wages and average number of years in school for different racial and ethnic groups. However, numerous other variables affect productivity, including such unmeasurable factors as individual initiative and motivation. Empirical efforts to verify the existence or absence of discrimination are limited by the inadequacy of statistics in capturing all components of productivity.

At the center of much controversy surrounding the issue of discrimination is the government program called "affirmative action." This program encourages employers to establish goals for minority employment and to vigorously search for qualified minority candidates. Each of the four perspectives has a different view of affirmative action and a different interpretation of the role of minority groups in society.

THE CLASSICAL LIBERAL PERSPECTIVE

Explanations of Discrimination

As an ideology originating in conjunction with the struggle of merchants and manufacturers to free themselves from control by church and state, Classical Liberalism upholds the right of all individuals to compete freely in the market. Classical Liberals affirm civil rights as protection against harm by the government or by other citizens; however, they do not view discrimination as a violation of civil rights unless it occurs within a public institution or facility. So, while they opposed laws prohibiting minorities from riding city buses or attending public schools, Classical Liberals defend the right of private individuals and firms to choose their associates. This freedom to choose includes the freedom to exclude; therefore, laws forcing individuals or firms to transact with minorities are regarded as violations of freedom and the rights of private property.

Although Classical Liberals defend the right to discriminate, they claim that a free market is the best antidote to discrimination because it distributes income in accordance with productive contribution and penalizes bigotry.[1] For example, a bigoted employer with a "taste for discrimination" may refuse to hire minority workers despite their willingness to work for lower wages. Yet, if markets are competitive and minority workers are as productive as other workers, this discriminating employer will sacrifice some profit by paying higher wages than necessary. Other nondiscriminating employers will hire minority workers at lower wages, earning more profit or selling the product at a lower price. Over time, the cost advantage gained by nondiscriminating firms will cause discriminating employers to lose market share and perhaps face bankruptcy. Eventually, competition among nondiscriminating employers will bid up wages for minority workers and discrimination will disappear. Classical Liberals conclude that profits speak louder than prejudice in motivating human behavior.

To measure the extent of discrimination, economists attempt to assess the "rate of return" for investments in education among different racial and ethnic groups. The rate of return is simply a measure of the additional future income attributable to increased years of schooling. Empirical data do reveal lower rates of return for minority persons, but Classical Liberals discount this evidence by arguing that years of schooling is only one of many variables affecting a person's productivity and income. The "pay gap" between workers from different groups drops significantly when the measurement of productivity includes other variables such as quality of schooling, age, geographic location, and job experience. In addition, the effect of intangible factors such as family background, motivation, and self-discipline is nearly impossible to measure, so statistical evidence of a racial pay gap cannot be taken as proof of discrimination.

Classical Liberals believe that the free market will not sustain discrimination and, therefore, suggest that the lower economic status of minority groups may be due to lower productivity which, in turn, reflects either lower ability or a preference for leisure and immediate gratification. However, this conclusion creates a dilemma for Classical Liberals. Any claim that inferior abilities and preferences are innate among minorities is tantamount to racism, a doctrine that is abhorrent to Classical Liberals. On the other hand, if abilities and preferences result from social conditioning, then individuals cannot be the autonomous, rational utility-maximizers portrayed in neoclassical economic theory. To avoid this dilemma and still explain the racial pay gap, Classical Liberals attribute persistent discrimination to imperfect competition. Employers with market power may discriminate without penalty because they can pass higher wage costs on to consumers in the form of higher prices. Because Classical Liberals believe that government regulations create and perpetuate monopolistic elements in the economy, they conclude that government is ultimately responsible for discrimination.

Three Classical Liberal economists, Thomas Sowell, Walter Williams, and Glenn Loury, have separately posited that government intervention, not bigotry and discrimination, has caused the lower economic status of minority groups in the United States. Sowell claims that government policies aimed at combating the effects of discrimination are unnecessary and actually detrimental to minorities.[2] As a result of antidiscrimination statutes and affirmative action programs, employers hire only the most highly qualified minority workers to minimize the likelihood of subsequent layoffs and resulting legal entanglements. Thus, government pressure to hire minorities creates a dual labor market: the gains of more educated persons come at the expense of those with fewer credentials. Segmentation of the minority labor market is evidenced by the fact that black female professionals earn more than their white counterparts, while black high-school dropouts earn considerably less than their white counterparts.

Walter Williams claims that legislation requiring equal pay for black and white workers in the same job actually closes off opportunities for minority workers because employers no longer face the penalty of paying higher wages to hire only white workers. As an example of a government-imposed barrier to minority advancement, Williams cites New York City's expensive license to own a taxi. The cost of the license effectively prohibits most minority persons from entering that line of business. In addition, municipal zoning laws and housing codes raise property values and effectively prevent low-income minority persons from moving into certain neighborhoods. If government would let the market operate freely, the talents and ingenuity of minority persons would enable them to rise from poverty.[3]

While Glenn Loury places much of the responsibility for minority problems on the attitudes, values, and behavior found within minority families and communities, he ultimately blames government welfare programs for undermining the initiative of minorities and creating a sense of dependency passed on from one generation to the next. Loury is particularly concerned about the decline of the traditional nuclear family in the black community, and he blames welfare programs that are more accessible for single mothers than for families headed by males.[4]

To summarize, Classical Liberals largely deny the existence of discrimination, arguing that most of the pay differential between majority and minority wages results from differences in productivity. These differences may be due to genetic inheritance or cultural norms, but Classical Liberals prefer to emphasize the role of individual attitudes and values. Those who are unable or unwilling to make productive contributions in the market are treated fairly when their rewards are correspondingly small. If discrimination does occur, government bears the blame because it perpetuates racism by providing welfare programs that reward irresponsible behavior, posing legal obstacles to the advancement of minority persons and facilitating monopolistic concentrations of power that shield discriminators from the disciplining force of competition.

Responses to Discrimination

Viewing competitive markets as the best defense against discrimination, Classical Liberals want government to eliminate nearly all regulations on business activity. Government aid to minority groups is also condemned because majority citizens should not be coerced through taxation to assist minority persons. Any person wishing to offer assistance may contribute to private charities. Furthermore, with less assistance from government, minority persons will be motivated to acquire more skills and work more diligently.

For Classical Liberals, equal opportunity exists when no individual or group is either advantaged or disadvantaged by government policies. Laws and public policies should be "color-blind," affecting members of all groups equally. Any reference to race, religion, gender, or ethnic background in the formation of public policy is discriminatory. In particular, affirmative action is simply "reverse discrimination" against nonminority members of society.[5] Besides unfairly penalizing nonminorities, affirmative action creates inefficiency by disrupting the market's allocation of persons to jobs for which they are qualified. Whenever employment is based on criteria other than productivity, efficiency will be lost.

Classical Liberals support publicly funded education to assure equal opportunity for all persons. Not only should government assure equal education for all children, but students should have equal access to borrowing money for higher education. When markets are free and the avenues for acquiring human capital are open to all, Classical Liberals assume that prejudice and bigotry cannot persist. They point to increasing opportunities for minorities in professional and managerial positions as evidence that discrimination is fading.[6] Eventually, equality of opportunity will create a society in which individuals are rewarded solely on the basis of productive contribution of their resources.

THE RADICAL PERSPECTIVE

Explanations of Discrimination

Radical explanations of discrimination are based on a particular interpretation of the historical transformation from feudalism to capitalism. In the medieval period, most individuals lived in relatively homogeneous communities where they filled a variety of overlapping roles. The rise of industry and commerce, however, ripped apart the social fabric of medieval society by turning labor into a mobile economic resource whose function and location were determined by profitability. Increasingly, people found themselves performing very routine tasks, surrounded by others with whom they shared no sense of tradition or community. Social relations became more impersonal as self-interested motives began to dominate all human interactions. Society became simply an aggregation of isolated individuals pursuing private goals. Other persons were no longer viewed as fellow citizens but as rivals and potential threats in the competitive struggle for survival.[7]

While Radicals claim that capitalism bears much of the responsibility for racial and ethnic conflict, paradoxically they also defend capitalism as a progressive force in integrating diverse groups. Profitability requires that barriers between nations, ethnic groups, and races be broken down so that commerce can proceed smoothly in a unified global market. Radicals half-jokingly claim that the leading proponents of "one-world government" are not communists but instead the chairpersons of multinational corporations who seek to end nationalist, racial, and religious hostilities impeding the free flow of capital. Capitalism breeds civility toward strangers by bringing diverse cultures into contact with one another and by making each person's livelihood dependent on peaceful exchange with others.

Radicals may be inconsistent in both praising and condemning capitalism, but they appeal to the dialectical logic developed by Hegel in which apparent opposites are actually parts of a larger unity. Because the primary force underlying capitalism is the accumulation of capital, racial and ethnic distinctions will diminish when they obstruct capital accumulation. For example, during the half century after the Civil War, the U.S. economy successfully absorbed millions of foreign immigrants who kept wages low and contributed to capital accumulation. Similarly, the Civil Rights movement in the United States was aided by the perception among influential members of the ruling class that continued segregation would jeopardize profitability and social order.

On the other hand, racial and ethnic distinctions provide an easy method to segregate the labor force and maintain hierarchy in the division of labor. Although capitalism has accomplished significant integration of the global population, the annexation of new sources of labor typically occurs under extremely inequitable conditions. Minority groups often find themselves ushered into the capitalist economy either as cheap labor or because they possess natural resources attractive to capitalists. Therefore, despite capitalism's potential for integration, the accumulation process often subordinates, exploits, and discriminates against newly assimilated groups.[8]

Even within the industrialized nations, capitalists manipulate hostility between racial and ethnic groups to undermine worker solidarity, thereby weakening the power of the working class. This "divide and conquer" strategy is exemplified by the practice of using black workers as "scabs" during strikes to motivate whites to return to work. In addition, minorities are easily relegated either to the most menial occupations or to the "reserve army of the unemployed" because their lack of power impedes their ability to exert political resistance.[9]

Racial hostility also legitimizes the inequality associated with capitalism. Race and ethnicity create distinct and identifiable groups in society, legitimizing poverty as the natural fate of people with personal deficiencies. If poor and unemployed persons are perceived as "outsiders" who are not part of the community, their presence is more easily tolerated. The frustrations of lower-class white workers are diffused by knowledge that they are relatively successful compared to unemployed minority persons.

In blaming discrimination on capitalism, Radicals do not deny the existence of racism. Yet this hostility has been formed by perceptions of self-interest created by the capitalist economy. For example, the belief that minorities pose a threat to wages and job security fuels racism. However, Radicals claim that antagonism toward minorities is misdirected. Economist Michael Reich assembled statistics showing that cities in which black wages lagged farthest behind white wages also tended to have the lowest wages for unskilled white workers, the highest profit rates, and the least amount of unionization.[10] Reich found capitalist employers to be the primary beneficiaries of discrimination, giving them an economic interest in its perpetuation. White workers, on the other hand, benefit from increased solidarity and bargaining power provided by greater racial equality and unionization.

Radicals attribute much of the persistence of discrimination to segmented labor markets. During the late nineteenth century, as capitalism annexed and assimilated new populations, profitability demanded the de-skilling and homogenization of labor. Tasks formerly requiring substantial skill and training were broken down into series of routine movements easily learned by any worker. The resulting gains in efficiency provided a stimulus to profits, but the homogenization of labor also fostered a growing solidarity among workers, resulting in demands for higher wages and better working conditions. In response to this militancy, capitalists stratified the workforce by imposing job ladders and segmenting various occupations within the firm, resulting in a dual labor market consisting of a primary sector with high-paying jobs and a secondary sector with low-paying, unskilled jobs.[11]

This historical change in the structure of the labor market substantially affected the economic status of minority persons. Since they typically begin their work-lives in the secondary sector, the experience of low wages, bad working conditions, and lack of opportunity for advancement is so discouraging that many develop records of absenteeism, frequent job changes, and poor productivity. In other words, the productivity of workers is based on more than ability or effort; it is conditioned by their job experience. The very nature of work in the secondary sector causes workers to become unfit for employment in the primary sector.

To summarize, capitalism's need for a hierarchical division of labor and a reserve army of the unemployed assures that many minority workers will lack productive skills. They become the victims of a systemic and institutional pattern of power requiring a powerless and subordinate group in society. Because profitability is enhanced by institutional discrimination, the competitive forces of the market will not secure equal opportunities for minority persons.

Responses to Discrimination

Within the context of capitalism, Radicals propose two strategies for combating discrimination and elevating the economic status of minorities. First, they encourage the formation of interracial coalitions to pressure employers and the government for programs to overcome the effects of discrimination. Radicals argue that both majority and minority persons have much to gain through cooperation. For example, the Congress of Industrial Organizations (CIO) made a concerted effort during the 1930s to include black workers in its unionization drives. As a result, the CIO achieved significant bargaining power and dramatic success in raising wages and improving working conditions for millions of workers. The Civil Rights movement of the 1960s provides another example of an interracial coalition yielding gains for both black and white citizens.

The second component of a Radical program to combat discrimination consists of government policies to promote full employment and economic growth. Without growth, the economy becomes a zero-sum game with the gains of one group coming at the expense of another. Similarly, unemployment exacerbates the tensions between marginally employed workers and those eager to take their jobs. With growth and full employment, the formation of interracial coalitions should proceed more rapidly.

Radicals acknowledge that these proposals challenge the interests of employers in maintaining cheap labor. If strategies for coalition-formation and full employment are successful, they may erode profitability and either trigger a recession or force employers to pursue new sources of cheap labor by relocating overseas or by hiring illegal aliens. If employers cannot annex new supplies of labor, Radicals expect a slowing of capital accumulation and renewed efforts by employers to regain control over wages and other production costs.

Recognizing these obstacles to eliminating discrimination within the confines of capitalism, Radicals call for greater public control over the means of production as a method for enabling citizens to collectively implement social justice. For most Radicals, including black activists such as Angela Davis, Jesse Jackson, and Manning Marable, coalition-building and full employment are viewed as essential to achieving the long-term goal of social justice. However, other black Radicals such as Malcolm X (1925–1965) and Louis Farrakhan have urged minorities to separate from white society by establishing their own political parties and economic structures.[12]

By appealing to socialism as the ultimate solution to discrimination, Radicals raise a thorny issue. Many of those nations experimenting with socialism have not treated minority groups particularly well. If socialism consists of eliminating markets in favor of government planning, the absence of competition may reinforce existing racial or ethnic hostilities. Managers and bureaucrats would be free of the restraint of market forces if they chose to exercise prejudice. On the other hand, if socialism consists of eliminating private ownership of the means of production while retaining markets, worker-controlled firms could continue to discriminate against minority groups. Prior to its disintegration, Yugoslavia had a market-socialist economy, yet intense ethnic hostilities consistently excluded certain groups from top positions in both industry and government.

Radicals respond to these criticisms by pointing out that socialism has evolved only in relatively undeveloped countries lacking industrialization and modernization under capitalism. As a result, the social structures and cultural practices of these countries remained linked to their recent past as quasi-feudal societies. Radicals conclude that socialism's potential for fostering cooperation and solidarity among diverse groups has not yet been given a genuine opportunity to develop.

THE CONSERVATIVE PERSPECTIVE

Explanations of Discrimination

The Conservative vision of a hierarchical community provides an appealing perspective for those who favor a racially and ethnically segregated society. Yet, while racists are often Conservative, Conservatism does not logically imply any particular attitude toward minority groups. Some Conservative theorists presume the innate inferiority of minority populations, and others do not.

Racism implies that race should be a relevant factor in determining a person's political, economic, or social status. Racists typically buttress their views by claiming that specific groups of people are genetically inferior and represent a lower stage in the evolution of the human species. Because of their diminished capacities, minority groups should be denied equal rights.[13]

Several prominent Conservative theorists have proposed that some minority groups are intellectually inferior to whites. William Shockley (the inventor of the transistor and winner of a Nobel prize in 1955), Arthur Jensen, Richard Herrnstein, and Charles Murray point to the fact that African-American students in the United States perform less well on IQ tests than do whites.[14] While the differences in test scores are indisputable, Modern Liberals and Radicals dismiss IQ tests as "culturally biased" measures of those aptitudes nurtured by the white middle class. More generally, the critics challenge the very notion of innate or objectively measurable intelligence.[15] Since intelligence denotes the ability to manipulate symbols in a manner judged to be correct by a specific culture, aptitudes associated with intelligence in one culture may be insignificant in another culture. Therefore no single test can objectively measure intelligence across cultures.

Those Conservatives who regard minority persons as innately inferior offer several explanations for discrimination. They claim that discrimination selects the superior over the inferior and is therefore neither immoral nor unjust. Also, discrimination and segregation discourage interracial marriages, which would result in "deterioration" of the gene pool. Finally, segregation protects the cultural achievements of the dominant society.

Nonracist Conservatives offer different explanations of discrimination. Because many minority groups originated in parts of the world with less exposure to capitalism, their cultures may not emphasize behaviors such as initiative, punctuality, and delayed gratification that contribute to success in a market economy. If cultural differences create barriers to social interaction, employers may be reluctant to hire minorities because an individual's productivity depends on the ability to function well within the dominant culture.

Conservatives also emphasize the importance of maintaining the integrity of various cultural heritages within a pluralistic society. Race and ethnicity, together with family, neighborhood, and nation, create meaning and identity for individuals. In addition, shared values and customs forge strong social bonds preserving traditional cultures and communities. Segregation may be necessary to protect minority cultures as well as the dominant culture.

Conservative opposition to integration is ultimately based on rejection of the Enlightenment ideal of a universal community, the "brotherhood of mankind," in which equally free and rational individuals pursue their interests in peace and harmony. By treating all persons equally, the universal community fails to sustain a sense of uniqueness, rootedness, and belonging needed for full human development. Conservatives fear that modern society will absorb minority cultures into a homogeneous mainstream representing no particular culture. The individualism and mobility of mass society rob everyone of a sense of community. Only close-knit, local communities, with all their prejudices, parochialism, and traditions, can provide socially defined roles through which individuals find meaning and purpose in their lives. Being cut off from one's "roots" causes isolation and alienation, leading to either a frustrated and potentially violent populace or a nation of passive pleasure-seekers.

From the Conservative perspective, efforts to integrate society are particularly damaging to minorities. Those who attempt to assimilate into mainstream culture are likely to face a dilemma. Failure to assimilate results in loss of self-esteem, while success breeds alienation as minority persons lose the security of their own culture but are unable to completely identify with the dominant culture. Some Conservatives urge minorities to develop separate community structures and business enterprises to sustain their cultural heritage. The separate social groupings established by racial and ethnic pluralism function as "intermediate institutions" to provide a sense of belonging and maintain social order.

As final evidence that segregation is natural, some Conservatives point out that different racial and ethnic groups were originally located in separate geographical areas. Also, humans seem inclined to associate with others who share their culture, experiences, and values. This instinct is claimed to be essential to social harmony because it keeps people in separate communities which, by providing local meaning and purpose, restrain the unbridled pursuit of self-interest. Edmund Burke praised the role of "prejudices" in establishing instinctive loyalty to particular institutions and values so that individuals need not rationally assess every judgment they make.

Responses to Discrimination

Conservatives are less concerned with alleviating discrimination than with reestablishing segregation to minimize interaction between different racial and ethnic groups. Those Conservatives who appeal to the innate inferiority of minorities may favor the practice of eugenics, which involves social control of human reproduction through sterilization of "deficient" persons and selection of "superior" persons for breeding. For example, government might require sterilization for individuals applying for welfare assistance. The Nobel prize-winning physicist William Shockley sought to promote selective breeding by establishing a sperm bank for Nobel prize winners.

Most Conservatives would like to end all government efforts to promote integration. Groups sharing sufficiently common cultural heritages will assimilate spontaneously, so if government coercion is required, Conservatives conclude that integration is unnatural. Government should act only to protect the rights of minorities against the "tyranny of the majority" as exemplified by the former South African government's policy of apartheid, which maintained racial segregation to preserve the culture and privileges of the white minority. When government forces integration, it creates a backlash of resentment from members of the majority and a flood of "rising expectations" from minority persons who feel they deserve a better quality of life.

Conservatives also oppose programs to benefit minorities because any perception that one group is being favored at the expense of others serves to undermine respect for governmental authority. This opposition to public assistance for minorities also extends to affirmative action policies. Like Classical Liberals, Conservatives view affirmative action as "reverse discrimination" and warn that it will generate animosity among whites toward minority groups. In addition, Conservatives claim that affirmative action damages the psyches of minority persons by tainting their accomplishments; they can never know whether their achievements are attributable to ability and effort or are simply the result of preferential treatment.[16]

Some Conservatives have proposed a strategy for government to aid minorities with minimal intervention. Inner-city neighborhoods would be designated as "enterprise zones," and businesses would be given tax breaks or other financial incentives to invest in these areas.[17] Conservatives claim that this policy restores the viability of minority neighborhoods by fostering local initiative and entrepreneurial energy. Conservatives have borrowed the leftist phrase "empowerment" to describe policies encouraging initiative and entrepreneurship in minority neighborhoods.

In defending segregation, Conservatives are fighting against strong historical currents. Since the Englightenment, ethnically and racially pure communities have been criticized as stultifying, repressive, and intolerant. However, Conservatives claim that a cohesive, homogeneous community enables individuals to form attachments to particular persons and places which are necessary for establishing personal identity. Freedom, Conservatives argue, is worthless unless people have purpose in their lives, and genuine freedom flourishes when individuals are enmeshed in a web of mutually supportive social relationships provided by racial and ethnic identity and other intermediate institutions.

THE MODERN LIBERAL PERSPECTIVE

Explanations of Discrimination

Modern Liberals trace the origins of racial and ethnic conflict in industrial societies to the inequitable conditions under which most minority groups entered. Having begun in a disadvantaged position, minority persons are caught in a debilitating cycle; a deprived background restricts opportunity for acquiring skills which, in turn, results in menial jobs, low income, and perpetuation of poverty. Blending Classical Liberal and Radical themes, Modern Liberals acknowledge that the plight of minority groups is partially attributable to choices concerning education and employment, but they argue that these decisions are made within a social system structured around the subordination of minority groups.

Modern Liberals doubt the market's ability to end discrimination. They view the market as an arena in which powerful groups seek to control competition to advance their own interests. Minority groups, having been systematically excluded from power, are therefore disadvantaged in the market. Although competitive forces may push for integration, the market is not the only institution shaping society. Economic activity is embedded in cultural practices and power relations, and competition is too imperfect to override deeply entrenched cultural biases and unequal power.

The mechanisms by which power circumscribes and limits the integrating forces of market competition are largely invisible. Discrimination may persist because the traditional values shaping human behavior reflect fear, ignorance, and the need to maintain social harmony within a community. For example, a nonracist employer may discriminate against minority job applicants, fearing that employees, customers, or other members of the community might react negatively to the presence of minority workers. Similarly, a nonracist homeowner may oppose the sale of a neighbor's house to a minority person based on knowledge that housing values often drop when a neighborhood is initially integrated. In both cases, discrimination results not from personal hostility toward minority persons, but from assessments of the economic realities of a racist society.

Even employers committed to hiring the best workers often lack information about the productivity of job applicants and, therefore, may rely on race or ethnicity as criteria for screening candidates. The employer could conduct extensive interviews and research to determine each person's qualifications, but this process would be efficient only if the benefits of hiring better employees exceed the costs of obtaining information. In many cases, employers rely on their personal opinions about the "typical behaviors" of different groups. Lacking perfect information about the productivity of each individual, this screening by race or ethnicity is consistent with profit-maximization and therefore can persist even in a competitive market. Economists call this practice "statistical discrimination."[18]

Modern Liberals also claim that discrimination occurs outside the labor market. Society's institutions reflect and perpetuate power relations and the subordinate status of minority groups. This "institutional discrimination" is sustained through both its material and psychological impacts. Many minority persons live in neighborhoods with inferior schools, high unemployment, high rates of crime, dilapidated housing, and broken families.

Segregation and discrimination adversely affect the aspirations of minority persons because one's social environment shapes one's self-image. People who consistently experience negative reactions from others are likely to develop low self-esteem and may even conclude that they are undeserving of equal rights. Low self-esteem is also perpetuated by a lack of minority persons in prominent social positions who might serve as role models for raising the aspirations of minorities. Finally, even those minority persons who maintain their self-esteem may be subject to a "feedback effect," causing them to invest less time and money in acquiring productive skills because they correctly perceive that members of their group earn lower financial returns on such investments.[19]

Responses to Discrimination

The Modern Liberal belief that discrimination is embedded in society's institutions means that viable solutions must involve legal and structural changes as well as changes in individual values. Modern Liberals were instrumental in the Civil Rights movement during the 1960s, pushing for legal reforms such as the Civil Rights Act, the Voting Rights Act, the Equal Opportunity Act, and desegregation of schools.

However, equal schooling and equal opportunity cannot fully compensate for the deprived family environments affecting many minority children trapped in a "cycle of poverty." During the 1970s, Modern Liberals focused on achieving greater "equality of result." Minority persons cannot take full advantage of the opportunities opened by legal reforms unless their income is sufficient to sustain normal human development. The most direct strategy for improving the material well-being of minority groups is redistribution of income and wealth. Although theoretical justification for such a policy has been provided by Keynes and Rawls, most Modern Liberals oppose large-scale redistribution as politically infeasible and damaging to incentives. Instead, they opt for less ambitious financial assistance and government intervention. Proposals include raising the minimum wage, providing greater public assistance, and enforcing legal safeguards against discrimination. Some Modern Liberals also join with Radicals in supporting full employment as a method for increasing minority opportunities.

As economic stagnation eroded support for direct government assistance to minority groups in the early 1970s, Modern Liberals turned to affirmative action to encourage employers to vigorously search for qualified minority candidates.[20] Critics claim that affirmative action sets hiring quotas, forcing employers to hire less-qualified job applicants, and that it constitutes "reverse discrimination" against whites. However, Modern Liberals defend affirmative action by arguing that whites, as a group, have benefitted from past injustices inflicted on minority groups. Had discrimination not occurred, many whites would not have attained their present income and status. Therefore, affirmative action simply counterbalances the injustices of the past.

Modern Liberals also think affirmative action provides minority children with adult role models in professional and managerial positions. They anticipate that racial stereotyping will diminish as people of all racial and ethnic backgrounds appear in high-status positions. Another justification of affirmative action is based on the concept of human rights, which entitle people to certain protections and benefits even if they cannot afford them. Because the market recognizes only property rights, the government must defend the human rights of those individuals disadvantaged in the market. Affirmative action protects the right of minority groups to be free from discrimination. Modern Liberals reject the criticism that affirmative action impedes efficiency by placing people in positions for which they are unqualified. Many job skills are acquired after a person is employed, so people become qualified by virtue of having a job. Affirmative action simply assures that minority persons have greater opportunities for access to good jobs.

In spite of these arguments in favor of affirmative action, Modern Liberals acknowledge the anger and resentment felt by many whites. Some Modern Liberals have withdrawn their support, claiming that affirmative action has already accomplished much of its original purpose to open doors for minority groups. Given the eroding support for affirmative action, Modern Liberals have recently adopted a new approach called "multiculturalism." Instead of redistributing income or jobs, multiculturalism entails public sharing and celebration of the uniqueness and worth of different cultures within society. As citizens learn to value and respect a wide variety of cultural practices, the fear and ignorance that fuel discrimination should subside. Multiculturalism also restores pride among minority groups by illuminating their contributions and achievements.

NOTES

1. See Gary Becker, *The Economics of Discrimination,* 2nd ed., Chicago: University of Chicago Press, 1971.

2. See Thomas Sowell, *Markets and Minorities,* New York: Basic Books, 1981. Other relevant works by Sowell include *Ethnic America: A History,* New York: Basic Books, 1981; *Race and Economics,* New York: David McKay, 1975; *The Economics and Politics of Race,* New York: William Morrow, 1983; *Race and Cultures: A World View,* New York: Basic Books, 1994; and *Migration and Cultures: A World View,* New York: Basic Books, 1996.

3. Walter Williams, *The State Against Blacks,* New York: McGraw-Hill, 1982.

4. Glenn C. Loury, "The Moral Quandary of the Black Community," *Public Interest* 79 (Spring 1985): 9–22.

5. See Alan H. Goldman, *Justice and Reverse Discrimination,* Princeton, NJ: Princeton University Press, 1979; Frederick R. Lynch, *Invisible Victims: White*

Males and The Crisis of Affirmative Action, New York: Greenwood Press, 1989; and Richard Epstein, *Forbidden Grounds: The Case Against Employment Discrimination Laws*, Cambridge: Harvard University Press, 1992.

6. See Dinesh D'Souza, *The End of Racism*, New York: The Free Press, 1995.

7. A Radical account of the effect of early capitalism on the lives of common people is presented in E. P. Thompson, *The Making of the English Working Class*, New York: Pantheon, 1963.

8. See Eric Williams, *Capitalism and Slavery*, New York: Putnam, 1966.

9. See William Tabb, *The Political Economy of the Black Ghetto*, New York: W. W. Norton, 1970; Manning Marable, *How Capitalism Underdeveloped Black America*, Boston: South End Press, 1983; and Lloyd Hogan, *Principles of Black Political Economy*, Boston: Routledge & Kegan Paul, 1984.

10. Michael Reich, *Racial Inequality: A Political Economic Analysis*, Princeton, NJ: Princeton University Press, 1981.

11. See David M. Gordon, Richard C. Edwards, and Michael Reich, *Segmented Work, Divided Workers: The Historical Transformation of Labor in the United States*, New York: Cambridge University Press, 1982.

12. The integrationist perspective is presented in Manning Marable, *Beyond Black and White*, New York: Verso, 1995. The separatist perspective is presented in John T. McCartney, *Black Power Ideologies*, Philadelphia: Temple University Press, 1992.

13. See Carleton Putnam, *Race and Reason*, Washington, DC: Public Affairs Press, 1961. For a critical analysis of the history of racist ideas, see Thomas F. Gossett, *Race: The History of an Idea in America*, New York: Schocken Books, 1963.

14. William Shockley, "Dysgenics, Geneticity, Raceology: A Challenge to the Intellectual Responsibility of Educators," *Phi Delta Kappan 53*, no. 5 (January 1972): 297–307; Arthur R. Jensen, *Genetics and Education*, New York: Harper & Row, 1972; and Richard Herrnstein, *Educability and Group Differences*, New York: Harper & Row, 1973. More recently, the idea of hereditary IQ has been defended in Richard J. Herrnstein and Charles Murray, *The Bell Curve: Intelligence and Class Structure in American Life*, New York: Free Press, 1994. Excellent summaries of these ideas and the debates surrounding them are found in Steven Fraser, ed., *The Bell Curve Wars: Race, Intelligence, and the Future of America*, New York: Basic Books, 1995; Russell Jacoby and Naomi Glauberman, *The Bell Curve Debate: History, Document, Opinions*, New York: Times Books, 1995; and Joe L. Kinchloe, Shirley R. Steinberg, and Aaron D. Gresson III, *Measured Lies: The Bell Curve Examined*, New York: St. Martin's Press, 1996. The history of efforts to scientifically establish racial differences in intelligence is detailed in Allan Chase, *The Legacy of Malthus: The Social Costs of the New Scientific Racism*, New York: Alfred A. Knopf, 1977; Pat Shipman, *The Evolution of Racism: Human Differences and the Use and Abuse of Science*, New York: Simon & Schuster, 1994; and Edward J. Larson, *Sex, Race and Science: Eugenics in the Deep South*, Baltimore: Johns Hopkins University Press, 1995. For a response by Arthur Jensen to his critics, see Arthur Jensen, *Straight Talk About Mental Tests*, New York: Free Press, 1981.

15. See Ashley Montague, ed., *Race and IQ*, New York: Oxford University Press, 1975; N. J. Block and Gerald Dworkin, eds., *The IQ Controversy*, New York: Pantheon, 1976; Carl Senna, ed., *Race and IQ*, New York: Third Press,

1973; James M. Lawler, *IQ, Heritability, and Racism*, New York: International Publishers, 1978; and Elaine Mensh and Harry Mensh, *The IQ Mythology: Race, Class, Gender, and Inequality*, Carbondale, IL: Southern Illinois University Press, 1991.

16. See Nathan Glazer, *Affirmative Discrimination: Ethnic Inequality and Public Policy*, New York: Basic Books, 1975. See also Nathan Glazer and Daniel Patrick Moynihan, *Ethnicity*, Cambridge, MA: Harvard University Press, 1975.

17. See Stuart Butler, *Enterprise Zones: Greenlining the Inner Cities*, New York: Universe Books, 1981; and Deborah K. Belasich, *Enterprise Zones: Policy Perspectives of Economic Development*, New York: Garland Publishers, 1993.

18. See Edmund S. Phelps, "The Statistical Theory of Racism and Sexism," *American Economic Review* 62, no. 4 (September 1972): 659–61.

19. See Kenneth J. Arrow, *Some Models of Racial Discrimination in the Labor Market*, Santa Monica, CA: Rand Corporation, 1971. See also Ray Marshall, "The Economics of Racial Discrimination: A Survey," *Journal of Economic Literature* 12, no. 3 (September 1974): 849–71.

20. For additional information on affirmative action, see Margaret C. Simms, ed., *Economics Perspectives on Affirmative Action*, Washington, DC: Joint Center for Political and Economic Studies, 1995; Nicolaus Mills, *Debating Affirmative Action*, New York: Delta, 1994; and Francis J. Beckwith and Todd E. Jones, eds., *Social Justice or Reverse Discrimination*, Amherst, NY: Prometheus Books, 1997.

ADDITIONAL READING

Boston, Thomas D. *Race, Class, and Conservatism*. Boston: Unwin & Hyman, 1988.

Carnoy, Martin. *Faded Dreams: The Politics and Economics of Race in America*. New York: Cambridge University Press, 1994.

Cherry, Robert. *Discrimination*. Lexington, MA: Lexington Books, 1989.

Franklin, Raymond, and Solomon Resnick. *The Political Economy of Racism*. New York: Holt, Rinehart and Winston, 1973.

Gabriel, John. *Racism, Culture, Markets*. New York: Routledge, 1994.

Hacker, Andrew. *Two Nations*. New York: Ballantine Books, 1992.

Jennett, Christine, and Randal G. Steward. *Three Worlds of Discrimination: Race, Class, and Gender*. South Melbourne, Australia: Macmillan, 1987.

Lauren, Paul Gordon. *Power and Prejudice: The Politics and Diplomacy of Racial Discrimination*, 2nd ed. Boulder, CO: Westview Press, 1996.

Leiman, Melvin M. *Political Economy of Racism*. Boulder, CO: Pluto Press, 1993.

Marable, Manning. *Beyond Black And White: Transforming African-American Politics*. New York: Verso, 1995.

Oliver, Melvin L., and Thomas M. Shapiro. *Black Wealth/White Wealth: A New Perspective on Racial Inequality*. New York: Routledge, 1995.

Reuter, Theodore, ed. *The Politics of Race*. Armonk, NY: M. E. Sharpe, 1995.

Schiller, Bradley. *The Economics of Poverty and Discrimination*, 5th ed. Englewood Cliffs, NJ: Prentice-Hall, 1989.

Van Dyke, Vernon. *Human Rights, Ethnicity, and Discrimination*. Westport, CT: Greenwood, 1985.

Chapter 12

The Political Economy of Gender

Traditionally, both political and economic theory have ignored the division of humans into two sexes. This oversight reflects one of two approaches to issues of gender. Either women and men are so equal in status and role designation that theory need not distinguish between them, or women's roles in the political and economic realm are so insignificant that theory may safely ignore them. Neither of these approaches is appropriate for modern industrial societies in which women are active participants in public life yet remain relegated to jobs with lower status and income. Even allowing for differences between men and women in educational background and number of hours worked, a gender wage gap of twenty-five to thirty percent remains.

Gender discrimination poses additional issues besides those associated with racial or ethnic discrimination. The anatomical differences between men and women are undeniable. Some theorists go further to claim that women's and men's behavior suggests different interests and values. The question remains whether women are economically and politically disadvantaged by these differences. Economists distinguish between "in-market" discrimination, which involves unequal treatment of equally productive persons, and "pre-market" discrimination, which arises from social institutions including schools, family structure, and traditional values. Pre-market discrimination may render women less productive, in which case their lower wages do not necessarily indicate in-market discrimination. Yet efforts to precisely assess the extent of in-market discrimination are hampered by the porous boundaries separating public life and private life. When employers discriminate against women, they often rely on prevailing stereotypes about women's productivity. These same stereotypes affect child-rearing practices, educational programs, and training opportunities for women. Thus in-market discrimination and pre-market discrimination may reinforce each other, making separate statistical analysis of discrimination in the labor market haphazard at best.

THE CLASSICAL LIBERAL PERSPECTIVE

Explanations of Gender Roles

Early Classical Liberals built their theories around the view of all persons as equally autonomous and self-interested; thus, no analysis of gender roles was offered. When Classical Liberals spoke of the "rights of man," they may have been referring only to males because women were largely excluded from public life.[1] However, early American feminists such as Sarah Grimke (1792–1873), Elizabeth Cady Stanton (1815–1902), Lucretia Mott (1793–1880), and Susan B. Anthony (1820–1906) interpreted these rights as applying to all persons and thus were attracted to Classical Liberalism.[2] Seeking the same legal rights to choice and self-determination as were held by men, they envisioned a society in which all individuals, regardless of sex, would be free to compete in the market for rewards distributed according to productivity.

Today, Classical Liberals are optimistic that the abolition of legal and political barriers will result in fair treatment of both sexes. The market economy, with its freedom of choice and opportunity, is the best guarantee that women's efforts and abilities will be fairly rewarded.[3] If women's productivity parallels that of men, then employers should prefer to hire women because past discrimination has suppressed women's wages. Any employer who continues to discriminate will experience higher wage costs, resulting in lower profit and inability to compete effectively. Competitive market forces will eventually establish "equal pay for equal work" regardless of who is performing the job.

Classical Liberals claim that even sexist attitudes among male workers cannot prevent the market from eliminating discrimination. Neoclassical economic theory suggests that if men resent working alongside women, they will demand higher wages for undergoing the "disutility" of an integrated workplace. However, the market will not permit an employer to pay higher wages to men without a corresponding loss of profit. Therefore, employers will seek to persuade male workers to accept women or, failing in that, they will establish segregated worksites where men and women earn equal wages but work separately. In either case, wage discrimination against women will end.

Classical Liberals rely on the following explanations for the differences between male and female social roles and earnings:

1. *Women's abilities.* While Classical Liberals prefer to deemphasize genetic differences between persons, they don't deny the existence of male and female aptitudes leading to differences in market success. They view the relative stability of gender roles over time as evidence that men and women have different aptitudes and tend to specialize in those roles for which they are best suited. Economist Gary Becker suggests that if women are better than men at homemaking, then economic efficiency dictates that women specialize in domestic labor and trade these services for a share of their husband's earnings.[4] The theory of comparative advantage demonstrates the inefficiency of husbands and wives sharing household tasks if men are more productive than women in the labor market. The husband can better utilize his time earning money outside the home. By contributing to efficiency, the sexual division of labor is beneficial to both men and women.

Extending Becker's analysis, economists Richard McKenzie and Gordon Tullock describe the family as a "producing unit" that operates like a profit-maximizing firm in seeking to establish the most efficient division of labor.[5] This analysis applies not only to the structure of the family, but also to occupational segregation. Competitive market forces will effectively preclude women from types of work for which they are unsuited. To the extent that occupational segregation and a gender wage gap reflect differences in abilities between men and women, Classical Liberals claim that no injustice occurs. They note that advancing technology is enhancing women's relative status in the workplace by reducing the value of physical strength. Some Classical Liberals even predict that women will increasingly fill managerial positions as communication and organizational skills become more important than physical prowess and use of intimidation in motivating employees.

2. *Women's preferences.* Classical Liberals attribute much of the difference between male and female roles and wages to the rational choices of self-interested individuals. All persons, whether male or female, choose social roles in accordance with their preferences. Classical Liberals note that many women are strongly oriented toward home and family and that this commitment often limits their acquisition of education and training, their choice of occupation, and their mobility. If women choose to marry and raise children rather than obtain education, job skills, and work experience, then their productivity in the market will be lower. If women's earning capacity is less than men's, efficiency dictates that women specialize in unpaid household labor while their more productive husbands work for wages.

For those women who do work outside the home, their child-bearing and child-rearing commitments may cause them to choose jobs such as retail sales or clerical work which permit intermittent employment and require skills that do not depreciate rapidly over time. Such jobs typically offer lower wages and few opportunities for advancement, leaving women with less experience and seniority than their male counterparts. Statistically, a significant portion of the gender wage gap is attributable to the concentration of women in these occupations. However, Classical Liberals argue that this occupational segregation and the resulting wage gap arise from women's preferences. They are willing to work in low-paying jobs because they value time to spend with their families.

3. *Market disequilibrium.* As the number of women entering the labor market has risen in recent years, the market has been unable to absorb quickly all persons seeking work. Moreover, the excess supply of women crowding into entry-level positions has depressed wages for such jobs even lower than usual. Classical Liberals offer several explanations for rising female participation rates in the labor force. Improvements in household technology have reduced the time necessary for housekeeping, freeing women to pursue employment outside the home. Moreover, the tendency for family size to decrease as standards of living rise has further reduced the domestic responsibilities of women. Finally, as women have gained equality in education, their increased earning potential makes working more attractive.

Classical Liberals remain confident that the concentration of women in low-paid occupations will dissipate as the market adjusts to increased supplies of female labor and steers women toward jobs corresponding to their abilities and preferences. More productive women will be rewarded with higher wages and promotions to better jobs. As evidence that the market is making these adjustments, Classical Liberals note that the gender wage gap is substantially smaller for young women than for older women.

4. *Government intervention.* Classical Liberals argue that efforts by government to protect or assist women are demeaning because they imply that women are less capable than men. In fact, these policies often represent attempts by men to protect their own privileges. Men can effectively reduce competition for their jobs by securing legislation aimed at restricting women's opportunities, thereby forcing women to crowd into "female occupations" and driving down wages for those jobs. Examples of such policies include laws prohibiting women from lifting heavy objects or working in hazardous conditions. Also, laws requiring equal pay for men and women discourage employers from hiring women since a man can be hired for the same cost. In general, Classical Liberals claim that all government restrictions on competition have distributive effects; some groups are advantaged and other groups are harmed.

Policy Proposals

Classical Liberals propose that discrimination against women can be eliminated by establishing a free market. Virtually all government intervention should be abolished, and public life should be made "gender-blind" by removing all references to gender in laws and public policies. While the proposed Equal Rights Amendment to the U.S. Constitution seems to promise equal treatment for men and women, most Classical Liberals oppose it, arguing that existing laws already protect the civil rights of women and that the ERA would lead to increased government regulation of business and a resulting loss of efficiency and freedom. This same argument has been extended by some Classical Liberals to criticize the entire feminist movement for seeking to use government to promote equality between the sexes through quota systems and other forms of government intervention.[6]

Classical Liberals also oppose "comparable worth" laws, which would establish fair wages for different occupations by evaluating jobs according to such criteria as skills required, level of responsibility, and working conditions. While Classical Liberals support "equal pay for equal work," they claim that only the market can determine the value of a job. The Classical Liberal case against comparable worth focuses on three arguments.[7] First, the assessed worth of any job depends on which criteria are used in its evaluation, but no objective method exists for selecting the criteria. Given this lack of objectivity, a bureaucratic evaluation of a job's worth would be no fairer than the market's assessment. Second, to the extent that comparable worth would raise wages in traditionally female occupations, it would reduce the incentives for women to enter male-dominated professions and therefore would perpetuate the current occupational segregation of women. Third, since male workers would resist efforts to reduce their wages, the effect of comparable worth would be to increase overall labor costs for employers, reduce profitability, eliminate jobs, and slow economic growth.

Some Classical Liberal economists have proposed policies to extend the logic of the market into the private realm of the family. In response to concerns about overpopulation, Classical Liberals have suggested that the most efficient way to limit population growth is to establish a market for the right to bear children. Adults would be granted a voucher for the right to produce one child, and then, depending on their preferences, they could buy or sell vouchers to reach their desired family size. Unlike China's efforts to control population growth by restricting the number of children in a family, this policy would retain the freedom to choose one's family size.

The development of artificial insemination and fetal transplants has already transformed child-bearing itself into a marketable service as some women contract to bear children in exchange for money. In the absence of legal obstacles, supply and demand will determine the appropriate price for "renting the womb" of a surrogate mother. Extending this logic, economist Richard Posner, who is also a federal judge, proposes that markets be established for babies so that couples can buy and sell to achieve their desired family size. This policy is consistent with economic efficiency, which dictates that any commodity be allocated to those who are most willing and able to pay for it.

THE RADICAL PERSPECTIVE

Explanations of Gender Roles

Some early feminists sought more than equal rights, arguing that women would remain oppressed until fundamental changes occurred in the institutions of marriage, family, and religion. Perhaps the most Radical of the early feminists was Mary Wollstonecraft (1759–1797), who claimed that women were socialized to be servants of men, preventing them from achieving full personal development. Mere legal reforms would not be sufficient to liberate women; genuine freedom would be attained only when women held equal power and were no longer dependent on men for financial support.

For the most part, however, Radicalism offered little analysis of gender roles until the late 1960s. At that time, three Radical versions of feminism emerged: Marxist feminism, radical feminism, and socialist feminism. During the 1970s and 1980s, intense and sometimes bitter debates occurred among proponents of these schools of thought. The debates were not so much resolved as transcended, so that contemporary feminist theorists working in the Radical tradition are less concerned about labels than about advancing the understanding of women's oppression and developing policies to end it. Today, the terms "Marxist," "radical," and "socialist" feminism are sometimes used interchangeably, but to review the debates of the past three decades, we shall examine each separately.

1. *Marxist feminism*. Karl Marx and Friedrich Engels claimed that the social roles available to both men and women are conditioned by society's production process. The earliest communal societies were sometimes matriarchal, but as soon as technological progress yielded production of a surplus beyond what was immediately consumed, men instituted private property to establish rights to the surplus. With the emergence of private property came male dominance over women, motivated partly by men's desire to control women's reproductive activities to assure transmission of property to legitimate heirs. Women became essentially the property of men, sometimes to the point of being bought and sold between different families and communities.

In the early years of capitalism, the sexual division of labor and the nuclear family were strengthened because they contributed to the accumulation of capital. By performing unpaid tasks such as childbearing and housekeeping, women enabled employers to, in effect, hire two workers for the price of one. Women also indirectly aided employers by providing a supportive home life so that their husbands were physically and emotionally prepared to face another day in the factory. For men, home and family became havens from the alienating experience of work.[8]

However, as capitalism matured and the demand for labor increased, market forces pulled women out of the home and into the workplace as a source of cheap labor. Yet the entry of women into the labor force had an unanticipated consequence: employers replaced a "family wage" with a wage adequate to support only a single person. The nuclear family became endangered as men could no longer earn enough to support their families, and women became increasingly capable of financial independence. From the Radical perspective, rising divorce rates, disintegration of families, and the blurring of gender roles are not symptoms of moral decline, but instead are consequences of capitalism. The accumulation process penetrates every sphere of human existence, breaking down bonds and obligations between people and replacing personal relations with a "cash nexus."

According to Marxists, the capitalist system is the enemy of both men and women. As long as capitalism continues, all members of the working class will lack control over their lives. Hostility between the sexes arises as capitalists seek to fragment and divide the working class to assure a steady supply of cheap labor. As long as men and women blame each other for bad relationships and financial problems, their attention is diverted from the real source of their frustration, which is the dominant power of capital over people.

In the late 1960s, a resurgence of interest in both Marxism and feminism led to "Marxist feminism," which holds that women's oppression is attributable to capitalism and that issues raised by feminists are best analyzed and understood using the Marxist critique of capitalism. Among the most prominent Marxist feminist theorists are Sheila Rowbotham and Michele Barrett.[9]

2. *Radical feminism.* Radical feminists find the Marxist explanation of women's roles to be implausible, claiming that the root of women's oppression is not economic but biological. Men are violent, aggressive, and domineering, and have always sought to oppress women. Women are made vulnerable to oppression by their childbearing function, which makes them dependent on men. Noting that women were oppressed long before capitalism appeared, radical feminists point to patriarchy, or male dominance, as the fundamental problem and argue that fighting against patriarchy must take precedence over any political struggle against capitalism. Capitalism is simply the most highly developed form of the various economic systems that have accompanied patriarchy, and any revolution that overthrows capitalism without simultaneously demolishing patriarchy will fail to liberate women. Radical feminists point to the former Soviet Union as evidence that abolishing private property and including women in the labor force are insufficient to secure women's liberation.[10]

Unlike Marxists, radical feminists view women rather than workers as the oppressed class in a patriarchal society. Men dominate women not for profit, they insist, but for ego gratification and a sense of power. Overthrowing patriarchy is justified not only because male aggression oppresses women, but because women's values, including nurturance, cooperation, and empathy are superior to the values emphasized by patriarchal societies. Radical feminists propose that major social problems such as war, hunger, and unemployment would not exist in a matriarchal society.

Theorists who founded Radical feminism, including Kate Millett and Mary Daly, focused on family life and religion as key sites in which women's subordination is experienced and reproduced in the attitudes of young children.[11] Whereas liberals strive to maintain separation between private and public life, radical feminists draw attention to family violence, marital rape, incest, and psychological abuse. These issues are not simply personal problems or isolated incidents, they claim, but symptoms of society's attitude toward women. In the words of French philosopher Simone de Beauvoir (1908–1986), "the personal is the political." The problems experienced by women as individuals are socially created and therefore require political solutions.

The power of patriarchy manifests itself not only in violence against women and job discrimination, but in the subtle conditioning of women's own self-image. The very concept of femininity is a "social construction" created largely by men to perpetuate male dominance. Femininity is associated with weakness, passivity, and self-denial. Because female identity is defined by men, the social roles available to women in a patriarchal society are inherently oppressive.

3. *Socialist feminism.* In an effort to synthesize Marxist feminism and radical feminism, socialist feminists propose that capitalism and patriarchy reinforce each other and thus constitute inseparable forms of female oppression. Socialist feminist theorists such as Juliet Mitchell, Zillah Eisenstein, and Nancy Hartsock affirm the critical insights provided by Marxism, particularly its emphasis on the social nature of human consciousness.[12] However, they join with radical feminists in criticizing Marxism for being tainted by a male perspective. By reducing all oppression in capitalist society to exploitation of workers by capitalists, Marxism fails to offer an analysis of the unique oppression faced by women.

Socialist feminists propose to augment Marxism by treating household production as an integral component of society's production process. Although not directly salaried, women's production in the home is essential for profitability and capital accumulation. The family is also the site of ideological and behavioral reproduction. Child-rearing practices serve to produce children who are suited for capitalism. In working-class families, women and children are traditionally taught to obey orders from male authority figures, while upper-class parents are more likely to stress creativity and self-direction for their children. As a result, the children of each class are socialized to fill their respective future roles in the hierarchy of capitalist production.

Policy Proposals

Because the Radical perspective encompasses three distinct types of feminism, Radicals offer a wide variety of proposals related to gender issues. Marxist feminists believe that the oppression of women can be solved only by ending capitalism and making the transition to a socialist society. Yet, in addition to the socialization of the means of production envisioned by Marx, they call for socialization of household production. Communal households would be able to take advantage of economies of scale and modern technology to accomplish such tasks as cleaning, shopping, food preparation, and child care. All adults would be expected to share in these responsibilities, and women would participate equally with men in the paid labor force. Marxist feminists believe that only when women and men have similar economic roles in society will male domination end. Women can be most effective in bringing about social change by joining with men in a working-class movement to end capitalism.

In contrast, radical feminists propose that the only viable strategy for the liberation of women is to develop separate "women-centered" institutions and communities that exclude patriarchal culture and male domination. Because Radical feminists view the nuclear family as a key institution in perpetuating patriarchy, some have suggested that the technology for producing "test-tube babies" offers an unprecedented opportunity for women to escape their biological dependence on men and to become autonomous, self-directing persons.[13]

Socialist feminists share much of the Marxist feminist skepticism concerning the possibility of reform within a capitalist society. Not only is government an instrument in the hands of the ruling class, but legal reforms cannot effectively end the institutionalized sexism shaping women's aspirations. The liberation of women and men requires a broad-based socialist movement to abolish both capitalism and patriarchy. While socialist feminists reject the separatist strategy of radical feminists, they also insist that feminist issues not be submerged in the struggle to end capitalism.

According to socialist feminists, capitalism is currently contributing to its own demise. As women enter the labor market, they are disillusioned by the alienating conditions of work and often face "double duty"—performing household labor in addition to wage labor. The hours devoted to housework are kept from declining by corporate marketing campaigns that create ever-higher standards of housekeeping and parenting.[14] Women's frustration with the roles available to them in capitalist society will foster growing support for socialism. In the meantime, some socialist feminists advocate wages for housework in recognition of the productive activities performed by people outside the formal labor market. These wages could be paid by spouses, by government, or by the spouse's employer. Other gender-related reforms supported by socialist feminists include public provision of child-care facilities, nationalized health care, increased public housing, government programs such as comparable worth to assure pay equity, and government efforts to expand job opportunities for women.

THE CONSERVATIVE PERSPECTIVE

Explanations of Gender Roles

While sexism is not logically implied by Conservatism, the Conservative emphasis on hierarchical authority often extends to encompass the roles of men and women. In describing women's roles in the social hierarchy, Conservatives emphasize the following characteristics:

1. *Sensitivity.* Women are "other-oriented"; they derive personal fulfillment through meeting the needs of other people. This sensitivity makes women ideally suited for roles requiring an ability to care, nurture, and mediate conflict (e.g., parenting, homemaking, teaching, and nursing). Conservative writer George Gilder describes the positive effect women have on men. Outside of marriage, he claims, men are "barbarians" who lack responsibility and purpose in their lives and therefore aimlessly pursue immediate pleasure. Women are able to channel the aggressive and potentially violent nature of men into productive work and parenting.[15]

2. *Irrationality.* Sigmund Freud (1856–1939) claimed that women have weak superegos, making them incapable of objective, dispassionate reasoning and, therefore, unfit for positions of responsibility and authority. Freud went so far as to portray women as subversive to civilization because they act on instinct and emotional impulse rather than making rational calculations of consequences. Women's irrationality is innate and cannot be changed by expanding educational or employment opportunities. In Freud's words, "anatomy is destiny."[16]

3. *Passivity.* Women are claimed to be physically weaker and more passive than men due to differences in hormonal balances. Specifically, a lower level of testosterone in women explains reduced aggressiveness and muscular development. To the extent that certain social roles require strength and forcefulness, women are disadvantaged in performing these tasks.

The differing temperaments and abilities of men and women dictate well-defined gender roles. Just as the human body requires different cells to function (such as bone, muscle, and skin), society needs differentiated gender roles to remain healthy. The sociologist Talcott Parsons claimed that women are best suited for "expressive" roles while men have greater aptitude for "instrumental" roles. Social harmony requires that women fill roles as wives, mothers, and members of the "helping professions" while men engage in physical or intellectual work manipulating the external world.

Conservatives insist that gender differences are naturally complementary. They view men as strong, aggressive, and inclined toward rational analysis, while women are nurturing and emotionally expressive. Men need women to raise children and provide a fulfilling home life, while women need men as sources of authority and financial support. So long as men and women accept one another's relative strengths and weaknesses, harmony will prevail. Indeed, the different capacities of men and women constitute the basis for sexual attraction and are therefore essential to reproducing the human species.

In analyzing the breakdown of traditional gender roles and gender identities, Conservatives place much of the blame on the deterioration of the nuclear family.[17] The family, as the basic unit of society and the primary site of socialization processes, prepares children for adulthood. Conservatives reject the Classical Liberal notion that humans develop through rational choice. The role models and socialization to which people are exposed as children shape individual preferences and behavior. For both children and adults, personal development requires involvement in a web of hierarchical social relations. The authority of parents conditions the child to later accept the authority of teachers, employers, and government. In addition, children's observation of the relation between their parents provides the basis for gender identity. When adult gender roles are vague or ambiguous, Conservatives fear that children will become confused and thwarted in the development of their own personalities.

Conservatives claim that blurring of gender roles and deterioration of the nuclear family contribute to immorality and economic stagnation. They blame this process on the following factors:

1. *Government.* When government intrudes into the everyday existence of citizens, traditional authority figures in the family, church, and community become less significant in people's lives. For example, the standardization of public-school curricula reduces the influence of parents and local authorities in determining the content of education. Mandatory sex education in schools diminishes parental discretion over childrearing. Welfare benefits and other publicly funded social services reduce women's dependence on men for financial support, thereby undermining male authority within the family. Finally, Conservatives blame government for the combination of inflation, high taxes, and foreign competition eroding male wages and forcing women to enter the labor market.

2. *The market.* Although most Conservatives accept the market as a lesser evil than government control of the economy, their long-held suspicions about the corrupting and disintegrating effects of competitive forces have resurfaced in their analysis of the family. From the Conservative perspective, the family and the market operate on diametrically opposed principles. The market fosters the individual pursuit of material self-interest, while the family depends on cooperation, sacrifice, and a sense of collective purpose and identity. The family should offer a haven of security and commitment in an otherwise fragmented, competitive, and individualistic society. The experience of growing up in a family with strong parental authority teaches children to place their duties above the pursuit of self-interest.

However, the market has become the dominant institution in modern societies, and its principles have penetrated and overwhelmed the virtues of family life. Once the market mentality pervades the home, calculations of self-interest displace the commitment and altruism essential to maintaining a stable family. Women and children adopt the autonomous and self-interested behavior previously reserved for men in the market, undermining the father's authority. In short, families cannot function as cohesive social units if all members are purely self-interested.

High divorce rates, single-parent households, runaway children, and juvenile delinquency provide testimony to the deterioration of commitment and obligation in the family. From the Conservative perspective, the Classical Liberal portrayal of marriage and childrearing as self-interested exchanges and contracts between individuals reveals the shortcomings of modern family life. In the absence of stable traditions and gender roles, individuals become calculators of self-interest in even the most personal aspects of their lives. Without the influence of closely knit families on childhood development, society will eventually degenerate into a chaotic battle among individuals unable and unwilling to control their selfish impulses.

3. *Feminism.* Both government and the market have contributed to feminism by undermining the ability of men to financially support their families and by offering women alternative sources of financial support. Conservatives find numerous faults with feminism, viewing it as symptomatic of the general trend toward narcissism and selfishness in modern societies.[18] Feminists are accused of shirking responsibility and commitment as they pursue "self-fulfillment" and seek to "find themselves." The basic error underlying feminism is a failure to perceive that the commitments and responsibilities accompanying family life result in personal fulfillment. What feminists call liberation is actually selfishness, and a society of selfish individuals cannot sustain itself.

Conservatives also claim that feminism undermines men's identity as providers, protectors, and authority figures within the family. Faced with the challenge of feminism, men lose self-esteem and become confused about their purpose in life. George Gilder argues that men's economic productivity has been adversely affected by feminism because when women are actively involved in the labor force, men no longer feel as compelled to work.[19] Not only are women bringing their earnings into the household, but their employment erodes men's attachment to work as a uniquely male source of self-esteem. Moreover, having lost authority over their own families, men feel inadequate to assert themselves in the business world. To the extent that feminism contributes to divorce, men are freed from most of their domestic responsibilities, causing further deterioration of their identities as providers and hence diminishing their productivity in the workplace.

Finally, Conservative women such as Phyllis Schlafly and Anita Bryant have claimed that the women's liberation movement consistently degrades women who choose the role of housewife and mother.[20] Women in traditional roles are made to feel inadequate in comparison with women who pursue careers. The resulting confusion and loss of confidence contributes to the blurring of gender roles as women feel compelled to prove their worth outside the home. Conservatives claim to be the true defenders of women's rights to keep the status and privileges attached to their traditional roles.

Policy Proposals

Because they blame both government and the market for undermining gender roles and threatening the family, Conservatives will not rely exclusively on either institution to solve the problem. Their goal in reforming government policies is to revitalize the market's potential for producing wealth while protecting women and families from the corrosive impact of market forces. Conservatives call on government to consciously promote traditional values and gender roles. For example, they support a Family Protection Act to reduce the pressures on women to work outside the home by granting tax breaks to families with nonworking wives. This law would also prohibit publicly funded lawyers from handling cases involving divorce, abortion, or homosexuality.

Conservative policy proposals also include making divorce more difficult, prohibiting abortion, and making welfare less accessible for single women. Public schools would be prohibited from using textbooks featuring nontraditional roles for women. Some Conservatives, concerned that feminism and narcissism have caused many young adults to shun the responsibilities of parenthood, want government to pursue pronatal policies to combat a "birth dearth." Such policies might include larger tax deductions for families with children and public financial assistance with childrearing. Conservatives have consistently opposed the Equal Rights Amendment, claiming that it would further erode the differentiation between gender roles and would abolish the legal requirement that men provide financial support to their wives. The ERA, they claim, would actually result in men's liberation from traditional responsibilities to their families.

Conservatives tend to be pessimistic about the future of gender roles and the family. The economy's increasing inability to provide a "family wage" for male workers contributes to the breakdown of the family, and, reciprocally, the breakdown of the family undermines the economy by producing self-centered, poorly socialized children who are ill-equipped to work effectively and to handle the responsibilities of adult life. This circular path of causation means that any effective Conservative strategy must simultaneously deal with misguided government policies, powerful economic forces, and the influence of feminism.

THE MODERN LIBERAL PERSPECTIVE

Explanations of Gender Roles

The Modern Liberal approach to gender issues has evolved through three distinct historical phases. In the early years of the feminist movement, some leaders doubted whether men and women should be treated equally. Both Margaret Fuller (1810–1850) and Charlotte Perkins Gilman (1860–1935) claimed that women are innately less aggressive and individualistic than men. These feminine traits contribute to a decent society by promoting nonviolence, cooperation, and civic virtue. Since women occupy a "separate sphere," female values should be protected by government from the competitive forces of the market. Early Modern Liberal feminists supported legal restrictions on women's working hours and on women's entry into certain occupations. Their rejection of equal treatment is illustrated by the fact that Eleanor Roosevelt, the National Women's Trade Union League, and the League of Women Voters opposed the Equal Rights Amendment when it was first proposed in the 1920s, fearing that it would abolish all legislative protection for women.

By the 1960s, a second phase of Modern Liberal feminism was articulated by Betty Friedan and was institutionalized with the founding of the National Organization for Women (NOW) in 1966.[21] Arguing that protective legislation perpetuates occupational segregation by forcing employers to treat women differently, Modern Liberals sought to eliminate all discriminatory laws and to dismantle the stereotype of women as uniquely suited for the roles of care-giver and homemaker. During this second phase, Modern Liberals attributed women's lower salaries and status to gender stereotypes and ignorance. They believed that employers should welcome equal rights for women since sexism effectively denies more than half the population a full opportunity to contribute to economic activity. However, to prevent unenlightened employers from continuing to discriminate, Modern Liberals advocated new laws and government regulation to make capitalism more efficient and fair.

By the end of the 1970s, many Modern Liberals became concerned that their commitment to equal rights and equal treatment was imposing unforeseen burdens on women. A third phase of Modern Liberal feminism reintroduced notions of difference between the sexes. For example, social psychologist Carol Gilligan claims that women view the social world as one of relationships, commitments, and responsibilities, whereas men view society as composed of separate individuals whose interaction is based on rules and rights.[22] If, in their quest for occupational success, women adopt the competitive individualism of men, they risk compromising their own valuable qualities. Gilligan does not propose that women remain at home, but suggests that institutional changes are necessary to accommodate the different needs and interests of women in the workplace.

Similarly, Nancy Chodorow claims that differences in male and female gender identity are determined at a very early stage of childhood development.[23] Boys develop more "rigid ego boundaries" because they must differentiate themselves from their mother. In the process, they form identities as separate individuals in competition with others. Girls, on the other hand, share the gender of their mother and, therefore, develop a more fluid sense of self that emphasizes interpersonal connections and sympathy with the needs of others. As a result, girls are prepared for the role of mother, while boys, with their sense of separateness and independence, are prepared to participate in the impersonal world of work and business.

Chodorow denies that gender differences are purely biological. If men were to become more involved in the early stages of childrearing, traditional distinctions between the psychosocial development of boys and girls might fade. In addition, if marriages provided greater emotional gratification, women would not feel compelled to focus their energies primarily on their children and would expect greater sharing of responsibilities between husband and wife. However, for the foreseeable future, the differences between adult gender roles are likely to be "reproduced" in children, and feminists should recognize these differences when proposing public policies related to gender issues.

While Modern Liberals acknowledge that competitive market forces create pressures to integrate women into the labor force, they challenge the Classical Liberal portrayal of the market as an adequate deterrent to discrimination. Discrimination is resistant to market forces for the following reasons:

1. *Social conditioning of preferences.* Modern Liberals emphasize the powerful forces of parental, peer, and societal influences that affect young women's aspirations and achievements. This socialization process is institutionalized in such practices as educational "tracking" that steers girls toward coursework preparing them for traditional female roles. Even more pervasive is the perception of particular occupations as "men's work" and

the corresponding stigma attached to women who aspire to those occupations. The choices of young women are also affected by "demonstration effects" whereby the occupational segregation of adult women in lower-status jobs creates an absence of role models for stimulating the aspirations of young women. Similarly, a "feedback effect" operates when young women rationally choose to bypass higher education because they observe that the financial rate of return to education is less for women than for men. Even women who attain professional positions may be deterred from further success by their isolation and visibility as challengers of traditional gender roles.

2. *Imperfect competition.* Market imperfections posed by labor unions, corporations, and government intervention establish various barriers to entry into certain occupations. An example of this "structural discrimination" is the informal practice by some firms of hiring only within an "old boy network." Information about job openings may not be widely publicized and job qualifications may include unnecessary education or experience, effectively screening out many female applicants. While Classical Liberals insist that such practices cannot survive in a market economy, Modern Liberals believe that market competition is sufficiently imperfect to permit discrimination and stereotypes to persist. The same self-interested motivation underlying market behavior also leads men to construct formal and informal barriers to female competition.

3. *Domestic responsibilities.* The division of labor within the family often leaves women with the majority of childrearing and homemaking responsibilities, and their choice of occupation is affected by these duties. Because so many women are faced with the same predicament of trying to balance family responsibilities and careers, they tend to crowd into those occupations offering flexible or part-time hours, ease of exit and reentry, and durable skills. This crowding results in lower wages and fewer opportunities for career development.[24] The occupational segregation of women does not necessarily reflect lower productivity or the individual preferences of women, but rather results from a social environment in which the burden of homemaking falls on women due to men's noncooperation and the lack of government-funded day care.

4. *Sexist attitudes.* When sexism is prevalent, discrimination against women may be practiced by all employers. Neoclassical economic theory suggests that at least one employer would break ranks to hire women in the pursuit of greater profit and that lower labor costs enjoyed by this employer would exert competitive pressure on other firms to cease discrimination. However, Modern Liberals question this analysis, pointing to the psychological impact of societal norms in restraining economizing

behavior. The employer who violates these norms by hiring women to perform "men's work" may be ostracized within the community or may feel guilt for having exploited women for the sake of greater profit. Discrimination can be disguised as protecting the dignity and virtue of women, and this attitude may be sufficiently strong to withstand competitive market forces.

Employers may also be reluctant to hire women due to concern about the morale of male workers. Employers may worry that the presence of women will distract men, disrupt their camaraderie, and create tensions between co-workers. Male employees engaged in strenuous or risky jobs are likely to feel particularly threatened by female co-workers whose presence undermines their enjoyment of work as a source of masculine pride. Employers must be sensitive to these reactions since time and money have been invested in training male workers. Hiring female workers will be unappealing if it lowers male workers' productivity.

5. *Statistical discrimination.* Even employers committed to hiring the best candidate for a job may lack information about the productivity of individual candidates, causing them to rely on preconceived notions about women as a group. For example, an employer may believe that female employees are likely to leave their jobs due to marriage or pregnancy and may therefore categorically reject all female applicants. Some highly qualified women may be bypassed, but if the costs of gathering complete information about candidates exceed the benefits of hiring more productive workers, then this "statistical discrimination" is efficient from the employer's viewpoint.[25]

In summary, Modern Liberals claim that nonmarket forces and imperfections in the market are sufficiently powerful to make competitive pressures resist putting an end to sex discrimination. Even when women's lower wages do reflect lower productivity or less permanent attachments to the labor market, Modern Liberals argue that these characteristics are themselves conditioned by the values and institutional structure of society. Women's choices are made in response to limited opportunities and incentives. Whereas Classical Liberals attribute lower female wages to lower productivity, Modern Liberals are more inclined to reverse the causal sequence and view lower productivity as a consequence of occupational structures and wage levels.

Policy Proposals

The initial orientation of Modern Liberal groups such as the National Organization for Women was to make all laws gender-neutral, and they were quite successful in accomplishing that goal. In the mid-1970s, however, Modern Liberals began to doubt the wisdom of perfectly gender-neutral public policy. This reorientation evolved from the realization that if women and men are treated equally in the job market, women may be penalized due to their unique status as childbearers and, in many cases, primary homemakers. The pitfalls of a purely "equal rights" strategy were highlighted in 1976 when the Supreme Court ruled that a proposed law requiring employers to grant paid leaves of absence to pregnant women was discriminatory because it treated women differently than men.

To move beyond formal equality under the law, affirmative action programs require employers to make concerted efforts to locate qualified female and minority applicants for jobs. Another proposal for addressing pay inequities is "comparable worth." While the wages attached to various jobs are theoretically determined by supply and demand, Modern Liberals claim that market-determined wages can be unfair due to discrimination and gender stereotyping. In addition, women's family responsibilities force them to crowd into occupations offering flexible hours, but this overcrowding keeps wages for these occupations permanently depressed.

Therefore, if the financial burden of childrearing is to be shared equitably by men and women, the market's determination of wages must be overridden. Comparable worth provides an alternative to the market in assessing the relative worth of different jobs. Each job would be evaluated according to criteria such as level of responsibility, physical difficulty, and amount of training required. By assigning points in each category, a numerical rating would be established for each job, and pay would correspond with that rating. The goal of comparable worth is to formulate an objective measurement of the value of different jobs independently of the market's valuation.[26]

Those Modern Liberals who support comparable worth claim that it would contribute to women's financial independence and enhance their self-esteem and power. By paying women more than their market-determined wages, society is acknowledging not only the unfairness of traditional wage structures, but also the value of women's productive contributions in the home. Modern Liberals claim that comparable worth can actually increase efficiency because women's child-rearing activities create positive externalities; the social benefits of good parenting exceed the private benefits to the individual child or family. Adults who grew up in nurturing families are more likely to work productively, vote intelligently, and contribute to the good of society. When an activity produces positive externalities, the market allocates insufficient resources to that activity, resulting in inefficiency. To correct this market failure, government should compensate women for their productive efforts in the home by setting their wages above the level determined by supply and demand.

Other Modern Liberal proposals related to gender include marital property reform to secure for married persons a legal right to half of any property acquired during the marriage, even if only one spouse was in the labor force. Such a law would recognize the productive contribution made by homemakers. A second proposal seeks reform of social security and unemployment compensation so that unpaid work outside the labor market would entitle persons to protections and benefits similar to those enjoyed by employed workers. A third proposal calls for government to improve the "social infrastructure" of health care, social services, day care, and facilities for youth and the elderly. These areas now absorb vast amounts of unpaid labor by women. Finally, some Modern Liberals want employers to offer more flexible work schedules, paid leaves of absence for parenting, fringe benefits for part-time work, and the option of job sharing between two or more persons.

NOTES

1. See Jean Bethke Elshtain, *Public Man, Private Woman: Women in Social and Political Thought*, Princeton, NJ: Princeton University Press, 1981; and Susan Moller Okin, *Women in Western Political Thought*, Princeton, NJ: Princeton University Press, 1979.

2. See Mari Jo Buhle and Paul Buhle, *The Concise History of Woman Suffrage*, Urbana, IL: University of Illinois Press, 1978; Judith Hole and Ellen Levine, *Rebirth of Feminism*, New York: Quadrangle Books, 1971; Richard J. Evans, *The Feminists*, Totowa, NJ: Rowman & Littlefield, 1979; Sara M. Evans, *Born for Liberty: A History of Women in America*, New York: Free Press, 1989; and Lois W. Banner, *Women in Modern America: A Brief History,* 3rd ed., Fort Worth: Harcourt Brace College Publishers, 1995.

3. Classical Liberal feminism is presented in Wendy McElroy, ed., *Freedom, Feminism, and the State*, Washington, DC: Cato Institute, 1982; Ellen Frankel Paul, *Equity and Gender*, Washington, DC: Cato Institute, 1988; and Joan Kennedy Taylor, *Women's Issues: Feminism, Classical Liberalism, and the Future*, Stanford, CA: Hoover Institution, 1993.

4. See Gary Becker, *A Treatise on the Family*, Cambridge, MA: Harvard University Press, 1981. See also Gary Becker, *The Economic Approach to Human Behavior*, Chicago: University of Chicago Press, 1976.

5. See Richard B. McKenzie and Gordon Tullock, *The Best of the New World of Economics*, 5th ed., Homewood, IL: Richard D. Irwin, 1989. See also Gary S. Becker and Guity Nashat Becker, *The Economics of Life*, New York: McGraw-Hill, 1997.

6. The Classical Liberal case against feminism is presented in Michael Levin, *Feminism and Freedom*, New Brunswick, NJ: Transaction Books, 1987.

7. For a Classical Liberal critique of comparable worth, see Richard E. Burr, *Are Comparable Worth Systems Truly Comparable?*, St. Louis: Center for the Study of American Business, Washington University, 1986. See also Jennifer Roback, *A Matter of Choice: A Critique of Comparable Worth by A Skeptical Feminist*, New York: Priority Press, 1986.

8. See Eli Zaretsky, *Capitalism, The Family and Personal Life*, New York: Harper & Row, 1976.

9. Sheila Rowbotham, *Woman's Consciousness, Man's World*, Baltimore: Penguin, 1973, and Michele Barrett, *Women's Oppression Today: The Marxist/Feminist Encounter*, rev. ed., New York: Verso, 1988. See also Edith Hoshino

Altbach, ed., *From Feminism to Liberation*, Cambridge, MA: Schenkman, 1971, and Evelyn Reed, *Problems of Women's Liberation: A Marxist Approach*, New York: Pathfinder Press, 1971.

10. See Hilde Scott, *Does Socialism Liberate Women?*, Boston: Beacon Press, 1974.

11. Kate Millett, *Sexual Politics*, New York: Avon, 1971, and Mary Daly, *Gyn/Ecology: The Metaethics of Radical Feminism*, Boston: Beacon Press, 1978. A retrospective assessment of radical feminism is presented in Alice Echols, *Daring To Be Bad: Radical Feminism in America 1967–1975*, Minneapolis: University of Minnesota Press, 1989. See also the collection of articles in Anne Koedt, Ellen Levine, and Anita Rapone, eds., *Radical Feminism*, New York: Quadrangle Books, 1973.

12. Juliet Mitchell, *Woman's Estate*, Baltimore, MD: Penguin, 1975; Zillah R. Eisenstein, ed., *Capitalist Patriarchy and the Case for Socialist Feminism*, New York: Monthly Review Press, 1979; and Nancy Hartsock, *Money, Sex and Power: Toward a Feminist Historical Materialism*, New York: Longman, 1983. See also Linda Jenness, ed., *Feminism and Socialism*, New York: Pathfinder Press, 1972; Batya Weinbaum, *The Curious Courtship of Women's Liberation and Socialism*, Boston: South End Press, 1978; and Lise Vogel, *Woman Questions: Essays for A Materialist Feminism*, New York: Routledge, 1995.

13. See Shulamith Firestone, *The Dialectic of Sex: The Case for Feminist Revolution*, New York: William Morrow, 1970.

14. See Arlie Hochschild, *The Second Shift*, New York: Viking, 1989; Juliet B. Schor, *The Overworked American: The Unexpected Decline of Leisure*, New York: Basic Books, 1991; and Lydia Morris, *The Workings of the Household*, Cambridge: Polity, 1990.

15. George Gilder, *Naked Nomads: Unmarried Men in America*, New York: Quadrangle Books, 1974. See also George Gilder, *Men and Marriage*, Gretna, LA: Pelican, 1986.

16. See Eli Sagan, *Freud, Women, and Morality*, New York: Basic Books, 1988.

17. See Ronald Fletcher, *The Abolitionists: The Family and Marriage under Attack*, New York: Routledge, 1988; Ronald Fletcher, *The Shaking of the Foundations: Family and Society*, New York: Routledge, 1988; and Ferdinand Mount, *The Subversive Family: An Alternative History of Love and Marriage*, London: Jonathan Cape, 1982. A historical account of the development of Conservative opposition to feminism is presented in Michele A. Pujol, *Feminism and Anti-feminism in Early Economic Thought*, Brookfield, VT: Edward Elgar, 1992. For a critique of the Conservative perspective, see Pamela Johnston Conover and Virginia Gray, *Feminism and the New Right: Conflict Over the American Family*, New York: Praeger, 1983.

18. Conservative critiques of feminism can be found in Nicholas Davidson, *The Failure of Feminism*, Buffalo, NY: Prometheus, 1988; Steven Goldberg, *The Inevitability of Patriarchy*, New York: William Morrow, 1973; Midge Decter, *The New Chastity and Other Arguments against Women's Liberation*, New York: Coward, McGann and Geoghegan, 1972; Arianna Stassinopoulos, *The Female Woman*, New York: Random House, 1973; and Elaine Storkey, *What's Right with Feminism*, Grand Rapids, MI: William B. Erdman, 1985.

19. George Gilder, *Wealth and Poverty*, New York: Basic Books, 1981.

20. Phyllis Schlafly, *The Power of the Positive Woman*, New Rochelle, NY: Arlington House, 1977.

21. Betty Friedan, *The Feminine Mystique*, New York: W. W. Norton, 1963. See also Betty Friedan, *The Second Stage*, New York: Summit Books, 1981.

22. Carol Gilligan, *In A Different Voice: Psychological Theory and Women's Development*, Cambridge, MA: Harvard University Press, 1982.

23. Nancy Chodorow, *The Reproduction of Mothering: Psychoanalysis and the Sociology of Gender*, Berkeley: University of California Press, 1978.

24. See Barbara Bergman, "The Economics of Women's Liberation," *Challenge* 21, no. 5, (May/June 1973): 11–17.

25. See Isabel V. Sawhill, "The Economics of Discrimination Against Women: Some New Findings," *Journal of Human Resources* 8, no. 3 (Summer 1973): 383–96.

26. See Elaine Johansen, *Comparable Worth: The Myth and the Movement*, Boulder, CO: Westview Press, 1984; Rita Mae Kelly and Jane Bayes, eds., *Comparable Worth, Pay Equity, and Public Policy*, Westport, CT: Greenwood, 1988; Steven L. Wilborn, *A Comparable Worth Primer*, Lexington, MA: Lexington Books, 1986; Henry J. Aaron and Cameron M. Lougy, *The Comparable Worth Controversy*, Washington, DC: Brookings Institution, 1986; Joan Acker, *Doing Comparable Worth*, Philadelphia: Temple University Press, 1989; Linda M. Blum, *Between Feminism and Labor: The Significance of the Comparable Worth Movement*, Berkeley: University of California Press, 1991; Paula England, *Comparable Worth: Theories and Evidence*, New York: Aldine de Gruyter, 1992; and Sara M. Evans and Barbara J. Nelson, *Wage Justice: Comparable Worth and The Paradox of Technical Reform*, Chicago, University of Chicago Press, 1989.

ADDITIONAL READING

Amott, Teresa. *Caught in the Crisis: Women and the U.S. Economy Today.* New York: Monthly Review Press, 1993.

Bartlett, Robin L., ed. *Introducing Race and Gender into Economics.* New York: Routledge, 1997.

Beneria, Lourdes, and Shelly Feldman, eds. *Unequal Burden: Economic Crises, Persistent Poverty, and Women's Work.* Boulder, CO: Westview Press, 1992.

Birch, Bettina. *The Endless Day: The Political Economy of Women and Work.* New York: Harcourt Brace Jovanovich, 1982.

Blau, Francine D., and Mariann A. Ferber. *The Economics of Women, Men, and Work*, 2nd ed. Englewood Cliffs, NJ: Prentice-Hall, 1992.

Burggraf, Shirley P. *The Feminine Economy and Economic Man.* Reading, MA: Addison-Wesley, 1997.

Chavetz, Janet Saltzman. *Gender Equity.* Newbury Park, CA: Sage, 1990.

Clayton, Susan D., and Faye J. Crosby. *Justice, Gender and Affirmative Action.* Ann Arbor: University of Michigan Press, 1992.

Donovan, Josephine. *Feminist Theory: The Intellectual Tradition of American Feminism.* New York: Frederick Ungar, 1985.

Eisenstein, Zillah. *The Color of Gender: Reimaging Democracy.* Berkeley: University of California Press, 1994.

Farganis, Sondra. *Situating Feminism: From Thought to Action.* Thousand Oaks, CA: Sage, 1994.

Ferber, Marianne A., and Julie A. Nelson, eds. *Beyond Economic Man: Feminist Theory and Economics.* Chicago: University of Chicago Press, 1993.

Ferguson, Kathy. *Self, Society and Womankind.* Westport, CT: Greenwood Press, 1980.

Folbre, Nancy. *Who Pays for the Kids? Gender and the Structures of Constraint.* London: Routledge, 1994.

Fuchs, Victor. *Women's Quest for Economic Equality.* Cambridge, MA: Harvard University Press, 1988.

Goldin, Claudia. *Understanding the Gender Gap: An Economic History of American Women.* New York: Oxford University Press, 1990.

Gordon, Linda, ed. *Women, the State and Welfare.* Madison: University of Wisconsin Press, 1990.

Humphries, Jane, ed. *Gender and Economics.* Brookfield, VT: Edward Elgar, 1995.

Jacobson, Joyce P. *The Economics of Gender.* Cambridge, MA: Blackwell, 1994.

Jenson, Jane, Elizabeth Hagen, and Ceallaigh Reddy. *Feminization of the Labor Force: Paradoxes and Promises.* New York: Oxford University Press, 1988.

Kelly, Rita Mae. *The Gendered Economy.* Newbury Park, CA: Sage Publications, 1991.

Martin, Susan Ehrlich. *Doing Justice, Doing Gender.* Thousand Oaks, CA: Sage Publications, 1996.

Mutari, Ellen, Heather Boushey, and William Fraher IV. *Gender and Political Economy: Incorporating Diversity into Theory and Policy.* Armonk, NY: M. E. Sharpe, 1997.

Nelson, Julie A. *Feminism, Objectivity and Economics.* New York: Routledge, 1996.

Okin, Susan Mollar. *Justice, Gender, and the Family.* New York: Basic Books, 1989.

Peattie, Lisa, and Martin Rein. *Women's Claims: A Study in Political Economy.* New York: Oxford University Press, 1983.

Peterson, Janice, and Doug Brown, eds. *The Economic Status of Women under Capitalism: Institutional Economics and Feminist Theory.* Brookfield, VT: Edward Elgar, 1994.

Phillips, Ann, ed. *Feminism and Equality.* New York: New York University Press, 1987.

Chapter 13

Education and Culture

Culture encompasses the values, beliefs, customs, and habits that guide human behavior. In the past, traditional divisions within social science relegated the study of culture to sociology and anthropology, placing it outside the proper scope of political economy. Furthermore, because education functions, in part, to transmit culture over time, political economists also devoted little attention to education. With the exceptions of school financing and the effect of education on individual earnings, economists were content to leave the study of society's educational process to other disciplines.

The problem with this restricted vision is that if education and culture play major roles in affecting human behavior, and if the economy and government are shaped by individual choices, then political economy is left with incomplete understandings of the very institutions it claims to analyze. Recognizing this deficiency, some political economists have recently sought to include education and culture within their purview to illuminate the effects of both institutions on the market and government. To examine these issues, the viewpoints of each of the four ideological perspectives are presented in this chapter.

THE CLASSICAL LIBERAL PERSPECTIVE

The Purpose of Education

Classical Liberals designate two groups as incapable of making rational decisions—children and "lunatics." So despite their commitment to free choice, Classical Liberals favor subjecting children to the authority and wisdom of parents and teachers. For this reason, education represents an anomaly within the Classical Liberal vision, functioning as an enclave of authority in a society otherwise committed to individual autonomy and choice.

Classical Liberals favor compulsory, publicly funded education as an exception to the general rule of laissez-faire. The explanation for this apparent violation of liberty lies in nineteenth-century history. As voting rights were extended to propertyless workers, Classical Liberals feared political turmoil unless all citizens were taught literacy, citizenship skills, and respect for society's basic values and institutions. Public schools and compulsory education were deemed to be the best solutions to the problems raised by democracy.

More recently, Classical Liberals have added an economic rationale for compulsory public education, claiming that private education based on ability to pay is undesirable because parents may not make rational choices about their children's education. This problem arises because parents would decide how much education to purchase, while the benefits accrue primarily to their children. To the extent that parents do not identify their children's interests with their own, they are likely to underinvest in education. This underinvestment leads to dynamic inefficiency in the economy because education is a form of capital accumulation yielding future benefits due to the increased productivity of the next generation. From this perspective, publicly funded education is justified by the resulting increases in earnings and tax revenue attributable to higher productivity. A final economic argument for public education rests on the role of schools in improving labor market efficiency by sorting and matching students with the types of training and employment for which they are best suited.[1]

Public education also offers an ideological attraction to Classical Liberals. The highly unequal distributions of income and wealth generated by free markets would appear to jeopardize the equal opportunity of all individuals to compete fairly because family background often plays a significant role in determining the educational and employment prospects of children. Classical Liberals view public education as the least intrusive method by which government can attempt to reconcile equal opportunity with unequal income and wealth. By providing the same basic education to all children, public schools promote equality of opportunity without any significant governmental redistribution of wealth or interference with labor markets. Government simply sets the stage for open and fair competition in which individual abilities and preferences determine future economic success. The Classical Liberal goal is a meritocratic society in which individual status and income are linked to productivity rather than race, ethnicity, sex, or religion.

Educational Policy

Despite their advocacy of public funding for education, Classical Liberals fear that government's monopoly over education results in high costs, low quality, and indifference toward students and parents. As long as public education remains monopolistic, administrators and teachers know that their salaries are not directly affected by the quality of education they offer or by the number of students they instruct. Conversely, if a student fails or drops out, the system does not penalize the school or teachers. As a result, teachers and administrators have little incentive to provide high-quality education. Public schools may become mere youth repositories where unmotivated teachers stand guard over bored pupils.

Classical Liberals also claim that problems with public schools reveal a serious flaw in democracy, which, because it is based on majority rule, may be insensitive to local or minority interests. In formulating educational policy, democratic governments typically rely on bureaucracy to formulate a standardized curriculum, but this centralized process limits the discretion of local school officials, teachers, and parents. As a result, innovation is stifled and local cultures and values may be suppressed.

In response to these concerns, Classical Liberals propose a method for providing education to all children without direct government involvement. Government can issue to parents a "voucher" redeemable for education at any public or private school.[2] This proposal eliminates government's monopoly over the provision of education while retaining public financing. Schools compete with one another, and those schools attracting more students receive additional government funding. The best teachers will presumably move to successful schools because, by attracting more students and redeeming more vouchers, these schools can offer higher salaries. Conversely, students will shun schools offering inferior education, and teachers' salaries at those schools will fall accordingly. To ensure maintenance of educational standards, vouchers should be redeemable only at accredited schools.

By removing the financial barrier to attending private schools, the voucher system permits families of all income levels to choose a school providing an education best suited to their children's needs. Vouchers eliminate the penalty currently imposed on parents who choose private education for their children and are forced to "pay twice"—once for taxes to fund public schools and again for tuition at a private school. If public schools face a large-scale exodus of students, administrators and teachers will presumably reassess their methods and offer a more effective program. Those schools unable to improve will gradually disappear as their best teachers are hired by successful schools, while ineffective teachers are forced to seek employment in other occupations. To summarize, the voucher system promotes competition, diversity of educational opportunities, efficiency, accountability, freedom of choice, and improved learning for students. All this is accomplished by bringing the competitive forces of the market into a previously monopolized industry.

Classical Liberals also advocate merit pay for teachers. By linking salaries with teaching effectiveness, they hope to elicit greater effort and to attract and retain the most skilled teachers. At the university level, Classical Liberals propose full and equal access to educational loans at market rates of interest. They are concerned that outright financial aid to students will distort the market and result in too many students pursuing too much education. Economic efficiency dictates that students should pursue additional education only if the present value of additional lifetime earnings exceeds the opportunity cost of education in terms of tuition, related expenses, and the value of foregone income or leisure. The best method to determine who should pursue higher education is to let individual students decide whether their education will result in sufficient additional earnings to justify its cost.

A Classical Liberal curriculum would be organized around the skills and knowledge deemed essential to good citizenship and productive employment. Because Classical Liberals reject the medieval notion of knowledge as certain, unchanging, and absolute, they demand that education be practical and useful. The natural and social sciences, history, mathematics, and communication skills are given priority, with less emphasis placed on training in literature and the arts. Horace Mann (1796–1859), who led the effort to reform U.S. education along Classical Liberal lines, sought to create a common curriculum for all students that emphasized practical knowledge and citizenship skills.

The Role of Culture

According to Classical Liberals, individuals should be free to pursue their interests and express their preferences so long as they do not harm others.[3] All social practices and cultural expressions arising from this free interplay of individual interests are considered equally legitimate. This libertarian stance is justified by the claim that humans possess no objective norms of "good taste" by which culture can be judged. What is vulgar to one person may be sublime to another. Humans have diverse tastes, and a free society will tolerate all behaviors and expressions that are harmless to others.

The difficulty posed by the Classical Liberal position lies with the definition of "harm." While merely offending another person's values or tastes is usually not considered harmful, such "victimless" practices as drug abuse, prostitution, and sale of pornography raise the question of whether harm occurs indirectly in the form of highway fatalities, increases in sexual assaults, and exploitation of powerless persons. To the extent that Classical Liberals acknowledge this indirect harm, they may support laws prohibiting such practices. However, they are philosophically predisposed to "live and let live," assuming that individuals are sufficiently rational to judge the benefits or harms of any particular act. For example, Milton Friedman and former Secretary of State George Schultz, both former members of the University of Chicago economics department, support the legalization of all drugs. They claim that by restricting supply, prohibition drives up prices and creates huge profits that attract organized crime and contribute to random violence affecting innocent citizens.

As a corollary of the principle of tolerance, Classical Liberals express little concern about either adverse or beneficial effects of culture on the individual. This indifference stems from a view of the individual as an autonomous entity whose preferences are internally generated and therefore independent of the social environment. As rational actors, individuals will gravitate toward those cultural forms meeting their preferences and self-interest and will shun cultural expressions perceived as irrelevant or detrimental. In short, people are the best judges of their own interests and therefore should be in control of their actions.

THE RADICAL PERSPECTIVE

The Purpose of Education

Radicals believe that capitalism periodically experiences difficulty in sustaining the conditions necessary for its survival. The conflict between classes poses the continual threat of a breakdown in the cooperation and consensus required for social stability. One possible strategy for the capitalist class would be to exert repressive force, but this would be costly and probably ineffective. A preferred method is to mask and defuse the tensions emanating from class conflict by structuring social institutions and ideology that promote the appearance of harmony. Schools, according to Radicals, are essential to maintaining and legitimizing the dominance of the capitalist class.

Although schools seem to provide children with equal opportunities to develop and display their abilities, Radicals argue that schools in capitalist societies actually perpetuate hierarchy by shaping students' personalities and consciousness in a manner that facilitates social control by one class over another. The two leading Radical economists in the field of education, Samuel Bowles and Herbert Gintis, challenge the Classical Liberal view of education as a vehicle by which talented and hardworking individuals rise to success regardless of their class background.[4] They claim that class background is the primary determinant of individual success, and that schools function to transmit the class status of families from one generation to the next. To support this argument, Bowles and Gintis offer statistical evidence that despite a significant trend toward equalization in years of schooling across social classes, there has been little change in income inequality during the past half-century.

The key to the intergenerational transmission of status is the close correspondence between the social relations of the classroom and the social relations of adult worksites. Like workers, most students are trained to follow rules, to accept authority, and to compete for external rewards such as grades. However, not all students are trained to respond passively to authority. The hierarchical division of labor also requires managerial and creative talent. To meet this need, public schools typically offer different forms of education to children depending on their class background and expected adult status. This strategy is feasible because the residential segregation of families according to income means that particular schools tend to reflect the economic status of the neighborhood in which they are located. Moreover, the financing of schools by the property tax assures that affluent areas are able to offer superior education. Finally, schools may use tracking to provide different educations for students with different demonstrated abilities, but these abilities are often linked to family status.

Radicals claim that schools in more affluent neighborhoods tend to stress creativity, independence, achievement, and leadership skills, while schools in lower-income neighborhoods emphasize conformity and obedience. This dual educational system reflects parental expectations for their children. White-collar parents have learned from their own work experience that leadership skills and innovative thinking are rewarded, whereas blue-collar parents know that their jobs often require perseverance at routine tasks and submission to authority. Parents typically want schools to instill in their children those personality traits that the parents have found to be important in their own lives.

Besides its role in legitimizing and reproducing hierarchy, education is functional to capitalism in several other ways. According to Radicals, a major force behind public education has always been the demands of employers that children be schooled in both the basic skills required for productive labor and an ideology supportive of capitalism. Employers want publicly financed education because the mobility of labor makes it unprofitable for individual firms to teach basic skills to workers who are then free to move to other firms. With public education, taxpayers bear the expense of much of the training of the labor force, thereby reducing business costs.

Radicals also emphasize the potentially disruptive and even revolutionary aspects of education. Schools may fail to reproduce the hierarchical social relations of capitalism because capitalism itself is internally contradictory. As a system of production, capitalism is characterized by hierarchy and dominance as owners exercise power over workers for the purpose of extracting profits. However, as a system of exchange, capitalism emphasizes the freedom of autonomous individuals to seek mutually beneficial transactions. The presence of both authoritarian and egalitarian social relations in capitalist society places conflicting demands on education to perform both a liberating/developmental function and a repressive/integrative function.

In preparing for the realm of exchange, children are taught respect for the rights and opinions of others and a sense of fair play. However, these messages conflict with training given in preparation for the realm of production, which teaches most children to submit to hierarchy and authority. To the extent that schools teach doctrines of equality and fairness, they undermine the reproduction of hierarchical social relations. Therefore, according to Radicals, education ultimately creates obstacles to capital accumulation by introducing students to ethical ideals and forms of human interaction inconsistent with capitalist production.[5]

Educational Policy

In proposing educational reforms, Radicals acknowledge that the functional role of education in sustaining hierarchy and privilege assures that most schools in a capitalist society are likely to remain repressive. Yet some Radicals are sufficiently optimistic to formulate proposals for educational reform within capitalist society. Education can be liberating if the authority of teachers and curricular requirements are minimized to enable students to pursue their own interests, to learn at their own pace, and to integrate their formal knowledge with practical aspects of their lives.[6] In "free schools," there is little emphasis on grades, routine memorization, or rule-following. Rather, students acquire a variety of skills, enabling them to function effectively in many different social roles as they apply their intelligence and creativity to learning, recreation, and work.

Radicals favor reliance on work-study programs to break down barriers between knowing and doing. The physical and creative abilities of students should be stimulated at the same time that intellectual capacities are expanding. Education should also be a life-long process; adults should continue to learn and develop, with paid work being merely one outlet for their productive energies.

Specific Radical proposals include Ivan Illich's idea of "deschooling society."[7] Illich believes that experts, including educators, scientists, bureaucrats, and administrators, have gained such total control over social institutions that most people no longer think or act independently. Freedom has been suppressed by the very institutions that were designed to create a rational and stable society. The only solution is to deschool society by challenging and ultimately overturning the authority of experts and the institutions they represent. Illich would have children work at least two hours a day, with access to factories, offices, laboratories, and farms where they could learn through experience. For Illich, even free schools are too institutionalized because they continue to rely on teachers and classrooms and therefore provide only the illusion of freedom. Genuine education cannot be confined to a particular building with particular authority figures, but rather must occur within the entire community as an ongoing process for children and adults alike.

Not all Radicals share Illich's antiauthoritarian perspective.[8] Some have criticized free schools and "schools without walls" as being both naively utopian and counterproductive in the sense that they produce not liberation, but maladjustment and confusion as students must inevitably face the demands of adult work in a capitalist society. Indeed, the free-school movement and other experiments with unstructured education peaked during the 1970s and have been under considerable attack since then. Radicals debate among themselves whether the collapse of free schools was due to inherent internal problems or to the fact that students were simply ill-prepared for life in capitalist society.

Surprisingly, some Radicals join with Classical Liberals in supporting educational vouchers.[9] In fact, the campaign for school choice has historical roots in the Black Power movement and alternative schools of the late 1960s. Radicals argue that if children from low-income families received larger vouchers and financial support for transportation, their mobility would challenge the monopoly of public schools, giving parents and local communities greater control over the content of education. Moreover, if parents and students chose to remain in local schools, the larger vouchers could fund excellent schools in low-income neighborhoods and the preservation of community values. From this perspective, educational vouchers could redistribute opportunity and future earnings in favor of children from low-income families and promote cultural diversity.

The Role of Culture

Much of the Radical analysis of culture stems not from Marx, who focused primarily on the process of capitalist production and exchange, but from a group of German theorists known collectively as "the Frankfurt school." The leading members of this group were Max Horkheimer (1895–1973), Theodor Adorno (1903–1969), and Walter Benjamin (1892–1940). Their works form the heart of much of the Radical interpretation of capitalist culture.[10] Radicals regard culture in a capitalist society as a component of society's "superstructure" and thus subject to contradictory forces emanating from the accumulation of capital. On one hand, culture perpetuates the hierarchy of capitalist production by offering shared traditions and values that reduce social conflict. On the other hand, culture contains disruptive forces that challenge capital accumulation and contribute to social disorder.

As an integrative and functional component of capitalism, culture encourages passive consumption and nondisruptive forms of emotional gratification. Radicals claim that the banal and insipid quality of much of television, film, literature, and music serves to pacify people and distract their attention from personal discontents. Culture is largely under corporate control and, like other commodities, is marketed through the use of advertising. Corporate dominance prevents culture from serving its legitimate purpose of creatively expressing the emotions and ideas emanating from the personal lives of citizens.

However, culture is not solely an instrument of the capitalist class. Culture also expresses working-class interests and aspirations. Capitalists may attempt to make these aspirations compatible with the status quo, but their success will never be complete. Television may be the modern "opiate of the masses," but writers and producers need high viewer ratings and therefore will cater to working-class interests, as demonstrated by the frequent portrayal of bosses as either tyrants or buffoons. A variety of popular films have sympathetically featured union organizers, factory workers, secretaries, or students as victims of incompetent or malevolent authority figures.

The capitalist class may condone subversive forms of culture that encourage people to assuage their frustration in theaters or living rooms rather than venting it at the workplace or the voting booth. Radical theorist Herbert Marcuse argued that capitalism's tolerance for nearly all forms of cultural expression is actually a form of repression because it focuses attention on apparent freedom of choice while disguising the powerlessness experienced by most people in work and politics.[11] Capitalism's enormous capability for absorbing and diverting anticapitalist sentiment is, however, not without limits. Beyond a certain point, subversive culture can jeopardize the stability of capitalist society. For example, songs calling for revolution and the murder of policemen are sold by the corporate giants of the entertainment industry, a practice confirming Lenin's claim that capitalists will sell the rope with which they are to be hanged.

If capitalist culture is so repressive, then why is it so popular in the United States and around the world? Radicals explain this paradox by appealing to Marx's concept of alienation. Alienated individuals do not desire to express themselves through society's institutions. Art, music, and literature become simply commodities manufactured by distant producers and consumed in a quest for status or emotional gratification. Culture is "reified"; it appears to exist independently of citizens who do not conceive of themselves as producers of culture, but only as consumers who choose whether to buy a particular cultural product. Radicals label this process "commodification"; culture is reduced to marketable objects sold at a profit.[12]

Citizens accept a reified culture because of "false consciousness." In the absence of genuine community and meaningful work, people no longer seek to realize their potential as emotional, intellectual, and physical beings. Instead, driven by alienation and unmet needs, they opt for a life of instant gratification through consumption and entertainment. Having adopted this orientation toward life, they view traditional social structures such as family and community as obstacles to the free pursuit of pleasure, resulting in further disintegration of social bonds. In the absence of fulfilling social relations, consumption is indeed the quickest and most direct form of pleasure. Ironically, this distorted form of human existence conforms with the Classical Liberal portrayal of humans as autonomous, pleasure-seeking creatures. Radicals, however, claim that such behavior is not intrinsic to human nature, but is instead a response to the isolation and alienation fostered by capitalism.

One of the hallmarks of capitalist culture is mass conformity, which Radicals attribute to the need by alienated individuals to latch onto any cultural expression seeming to offer solidarity with fellow citizens. At the same time, fads and changing fashion prevail as individuals try to escape the traditional hierarchy to establish a sense of autonomy and dignity. Ultimately, though, the novelty and variety offered by capitalism may prove dangerous to the system. Because profitability thrives on sales generated by continual changes in culture, people are conditioned to believe that the past and present are never satisfactory; novelty becomes desired purely for its own sake. In such a world, the very notion of a stable personal identity is undermined as continuity and tradition slip from memory. On this point, Radicals agree with Conservatives; a focus on consumptive pleasure makes satisfaction elusive. In the unceasing pursuit of pleasure, individuals neglect social bonds and institutions essential to genuine fulfillment. Moreover, pleasure-seeking individuals will resent the demands for routinization and delayed gratification placed on them by bosses and other authority figures. Capitalism therefore creates a culture that ultimately creates frustration with and even rejection of the system.[13]

Radicals affirm the worth of cultural expression that contributes to subverting capitalist hierarchy and control. Conversely, cultural expressions are condemned if they seem to reinforce and perpetuate the privileges of dominant groups. Some Radicals have proposed that free speech should be restricted to prevent language deemed offensive to subordinate groups such as women and minorities.[14] Several colleges and universities in the United States have established sanctions against "hate speech," including possible expulsion. Radicals have disrupted public lectures by speakers with whom they disagree and have defaced art that is deemed oppressive. All of these actions can be explained by the Radical belief in objective standards of value that supersede individual preferences. Like Conservatives, some Radicals feel morally obliged to defend the good and suppress the bad. In practice, however, many Radicals, particularly in the United States, are so wedded to the liberal principle of tolerance that they condemn cultural repression of any sort.

THE CONSERVATIVE PERSPECTIVE

The Purpose of Education

The Conservative view of education is shaped by a belief that most humans have limited capacity for autonomously exercising reason and virtue. In the absence of tutelage and guidance by authority figures, the flaws of human nature may overwhelm mankind's potential for constructing a stable and orderly society. Education represents the transmission from generation to generation of the wisdom and cultural achievements of the past. Formal education shapes youth into responsible adults prepared to fill appropriate positions in the social hierarchy.

Education should impart knowledge of the timeless, objective values guiding society toward virtue and order. Knowledge consists not simply of skills and techniques, but encompasses morality, discipline, and culture. By teaching traditional values such as patriotism, obedience, respect, honor, reverence, civility, and loyalty, education serves to preserve and legitimize the hierarchical society.

The Conservative view of education has been clearly articulated by Allan Bloom (1930–1992), who was a Classics professor at the University of Chicago. Bloom claimed that higher education in the United States was badly damaged by egalitarian attacks on authority launched during the 1960s.[15] As students demanded and were granted greater participation in university governance and design of the curriculum, they proceeded to dismantle the hierarchical structure that made genuine education possible. Universities seeking to become more "relevant" abandoned the study of the classic texts forming the core of Western civilization. The knowledge held by professors was devalued as the classroom became an open forum in which everybody's opinion was considered equally valid. Bloom extended his criticism to include many professors, themselves products of the 1960s, who encourage students to rely on their own opinions and judgment. As a Conservative, Bloom believed that young minds must be carefully cultivated by skilled educators. Students should have little input in determining the nature of their education because they have not yet attained sufficient wisdom to discern truth and virtue. Therefore, the university curriculum and classroom must remain under the control of scholars and professional administrators.

Educational Policy

The Conservative educational agenda focuses on three issues. First, true knowledge and absolute values must be protected from the corrosive effects of individualism, materialism, and the liberal notion that pleasure is the sole criterion of value. Second, the unequal capacities of students for learning must be fully acknowledged in structuring the educational system. Third, control over education must be placed securely in the hands of proper authorities. We shall examine each of these principles and the specific policies flowing from them.

1. *Preservation of knowledge.* Conservatives favor a curriculum built around the literary classics, including the works of Plato, Aristotle, Cicero, Homer, Augustine, and Aquinas. These thinkers presented enduring truths, and Conservatives view them as essential to education. This commitment to the classics has been labeled "perennialism" because it insists on the unchanging nature of true knowledge and opposes curricular reforms reflecting the latest trends.

Conservatives also emphasize instruction in values as integral to the education process. Students need moral education because their untutored instincts are not reliable guides to virtue. Conservatives worry that independent, critical thinking will lead to ethical relativism. To facilitate the teaching of values, many Conservatives favor prayer and at least the option for religious instruction in public schools. In addition, they support tax credits for tuition paid to private schools where religious education can be integrated into the entire curriculum. Some Conservatives, particularly those with a fundamentalist religious orientation, have sought to control the selection of textbooks in the public schools, claiming that most current texts present the viewpoints of only ethical relativism and secular humanism.

Conservatives also want schools to promote patriotism, claiming that loyalty to one's country is essential to political unity and strength. Conservatives typically oppose bilingual education in public schools, fearing that a multi-language society would lack the cohesiveness and common purpose required for both internal order and defense against external threats.

2. *Unequal education.* Conservatives seek to provide different forms of education for students of different ability.[16] They rely on IQ tests as measures of innate intelligence and advocate assigning young students to educational tracks designed to prepare them for adult roles which best suit them. University education for future elites should consist of rigorous intellectual training in the arts, humanities, and sciences, while deemphasizing vocational training and extracurricular activities. Less capable students should be placed in tracks leading to professional training in business or industry, while the least able students should be steered toward vocational training and manual skills.

Equal education not only fails to provide the best students with challenges suited to their abilities, but overwhelms and discourages less able students. According to Allan Bloom, the commitment to equal educational opportunity has ruined the modern university. He claimed that only a select number of students are suited to a genuinely scholarly education. By accepting most high-school graduates, universities have transformed themselves from institutions of higher learning into glorified vocational schools preparing students to earn a living. The ideal of the university as a community of scholars in search of truth has been sacrificed to the egalitarianism of mass society.

Even more objectionable than equal education is compensatory education, with its attempt to assist underperforming students. Compensatory education is regarded by Conservatives as a waste of resources because some students are incapable of learning more than routine vocational skills. Moreover, both equal and compensatory education result in too many people graduating with degrees and correspondingly high expectations for future earnings. The jobs requiring a college or university education are limited, and students will become frustrated and resentful as they discover that their newly acquired knowledge and skills are not in demand by society. Large numbers of underemployed persons threaten social stability. To prevent excess education, Conservatives would limit the number of students accepted by universities and increase enrollments in vocational and technical schools.

3. *Hierarchical control.* Control over the structure and content of education at the university level should rest in the hands of professional administrators and senior faculty members because only they have the knowledge and experience to educate the elite students who will lead the next generation. The issue of control over public grade schools, on the other hand, poses a dilemma for Conservatives. With religion and family life in decline, elementary schools play a significant role in socializing children. Yet Conservatives are uncertain who should determine the curriculum and teaching methods of public schools. Teachers and administrators, often unionized, may exhibit the same narrow materialism that infects society as a whole. Government control results in a mandated curriculum that is insensitive to the cultural heritages of communities. Parents and community leaders lack the professional expertise to design curriculum. Therefore, Conservatives appeal to administrators to work with teachers and parents to assure that schools reinforce the moral instruction received by children at home.

The Role of Culture

Conservatives view culture as essential to creating social bonds between individuals and preserving the wisdom and achievements of past generations. Culture is based on shared meanings and therefore provides a context within which individuals develop their values and interests. Without culture, individuals are isolated and removed from the sustenance of society's collective wisdom and traditions. While schools represent one mechanism for transmitting culture, the process of acculturation is lifelong and occurs in all dimensions of existence. Any society's culture will reflect the diversity of groups, but a healthy society should manifest sufficient cultural homogeneity to generate the allegiance of all citizens.

Conservatives have always expressed deep concern about the quality of culture. In the nineteenth century, critics such as Matthew Arnold (1822–1888) and Henry Adams (1838–1918) decried the banality and crassness of modern culture. In the twentieth century, Conservative writers have developed the notion of "mass society" to describe the conformity and mindlessness in modern life. Spanish writer José Ortega y Gasset (1883–1955) attributed the rise of totalitarianism to the loss of meaning and personal identity that accompanies mass society,[17] while T. S. Eliot (1888–1965) referred to modern culture as "the waste land."

Conservatives view culture as the visible expression of the state of mind of the populace. A crude and decadent culture reveals more than just bad taste; if culture is in decline, then people's inner lives are in turmoil and the economic and political strength of the nation is jeopardized. Nineteenth-century Conservatives blamed both democracy and capitalism for the deterioration of culture. Democracy places crude and ignorant citizens on an equal footing with wise and virtuous citizens. Similarly, capitalists, with their insatiable drive for profits, inundate society with commodities and "inflame the appetites" of consumers through advertising. Both democracy and capitalism lower the quality of culture by permitting the values and tastes of the masses to establish norms for society.

Most Conservatives in the twentieth century, after witnessing both communism and fascism, have suppressed their qualms about democracy and capitalism. Instead, they now join with Classical Liberals in blaming government for many social problems.[18] With political power concentrated at the national level, government programs to provide welfare and security have the unintended consequence of undermining the intermediate institutions of family, church, and neighborhood. As the authority of these institutions declines, isolated individuals face the intimidating task of fashioning personal identities and meaningful lives in a world offering few guidelines. Conservatives attribute obscene language, sexual promiscuity, and drug use to the anxiety arising from individuals who cannot find purpose in life.

Conservatives look to the classics of literature, music, and art as standards of eternal excellence. Culture should express shared values and traditions, but when society is increasingly fragmented and devoid of standards, culture instead reflects anger, resentment, cynicism, skepticism, and a sense of the absurd. Lacking traditional forms to honor and develop, artists, musicians, and writers produce abstract, surreal, dissonant, and shocking expressions. Conservatives criticize rock music for its pulsing beat and suggestive lyrics designed to arouse the passions and alleviate the anxieties of alienated youth. Conservatives regard movies as inferior to books because the picture overwhelms the mind and suppresses creative thought.

The drug culture pervading modern societies is, for Conservatives, the logical culmination of liberal utilitarianism in which pleasure is the sole criterion of value. Conservatives regard many contemporary intellectuals, writers, musicians, and artists as members of a "new class" or "adversary culture" consciously seeking to subvert traditional society. Sociologist Daniel Bell describes an inherent conflict between a capitalist economy and the culture it spawns. The market demands workers who are self-disciplined, stable, and able to delay gratification, while capitalist culture emphasizes hedonism and rejection of authority.[19]

Conservatives are not simply cultural snobs who insist on the superiority of classical music, art, and literature. They acknowledge the value of popular culture if it emerges from traditional communities. For example, folk music is treated as a genuine expression of rural culture. Quilting and woodworking are legitimate art forms. Storytelling is crucial in transmitting society's cultural heritage. Conservatives ultimately judge culture by its contribution to maintaining social order; both high culture and popular culture are valuable if they serve that task.

THE MODERN LIBERAL PERSPECTIVE

The Purpose of Education

The Modern Liberal view of education owes much to the American philosopher John Dewey.[20] Dewey's educational philosophy, which came to be known as "progressivism," expresses confidence in the natural intelligence of each child. What concerned Dewey was the evolution of society from the rugged individualism of the nineteenth century to the corporate capitalism of the twentieth century. He sought to prepare children for this new society by cultivating the capacity for critical and independent thinking. This emphasis on critical thinking reflects the Modern Liberal skepticism toward the notion of eternal truths and values. Students are encouraged to objectively assess the facts of any situation and the potential consequences of any action.

Extending Dewey's ideas, Modern Liberals currently emphasize the following three purposes of education:

1. *Personal development.* Modern Liberals believe that education can awaken talents and aspirations that might otherwise remain dormant. Education encourages individuals to reach beyond their current interests and social status. In addition, education teaches respect for other persons and cultures, fostering social relationships based on mutual esteem and reciprocity. Personal development has been the focus of three developmental psychologists: Jean Piaget (1896–1980), Lawrence Kohlberg (1927–1987), and Abraham Maslow.[21] Their research led them to conclude that humans

pass through stages of moral and emotional maturation, potentially culminating in a full and stimulating life that Maslow called "self-actualization." However, this evolution can be blocked by poverty, ignorance, and repression. Therefore, equal access to high-quality education is considered essential to enabling both children and adults to achieve their full potential.

2. *Social equality.* Modern Liberals assume that human abilities are more nearly equal than the present distribution of income would suggest. If every child is given equal education and equal access to jobs, then ability and effort, rather than family background, will become the key determinants of economic success, and the distribution of income should become more equal over time. Education can help break the generational cycle that causes many children to remain bound by the impoverished circumstances of their parents. Public education also fosters a sense of shared culture among children from widely divergent family backgrounds, thereby contributing to the cohesiveness and stability of society.

3. *Efficiency.* Using the metaphor of America as "the great melting pot," Modern Liberals view education as the flame that keeps the broth bubbling so talented individuals can rise to make their greatest possible contribution to society. Modern Liberals do not perceive any conflict between this economic role of education and its developmental and egalitarian roles because more highly developed citizens and greater social equality are deemed to promote economic growth. Public funding for education promotes efficiency by correcting a positive externality. In addition to the benefits conferred on individual students in the form of higher future earnings and enhanced personal development, education creates benefits for society as a whole such as lower crime rates, less need for welfare, increased tax revenue from the higher earnings of educated citizens, and improved democracy due to widespread literacy and involvement in public affairs. Because the social benefits of education exceed the private benefits, the market will fail to produce an efficient amount of education. Government funding is essential to achieve economic efficiency.

Educational Policy

Modern Liberals want education to be both compulsory and compensatory. Because formal education is only one component of children's socialization, providing identical educational experiences to children from vastly different family backgrounds will not secure genuine equality of opportunity. The purpose of compensatory education is to provide instruction designed to overcome the disadvantages facing children from deprived backgrounds. These disadvantages may include not only low academic skills, poor health, and inadequate nutrition, but also lack of motivation due to the absence of role models or prospects for success. Modern Liberals stress that education cannot bear the entire burden of ending poverty, and therefore compensatory programs must be accompanied by a broader attack on the causes of poverty.

With regard to curriculum, Modern Liberals emphasize the importance of extracurricular activities such as student government and clubs. They also propose that democratic ideals can be taught by democratizing the classroom, giving students a greater voice in determining the structure and content of their curriculum. Modern Liberals were instrumental in introducing the "open classroom," allowing students to pursue their strongest interests and to advance at their own pace.[22]

Modern Liberals are strongly committed to the public school system and have been critical of proposals for either a voucher system or tuition tax credits.[23] Both policies, they claim, would encourage increased racial segregation of students, reduce governmental control over the quality of education, and violate the Constitution's separation of church and state. If the government offered to pay for education at any school selected by the family, children of affluent families would flock to suburban and private schools. In contrast, children of low-income families, unable to afford transportation, would be forced to attend their neighborhood school, and inner-city public schools would become the repositories for those unable to afford an alternative. The best teachers would relocate to the more attractive suburban and private schools, and the goal of equal education for all students would be sacrificed.

Modern Liberals also typically oppose merit pay for teachers, citing the difficulty in measuring teacher productivity. The use of any particular criterion of productivity, such as student scores on standardized tests, might cause teachers to orient their efforts toward preparing students to perform well on the tests while neglecting other areas of instruction. Merit pay is also accused of having a divisive and demoralizing effect on teachers.

Many Modern Liberals have favored busing students to achieve racial balance throughout a school district.[24] They argue that neighborhood schools cannot possibly provide equal education for all students when neighborhoods are segregated and funding for public schools is dependent on property taxes. Also, integrated classrooms expose children to members of other racial groups, diminishing the likelihood of racial conflict in the future.

Conservative and Classical Liberal critics of busing claim that children cannot learn effectively in a hostile and foreign environment and that busing often contributes to increased residential segregation as some parents choose to move rather than comply with the new regulations. They also claim busing causes an exodus of students from public schools as parents enroll their children in private schools. Another concern is the disruption of neighborhood unity as children are relocated to distant schools. Modern Liberals acknowledge these concerns and have recently softened their advo-

cacy of busing. Even if busing achieves the goal of providing equal education for all children, it provides no ultimate solution to poverty and
inequality. Formal education is only one component of the socialization
process leading to acquisition of skills and personality traits essential to
future success. The family and the neighborhood often overshadow the
impact of the school on children's maturation.

Modern Liberals have recently begun to share with Conservatives the
desire to introduce moral education into the public school curriculum.
However, while Conservatives typically link moral education with religious
education, Modern Liberals simply want to provide students with a forum
in which they can clarify their own values through discussion of hypothetical situations. This process of "values clarification" assumes that with
increased awareness developed through classroom discussions, children
will learn the Modern Liberal values of tolerance, sensitivity, honesty, and
respect for the rights of others.

In the face of growing concern about the United States' ability to compete in global markets, Modern Liberals are shifting their focus from the
developmental and egalitarian roles of education to the economic role of
education in enhancing efficiency and growth. To assess the efficiency of
education, Modern Liberal economists rely on cost–benefit analysis to
compare the financial benefits of education with other forms of public
investment. They also compare the financial payback to dollars spent on
different departments within universities and on university education as
opposed to vocational education. Faced with intensifying competition from
abroad, government should reallocate public funding to those forms of
education yielding the largest gains in future productivity. However, some
Modern Liberals warn that by focusing on measurable changes in individual earnings and GDP, cost–benefit analysis of education can easily overlook the intangible benefits of social equality, political stability, and
personal growth.

The Role of Culture

Ambiguity in the Modern Liberal approach to culture can be traced
back to John Stuart Mill. On one hand, Mill expressed the Classical Liberal
view that cultural diversity is a sign of a vital society and that individuals
are obliged to tolerate even the most distasteful of cultural expressions so
long as nobody is harmed. On the other hand, Mill appealed to the notion
of a hierarchy of pleasures based on "the permanent interests of man as a
progressive being." According to Mill, although humans are capable of
experiencing pleasure from a variety of sources, some pleasures are
demeaning and ultimately destructive while other pleasures are uplifting
and contribute to the full realization of human potential. Mill claimed that

superior pleasures are to be found in intellectual and artistic expression that exercise the uniquely human capacities for reason and creativity.

Today, Modern Liberals waver between Mill's tolerance of nearly all forms of cultural expression and his tendency to establish moral criteria for distinguishing between "good" and "bad" culture. The instinct for tolerance prevails unless some aspect of culture is viewed as potentially dangerous to the well-being of uninvolved persons. Modern Liberals defend tolerance for two reasons. First, they value the experience of choosing among diverse alternatives. Cultural alternatives enable individuals to develop their capacity for judgment and choice. Even if the choice is unwise, the experience of choosing is educational and enhances personal growth. Only through experimentation with alternatives will individuals come to know and value that which is good. Second, Modern Liberals are concerned that efforts to regulate culture may lead to abuse of government power. In the absence of a social consensus on criteria of good culture, the government would inevitably repress some valuable forms of expression. While Mill's notion of a hierarchy of pleasures gives Modern Liberalism a rough criterion on which censorship might be based, the commitment to tolerance leaves most Modern Liberals with little inclination to suppress any form of culture.

However, Modern Liberals believe that government does play an important role in promoting culture. Government should financially support a variety of artistic forms ranging from public television to symphony orchestras. This support is justified by the positive externalities associated with exposing a broad spectrum of the population to the arts. Public funding for the arts contributes to the personal development of most citizens. Modern Liberals also believe that government can indirectly affect culture by remedying the unemployment and poverty that contribute to frustration and nihilism in modern societies. When economic security is out of reach, people vent their anger in various distorted forms of cultural expression. Rather than attacking the symptoms of alienation through repression or censorship, Modern Liberals propose economic revitalization as the only viable solution to cultural decline.

NOTES

1. The Classical Liberal perspective on the economic benefits of education is presented in Fritz Machlup, *Education and Economic Growth*, Lincoln: University of Nebraska Press, 1970; Richard B. McKenzie, *The Political Economy of the Educational Process*, Boston: Martinus Nijhoff, 1979; and Martin O'Donoghue, *Economic Dimensions in Education*, Chicago: Aldine-Atherton, 1971.

2. The original proposal for school choice appeared in Milton Friedman, "The Role of Government in Education," *in* Robert A. Solo, ed., *Economics and the Public Interest*, New Brunswick, NJ: Rutgers University Press, 1955. For additional

details on proposed educational voucher systems and school choice, see Myron Lieberman, *Privatization and Educational Choice*, New York: St. Martin's, 1989; David R. Henderson, *The Case For School Choice*, Stanford: Hoover Institution, 1993; and John E. Chubb and Terry M. Moe, *Politics, Markets and America's Schools*, Washington, DC: The Brookings Institution, 1990.

3. See John Stuart Mill, *On Liberty*, New York: Liberal Arts Press, 1956.

4. Samuel Bowles and Herbert Gintis, *Schooling in Capitalist America*, New York: Basic Books, 1976.

5. Radical interpretations and critiques of education are presented in Martin Carnoy, *Schooling in a Corporate Society*, New York: McKay, 1972; Madan Sarup, *Marxism and Education*, Boston: Routledge & Kegan Paul, 1978; and Kenneth A. Strike, *Liberal Justice and the Marxist Critique of Education*, New York: Routledge, 1989.

6. See Allen Graubard, *Free the Children: Radical Reforms and the Free School Movement*, New York: Random House, 1972. See also Peter Marin, Vincent Stanley, and Kathryn Marin, *The Limits of Schooling*, Englewood Cliffs, NJ: Prentice-Hall, 1975.

7. Ivan Illich, *Deschooling Society*, New York: Harper & Row, 1971.

8. See Robin Barrow, *Radical Education: A Critique of Freeschooling and Deschooling*, New York: John Wiley & Sons, 1978. See also Herbert Gintis, "Towards a Political Economy of Education: A Radical Critique of Ivan Illich's Deschooling Society," *Harvard Educational Review* 42, no. 1 (February 1972): 70–96.

9. See Herbert Gintis, "The Political Economy of School Choice," *Teachers College Record*, 96, no. 3 (Spring 1995): 492–511; and Christopher Jencks, *Rethinking Social Policy: Race, Poverty and the Underclass*, Cambridge, MA: Harvard University Press, 1992.

10. Important works on culture by members of the Frankfurt school include Walter Benjamin, *Illumination*, New York: Harcourt Brace & World, 1968; Theodor W. Adorno, *Aesthetic Theory*, Boston: Routledge & Kegan Paul, 1983; and Herbert Marcuse, *The Aesthetic Dimension: Toward a Critique of Marxist Aesthetics*, Boston: Beacon Press, 1978. For a collection of writings from the Frankfurt school, see Andrew Arato and Eixe Gebhardt, eds., *The Essential Frankfurt School Reader*, New York: Continuum, 1982. For a review and assessment of the Frankfurt school, see Ronald J. Schindler, *The Frankfurt School Critique of Capitalist Culture*, Aldershot: Avebury Publishers, 1996.

11. Herbert Marcuse, *One Dimensional Man*, Boston: Beacon Press, 1964. See also Robert Paul Wolff, Barrington Moore, Jr., and Herbert Marcuse, *A Critique of Pure Tolerance*, Boston: Beacon Press, 1969.

12. For greater detail on the Radical analysis of culture, see Cary Nelson and Lawrence Grossberg, eds., *Marxism and the Interpretation of Culture*, Urbana, IL: University of Illinois Press, 1988. See also Louis Dupré, *Marx's Social Critique of Culture*, New Haven, CT: Yale University Press, 1983.

13. This argument is elaborated in Christopher Lasch, *The Culture of Narcissism: American Life in an Age of Diminishing Expectations*, New York: W. W. Norton, 1978.

14. See Catherine MacKinnon, *Only Words*, Cambridge, MA: Harvard University Press, 1993, and Cass R. Sunstein, *Democracy and the Problem of Free Speech*, New York: The Free Press, 1993.

15. Allan Bloom, *The Closing of the American Mind*, New York: Simon & Schuster, 1987.

16. See Arthur R. Jensen, *Educability and Group Difference*, New York: Harper & Row, 1973.

17. José Ortega y Gasset, *The Revolt of the Masses* [1932], Notre Dame, IN: University of Notre Dame Press, 1985. For more recent analyses of the phenomenon of mass society, see William Kornhauser, *The Politics of Mass Society*, Glencoe, IL: Free Press, 1959; Salvador Giner, *Mass Society*, London: Martin Robertson, 1976; and Peter Davison, Rolf Meyersohn, and Edward Shils, eds., *Culture and Mass Culture*, Teaneck, NJ: Somerset House, 1978.

18. Conservative critiques of contemporary U.S. culture are presented in William J. Bennett, *The De-valuing of America: The Fight for Our Culture and Our Children*, New York: Summit Books, 1992; Robert Hughes, *The Culture of Complaint: The Fraying of America*, New York: Oxford University Press, 1993; and Robert H. Bork, *Slouching Towards Gomorrah: Modern Liberalism and American Decline*, New York: Regan Books, 1996.

19. See Daniel Bell, *The Cultural Contradictions of Capitalism*, rev. ed., New York: Basic Books, 1996. Bell's thesis that capitalism tends to generate opposition from intellectuals was also an important theme in Joseph Schumpeter, *Capitalism, Socialism, and Democracy*, New York: Harper & Row, 1950.

20. For an assessment of Dewey's impact on American education, see Reginald D. Archambault, ed., *Dewey on Education*, New York: Random House, 1966.

21. Jean Piaget, *The Essential Piaget*, edited by H. E. Gruber and J. J. Voneche, New York: Basic Books, 1977; Lawrence Kohlberg, *Essays on Moral Development*, San Francisco: Harper & Row, 1981; and Abraham H. Maslow, *Motivation and Personality*, 3rd ed., New York: Harper & Row, 1987.

22. See Terrence E. Deal and Robert R. Nolan, eds., *Alternative Schools: Ideologies, Realities, Guidelines*, Chicago: Nelson-Hall, 1978.

23. The Modern Liberal opposition to school choice is presented in Bruce Fuller and Richard F. Elmore, *Who Chooses? Who Loses?*, New York: Teachers College Press, 1995; Peter W. Cookson, Jr., *School Choice: The Struggle for the Soul of American Education*, New Haven: Yale University Press, 1994; Jeffrey R. Henig, *Rethinking School Choice: Limits of the Market Metaphor*, Princeton: Princeton University Press, 1994; and Kevin B. Smith and Kenneth J. Meier, *The Case Against School Choice: Politics, Markets, and Fools*, Armonk, NY: M. E. Sharpe, 1995.

24. On the issue of school busing, see Gary Orfield, *Must We Bus?: Segregated Schools and National Policy*, Washington, DC: Brookings Institution, 1978; Emmett H. Buell, Jr., *School Desegregation and Defended Neighborhoods*, Lexington, MA: Lexington Books, 1982; and Edward J. Hayes, *Busing and Desegregation: The Real Truth*, Springfield, IL: Charles C. Thomas, 1981.

ADDITIONAL READING

Aronowitz, Stanley, and Henry Giroux. *Education Under Siege: The Conservative, Liberal and Radical Debate over Schooling*. South Hadley, MA: Bergin & Garvey, 1985.

Bernier, Norman R., and Jack E. Williams. *Beyond Beliefs: Ideological Foundations of American Education*. Englewood Cliffs, NJ: Prentice-Hall, 1973.

Carnoy, Martin, and Henry M. Levin. *Schooling and Work in the Democratic State.* Stanford, CA: Stanford University Press, 1985.

DeYoung, Alan J. *Economics and American Education.* New York: Longman, 1989.

Edel, Abraham. *Interpreting Education: Science, Ideology, and Value.* New Brunswick, NJ: Transaction Books, 1985.

Feinberg, Walter, and Jonas S. Soltis. *School and Society.* New York: Teachers College Press, 1985.

Freire, Paulo. *The Politics of Education.* South Hadley, MA: Bergin & Garvey, 1985.

Giroux, Henry. *Ideology, Culture, and the Process of Schooling.* Philadelphia: Temple University Press, 1981.

Gutman, Amy. *Democratic Education.* Princeton, NJ: Princeton University Press, 1987.

Karabel, Jerome, and A. H. Halsey, eds. *Power and Ideology in Education.* New York: Oxford University Press, 1977.

Katz, Michael B. *Reconstructing American Education.* Cambridge, MA: Harvard University Press, 1987.

Persell, Caroline H. *Education and Inequality.* New York: Free Press, 1977.

Shaw, G. K., ed. *Economics, Culture and Education.* Brookfield, VT: Edward Elgar, 1991.

Sowell, Thomas. *Inside American Education.* New York: Free Press, 1993.

Spring, Joel. *American Education: An Introduction to Social and Political Aspects.* New York: Longman, 1982.

Webb, Rodman B. *Schooling and Society,* 2nd ed. New York: Macmillan, 1989.

Chapter 14

Pollution and the Environment

Economists have traditionally viewed the environment as a source of raw materials and energy for producing goods and services. Kenneth Boulding (1910–1993) coined the term "cowboy economy" to describe a situation of limitless resources and unproblematic waste disposal. However, the modern economy, according to Boulding, is more aptly viewed as "spaceship earth" whose resources are finite and whose waste must be managed. In light of past and potential damages posed by global warming, acid rain, deforestation, destruction of the ozone layer, desertification, air and water pollution, and the accumulation of toxins in the food chain, environmental issues have come to the forefront of political economy.

As the global economy expands, pressures on the environment will increase. Popular support for protecting nature will be partially determined by the extent to which citizens perceive environmental policies as threats to their jobs and income. However, ignoring pollution and resource depletion might pose even more serious consequences for standards of living. In 1972, a group of scientists at the Massachusetts Institute of Technology ran computer simulations using variables such as population, food supply, industrial production, pollution, and resource depletion.[1] They concluded that economic growth will be halted by a series of ecological catastrophes during the twenty-first century unless current trends are changed dramatically. This dire prediction has been challenged by other researchers, and political economists continue to debate the causes of and appropriate policies for coping with environmental degradation.

THE CLASSICAL LIBERAL PERSPECTIVE

Causes of Pollution

Classical Liberalism reflects the Enlightenment view of nature as physical matter to be controlled and manipulated for the purpose of serving human interests. Despite the scarcity of natural resources, Classical Liberals remain optimistic that standards of living can continue to rise if the market economy is left essentially free of government regulation. When pollution and resource depletion occur, Classical Liberals focus on the following causes:

1. *Consumer preferences.* Consumers are free to choose between goods kept less expensive by the free disposal of waste into the environment or more expensive goods whose higher costs result from pollution controls. When pollution occurs, consumers are partly to blame because corporations must cater to consumer preferences. Consumers vote with their dollars, and if they value lower-priced goods more than a clean environment, then pollution will occur. Classical Liberals defend the right of individuals to place a higher value on consumption of material goods than on environmental purity.

2. *Public property.* In the absence of government regulation, the lack of well-defined private property rights over certain domains such as rivers, lakes, and atmosphere permits them to be used as free disposal sites. Firms seeking to minimize costs will take advantage of the opportunity to dispose of wastes by dumping them into the public domain. However, if disposal sites were privately owned, polluters would have to negotiate with owners over payment for damages. Classical Liberal economist Ronald Coase has argued that, under certain restrictive assumptions, the bargaining between polluters and owners of disposal sites would result in an "optimal level of pollution" regardless of who owns the site.[2] For example, if government granted ownership of a lake to a polluting corporation, then local citizens who want clean water could "bribe" the corporation to reduce its use of the lake for waste disposal. Citizens would pay to reduce pollution until the cost of further pollution abatement is equal to the additional benefits of a cleaner lake. Any further reduction in pollution would be economically inefficient because the additional cost would exceed the additional benefit. Alternatively, a citizen could be given the property right over this same lake

and the corporation could "bribe" the citizen for the use of the lake as a waste disposal site. Again, Coase argues, the optimal level of pollution would result since the corporation would pay for the right to pollute until the cost to the firm of additional pollution equals the additional benefit. Thus, the assignment of private property rights over common resources creates a market for the right to pollute, resulting in an efficient allocation of resources without the need for environmental regulations.

3. *Transaction costs.* Transaction costs are the expenses associated with gathering information, specifying contracts, and enforcing the terms of contracts. In the case of pollution, citizens willing to pay for a cleaner environment may incur substantial transaction costs in organizing themselves to collectively express their preferences and to monitor compliance with any contract between citizens and corporations to reduce pollution. Coase acknowledges that in the presence of transaction costs, markets fail to establish an optimal level of pollution.

4. *Public goods.* Most Classical Liberals acknowledge that some natural resources are public goods with significant external benefits. For example, a river flows downstream, dispersing the benefits of clean water among large numbers of people. To the extent that natural resources remain in the public domain, Classical Liberals usually concede that pollution and resource depletion are partially attributable to the market's inability to achieve efficiency when public goods are present.

5. *Lack of development.* Classical Liberals reject the argument that economic growth is the principal cause of pollution. Instead, they claim that environmental destruction is more closely linked to lack of economic development. Less developed countries (LDCs) typically have higher rates of population growth, less education, less efficient use of raw materials, fewer synthetic materials, and lower technical capacity for protecting the environment. The pressures of subsistence living often force citizens in LDCs to engage in practices harmful to the environment. Development should therefore reduce pollution, and the free market is the optimal institution for achieving prosperity.

Environmental Policy

Classical Liberals defend the ability of the market to protect the environment.[3] If a particular resource is being depleted, its price will rise not only in response to its current scarcity, but also to the anticipated higher costs of extracting that resource in the future. This "scarcity pricing" causes consumers and producers to search for cheaper alternatives and provides strong incentives to develop new technology for producing synthetic substitutes, locating additional reserves of resources, and using resources more efficiently. Classical Liberals find much of the public concern over resource depletion unwarranted because market incentives will spur entrepreneurs to respond to the problem.

The market's propensity to foster rising standards of living provides both the resources and incentives to respond to pollution. Consumers with high levels of disposable income have met their basic needs and are therefore more likely to value a clean environment. Corporations cater to these consumer preferences, making environmentalism a profitable corporate strategy. In a robust economy, high corporate profits will permit the adoption of cleaner, more efficient technologies. Finally, the historical record demonstrates that rising standards of living are associated with lower birth rates, thus reducing population pressures.

Recently, Classical Liberals have argued that private entrepreneurs can solve many environmental problems by negotiating contracts between polluters and those affected by pollution. The benefits of reducing pollution often exceed the direct costs, but the presence of transaction costs discourage citizens from organizing to take action. However, an "enviro-capitalist" can act as a middle man, locating opportunities in which the willingness to pay for reduced pollution is sufficient to compensate firms for switching to cleaner production methods and to provide a profit margin for the enviro-capitalist. Obviously, this strategy is most feasible when dealing with a few large organizations. For example, an association of commercial salmon fishers might pay a lumber mill to reduce effluents harmful to fish.[4]

Another environmental strategy favored by Classical Liberals is the sale of public property to private owners. Once a resource is privately owned, individuals have a strong interest in protecting the value of their property and will either charge for its use or rely on the legal system to sue for damages. However, the conversion of public property to private ownership cannot entirely resolve the problem of pollution due to transaction costs and the "public good" aspect of rivers, lakes, oceans, and the atmosphere.

If government regulations are imposed, Classical Liberals insist that government should simply alter the financial incentives facing private decisionmakers rather than dictate standards. By relying on incentives, individuals remain free to act in their own self-interest, with government merely changing the signals to which they respond. For example, government could impose "effluent fees" as a tax on waste disposal to reflect the cost imposed on society. The fee enables businesses to freely choose what method of waste disposal and what level of production would maximize their profits.

Classical Liberals also favor auctioning licenses to pollute as an alternative to existing environmental regulations. Once the government has determined an acceptable level of pollution, a limited number of licenses would be sold to the highest bidders. Those firms for whom pollution is most costly to control would presumably bid highest for licenses, forcing other firms to eliminate lower-cost forms of pollution. After licenses are auctioned by government, firms could resell them, creating a market for the right to pollute and enabling firms to adjust waste disposal in response to changing patterns of technology, resource availability, or consumer demand.

Classical Liberals have generally been critical of the notion of market failures, but they buttress their faith in the market by appealing to the concept of "government failure."[5] Bureaucrats, they claim, lack detailed information with which to formulate efficient policies. Moreover, without personal responsibility for the consequences of their policies, bureaucrats lack incentive to formulate optimal policies. Bureaucrats favor uniform pollution standards applicable to all industries because of the relative ease of enforcement. However, economic efficiency is more likely to be attained through different standards for different industries, a goal that can be achieved by auctioning pollution licenses.

Government is also susceptible to manipulation by special-interest groups. The firms most affected by environmental regulations have a strong incentive to influence legislation. Certain industries may even be successful in capturing control of a governmental agency by contributing money, lobbying, and promising lucrative jobs to bureaucrats when they leave government. Classical Liberals believe that government is unduly influenced by the lobbying of environmental organizations such as the Sierra Club and the Wilderness Society. Environmentalists, they claim, seek to increase donations to their organizations by frightening the public with exaggerated warnings of impending environmental disaster. When environmental lists are successful in using government to coerce everyone to comply with their values, they cripple the economy with restrictive regulations and create a disadvantage in international competition.

Another Classical Liberal strategy for reducing environmental regulations is based on the Fifth Amendment to the U.S. Constitution, which states: "nor shall private property be taken for public use without just compensation." This "takings clause" is interpreted to mean that any government regulation reducing the value or profitability of property requires payment to the owner for financial losses.[6] Classical Liberals assume that forcing government to pay for losses imposed by every regulation would result in considerably less regulation. For example, zoning laws, laws to protect endangered species, and laws to protect wetlands would become prohibitively expensive for government. A related strategy for minimizing regulation comes from Classical Liberals calling for "wise use" of the environment.[7] They propose that every regulation should be examined to determine whether its benefits exceed its costs. For example, the government would have to demonstrate that the dollar value of a protected species exceeds the dollar value of the resources that could be removed from a natural area. Any regulation failing to meet this standard would be scrapped.

In response to those who defend government intervention on the grounds that future generations have a right to adequate resources and a sound environment, Classical Liberals claim that individual liberty and free markets are the best guarantee of well-being for our descendants. The incentives and efficiency associated with free markets propel economic growth, which facilitates efforts to protect and restore the environment. Not only will firms be hard-pressed to deal with ecological problems when the economy is stagnant, but public support for environmental protection will weaken as citizens focus on defending their current levels of consumption. Ultimately, then, there is no trade-off between economic growth and environmental integrity.[8]

THE RADICAL PERSPECTIVE

Causes of Pollution

Two distinct forms of Radical environmentalism can be identified—"traditional Marxism" and "deep ecology." Traditional Marxists uphold the Enlightenment view of mankind's domination over nature. Marx himself explicitly supported continued economic expansion and the use of large-scale technology to gain mastery over the environment. Considering that Marx was writing in the middle of the nineteenth century, it would be surprising if he had not supported the notion of unlimited material progress.

According to traditional Marxists, the cause of pollution is not economic growth, but rather capitalism.[9] The structure of capitalism encourages waste and abuse of resources in the following ways:

1. *Private property*. Marxists believe that private property narrows human consciousness so that people focus only on matters directly affecting them. Rather than expressing social concern for the environment in which all humans must live, individuals in capitalist society concentrate on protecting their personal property while remaining indifferent to the circumstances of others.

2. *Competition*. When firms operate in a market, competitive pressures force them to adopt the lowest cost production method, including the free disposal of waste into the environment. A particular capitalist might value clean air and water, but reducing pollution raises the firm's costs and erodes its competitive position in the market. If the owner persists, the firm, lacking financial resources for research and innovation, could eventually be driven out of business. Competition also manifests itself in the drive to create new desires for commodities through advertising. Production to meet these "false needs" contributes to deterioration of the

environment. Another corporate strategy for increasing sales and profits is planned obsolescence, which forces consumers to replace products more frequently and contributes to waste in the system.

3. *Class conflict.* Capitalism generates conflicting interests between capitalists and workers. In the twentieth century, the preferred solution to class conflict has been "buying off" worker discontent with higher wages to maintain comfortable standards of living. However, this strategy places immense burdens on the ecosystem to sustain high levels of production. Households are filled with frivolous commodities as workers seek to relieve their job frustrations through the pride of ownership.

4. *Lack of political control.* Because capitalism fails to recognize preferences that can't be satisfied with profitable commodities, individuals remain powerless to express their desire for a clean environment in the market. Even when voters elect representatives who favor pollution control, politicians lack sufficient power to regulate large corporations effectively. Moreover, because capitalism is oriented toward providing commodities for private consumption, individuals learn to structure their lives around consumption as the primary source of satisfaction. Conversely, because capitalism is ill-suited to provide public goods such as a clean environment and mass-transit systems, individuals tend to devalue those goods and rely instead on commodities such as water purifiers and automobiles.

5. *Alienation.* Capitalism erodes traditional communities and social bonds, leaving individuals isolated and insecure. One response to this insecurity is the quest for ownership and consumption of commodities. When the worth of individuals is measured by their wealth and consumption, people seeking recognition and social acceptance will engage in "conspicuous consumption." However, this consumption does not reflect genuine human needs because it is a response to the powerlessness created by capitalism. In a better society, the pleasures associated with consumption would rank below fulfillment gained through developing and exercising the human capacities for creativity, artistic expression, athleticism, appreciation of nature, and cultivation of friendships. Furthermore, since these expressive activities require relatively few natural resources, they need not impose significant burdens on the environment.

The term "deep ecology" was coined in 1972 by Swedish ecologist Arne Naess, who views nature as a highly complex system of diverse yet interdependent species and elements.[10] Nature seeks equilibrium between all subsystems, so any disruptive force in one area may have extensive and unforeseen repercussions. Deep ecologists seek to grasp the functioning of nature as a holistic system. They blame environmental degradation on the anthropocentric worldview inherited from the Enlightenment, which treats nature as matter to be manipulated for human purposes. Instead, deep ecologists offer an ecocentric view of nature; humans are simply one part of a larger ecosystem. From this perspective, humans have a duty to treat nature with reverence and humility, valuing environmental protection above additional consumption.

The implications of deep ecology can be startling. If all species are equally privileged, then animals, insects, and perhaps plants possess the same rights as humans. Painful experiments on animals to test products for human use are condemned, and some deep ecologists even include soil and water as components of a "moral community."[11] The world is a living organism, and all species and elements are simply parts of the whole. British ecologist James Lovelock has named this organism "Gaia" and suggests that any species damaging the environment will be eliminated by Gaia just as the human body destroys a virus.[12]

The defining difference between deep ecologists and liberal environmentalists is their conflicting rationale for protecting nature. Environmentalists believe in preserving nature to make the world more useful for humans. For example, humans can enjoy wilderness experiences, recreation, inspiration, healthful food, clean water and air, and continued availability of resources. Deep ecologists, in contrast, claim that the spiritual value of the planet demands protection of the environment even if doing so requires sacrifices. Deep ecologists might restrict human access to wilderness areas to preserve the integrity of the environment. As an extreme example, some deep ecologists have suggested that protecting nature from overpopulation might require "harvesting" humans to reduce pressures on the environment. From this perspective, AIDS might be viewed as one of Gaia's harvesting methods.

To illustrate the weaknesses of Marxism, deep ecologists point to the poor environmental record of countries purportedly based on Marxist ideals. Marxists respond by noting that socialism has typically existed in less developed countries where rapid industrialization was essential to win political support for new revolutionary governments. Marxists assume that socialism can be more sensitive to the environment once a moderate level of affluence and political stability has been achieved.

Deep ecologists make the more serious charge that capitalism and communism are simply two alternative strategies for achieving the same Enlightenment goal of mastery over nature and expanding levels of consumption. Some Marxists refute this claim, arguing that Marx's view of reality was "relational" in the sense that objects and people are shaped and defined by their relation to other objects or persons.[13] Marx, they claim, did not view nature as inert matter to be manipulated by humans, but instead viewed man and nature as dialectically intertwined. If this interpretation is valid, the effort to completely dominate nature was not condoned by Marx and is another symptom of alienation in capitalist society.

Environmental Policy

Marxists and deep ecologists agree on the necessity of transcending capitalism, but they offer quite different visions of socialism. Marxists emphasize socialism's capacity for attainment of collective goals through conscious planning of society's production. Unlike the market, a planned economy can recognize noncommodity preferences such as the desire for a clean environment and can translate such preferences into social policy. With production guided by planning rather than profitability, resources can be allocated to protect and restore the environment. By acting collectively, citizens empower themselves to shape their society and their natural environment in a manner most conducive to human development.

Collective planning could even extend across national borders. To protect countries from the pressures of global competition, international governing bodies might establish environmental standards to which all countries must comply. Within each country, environmentalism might require stringent controls on population growth, immigration, and consumption. Even at the local level, the imperative of environmental integrity may lead governments to narrowly circumscribe the freedom of individuals to use and dispose of resources.[14]

Deep ecologists, in contrast, reject a planned economy. They envision a future society consisting of decentralized and largely self-sufficient communities free from the coercive pressures of market and state. These communities might consist of fewer than ten thousand people with communal ownership of land and highly egalitarian and participatory social relations. The experience of living in close-knit communities should steer individuals away from material consumption, reducing pressures on the natural environment.[15]

Marxists point to the similarities between deep ecology and Conservatism. Both are wary of technology and materialism, both appeal to objective values found in a spiritualized nature, and both envision a society composed of relatively autonomous communities. Marxists are concerned that small communities offer limited opportunities for personal development, mobility, and creativity. Moreover, independent communities might compete against one another, reviving the market conditions of capitalism. Finally, Marxists criticize deep ecologists for diverting attention from the class origins of environmental problems. According to Marxists, the ultimate cause of pollution and exhaustion of resources is not the flawed values of mankind but the division of society into owning and working classes, with individual survival dependent on producing commodities for sale in the market.

Marxists and deep ecologists also disagree on short-term strategies and policies. Marxists may hesitate to join forces with environmental groups seeking to limit economic expansion without challenging the class structure of capitalism. According to Marxists, capitalism without growth is not feasible. Capitalism must expand to maintain profitability and avoid collapse. Any effort to halt growth within the context of capitalism would, at best, freeze the current class structure and condemn the working class to permanent deprivation. Deep ecologists, on the other hand, are more likely to participate in political action and civil disobedience to protect the environment by curtailing industrialization and growth. They view the groups coalescing around environmental issues as embryonic communities planting seeds of the future society.

All Radicals support government regulations and standards to protect the environment. However, they simultaneously express skepticism about the viability of such regulations when private corporations wield more power than the governmental agencies responsible for enforcing public policy. Corporations can resist regulation by exerting influence over government agencies, the media, and employees. To challenge corporate power, some Radicals call for a comprehensive national policy to make environmental quality rather than private profit the guiding force in determining the use of natural resources.[16] A key component of such a policy would be the nationalization of energy companies to reduce the conflict between private profitability and the public interest.

THE CONSERVATIVE PERSPECTIVE

Causes of Pollution

Conservatives believe that nature provides guidance in structuring human institutions and relations. In nature, they observe diversity of species, survival of the fittest, the importance of instinct, hierarchical relations between members of the same species, and homeostasis—movement toward stable equilibria. Because humans are ultimately part of nature, these same characteristics are appropriate for society. Conservatives reject "secular humanism," which makes human purposes the only source of values. Instead, they locate objective values in nature and view humans as morally obliged to conform to these values.

The degradation of nature is linked to the Enlightenment claim that human reason is capable of restructuring nature to serve human interests. This "arrogance of humanism" leads to a disregard for the sanctity of nature and the proper place of humans within it. Conservatives prefer the notion of "stewardship," which places on humans a custodial responsibility to live in harmony with nature and to minimize abuse.

Conservatives view environmental problems as symptoms of more funda-mental disorders associated with seeking social perfection and mastery over nature.[17] Modern society generates excessive pollution for several reasons:

1. *Decline of hierarchy*. Industrialization and modernization have undermined traditional authority and hierarchy. When hierarchy is no longer accepted as natural, humans become dissatisfied with their status, leading to widespread envy and resentment. The homogeneity of "mass society" strips individuals of their identities, compelling them to compete for status and recognition in the quest for self-esteem. However, self-esteem will remain elusive because the standards by which people assess individ-ual worth rise along with their wealth and status. Moreover, the apparent pleasure associated with consumption derives more from the easing of anx-ieties created by modern society than from any practical usefulness of com-modities. Ultimately, the environment is being sacrificed to high levels of consumption that bring little joy and would be considered frivolous in a well-ordered society.[18]

2. *Decline of community*. As individualism and materialism erode tra-ditional communities, humans become isolated pleasure-seekers, losing all capacities for satisfaction except accumulating commodities and gratifying sensual appetites. The values of cooperation, loyalty, and friendship are replaced by the pursuit of material gain and individual achievement. The modern obsession with ownership and consumption of material goods rep-resents a futile effort to compensate for loss of community by possessing as much of the world as possible.

3. *Capitalism*. Although Conservatives defend private property and a market economy, they fear that competitive individualism contributes to pollution. Profit-seeking corporations create new needs and persuade con-sumers that happiness comes primarily from consumption. This strategy may be good for business but conflicts with the finite capacity of nature to sustain human life. Modern societies are destroying the environment while consumers and capitalists remain absorbed in their private pursuit of plea-sure and profit.

4. *Democracy*. Conservatives argue that democracy has degenerated into struggles among interest groups, each pursuing its own narrow goals with little consideration for the public good. Policies to protect the envi-ronment are likely to entail some sacrifices in consumption, yet in a society oriented toward immediate gratification of desires, politicians calling for sacrifice endanger their careers. Therefore, democratic governments con-sistently favor economic expansion over environmental protection.

Environmental Policy

In their optimistic moments, Conservatives retain a confidence that nature, including the human species, is ultimately a self-equilibrating system. As environmental degradation worsens, humans can be expected to respond with new values upholding moral obligations to adopt ecologically sound lifestyles. Signs of such a shift are apparent in growing public support for recycling and controls on pollution.

However, Conservatives are typically less optimistic and, when proposing environmental policy, they often favor political rather than economic solutions to pollution.[19] Economic analysis focuses only on the preferences of individuals and ignores society's interest in a healthy and sustainable natural environment. Only the political process can promote such collective interests. In advocating political action, Conservatives envision a different type of politics from that of today's Western democracies.[20] To remedy the short-comings of democracy, political authority must be insulated from the pressures of interest groups, and positions of leadership must be filled by charismatic, wise, and virtuous persons. With political authority in the hands of natural leaders, government can maintain a well-ordered society, reducing alienation, the desire for consumption, and pressures on the environment.

In addition to reforming the political process, Conservatives would protect the environment by improving the socialization process shaping individual desires. This strategy requires that schools, families, neighborhoods, and churches be restored to their former roles as sources of authority and meaning in the lives of individuals. A strong sense of identity and belonging will dramatically reduce consumption and status-seeking. The pursuit of wealth will become less important than the self-esteem and respect of others gained through performing duties attached to one's social role. With artificial desires for consumption suppressed, humans can reestablish a harmonious relationship with nature.

THE MODERN LIBERAL PERSPECTIVE

Causes of Pollution

Modern Liberals claim that rapid growth cannot continue indefinitely. The first law of thermodynamics states that matter can be neither created nor destroyed. Therefore, unless humans colonize other planets or make dramatic strides in the development of solar or nuclear technology, limits to growth are inevitable. Moreover, the effectiveness of recycling is called into question by the second law of thermodynamics, which states that rearranging matter continually reduces its potential for further use.[21] Modern Liberals conclude that the long-term viability of human society hinges on protecting the environment, and they attribute pollution and resource depletion to the following failures of the market to allocate resources in a socially optimal manner:

1. *Externalities*. The market generates "externalities" in which the price of a commodity does not reflect all the costs and benefits associated with its production and consumption. Cambridge economists of the late nineteenth century originally developed the analysis of externalities. Henry Sidgwick (1838–1900) noted that the market would fail to provide lighthouses because a private owner would be unable to charge ships for the benefits provided by the lighthouse. A. C. Pigou generalized Sidgwick's observation to conclude that markets are inefficient whenever externalities are present. In the case of pollution, the use of air and water as waste disposal sites creates negative externalities because polluting firms are not charged and affected citizens are not compensated.

2. *Absence of future generations*. Future generations cannot express their interests, and therefore the market consistently devalues future consumption in favor of present consumption. If people of the future could hypothetically bid on environmental preservation, the price of using nature as a source of raw materials and as a disposal site would presumably rise substantially. In other words, the absence of future persons leads to overutilization of resources by the current generation.[22]

3. *Lack of information*. Consumers may not be aware of environmental damage caused by consumption of certain products or disposal of waste. Without full information concerning all costs and benefits, consumers cannot make rational decisions. Even when consumers do recognize potential damage associated with certain activities, they may be ignorant of thresholds beyond which pollution triggers unanticipated and irreversible ecological reactions. Also, when government lacks full information about the harmful effects of industrial waste, legal restrictions on pollution may be inadequate.

4. *Lack of competition*. If the market contains oligopolistic and monopolistic elements, resources are diverted from their optimal use. For example, corporations may devote resources to lobby against environmental regulations rather than install pollution-control devices. Resources may be used for advertising to create an image that corporations are environmentally sensitive. Moreover, monopoly power can contribute to unemployment and inflation, causing workers to focus on immediate survival rather than environmental protection. Finally, limited competition places less pressure on corporations to respond to the demands of citizens seeking environmentally sound products.

5. *Transaction costs*. If citizens negotiate directly with corporations to reduce pollution, they face huge costs of organizing themselves, gathering information, preparing legal documents, and monitoring compliance. Rather than endure this lengthy and expensive process, most people will simply move to a less polluted area. Economist Albert O. Hirschman suggests that individuals facing an undesirable situation have the options of "exit, voice, or loyalty."[23] In the case of pollution, exiting means moving away from environmental damage, and the market encourages exiting by fostering a society in which community bonds are weak, political action is difficult, and mobility is highly valued. The ease of exiting makes people less likely to voice their grievances by becoming politically involved or to remain loyal to their neighborhood, town, or region.

Environmental Policy

Modern Liberals view government intervention as essential to environmental protection. Citizens and firms have little incentive to make private sacrifices to control pollution because their individual actions have little impact on the level of pollution. Government, on the other hand, can gather information, assess damages, collect fees or taxes, and monitor the enforcement of environmental laws more effectively and efficiently than private citizens.

A. C. Pigou, who originally developed the theory of externalities, proposed that government should respond to pollution with a tax on the polluting firm equal to the value of environmental damage. The revenue from the tax could be used to repair the damage or to subsidize citizens harmed by pollution. However, this strategy assumes that government has perfect information about the extent of pollution and its source. In the real world of imperfect information, Modern Liberals advocate the establishment of legal pollution standards to which industry must conform. They worry that proposals to sell pollution licenses will give pollution the same ethical status as hunting, fishing, driving a car, or getting married. To maintain a strong social stigma against polluting, they want to keep it illegal beyond specified levels.[24] Modern Liberals also defend standards as essential to maintaining equity; all regions or neighborhoods must meet the same standards, so pollution cannot be concentrated in a few sites.

Modern Liberals insist that environmental protection can be compatible with economic growth and rising standards of living. This optimism is based partially on the Keynesian view that additional spending—in this case, on pollution control—serves to stimulate the economy by creating greater demand for goods, more jobs, and higher incomes. Unemployed workers might be hired to construct pollution-control devices or repair environmental damage. Growth and environmental protection are also compatible because countries pioneering in pollution control can export ecologically sound or "green" technology and products to other countries.

However, Modern Liberals also share Conservative and Radical concerns that too much growth may harm the environment. In 1987, the United Nations' World Commission on Environment and Development formulated the notion of "sustainable development."[25] Growth should not exceed levels consistent with the health and well-being of future generations. In other words, sustainable development would not diminish the planet's capacity for supporting human life. This highly influential concept has gained support from governments, corporations, and environmental groups around the world. However, the widespread appeal of sustainable development may lie in its ambiguity. How many resources should be left to sustain future generations? How many future generations should be sustained? What standard of living should future generations attain? Can capital and technology substitute for depleted natural resources? The notion of sustainable development offers few guidelines to answer these questions and hence can be interpreted to support either growth or preservation.

In proposing environmental policies, Modern Liberals value both equity and efficiency. Equity could be promoted by treating a clean environment as a human right to which all persons are entitled regardless of their ability to pay. Alternatively, a larger share of the financial burden of pollution control could be placed on the more affluent members of society.[26] To promote efficiency, Modern Liberals favor policies designed to correct market failures such as missing markets, externalities, or lack of information. The major method for formulating efficient policies is cost–benefit analysis.[27]

Modern Liberals portray cost–benefit analysis as an objective, scientific method for designing efficient public policies. This procedure gives priority to policies offering maximum benefits per dollar of cost or, alternatively, achieving specified goals with the least cost. In practice, cost–benefit analysis faces the problem of establishing dollar values for costs or benefits external to the market.[28] In the case of pollution, policy analysts measure the value of a cleaner environment by assessing the price citizens would be willing to pay for lower levels of pollution. Such a procedure, however, has two major shortcomings.

First, citizens may not reveal their true preferences, anticipating the possibility of being a "free rider" by enjoying the benefits of a cleaner environment without paying. Second, the current distribution of wealth affects the willingness of individuals to pay. Low-income families may appear indifferent to a clean environment simply because their lack of money and education causes them to concentrate on more immediate concerns such as food and clothing. However, a different distribution of wealth might dramatically alter demands for environmental quality. So the quest for efficient policies is necessarily linked to considerations of fairness in the distribution of income and wealth.

Because many costs and benefits of government policies occur in the future, the analyst must choose a "social discount rate" to determine the present value of future effects. If the goal of cost–benefit analysis is to replicate the allocation of resources occurring in a perfectly functioning market, then the social discount rate should reflect the private discount rates of citizens. However, the future is likely to be valued more highly by society as a whole than by individuals. Individuals do not survive to experience the distant future, but society presumably will. Also, individuals may shirk responsibility for the well-being of subsequent generations. Society as a whole cannot ignore this duty without jeopardizing the survival of the species. For these reasons, the policy analyst justifiably assigns a lower discount rate to future costs and benefits than would individual citizens. However, the method of cost–benefit analysis offers no guidance as to how low the social discount rate should be set. Only the morality of intergenerational justice can shed light on this difficulty.

A final problem with cost–benefit analysis is the unavoidably arbitrary decision by the policy analyst to circumscribe the length of time, the geographical area, and the types of benefits and costs to be considered. If all the costs of pollution to all future generations were counted, then today's optimal level of pollution would probably be quite low. If intangible costs and benefits associated with beauty, serenity, and spiritual uplift are included in cost–benefit analysis, then dollar values must be assigned to these sensations. By attaching sufficient value to intangible costs or benefits, analysts can justify any policy they choose. This latitude, along with the ethical considerations involved in choosing a social discount rate, casts doubt on the proclaimed objectivity of cost–benefit analysis.

NOTES

1. Donella H. Meadows, Dennis L. Meadows, Jorgen Randers, and William W. Behrens, *The Limits to Growth*, New York: University Books, 1972. For a rebuttal to the pessimistic predictions of Meadows *et al.*, see Edward Pestel, *Beyond the Limits to Growth*, New York: University Books, 1989. The sequel to *Limits to Growth* is Donella H. Meadows, Dennis L. Meadows, and Jorgen Randers, *Beyond the Limits: Confronting Global Collapse; Envisioning A Sustainable Future*, Post Mills, Vermont: Chelsea Green Publishing Company, 1992.

2. Ronald H. Coase, "The Problem of Social Cost," *Journal of Law and Economics* 3 (October 1960): 1–44. For more accessible accounts, see William F. Baxter, *People or Penguins: The Case for Optimal Pollution*, New York: Columbia University Press, 1974, and Wilfred Beckerman, *Pricing For Pollution*, 2nd ed., London: Institute for Economic Affairs, 1990.

3. See Doug Bandow, ed., *Protecting The Environment: A Free Market Strategy*, Washington: Heritage Foundation, 1986; David Glasner, *Politics, Prices and Petroleum: The Political Economy of Energy*, Cambridge, MA: Ballinger, 1985;

and Terry L. Anderson and Donald R. Leal, *Free Market Environmentalism*, Boulder, CO: Westview Press, 1991.

4. See Terry L. Anderson and Donald R. Leal, *Enviro-Capitalists: Doing Good While Doing Well*, Savage, MD: Rowman & Littlefield, 1997.

5. A Classical Liberal critique of the concept of market failure is presented in Tyler Cowen, ed., *The Theory of Market Failure*, Fairfax, VA: George Mason University Press, 1988.

6. See Richard Epstein, *Takings: Private Property and the Power of Eminent Domain*, Cambridge: Harvard University Press, 1985; Richard Epstein, *Bargaining with the State*, Princeton: Princeton University Press, 1993; and Richard Epstein, *Simple Rules for A Complex World*, Cambridge, MA: Harvard University Press, 1995.

7. See John Echeverria and Raymond Booth Eby, eds., *Let the People Judge: Wise Use and the Private Property Rights Movement*, Washington, DC: Island Press, 1995.

8. See Wilfred Beckerman, *Two Cheers for the Affluent Society: A Spirited Defense of Economic Growth*, New York: St. Martin's, 1974.

9. A traditional Marxist account of environmental problems can be found in Barry Weisberg, *Beyond Repair: The Ecology of Capitalism*, Boston: Beacon Press, 1971. See also Reiner Grundmann, *Marxism and Ecology*, New York: Oxford University Press, 1991.

10. See Arne Naess, *Ecology, Community and Lifestyle*, Cambridge: Cambridge University Press, 1989; Bill Bevall and George Sessions, *Deep Ecology: Living As If Nature Mattered*, Layton, UT: G. M. Smith, 1985; Murray Bookchin, *Deep Ecology and Anarchism: A Polemic*, London: Freedom Press, 1993; David Pepper, *Eco-Socialism: From Deep Ecology to Social Justice*, New York: Routledge, 1993; and Alan S. Miller, *Gaia Connections: An Introduction to Ecology, Ecoethics and Economics*, Savage, MD: Rowman & Littlefield, 1991.

11. See Peter Singer, *Animal Liberation*, New York: Random House, 1975, and Aldo Leopold, *The Land Ethic*, Oxford: Oxford University Press, 1949.

12. James Lovelock, *Gaia*, Oxford: Oxford University Press, 1979.

13. See Bertell Ollman, *Alienation: Marx's Conception of Man in Capitalist Society*, New York: Cambridge University Press, 1971.

14. Proposals for government control of production and consumption to protect the environment are found in Barbara Ward and Rene Dubos, *Only One Earth: The Care and Maintenance of a Small Planet*, London: Andre Deutsch, 1972; William Ophuls, "The Politics of a Sustainable Society," *in* Dennis Pirages, ed., *The Sustainable Society*, New York: Praeger, 1977; Fritjof Capra, *The Turning Point*, London: Flamingo, 1985; and Robert Heilbroner, *An Inquiry into the Human Prospect*, New York: W. W. Norton, 1980.

15. The Radical portrayal of socialism as a system of decentralized communities is presented in Ernest Callenbach, *Ecotopia*, Berkeley, CA: Banyan Tree Press, 1975. See also Murray Bookchin, *Remaking Society: Pathways To A Green Future*, Boston: South End Press, 1990; Rudolph Barro, *Building the Green Movement*, London: Green Movement Press, 1986; and Kirkpatrick Sale, *Dwellers in the Land: The Bioregional Vision*, San Francisco: Sierra Club, 1985.

16. See Barry Commoner, *The Politics of Energy*, New York: Alfred A. Knopf, 1979, and Robert Engler, *The Brotherhood of Oil: Energy Policy and the Public Interest*, Chicago: University of Chicago Press, 1977.

17. A Conservative analysis of pollution is presented in Francis A. Schaeffer, *Pollution and the Death of Man: The Christian View of Ecology*, Wheaton, IL: Tyndale House, 1970.

18. A fuller account of the shortcomings of material consumption can be found in Tibor Scitovsky, *The Joyless Economy: An Inquiry into Human Satisfaction and Consumer Dissatisfaction*, New York: Oxford University Press, 1976.

19. See John Gray, *Beyond the New Right*, New York: Routledge, 1993.

20. See Anna Bramwell, *The Fading of the Greens: The Decline of Environmental Politics in the West*, New Haven: Yale University Press, 1994.

21. See Nicholas Georgescu-Roegen, *The Entropy Law and the Economic Process*, Cambridge, MA: Harvard University Press, 1971.

22. See Brian Barry and Richard Sikora, eds., *Obligations to Future Generations*, Philadelphia: Temple University Press, 1978. See also Ernest Partridge, ed., *Responsibilities to Future Generations*, New York: Prometheus Books, 1981.

23. Albert O. Hirschman, *Exit, Voice, and Loyalty: Response to Declines in Firms, Organizations, and States*, Cambridge, MA: Harvard University Press, 1970.

24. The argument against market-oriented solutions to pollution is presented in Steven J. Kelman, *What Price Incentives?: Economists and the Environment*, Boston: Auburn House, 1981.

25. World Commission on Environment and Development, *Our Common Future*, Oxford: Oxford University Press, 1987. See also Michael Jacobs, *The Green Economy: Environment, Sustainable Development and the Politics of the Future*, Concord, MA: Pluto Press, 1991; Edward Barbier, ed., *Economics and Ecology: New Frontiers and Sustainable Development*, New York: Chapman & Hall, 1993; Jeroen van den Bergh, *Ecological Economics and Sustainable Development*, Brookfield, VT: Edward Elgar, 1995; Johan Holmberg, *Making Development Sustainable: Redefining Institutions, Policy and Economics*, Washington, DC: Island Press, 1992; R. Kerry Turner, ed., *Sustainable Environmental Economics and Management: Principles and Practice*, London: Belhaven, 1993; Dennis C. Pirages, ed., *Building Sustainable Societies: A Blueprint for a Post-Industrial World*, Armonk, NY: M. E. Sharpe, 1996; and Herman E. Daly, *Beyond Growth: The Economics of Sustainable Development*, Boston: Beacon Press, 1996.

26. See Daniel R. Mandeiker, *Environment and Equity: A Regulatory Challenge*, New York: McGraw-Hill, 1981.

27. The basics of cost–benefit analysis are presented in E. J. Mishan, *Cost–Benefit Analysis: An Introduction*, 3rd ed., Boston: Allen & Unwin, 1982.

28. For more detailed critiques of cost–benefit analysis, see James T. Campen, *Benefit, Cost, and Beyond: The Political Economy of Benefit–Cost Analysis*, Cambridge, MA: Ballinger, 1986, and A. Allan Schmid, *Benefit–Cost Analysis: A Political Economy Approach*, Boulder, CO: Westview Press, 1989.

ADDITIONAL READING

Ashworth, William. *The Economy of Nature: Rethinking the Connections Between Ecology and Economics*. Boston: Houghton Mifflin, 1995.

Baumol, William J., and Wallace E. Oates. *The Theory of Environmental Policy*, 2nd ed. New York: Cambridge University Press, 1988.

Bromley, Daniel. *Environment and Economy.* Cambridge, MA: Blackwell, 1991.

Caldwell, Lynton K. *Between Two Worlds: Science, the Environmental Movement, and Policy Choice.* New York: Cambridge University Press, 1990.

Daly, Herman E., and Kenneth Townsend, eds. *Valuing the Earth: Economics, Ecology, Ethics.* Cambridge, MA: MIT Press, 1993.

Dobson, Andrew. *Green Political Thought,* 2nd ed. Winchester, MA: Unwin Hyman, 1996.

Foster, John, ed. *Valuing Nature: Economics, Ethics and Environment.* New York: Routledge, 1997.

Goodin, Robert E., ed. *The Politics of the Environment.* Brookfield, VT: Edward Elgar, 1994.

Hardin, Garrett. *Living Within Limits: Ecology, Economics and Population Taboos.* New York: Oxford University Press, 1993.

Hirsch, Fred. *Social Limits to Growth.* Cambridge, MA: Harvard University Press, 1976.

Johnston, Ronald J. *Nature, State and Economy: A Political Economy of the Environment,* 2nd ed. New York: John Wiley, 1996.

Kapp, K. William. *The Social Costs of Private Enterprise.* New York: Schocken, 1971.

Krishnan, Rajaram, Jonathan M. Harris, and Neva R. Goodwin. *A Survey of Ecological Economics.* Washington, DC: Island Press, 1995.

Kula, E. *History of Environmental Economic Thought.* New York: Routledge, 1998.

O'Neil, John. *Ecology, Pollution and Politics.* New York: Routledge, 1993.

Power, Thomas M. *Environmental Protection and Economic Well-Being: The Economic Pursuit of Quality.* Armonk, NY: M. E. Sharpe, 1996.

Sagoff, Mark. *The Economy of the Earth: Philosophy, Law and the Environment.* New York: Oxford University Press, 1988.

Simpson, David. *The Political Economy of Growth.* New York: St. Martin's, 1983.

Wenz, Peter S. *Environmental Justice.* Albany: SUNY Press, 1988.

Chapter 15

International Trade
and Development

The increasing interdependence of nations has brought issues of international trade and development to the forefront of political economy. Modern transportation and communication systems facilitate the rapid flow of resources, products, and information across national borders, resulting in a highly integrated global economy. With increased trade has come concerns about diminished national sovereignty. International flows of capital and commodities make government efforts to fine-tune domestic economies using fiscal and monetary policies less reliable due to their effects on international trade, capital flows, and the value of a country's currency.

The trade problems facing industrialized countries are overshadowed by the developmental challenges confronting Asia, Africa, Latin America, and the Middle East. For the less developed countries (LDCs), the 1980s were a "lost decade." Higher oil prices and global recession caused declining commodity prices, high interest rates, and shrinking export markets. Unable to earn sufficient foreign exchange to service their debts, many LDCs were forced to accept dramatically lower growth rates. The 1990s have witnessed impressive comebacks by some countries and continued stagnation by others. Political economy is particularly well-suited for analyzing issues surrounding international trade and development because markets in LDCs tend to be deeply embedded in cultural and political contexts.

THE CLASSICAL LIBERAL PERSPECTIVE

Explanations of Underdevelopment

Classical Liberals attribute underdevelopment to a combination of the following four factors:

1. *Inadequate resources.* Classical Liberals view the economy as a technical production process in which output is a function of the quantity and quality of productive inputs. From this perspective, the LDCs are poor because they have insufficient skilled labor, natural resources, capital, and entrepreneurial ability. Any one of these four categories can, by its absence, create a bottleneck in the development process. A country may be unable to tap abundant natural resources if it lacks capital or entrepreneurship. In what is called "geographical determinism," a country's economic fate may be sealed by the quality of its climate, topography, and natural resources.

2. *Inadequate saving and investment.* In many LDCs, incomes are so low that people are unable to save. Because saving is the source of funds for investment in capital, inadequate saving dooms a country to continual poverty. LDCs are caught in a "vicious circle." Saving is low because incomes are low, and incomes cannot grow without more saving and investment. This dilemma forces LDCs to rely on foreign investment as a source of capital in the early stages of development. Once growth has begun, internal saving will increase due to rising incomes. However, even if adequate saving occurs, the small size of internal markets provides few outlets for investors. Therefore, in addition to infusions of foreign capital, LDCs need to broaden their markets by producing for export.

3. *Lack of international trade.* Some countries seek to preserve national autonomy and protect domestic markets by restricting trade with other nations. Classical Liberals argue that protectionism retards the development process. They defend free trade for industrialized nations and LDCs by appealing to the theory of comparative advantage formulated by English economist David Ricardo in the early nineteenth century. Ricardo encouraged each country to specialize in producing commodities for which it is best suited and then trade with other countries to obtain a wide variety of goods. The increased efficiency of production within each country makes greater worldwide consumption possible. This theory suggests that all nations have an interest in opposing restraints on trade. If LDCs remain isolated and closed to foreign trade and investment, they lose opportunities to benefit from the technology, capital, and consumer goods offered by industrialized nations.

4. *Government intervention.* Classical Liberals believe that government efforts to promote development do greater harm than good. Government, they claim, cannot possess sufficient knowledge to efficiently allocate resources; therefore, intervention inevitably results in waste and slower growth.

Classical Liberals rely on the theory of rent-seeking to demonstrate the shortcomings of government action. Wealthy elites in the LDCs use government to protect their status and to advance private interests. Corruption is endemic in many LDCs as people seek to buy government-protected privileges. Urban residents, who tend to be most visible and organized in national politics, pressure government for lower food prices at the expense of rural farmers. "Monument-building" for personal and national glorification diverts resources that could have been channeled by the market into profitable and productive use. Government officials funnel money from the public treasury to private estates, personal investments abroad, and purchases of imported luxury goods.

Rent-seeking is prevalent in LDCs because politicians must curry favor with powerful groups to remain in office. Yet, as individuals successfully obtain money and privileges through the political process, they steer more resources away from private production and toward additional rent-seeking. More seriously, successful rent-seeking delegitimizes the government and jeopardizes political stability. If citizens come to believe that control of government is the key to economic advancement, they will wage violent battles for political supremacy. Classical Liberals attribute most of the conflict in LDCs to struggles for control of a "transfer state" that redistributes income. If government were confined to its proper role of protecting property and enforcing contracts, there would be no motive to fight for control of the state. Corruption would virtually cease because politicians would have no favors or privileges to sell and the amount of revenue collected by government would be minimal.

The mistrust of politics places Classical Liberals in an awkward position with regard to democracy in LDCs. During much of the twentieth century, they remained silent about abuses of civil rights by authoritarian governments in noncommunist nations. In the mid-1970s, Milton Friedman and other Chicago economists served as advisors for the military junta that overthrew a democratically elected president in Chile. Authoritarianism was rationalized as a distasteful but necessary stage to suppress conflict, forge a national consensus, create investor confidence, and pave the way for development. Classical Liberals proudly note that Chile is now one of the most prosperous and democratic countries in Latin America. As LDCs mature and communism continues to recede, Classical Liberals expect constitutional democracy to be accepted throughout the world.

LDCs can also be harmed by the policies of governments in the industrialized countries.[1] For example, government efforts to preserve jobs may include tariffs on goods imported from LDCs. The use of fiscal or monetary policy to stimulate demand may inadvertently trigger inflation, resulting in higher prices for exports to LDCs. Finally, governments responding to hunger and misery in LDCs may send aid in the form of capital or food. According to Classical Liberals, this aid has the same effect on the global economy as welfare programs have on domestic growth. Redistribution from rich to poor undermines incentives and causes inefficiency by moving resources away from their most productive use. Foreign aid effectively slows the engines of the global economy and makes LDCs dependent on industrialized nations.

Development Policy

Classical Liberal policies on trade and development have been articulated by neoclassical economists such as Jacob Viner (1892–1970), Harry Johnson (1923–1977), Gottfried Haberler, and Sir Peter Bauer.[2] From their perspective, the same economic principles apply to both developed and developing countries, so free trade and competitive markets are the optimal strategies for raising standards of living anywhere in the world. Development proceeds as the quantity and quality of economic resources increase, and the market, with its strong incentives for providing productive resources, is the best mechanism to mobilize a nation for economic growth. Policymakers should oppose social, cultural, and political forces impeding the market's operation.

Classical Liberals are so confident of the benefits of free trade that they urge countries to drop all trade barriers even if trading partners continue to practice protection. Free trade permits a country to obtain cheaper goods; the fact that other countries have restrictions on trade does not alter the positive effects of lower-priced imports in restraining inflation, stimulating innovation, and enabling citizens to enjoy higher standards of living. Since all trade is voluntary, a country cannot possibly harm itself by expanding its opportunities to buy from foreigners.

Classical Liberals acknowledge that the transformation from a traditional, agrarian society to a market economy is inevitably a wrenching experience, but the trauma can be eased by free trade with the industrialized nations. Foreign trade serves to strengthen the merchant and manufacturing classes within LDCs, breaking the grip of traditional elites on the economy. Market forces also shift peasants out of subsistence farming and into factories where, through enhanced productivity, their standard of living can rise. Agricultural production should be performed by more efficient, large-scale farmers. Finally, untapped natural resources will be transformed into productive inputs once the incentive of profit and the availability of capital make their extraction both attractive and feasible. Classical Liberals are so certain of the ability of free markets to spur development that they reject all policies relying on planned strategies by government. The theory of free trade is their theory of development.[3]

The Classical Liberal view of development, sometimes referred to as "diffusion," envisions the gradual spread of capitalism throughout the world. Only political barriers such as trade restrictions or nationalization of property can halt capital diffusion to LDCs. Classical Liberals claim that capitalism is the only "natural" economic system, and they are confident that LDCs will follow a development path similar to that of the West. Experiments with socialism are interpreted by Classical Liberals as analogous to England's reliance on mercantilism in the seventeenth and eighteenth centuries. LDCs initially fear the destabilizing effects of free markets and enact policies to protect themselves. However, the demonstrated power of the market to provide rising standards of living will inevitably lead to disillusionment with socialist policies.

Classical Liberals oppose foreign aid, claiming that the most efficient form of assistance is investment by multinational corporations to provide jobs, capital, vocational training, tax revenue, and, in some cases, roads and other infrastructure. The presence of multinational corporations in LDCs also imparts Western values and lifestyles, promoting entrepreneurial energy and individual achievement.

In response to concerns that open borders and the mobility of multinational corporations will harm workers in the industrialized nations, Classical Liberals offer the following defenses of free trade:

1. *Efficiency*. Free trade and capital mobility permit global resources to flow to their most valued uses. The resulting gains in output permit all countries to enjoy higher standards of living.[4] Although a textile worker in the United States may temporarily be hurt by free trade, all consumers benefit from cheaper textiles, and the stimulus of free trade will create job opportunities in other industries. The primary obstacle to free trade is posed by politicians. The benefits of trade are long-term and dispersed across the entire population, while the losses are immediately visible and concentrated in particular industries or occupations. Therefore, groups temporarily harmed by free trade will organize to demand protective legislation, while the majority of citizens are likely to remain passive in defending free trade. Classical Liberals seek to educate both politicians and citizens about the virtues of free trade to thwart the political tendency toward protectionism.

Protection causes inefficiency by preventing resources from reaching their most productive uses and by shielding firms from the discipline of market competition. If a few seemingly justifiable tariffs or quotas are allowed, other interest groups will pressure politicians for additional protection, eventually sealing the nation from both access to low-priced imports and competitive pressures to innovate. Protectionist policies simply perpetuate inefficiency by maintaining the high costs and low productivity responsible for trade problems in the first place.[5]

2. *Reduced inflation.* Free trade restrains inflation by providing consumers and firms with low-priced alternatives to domestic products and resources. The ability of labor unions and oligopolistic firms to raise wages and prices is undercut by free trade.

3. *Peace.* Free trade contributes to global interdependence, fostering shared interests among nations and reducing the risk of war. Conversely, protective trade barriers may cause retaliation by other nations and increased international tensions.

4. *International stability.* The growing indebtedness of LDCs increases the importance of free trade. If the United States were to increase trade barriers, LDCs would lose export markets and be unable to earn sufficient foreign currency to pay interest on their debts. The ensuing defaults might trigger financial chaos in credit markets and possibly a global depression. Free trade remains essential for the long-term stability of all countries.

Classical Liberals acknowledge that problems arise if some countries renege on contracts or confiscate foreign property within their borders. Friedrich Hayek proposed the establishment of an international governing body to assure that countries don't harm one another.[6] Although this proposal for world government seems inconsistent with Classical Liberalism, the authority of the governing body would be limited to enforcing contracts and settling disputes. According to Hayek, a minimal international state is necessary to prevent anarchy.

THE RADICAL PERSPECTIVE

Explanations of Underdevelopment

Within the Radical perspective, two distinct views on underdevelopment coexist. Both can be traced to the writings of Marx.

Diffusion theory. In *The Communist Manifesto*, Marx and Engels praised capitalism for accomplishing the historically necessary task of mobilizing resources and destroying traditional social and political structures to pave the way for modernization. Marx had little sympathy for romantic visions of traditional culture, claiming that capitalism had rescued "a considerable part of the population from the idiocy of rural life." He anticipated that capitalism, by stimulating innovation and cost-cutting, would promote capital accumulation and economic development. Increased availability of resources, coupled with new attitudes toward profitmaking and individual initiative, would set the stage for a dynamic and efficient system for lifting society out of poverty.

This version of the Radical theory of development is remarkably similar to the Classical Liberal view and hence is also called "diffusion theory." The relationship between the industrialized nations and the LDCs is claimed to be mutually beneficial. Capitalism spreads outward from the industrialized countries to the LDCs, eventually incorporating the latter into a global economic system promoting the development of all countries. The industrialized nations can export surplus goods and import cheap raw materials to maintain profits, while the LDCs gain both markets for their raw materials and the capital essential for modernization. Increased exposure to capitalism will eventually ensure worldwide industrial development.

Marx did observe that certain countries were more resistant than others to capitalist penetration. In particular, he attributed the lack of industrialization in Asia to the need for large-scale irrigation projects requiring extensive political authority to mobilize resources. The power of the state suppressed the entrepreneurial and commercial activity essential to the formation of capitalism. Marx labeled such systems "oriental despotism" or the "Asiatic mode of production."

The view that capitalism is ultimately beneficial to LDCs does not deny that competitive international markets often wreak havoc on traditional economies and social structures, but this disruption is necessary for the transition to a modern capitalist society. Standards of living in the LDCs will rise as industrial development and trade with other countries create employment opportunities.

Dependency theory. In Marx's later writings, he argued that the continued accumulation of capital in the developed countries requires an underdeveloped "periphery" of nations to serve as markets for excess goods, sources of cheap resources, and profitable investment outlets. Therefore, capitalism in one region requires the presence of a precapitalist region, giving the developed countries a strong interest in keeping parts of the world dependent and backward. Marx illustrated this point with the British tactic of smashing handlooms and cutting off the thumbs of weavers in India to assure that country's continued reliance on British textiles.

Historical roots of dependency theory are also found in the writings of Lenin.[7] Seeking to justify revolution, Lenin argued that Russia was being damaged by its subordinate status among the European nations. He claimed that western European firms had entered Russia in search of new markets for their products and cheap labor. Whereas Marx originally predicted revolutions in the most industrialized capitalist nations, Lenin argued that exploitation of foreign labor enabled capitalist firms to pay higher wages in Europe and North America. These high wages served to quell revolutionary discontent, turning North American and European workers into an "aristocracy of labor" whose privileged position explained their political passivity. Lenin proposed that revolution must begin in Russia, the "weakest link" in the chain of capitalist nations.

The assertion that development in the industrialized countries retards development elsewhere has gained increasing acceptance among Radicals. In the 1950s, American economist Paul Baran argued that development of Africa, Asia, and Latin America was blocked by the trade and investment practices of developed capitalist countries.[8] Foreign capitalists seeking security for their assets in LDCs form political alliances with feudal landowners, resulting in authoritarian governments opposed to labor unions, civil rights, and democracy. Baran also claimed that economic interaction with capitalist nations drains wealth from the LDCs. Goods previously manufactured in the LDCs are replaced by imports, and self-sufficient agriculture is replaced by commercial crops grown for export.

The argument that Western capitalism is responsible for the plight of LDCs forms the core of "dependency theory" developed during the 1970s by André Gunder Frank, Celso Furtado, Osvaldo Sunkel, and Theotonio dos Santos.[9] Variants of the same theme are found in the theory of "unequal exchange" formulated by Samir Amin and Arghiri Emmanuel and the "world systems theory" of Immanuel Wallerstein.[10] These theorists agree that the primary problem confronting LDCs is not lack of capitalist trade and development, but exposure to global capitalism.

Dependency theorists trace the origins of underdevelopment to the fifteenth and sixteenth centuries, claiming that the development of Europe, and later North America, was achieved with wealth appropriated from Africa, Asia, and Latin America. Colonialism destabilized indigenous social and economic structures, subverting the normal development process. Europeans installed or protected local rulers who were receptive to foreign interests, and Europeans themselves populated the LDCs as plantation managers, factory bosses, and government officials. This dominance by foreigners concentrated development in specific industries such as mining, timber, or rubber, making the LDCs vulnerable to changing patterns of international demand. Moreover, profits were often either repatriated to Europe or used for consumption of imported luxury goods. This system of "peripheral capitalism" stalled the development process as both foreign and domestic elites, largely free from competitive pressures, used profits to insulate themselves from challenges to their power and privilege.

To verify the claims of dependency theory, Argentinean economist André Gunder Frank examined the historical relation between rates of growth in LDCs and the degree of economic interaction among those nations and developed capitalist countries. He found that LDCs experienced some of their highest growth rates during periods when the capitalist countries were absorbed in war or depression. Conversely, during times of peace, when trade and investment activities were greatest, LDCs fared relatively poorly.[11]

These findings challenge both the Classical Liberal and Radical views that capitalism results in a diffusion of development throughout the world.

Development Policy

Radical policies for promoting economic development reflect the schism between diffusion theory and dependency theory. Diffusion theory views capitalism as a progressive force in global development, so the business class in LDCs should be supported in its efforts to overthrow feudal oligarchies. Insurgent movements by peasants and workers are not encouraged because LDCs will not be ready for socialist revolution until capitalism has performed its historical task of accumulating capital and preparing people for industrial society. An illustration of policies emanating from diffusion theory is presented by the former Soviet Union's initial reluctance to support Fidel Castro's efforts to overthrow the Batista regime in Cuba. Soviet policy also approved of multinational corporations for performing the necessary task of injecting capital and technology into the LDCs.

In sharp contrast, dependency theorists encourage LDCs to minimize contact with the mature capitalist countries to develop internal economic structures consistent with their specific needs. Dependency theorists favor national autonomy or "collective self-reliance" among groups of LDCs to foster economic development and national pride. This focus on psychological liberation reflects a belief that LDCs have suffered from cultural as well as economic imperialism. Exposure to Western lifestyles and consumption patterns has alienated people in LDCs from their own cultures and has created a deep sense of inferiority. Restoring national pride will release the productive energies of people who are presently crippled by a sense of powerlessness.

Other policy proposals from dependency theorists include a reorientation of agriculture away from production for export and toward meeting the needs of local citizens, the use of labor-intensive or small-scale technology to increase employment, public investment in infrastructure, and the substitution of domestically manufactured goods for foreign imports.

During the 1980s, a coalition of Radicals and Modern Liberals proposed a dramatic realignment of international relations called the New International Economic Order (NIEO).[12] This strategy emerged from the perception that domestic development policies are futile without major revisions of the international political economy. The NIEO would entail greater political control over multinational corporations, an enlarged role for LDCs in international institutions such as the World Bank and the International Monetary Fund, easier credit terms for LDCs, reduced trade barriers for exports, increased foreign aid and technical assistance, and taxes on the extraction of nonrenewable resources.

Radicals exhibit ambiguity in their position on free trade. They view it as potentially damaging to LDCs, but they also condemn many protectionist policies in the industrialized nations as preserving privilege against competitive pressures from abroad. Radicals will support protection when it facilitates development of LDCs by sheltering them from global competition, but they claim that protection cannot solve the trade problems of the industrialized nations caused by failure to innovate and lagging productivity. This ambiguity on trade policy reflects an unresolved issue of whether workers in capitalist nations share common interests with workers in LDCs. To the extent that Radicals view workers in the United States and Western Europe as an "aristocracy of labor," they are likely to support trade policies beneficial to LDCs even at the expense of workers in the industrialized nations. On the other hand, those Radicals who view industrial workers in the West as the primary constituency for an eventual transition to socialism will favor trade policies to protect mature industries in the advanced capitalist nations.

THE CONSERVATIVE PERSPECTIVE

Explanations of Underdevelopment

Conservatives have not devoted much attention to issues of international development and trade. Historically, Conservatism focused on preserving Western culture by resisting industrialization and democracy. Given their dissatisfaction with the course of development in the West, Conservatives remain skeptical about efforts to move LDCs along a similar route that fosters disintegration of traditional social structures, decline of authority, and the emergence of a rootless, mobile population focused primarily on the pleasures of consumption. Conservatives trace these changes to the Enlightenment view that human reason can restructure society. Development should instead follow a natural path unique to each culture.[13]

To avoid the excesses of modern society, some aspects of precapitalist cultures should be preserved. A low level of production need not imply underdevelopment. Cultural, religious, and social institutions may provide a secure and stable existence for most citizens. Efforts to stimulate industrialization may actually ruin the existing culture by undermining traditional economic structures and practices.

However, recognizing that some countries have not yet achieved an adequate standard of living for the general populace, Conservatives offer the following explanations of underdevelopment:

1. *Environmental factors.* Climate affects the physical resources of a country as well as human behavior. Some Conservatives claim that people living in warm climates lack ambition because they can attain subsistence living so easily. Whereas the harsher climate of Europe and North America spurs people to work and innovate, people in the LDCs may devote more of their time to other aspects of life such as leisure, ritual, and community social life.

2. *Psychological traits.* Conservatives point to certain psychological predispositions causing people in LDCs to resist development. A lack of "achievement orientation" explains why individuals make little effort to distinguish themselves from their social group.[14] Conservatives point out that countries with warmer climates tend to be less developed. With a hospitable environment, people from tropical countries were never forced to plan for the future and organize themselves to conquer nature.[15] Also, when people are content simply to fulfill their biological and social needs, material incentives are less effective in changing behavior. Workers may respond to higher wages by working less because they can meet their basic needs with fewer hours of work. This response leads to a backward-bending supply curve of labor, suggesting that higher wages fail to spur additional productive activity.

People in LDCs also purportedly lack initiative and willingness to take risks. Life in traditional societies tends to be unchanging over time as individuals seek harmony with nature rather than mastery over it. Conservatives attribute this attitude to the prevalence of close-knit tribal communities and extended families in which responsibilities and rewards are dispersed over large numbers of people so that no individual has an incentive to change the pattern of living.

Psychological attachment to ritual and mysticism impedes the rational, calculating mentality essential to a market economy. High birth rates can be attributed to an unwillingness or inability to consider future consequences of actions. Finally, Conservatives note that people in LDCs often exhibit a preindustrial attitude toward time, making them unable to conform to schedules and therefore ill-suited to work in a market economy.

3. *Imperialism.* During the early nineteenth century, Conservatives supported cultural and religious excursions into Africa, Asia, and Latin America. The "white man's burden" obligated Europeans and North Americans to introduce Christianity and civilization to native cultures. However, as missionary work evolved into imperialism, Conservatives became concerned that corrosive market forces were being imposed on LDCs by corporations seeking cheap raw materials and outlets for their products. These concerns were undoubtedly amplified because the economic benefits of imperialism accrued primarily to manufacturers and merchants who Conservatives viewed as the enemy of traditional society both at home and abroad. Some Conservatives also condemned the military expenditures required to defend a global empire as a waste of resources. From their perspective, imperialism was responsible for decline in the West as well as destruction of traditional cultures throughout the world. By the early twentieth century, this opposition to imperialism led Conservatives to adopt an isolationist stance toward foreign involvements.

4. *Democracy*. After gaining independence from colonialism, many LDCs were confronted with arbitrarily drawn borders encompassing historically separate and sometimes hostile groups. Conservatives claim that if newly established governments are open to democratic participation, the variety of conflicting interests results in political stalemate at best, and possibly violence and anarchy. In short, while conservatives have come to terms with democracy in the industrialized world, they view political participation as a luxury that LDCs cannot yet afford.

Democracy fosters demagogy, as politicians pander to the masses, and instability when no coalition can gain a sufficient majority to rule effectively. Democracy also discourages political leaders from taking economically necessary but unpopular actions. Democratic governments focus on short-term measures to win the next election rather than the long-term performance of the economy. India is commonly used as an example of a democratic country with political instability, corruption, and relatively poor economic performance. In contrast, Conservatives point to Brazil, Chile, and South Korea as countries successfully combining authoritarian government with economic development.

Development Policy

Conservatives remained largely isolationist until the 1950s, opposing nearly all commitments to and interventions in foreign countries. They considered foreign aid to developing countries as counterproductive because, by increasing food supplies and promoting public health, it could lead to explosive population growth, which might impede development. More generally, foreign aid would cause a flood of rising expectations, resulting in social disorder.

During the 1950s, however, Conservatives began to reassess their isolationist policies in light of the growing threat of communist expansion. Indeed, Conservatives became leading proponents of internationalism, calling on the United States to assert its strength as leader of the "Free World." According to Conservatives, global peace and security require that one country gain "hegemony" with sufficient power to establish and enforce the rules of international relations.[16] Without hegemony, the struggle among nations for dominance leads to international tensions and conflict. Despite this new "internationalist" orientation, Conservatives reject shared international governance through representative organizations such as the United Nations because LDCs outnumber the industrialized countries and could therefore effectively wield power.

Conservatives want the United States to ally itself with those foreign governments protecting private property and promoting trade with the West.[17] These governments need not be democratic because the LDCs need strong governmental authority to control ethnic and religious strife, to protect domestic and foreign investment from excessive risk, and to actively resist insurgent political movements. In determining which governments deserve U.S. support, Conservatives distinguish between "authoritarian" and "totalitarian" regimes.[18] Totalitarian governments pursue egalitarian or socialist ends, but authoritarian governments promote favorable investment climates and capitalist development while restricting free elections and democratic participation. Conservatives oppose totalitarian regimes but tolerate the abuses of civil liberties in authoritarian countries, hoping that economic development will eventually create sufficient political stability to permit free elections.

The Conservative attitude toward foreign aid has changed along with the transition from isolationism to internationalism during the 1950s. To halt the spread of communism, Conservatives have supported military and economic aid to vulnerable countries. However, as the threat of communism recedes, Conservatives are retreating to their former isolationism, opposing virtually all government involvement with foreign countries. Instead, they encourage churches, civic groups, and other private organizations to provide humanitarian aid to the citizens of LDCs.

Conservatives condemn free trade for subjecting countries to competitive pressures over which they have little control. In the nineteenth century, the German economist Friedrich List argued that less industrialized countries should place tariffs on goods from more advanced countries to give "infant industries" time to mature and eventually become competitive in international markets. Even when Conservatives acknowledge the potential economic gains from free trade, they claim that the preservation of traditional culture, standards of living, and national security may require protectionist policies. Conservatives note that both the United States and Germany practiced extensive protectionism during the late nineteenth and early twentieth centuries while rapidly surpassing England, the country most devoted to free trade at the time.[19]

To summarize, Conservatives welcome trade when it contributes to the vitality of both trading partners and does not undermine traditional culture, but they favor protectionist policies to prevent standards of living in the industrialized countries from being undermined by competition with low-wage manufacturers in the LDCs.

THE MODERN LIBERAL PERSPECTIVE

Explanations of Underdevelopment

In the aftermath of World War II, Modern Liberals were concerned that the rapid transformation of the Soviet Union into a global power might provide an appealing model to LDCs. This concern increased when communists gained control of China in 1949. For post-war Modern Liberals, the best protection against the spread of communism was rapid growth in the LDCs to end hunger and misery that drive people to political extremes. During the 1950s and 1960s, economists such as Gunnar Myrdal (1898–1987), Ragnar Nurkse (1907–1959), Raul Prebisch (1901–1985), Paul Rosenstein-Rodan (1902–1985), William Arthur Lewis (1911–1991), and Albert O. Hirschman constructed the new field of development economics. These theorists sought to develop a synthesis of Classical Liberal and Radical views. Like Classical Liberals, Modern Liberals accept the need to mobilize resources and instill Western values of individual initiative and achievement. However, Modern Liberals also validate the Radical view that imperialism has been a major factor in blocking development, and they propose that governments in both the industrialized countries and the LDCs should pursue active policies to correct past injustices and hasten the development process.

Modern Liberals attribute underdevelopment to the following causes:

1. *Market failures*. Because markets have been suppressed in LDCs, the typical shortcomings of markets are magnified. Resources are relatively immobile, information is limited, and competitors are sometimes few. Moreover, capitalist notions of individual initiative, risk-taking, and entrepreneurship lie dormant.

2. *Extreme inequality*. Modern Liberals argue that excessive inequality in the distribution of wealth and income results in a structure of demand favoring imports. Even domestic production is geared toward luxury goods for the wealthy elite rather than food, clothing, and shelter for the bulk of the population. The low demand for basic necessities means that markets for these products remain small and undeveloped, with resulting inefficiency. To make matters worse, the concentration of wealth and income often fails to generate high levels of saving and investment because elites are prone to a "demonstration effect" as they emulate consumption patterns in the developed countries. Money that could have been channeled into capital formation goes instead for imported luxury goods serving primarily as status symbols.

Inequality retards development in other ways. Poverty prevents many farmers from experimenting with new agricultural techniques because a single crop failure could mean starvation. Poverty also causes overpopulation as families seek to increase the number of hands available to provide immediate subsistence. Finally, the development of human resources is hindered by inability to afford adequate nutrition, health care, and education.

3. *Free trade*. While Modern Liberals acknowledge that international trade between similarly developed nations can be mutually beneficial, they believe that free trade may harm LDCs. Swedish economist Gunnar Myrdal claimed that free international trade operates to the advantage of the

developed countries and perpetuates stagnation in the LDCs.[20] This hypothesis, elaborated by Raul Prebisch and Hans Singer, states that the terms of trade between developed countries and LDCs will shift over time in favor of the developed countries. Prebisch and Singer based their claim on Engel's Law, a well-established economic principle stating that the percentage of income spent on food becomes smaller as GDP rises. Since many of LDCs' exports are agricultural products, Prebisch and Singer concluded that demand for these products would fail to keep pace with rising incomes in the industrialized countries, suppressing the prices of LDCs' exports relative to the prices of manufactured goods from Europe and North America. In addition, the market power of corporations and labor unions in the developed countries pushes the prices of their exports up. Conversely, the largely nonunionized workers and small businesses of the LDCs have little control over the prices of their exports.

4. *Ineffective government.* As imperialist powers colonized Africa, Asia, and Latin America, they often installed puppet governments to give the appearance of local rule. Not only were these governments subservient to the mother country, they were closely aligned with a relatively small number of wealthy families who actually benefited from imperialist control of their country. As increasing numbers of LDCs gained independence after World War II, the new governments reflected the legacy of imperialism. Instead of providing social infrastructure including adequate health care, education, transportation, and communication systems, governments in LDCs blocked economic reforms threatening the status quo. They also diverted resources toward the military, glorification of the state, and displays of wealth and status. The industrialized nations overlooked this waste and corruption because they relied on LDC governments to maintain a secure investment climate and to repress guerrilla forces.

Development Policy

During the past half-century, Modern Liberals have formulated various strategies for government to supplement the market in promoting economic development. Although early European industrialization was based on exports, economist Ragnar Nurkse claimed that export-led growth was inappropriate for LDCs because of competition from more advanced industries in the West. LDCs should instead pursue a policy of import-substitution by promoting the domestic manufacture of formerly imported goods.[21]

To break the cycle of poverty, Paul Rosenstein-Rodan advocated a "big push" with widespread investment by government and development of an infrastructure of schools, highways, and communications systems.[22] This initiative is designed to take advantage of the positive and reinforcing interactions of simultaneous development throughout the country. The "external economies" generated by developments in each industry would enhance development of other industries. However, Albert Hirschman questions the viability of a big push. Such a policy requires significant government planning as well as large infusions of capital through foreign investment and aid from the industrialized nations. Arguing that sufficient capital will not be available, Hirschman advises that LDCs target their scarce capital on a few select projects with linkages to other industries throughout the economy.[23]

Modern Liberals criticize Classical Liberals for equating economic growth with development. As noted by Simon Kuznets (1901–1985), the early stages of growth are typically accompanied by increasing inequality and a worsening of conditions for the poorest members of society as the agricultural sector declines relative to the manufacturing sector.[24] To counteract this trend, Modern Liberals call for "growth with equity," focusing on the achievement of social goals such as reducing infant mortality, raising the literacy rate, and meeting the basic needs of the population.[25] Modern Liberals propose to focus assistance on the development of human resources through provision of adequate food, clothing, shelter, health care, and education. This "bottom-up" approach to development relies heavily on participatory efforts by local citizens. For Modern Liberals, projects using local resources and producing goods intended for local markets are essential to the development process. English economist E. F. Schumacher (1911–1977) insisted that investment projects should utilize "intermediate technology" lying somewhere between the capital-intensive techniques of the West and the traditional labor-intensive techniques of the LDCs.[26] Otherwise, new investments are likely to exacerbate unemployment by reducing the amount of labor required for production.

Another facet of "growth with equity" is land reform. In many LDCs, ownership of land is concentrated in the hands of a few wealthy families and is used primarily for export crops. As a result, peasants are often denied access to land and must migrate to urban areas where poverty and disease are rampant. Modern Liberals advocate government efforts to disperse the ownership of land by breaking up large estates into small peasant holdings. Because wealthy families exert considerable political pressure on local governments to block land reform, Modern Liberals have suggested that foreign aid be contingent on significant progress in land reform.

Although Modern Liberals advocate foreign aid to LDCs, they have criticized the method of delivery. Typically, much of the money and food ends up in the hands of ruling elites. In some instances, foreign aid actually disrupts viable production processes. For example, food shipments might be distributed from a central location, requiring people from remote areas to travel for several weeks to obtain the food. This journey disrupts farming efforts, creating greater dependence. Even if aid is granted in the form of technology transfers, traditional production processes may be eliminated, causing unemployment and the disintegration of stable communities and families. Modern Liberals favor aid in the form of technical assistance and resources to initiate local projects leading toward self-sustaining agriculture and industry.

As for trade policy, Modern Liberals seek a middle course between free trade and protectionism. They are skeptical about the effects of free trade on both LDCs and industrialized nations. Keynes proposed that mature capitalist economies should strive for "national self-sufficiency" by protecting themselves from foreign competition to encourage a diversity of industries.[27] He feared that competition from cheap foreign labor would jeopardize efforts to maintain high levels of employment and high wages in the developed countries. Whereas Classical Liberals applaud free trade's disciplining effect on wages in the industrialized countries, Keynes viewed high wages as essential to maintaining sufficient aggregate demand. Any increased international competitiveness gained through low wages would be offset by domestic stagnation due to inadequate demand from consumers in the developed countries.

During the 1980s, Modern Liberal economists such as Paul Krugman, John Culbertson, and Robert Kuttner formulated "strategic trade theory" to provide rationales for limited trade protection.[28] Refuting the Classical Liberal claim that any losses from trade will be more than offset by gains elsewhere in the economy, Modern Liberals argue that the theory of comparative advantage rests on the unrealistic assumption of a perfectly competitive economy with no externalities, full information, and perfect mobility of resources. In the real world, adjustment to dislocations caused by free trade can be painful and prolonged. Entire industries may stagnate for decades. Moreover, certain high-tech industries generate positive externalities by stimulating product development in other industries. The country with comparative advantage in those industries is likely to experience higher growth rates, so government action is justified to assure comparative advantage in selected industries.

A related argument favoring subsidies is that firms relying on extensive research and development are typically unable to reap the full social benefits of their efforts due to the dissemination of information. As a result, they will engage in less than the optimal amount of R&D. To encourage firms and industries to extend their research efforts, government may offer subsidies, tax breaks, or other forms of protection against competition.

Strategic trade theorists claim that comparative advantage can be created through public policy. As production becomes less dependent on climate and natural resources, and as capital and technology become increasingly mobile, the key determinant of comparative advantage is the quality of human resources. Government can exert considerable influence on human resource development through subsidies for education and job training. The country with a highly skilled labor force and innovative entrepreneurs will reap higher profits from production because these factors are the most scarce and least mobile in the global economy. Stated differently, countries with more skilled labor will specialize in higher "value-added" production, which generates greater profits and economic growth. As a result, all of society benefits from government efforts to create a more productive labor force.

Another Modern Liberal argument for government assistance to industries harmed by free trade is based on considerations of equity. If society as a whole benefits from the lower prices, increased efficiency, and innovation fostered by free trade, then society as a whole should share the burden of unemployment and business failures in industries suffering a loss of comparative advantage. This social assistance might take the form of subsidies for job training or relocation, low-interest loans, or temporary trade restrictions to give industries more time to adjust to changing market conditions.

Modern Liberals also warn that unfettered trade creates the dangerous potential for a "race to the bottom" as each nation is pressured to reduce wages and benefits in the quest for international competitiveness. Instead, Modern Liberals encourage government to take the "high road"; protection of high wages can actually improve competitiveness by providing corporations with strong incentives to invest in productivity-enhancing technology and by motivating employees to upgrade their skills and to increase the intensity of their work efforts. Modern Liberals claim that wage-cutting, union-busting, and deregulation lead to greater income inequality without improving international competitiveness.

A final argument for trade protection is based on the size of modern corporations. Firms engaged in large-scale production require stable costs and prices to plan long-term investments. By increasing uncertainty, free trade discourages investment and contributes to industrial decline. Even when an industry is in decline, trade protection may provide time to innovate, renegotiate contracts, modernize facilities, and return to competitive status.

However, the Modern Liberal case against free trade is not an unqualified endorsement of protection. Modern Liberals accept much of the Classical Liberal argument that protection encourages inefficiency and retards innovation. Paul Krugman, the leading theorist of strategic trade policy, became so concerned that his ideas were being used by advocates of widespread protection that he declared his support for free trade with only minor exceptions of limited duration and scope.[29] Modern Liberals acknowledge that a substantial portion of existing protection reflects lobbying efforts by special-interest groups. Government should carefully consider all such requests to determine which forms of protection serve the national interest in maintaining a healthy and diversified economy.

In attempting to move toward freer trade, Modern Liberals seek multilateral or reciprocal agreements between nations to lower trade barriers. Even if the economic arguments for free trade are valid, politicians cannot ignore the reality of closed factories and unemployed workers. To create popular support for lower trade barriers, each country must secure similar concessions from trading partners. Public acceptance of free trade can also be cultivated by government policies to deal with unemployment and wage depression created by international trade and by negotiating trade agreements containing stipulations about environmental protection, human rights, and labor unions in other countries. If trading partners refuse to negotiate, politicians may choose to retain domestic protection, pursuing "fair trade" rather than free trade. However, to prevent protectionism from degenerating into trade wars and "beggar thy neighbor" policies, Modern Liberals seek cooperative strategies among nations to develop rules governing international trade.[30]

The North American Free Trade Agreement (NAFTA) has been a deeply divisive issue for Modern Liberals. Proponents view the creation of a free trade zone between Canada, Mexico, and the United States as a necessary response to emerging free trade zones in Europe and Asia, while opponents worry that lower wages and less restrictive environmental, health, and safety standards in Mexico will give Mexican firms an unfair advantage and cause U.S. firms to move south or to cut wages and benefits.[31]

NOTES

1. See Anne O. Krueger, *Economic Policies at Cross-Purposes: The United States and Developing Countries*, Washington, DC: Brookings Institution, 1993; Ryan C. Amacher, Gottfried Haberler, and Thomas D. Willett, eds., *Challenges to a Liberal Economic Order*, Washington, DC: American Enterprise Institute, 1979; and Deepak Lal, *Against Dirigisme: The Case for Unshackling Economic Markets*, San Francisco, ICS Press, 1994.

2. For a collection of essays representing the Classical Liberal perspective on economic development, see David Wall, ed., *Chicago Essays in Economic Development*, Chicago: University of Chicago Press, 1972.

3. See Deepak Lal, *The Poverty of Development Economics*, Cambridge, MA: Harvard University Press, 1985; Peter T. Bauer, *Dissent on Development*, London: Weidenfeld & Nicolson, 1971; and Peter T. Bauer, *Reality and Rhetoric: Studies in the Economics of Development*, Cambridge, MA: Harvard University Press, 1984. For a critique of Classical Liberal development theory, see John Toye, *Dilemmas of Development: Reflections on the Counter-revolution in Development Theory and Policy*, Oxford: Blackwell, 1987.

4. A Classical Liberal response to concern about plant closings and job loss due to international competition is presented in Richard B. McKenzie, *Fugitive Industry: The Economics and Politics of Deindustrialization*, Cambridge, MA: Ballinger, 1984.

5. See Melvyn B. Krauss, *How Nations Grow Rich: The Case for Free Trade*, New York: Oxford University Press, 1997; Anne O. Krueger, *The Political Economy of Protection*, Chicago: University of Chicago Press, 1996; and Charles K. Rowley, Willem Thorbecke, and Richard E. Wagner, *Trade Protection in the United States*, Brookfield, VT: Edward Elgar, 1995.

6. Friedrich A. Hayek, *The Road to Serfdom*, London: Routledge & Kegan Paul, 1979.

7. V. I. Lenin, *Imperialism: The Highest Stage of Capitalism*, New York: International Publishers, 1969. For more recent Radical analyses of imperialism, see Anthony Brewer, *Marxist Theories of Imperialism: A Critical Survey*, 2nd ed., New York: Routledge, 1992, and Chronis Polychroniou, *Marxist Perspectives on Imperialism*, New York: Praeger, 1991.

8. Paul Baran, *The Political Economy of Growth*, New York: Monthly Review Press, 1967.

9. For surveys of dependency theory, see Vincent A. Mahler, *Dependency Approaches to International Political Economy*, New York: Columbia University Press, 1980; Mary Ann Tetreault and Charles Frederic Abel, eds., *Dependency Theory and the Return of High Politics*, Westport, CT: Greenwood, 1986; and Dudley Seers, ed., *Dependency Theory: A Critical Reassessment*, London: Pinter, 1981.

10. Samir Amin, *Accumulation on a World Scale*, New York: Monthly Review Press, 1974; Arghiri Emanuel, *Unequal Exchange: A Study of the Imperialism of Trade*, New York: Monthly Review Press, 1972; Immanuel Wallerstein and Terence K. Hopkins, *World-systems Analysis: Theory and Methodology*, Beverly Hills, CA: Sage, 1982; and André Gunder Frank and Barry K. Gills, eds., *The World System*, New York: Routledge, 1993.

11. André Gunder Frank, *Capitalism and Underdevelopment in Latin America*, New York: Monthly Review Press, 1969. See also André Gunder Frank, *Crisis in the Third World*, New York: Holmes & Meier, 1981.

12. For more detail on proposals for an NIEO, see Jagdish Bhagwati, ed., *The New International Economic Order*, Cambridge: MIT Press, 1977; William R. Cline, *Policy Alternatives for a New International Economic Order: An Economic Analysis*, New York: Praeger, 1979; Pradip K. Ghosh, *NIEO: A Third World Perspective*, Westport, CT: Greenwood, 1984; and Prakash N. Agarwala, *The New International Economic Order: An Overview*, New York: Pergamen, 1983.

13. See J. H. Boeke, *Economics and Economic Policy in Dual Societies*, New York: Institute for Pacific Relations, 1953. See also S. H. Frankel, *The Economic Impact on Underdeveloped Societies*, Oxford: Basil Blackwell, 1953.

14. See David McClelland, *The Achieving Society*, Princeton, NJ: Van Nostrand, 1961.

15. See Ellsworth Huntington, *Civilization and Climate*, New York: Arno Press, 1977. See also, Edward C. Banfield, *The Moral Basis of a Backward Society*. Glencoe, IL: The Free Press, 1958.

16. The argument for a single hegemonic leader in the global economy is examined in Robert Gilpin, *War and Change in World Politics*, Cambridge: Cambridge University Press, 1981. The claim that cooperation and coordination between a few great powers can serve as a substitute for hegemonic leadership is made in Robert O. Keohane, *After Hegemony: Cooperation and Discord in the World Political Economy*, Princeton, NJ: Princeton University Press, 1984.

17. See Norman Podhoretz, *The Present Danger*, New York: Simon & Schuster, 1980. See also Jeane J. Kirkpatrick, *Legitimacy and Force*, New Brunswick, NJ: Transaction Books, 1988.

18. See Jeane J. Kirkpatrick, *Dictatorships and Double Standards*, New York: Simon & Schuster, 1982.

19. See Alfred E. Eckes, *Opening America's Markets*, Chapel Hill, NC: University of North Carolina Press, 1995. See also Clyde V. Prestowitz, Jr., *Trading Places*, New York: Basic Books, 1988.

20. Gunnar Myrdal, *Development and Underdevelopment*, Cairo: National Bank of Egypt, 1956. See also Gunnar Myrdal, *The International Economy*, New York: Harper, 1956.

21. Ragnar Nurkse, *Problems of Capital Formation in Underdeveloped Countries*, Oxford: Basil Blackwell, 1953.

22. Paul Rosenstein-Rodan, *Philosophy and Practice in Latin American Development*, Cambridge: MIT Press, 1972.

23. Albert O. Hirschman, *The Strategy of Economic Development*, New Haven, CT: Yale University Press, 1959.

24. Simon Kuznets, "Economic Growth and Income Inequality," *American Economic Review* 45 (1955): 1–28.

25. See Irma Adelman and Cynthia Taft Morris, *Economic Growth and Social Equity in Developing Countries*, Stanford, CA: Stanford University Press, 1973, and Martin Neil Baily, Gary Burtless, and Robert Litan, *Growth with Equity*, Washington, DC: Brookings Institution, 1993.

26. E. F. Schumacher, *Small Is Beautiful: Economics As If People Mattered*, New York: Harper & Row, 1973.

27. John Maynard Keynes, "National Self-sufficiency," *The Yale Review* 22, no. 4 (June 1933): 155–69.

28. See Paul Krugman, ed., *Strategic Trade Policy and the New International Economics*, Cambridge: MIT Press, 1986; John M. Culbertson, "The Folly of Free Trade," *Harvard Business Review* (Sept./Oct. 1986): 122–28; and Robert Kuttner, *Managed Trade and Economic Sovereignty*, Washington, DC: Economic Policy Institute, 1989.

29. Paul Krugman, "Is Free Trade Passe," *Journal of Economic Perspectives* 1987, 131–44. See also Paul Krugman, *Pop Internationalism*, Cambridge: MIT Press, 1996.

30. The Modern Liberal debate over free trade and protectionism is presented in Alex Oxley, *The Challenge of Free Trade*, New York: Harvester Wheatsheaf, 1990; H. Peter Gray, *Free Trade or Protection?: A Pragmatic Analysis*, New York: St. Martin's, 1985; and Gunnar Sjostedt and Bengt Sundelius, eds., *Free Trade-Managed Trade?: Perspectives on a Realistic International Trade Order*, Boulder, CO: Westview Press, 1986. For a Classical Liberal critique of the concept of fair trade, see James Bovard, *The Fair Trade Fraud*, New York: St. Martin's, 1991.

31. See Ricardo Grinspun and Maxwell A. Cameron, eds., *The Political Economy of North American Free Trade*, New York: St. Martin's, 1993; M. Delal Baer and Sidney Weintraub, eds., *The NAFTA Debate*, Boulder, CO: Lynne Rienner Publishers, 1994; A. R. Riggs and Tom Valk, eds., *Beyond NAFTA: An Economic, Political and Sociological Perspective*, Vancouver: The Fraser Institute, 1993; and William J. Orme, Jr., *Understanding NAFTA: Mexico, Free Trade and the New North America*, Austin: University of Texas Press, 1996.

ADDITIONAL READING

Arndt, H. W. *Economic Development: The History of an Idea*. Chicago: University of Chicago Press, 1987.

Axford, Barrie. *The Global System: Politics, Economics, and Culture*. New York: St. Martin's, 1995.

Balaam, David N., and Michael Veseth. *Introduction to International Political Economy*. Upper Saddle River, NJ: Prentice Hall, 1996.

Balassa, Bela. *New Directions in the World Economy*. New York: New York University Press, 1989.

Bates, Robert H., ed. *Toward a Political Economy of Development*. Berkeley: University of California Press, 1988.

Blecker, Robert A., ed. *U.S. Trade Policy and Global Growth: New Directions in The International Economy*. Armonk, NY: M. E. Sharpe, 1996.

Chilcoate, Ronald. *Theories of Development and Underdevelopment*. Boulder, CO: Westview Press, 1984.

Cowan, Michael P., and Robert W. Shenton. *Doctrines of Development*. New York: Routledge, 1996.

Cowling, Keith, and Roger Sugden. *Transnational Monopoly Capitalism*. New York: St. Martin's, 1987.

Crane, George T., and Abla Amawi, eds. *The Theoretical Evolution of International Political Economy*, 2nd ed. New York: Oxford University Press, 1997.

Dell, Edmund. *The Politics of Economic Interdependence*. New York: St. Martin's, 1987.

Frey, Bruno. *International Political Economy*. Oxford: Basil Blackwell, 1984.

Frieden, Jeffrey A., and David A. Lake, eds. *International Political Economy: Perspectives on Global Power and Wealth*. New York: St. Martin's, 1987.

Gill, Stephen, and David Law. *The Global Political Economy*. New York: Harvester Wheatsheaf, 1988.

Gilpin, Robert. *The Political Economy of International Relations*. Princeton, NJ: Princeton University Press, 1987.

Godard, C. Roe, John T. Passe-Smith, and John G. Conklin, eds. *International Political Economy: State-Market Relations in the Changing Global Order*. Boulder: Lynne Rienner, 1996.

Hunt, Diana. *Economic Theories of Development*. Totowa, NJ: Rowman & Littlefield, 1987.

Kapstein, Ethan B. *Governing the Global Economy: International Finance and the State*. Cambridge, MA: Harvard University Press, 1994.

Long, David. *Towards A New Liberal Internationalism*. New York: Cambridge University Press, 1996.

Mander, Jerry, and Edward Goldsmith, eds. *The Case Against the Global Economy*. San Francisco: Sierra Club Books, 1996.

Martinussen, John. *Society, State and Market: A Guide to Competing Theories of Development*. London: Zed Books, 1997.

Mason, Mike. *Development and Disorder: A History of the Third World Since 1945*. Hanover, NH: University Press of New England, 1997.

Pirages, Dennis C., and Christine Sylvester, eds. *Transformations in the Global Political Economy*. New York: St. Martin's, 1990.

Sears, Dudley. *The Political Economy of Nationalism*. Oxford: Oxford University Press, 1983.

Smith, David A., and Jozsef Borocz. *A New World Order?: Global Transformation in The Late 20th Century*. Westport, CT: Greenwood Press, 1995.

Spero, Joan E. *The Politics of International Economic Relations*, 4th ed. New York: St. Martin's, 1990.

Strange, Susan. *States and Markets: An Introduction to International Political Economy*, 2nd. ed. New York: Pinter Publishers, 1994.

Thurow, Lester. *Head to Head: The Coming Battle Among Japan, Europe and America*. New York: William Morrow, 1992.

Chapter 16

Science, Ideology, and Political Economy

Every human being has ideological, moral and political views. To pretend to have none and to be purely objective must necessarily be either self-deception or a device to deceive others.
Joan Robinson

The way we see things can hardly be distinguished from the way we wish to see them.
Joseph Schumpeter

In the decades following World War II, it became intellectually fashionable to proclaim "the end of ideology."[1] Ideology was blamed for raising visions of heaven on earth, which fueled fanaticism and ultimately contributed to the rise of totalitarian systems on both the political left and right. At the time, fascism had been defeated and communism was presumed to be geographically contained until it would exhaust itself in a morass of economic inefficiency and political brutality. The divisive issues facing modern societies had seemingly been resolved in favor of democratic capitalism, and politics would subsequently consist of the administration of public functions by elected officials and appointed bureaucrats.

This vision proved to be premature. While international relations have been relatively peaceful and communism has indeed collapsed as predicted, ideological debate over economics, politics, and culture continues unabated. Most people profess to dislike ideology, viewing it as an intellectual strait jacket obscuring clear thinking. However, no person can escape ideology because humans are interpretive creatures struggling to make sense of what William James called the "buzzing, blooming confusion" of the external world. Ideology is simply a name for the mental constructs used by humans to guide their thinking and behavior. In premodern times, religion served this purpose, but with the advent of science and democracy, ideas about the world had to be legitimized in secular and rational terms to gain serious consideration by scholars, policymakers, and the public.

The distaste for ideology can be traced back to the scientific revolutions of the sixteenth through eighteenth centuries. The medieval era had provided humans with certainty that reality was a well-ordered system operating in accordance with natural laws of divine origin. The only prerequisite for correctly interpreting the external world was religious faith and openness to revelation. However, the cumulative impact of the Renaissance, the Protestant Reformation, commerce, and technology shattered medieval knowledge. Out of the ruins emerged a growing confidence that human reason was sufficiently acute to interpret the world without the aid of established religious authority. The French philosopher René Descartes (1596–1650) and the English physicist Isaac Newton (1642–1727) affirmed the existence of God and an orderly universe operating in accordance with natural laws, but their determination to combat dogma and superstition compelled them to seek a method for uncovering truth that was verifiable and therefore persuasive to all reasonable persons.

Descartes was haunted by the suspicion that his ideas were the work of a demon intent on deceiving him. Trust in sensory perception had been shaken by Copernicus's discovery that a world appearing to be flat and motionless was actually round and spinning. Mistrusting his senses, Descartes advocated doubt and skepticism as essential to scientific inquiry. In an effort to penetrate to a deeper level of reality than the senses could reach, he expressed physical dimensions such as mass and speed with mathematics and then applied logic to discover the laws of nature. Since only quantifiable aspects of the world could be captured by mathematics, Descartes's method created a distinction between an abstract, theoretical conception of reality and the actual world of objects and persons. Nonquantifiable aspects of reality were considered superficial and irrelevant for scientific knowledge. Thus, the Cartesian method, called "rationalism," relies on the logic of human reason to discover truth.

Although Newton shared many of Descartes's assumptions and methods, he insisted that verification of theories must ultimately entail testing against observed reality. The Newtonian method, known as "empiricism," recognizes that mathematics and reason may lead to a logical theory, but that theory may not be valid in its correspondence to reality. Newton accepted the role of reason in forming ideas, hypotheses, and theories, but demanded that these mental constructs be tested against facts to verify their status as scientific knowledge.

Scientists utilize both rational and empirical methods. The former relies on deductive reasoning to derive specific conclusions from general laws or principles. In contrast, empiricism uses inductive reasoning to construct general rules on the basis of accumulated observations of facts. Both mathematical proofs and controlled experimentation are components of the process of scientific verification, and ideally each can be used to confirm the results of the other. This scientific method instilled confidence that humans could understand the external world and, working within the laws of nature, improve the conditions of life.

Early political economists were tremendously impressed by achievements in the natural sciences. However, the complexity of human society made empiricism, inductive reasoning, and controlled experimentation problematic. The social world contains so many interacting variables that efforts to isolate cause and effect in a verifiable fashion are exceedingly difficult. As a result, political economists were attracted to rationalism. They formed an abstract conception of humans by focusing on the most consistent and easily measurable aspect of behavior—the pursuit of wealth. This image of man as *homo economicus* was the starting point of classical political economy. Yet John Stuart Mill acknowledged the fiction of *homo economicus* when he wrote:

Political economy does not treat of the whole of man's nature as modified by the social state, nor the whole conduct of man in society. It is concerned with him solely as a being who desires to possess wealth, and who is capable of judging of the comparative efficiency of means for obtaining that end.[2]

Having made this concession, Mill defended continued reliance on the concept of *homo economicus* "not (because) any political economist was ever so absurd as to suppose that mankind are really thus constituted; but because this is the mode in which science must necessarily proceed."[3] This statement is revealing, for it demonstrates that a commitment to the scientific method has dictated the scope and content of political economy by effectively precluding consideration of those dimensions of life unsuitable for quantification and measurement.

If ideology is defined as reliance on values to interpret reality, then despite its aspirations to scientific status, political economy has been ideological from the beginning. Early political economists were clearly engaged in efforts to promote the interests of an emerging business class in its struggle against government control and remnants of feudal authority. Most modern economists might agree that every political economist prior to

1870, or perhaps even 1930, was an ideologue. Yet even modern economists cannot avoid ideology. Theorizing necessarily entails abstraction, and
science offers no certain guidelines as to which aspects of reality are most
relevant. Facts have significance in proportion to their usefulness in achieving human goals, and those goals are based on values. Therefore, the decision to focus on particular aspects of reality for the purpose of constructing
theories is a value judgment. Even in empirical research, values influence
which aspects of reality will be observed and what will be considered a
"fact." In the social sciences, researchers deal with issues about which all
humans have value-laden preconceptions, and these commitments cannot
be kept separate from scientific inquiry.

Criticism of the scientific method in political economy has a long history. Nineteenth-century French and German writers claimed that British
political economy was based on faulty assumptions and fallacious reasoning. In fact, the field of sociology was established, in large part, as a reaction to political economy by French and German theorists such as Emile
Durkheim (1858–1917), Max Weber (1864–1920), and Ferdinand Tönnies
(1855–1936). Many, if not most, U.S. economists in the nineteenth century
favored the empiricist and historical method developed in Germany over
the rationalist and deductive reasoning of English economists. Even in
England, prominent economists such as Philip Wicksteed (1844–1927), F.
Y. Edgeworth (1845–1926), and John A. Hobson (1858–1940) argued that
economics was too abstract and narrowly defined to provide practical
guidance in public policymaking. The most renowned English economist of
the late nineteenth century, Alfred Marshall, was praised by A. C. Pigou for
realizing that:

excessive reliance on (mathematics) might lead us astray in pursuit of intellectual
toys, imaginary problems not conforming to the conditions of real life: and further,
might distort our sense of proportion by causing us to neglect factors that could not
easily be worked up in the mathematical machine.[4]

Despite these reservations, economics subsequently became even more
abstract and mathematical. During the 1930s and 1940s, the spread of
fascism and communism motivated neoclassical economists to renew their
commitment to the scientific method. The atrocities occurring within
totalitarian systems created widespread disillusionment with all collec-
tivist schemes, so increasing numbers of economists rejected the use of
economics as a tool for fashioning activist public policies aimed at improving society. Intent on keeping ideology out of scientific research and analysis, these economists were attracted to a philosophy called logical
positivism developed in Vienna during the 1920s. This approach is based
on the notion of a clear distinction between *is* and *ought*, between fact and
value, between *de*scription and *pre*scription. Only positive statements

dealing with the world as it is can potentially be proved wrong (falsified) by comparison with facts. In contrast, normative statements, or judgments concerning what ought to be, are based on individual opinion and can therefore be neither confirmed nor falsified. Neoclassical economists welcomed logical positivism as a philosophical defense against totalitarian ideologies because it treats normative claims about how society ought to be structured as "meaningless" and therefore unworthy of serious consideration by economists.

This opposition to values applied only to the realm of science. Individuals would still be free to express personal tastes or preferences in the market or in their social activity. Logical positivists were determined to keep values out of science so that science could not be used to legitimize government policies conflicting with the private values of individuals. Led by Lionel Robbins in England, neoclassical economists sought to purge economics of all remnants of normative thinking; the world would be analyzed as it is, not as it should be.[5] By restricting their analysis to logic and facts, they intended to distinguish themselves from mere ideologues seeking to impose unsubstantiated opinions and arbitrary values on the general public. By the 1950s, neoclassical economists had incorporated Keynesianism into their theoretical framework and effectively captured control of the economics profession.

The legacy of this turning point in the evolution of economics is apparent today. Economic theory has become an almost completely mathematical exercise in logic, insulated from many of the forces shaping actual economic processes. In 1991, a group of economists commissioned by the American Economic Association to assess the conditions of graduate economic education in the United States concluded that "graduate programs may be turning out a generation with too many *idiot savants*, skilled in technique but innocent of real economic issues."[6] In modern economics, the influence of new ideas often depends more on their internal logic and the sophistication of their mathematical expression than on their relevance to resolving real-world problems. Even the most prominent of mainstream economists are occasionally frustrated with the current state of affairs in their profession. Nobel laureate Ronald Coase recently wrote: "In my youth it was said that what was too silly to be said may be sung. In modern economics it may be put into mathematics."[7]

ECONOMICS AS IDEOLOGY

Despite the concerted efforts of several generations of economists to create a pure science of economics, values remain implicit in economic theory. (Note: the terms "economics," "economist," and "economic theory" shall hereafter refer to the neoclassical variants of these terms.) Examples of these values include the following:

1. *Humans should be free to pursue their individual interests as long as they do not violate the rights of others.* In addition to being obviously normative, this statement contains two hidden values. First, the term "individual interests" is interpreted to mean desires for private goods, services, and experiences; it does not include desires for the type of institutional context or societal values within which private activity occurs. Second, economists interpret "rights" to mean only property rights and those civil rights such as free speech that bestow no entitlement to economic resources. However, if rights were defined more broadly to include rights to economic benefits such as health care, a job, or a clean environment, then the individual pursuit of self-interest would fail to protect the rights of citizens.

2. *Humans are rational maximizers of utility.* Economists have struggled for two centuries to decide exactly what *homo economicus* is seeking. The original claim that humans seek to maximize wealth was contradicted by everyday observations that many people do not direct their lives toward this goal. Beginning in the mid-nineteenth century, economists used the word "utility" to describe the goal of economic behavior, but even this concept was criticized for portraying humans as pleasure-seeking hedonists. In the twentieth century, economists tried to free themselves from any association with hedonism by developing the concept of "revealed preference." People's choices reveal their wants; if they had wanted something else, they would have made different choices. By resorting to revealed preference, economists implicitly acknowledge the circular meaning of utility. If utility is whatever people seek, then the claim that people maximize utility is tautological; it cannot be contradicted by fact because utility is defined to cover all possible behaviors. The same criticism can be made of the term "rational." For an economist, behavior is rational if it is directed toward the attainment of maximum utility. But because individuals are assumed to be the only judges of their own utility, no behavior can be called irrational. Like utility maximization, the claim that humans are rational is a tautology. Since tautologies are immune to falsification, they function as ideology.

3. *Individual preferences are independent of the social environment.* Economic theory treats preferences as originating within the biological and psychological drives of the individual. This view contrasts sharply with the perspective of most sociologists and psychologists who emphasize the role of social conditioning and acculturation in shaping individual preferences. Why do economists adamantly defend such an implausible argument? Again, the desire to emulate natural science dictates this assumption. If preferences were treated as dependent variables, economists could no longer analyze the economy as a closed system separate from the political

and sociocultural systems, and much of the precision and logic of economics would be lost. For example, economist Tibor Scitovsky demonstrated that if preferences are dependent on the social environment, individuals in situation A might prefer situation B, but if situation B were attained, the different environment might cause the same individuals to prefer situation A.[8] Economists could no longer claim that markets generate a unique and stable equilibrium reflecting individual preferences, resource availability, and technology.

4. *All preferences for private goods or services are equally valid but deserve fulfillment only to the extent that they are backed by money.* The equal validity of preferences assumes that individuals are the best judges of their own interests. This claim appeals to our sense of human dignity by recognizing the capacity of individuals to direct their own lives. However, it is ideological because it cannot be tested or even potentially falsified using standard scientific methods. Any action can be interpreted as serving a person's best interests because no method exists for assessing private interests. Moreover, this assumption blinds economists to both the private and social processes through which preferences arise. Individuals often struggle with their own preferences, experiencing conflict between immediate desires and prior commitments to other persons or moral principles. In addition to their preferences, individuals have "metapreferences" guiding them in choosing which of their desires to express and which to suppress. These metapreferences reflect the type of person the individual aspires to become. Treating all preferences as equally valid is thus unscientific because it fails to grasp essential aspects of preference formation. The claim that preferences deserve fulfillment only to the extent that they are backed by money is a corollary of economists' definition of rights as including only property rights and those civil rights making no demands on economic resources. This claim is unscientific because the definition of rights is a value judgment.

5. *A perfectly competitive market yields an efficient allocation of resources.* This statement, which constitutes the core proposition of neoclassical economic theory, is nonscientific because the definition of efficiency is itself value-laden. Markets may be inefficient if efficiency is defined as maximizing the total level of human satisfaction, as maximizing the attainment of societal goals, as maximizing the development of human capacities, or even as maximizing the expansion of output over time. Markets are only efficient in meeting economists' definition of efficiency: a situation in which all individuals have completed all mutually beneficial transactions. Based on this definition, the claim that markets generate efficiency is another tautology. To grasp this point, consider the following reasoning:

Assumption 1: A perfectly competitive market permits individuals to engage in all mutually beneficial transactions.

Assumption 2: Efficiency is a situation in which all mutually beneficial transactions have been completed.

Conclusion: A perfectly competitive market is efficient.

Since the conclusion is implied by the premises, the claim that markets are efficient is tautologous. Economists rely on this empty definition of efficiency due to scientific and ideological problems encountered in the late nineteenth century. At that time, efficiency was hazily linked with the maximization of social utility. The claim that markets maximize the overall level of well-being in society provided a powerful argument in support of markets. However, economists soon recognized that the notion of maximizing social utility presupposed the summing up of individual utilities, which would require interpersonal comparisons of utility. Since utility cannot be measured in any absolute sense, they rejected social utility as an unscientific concept. A second objection to maximizing social utility was created by applying the law of diminishing marginal utility to money. If wealthy people get less satisfaction from an additional dollar of income than do poor people, maximization of social utility would seemingly require massive redistribution of income from rich to poor. Most economists were unwilling to validate this conclusion and, led by Vilfredo Pareto, they proceeded in the early twentieth century to redefine efficiency as a situation in which all mutually beneficial transactions have been completed so that no person can be made better off without making someone else worse off.

Economists defend their concept of efficiency as value-free and scientific, yet considerations of efficiency form the basis for virtually all their policy recommendations. How can a science with no values shed light on what government ought to do without violating logical positivism's separation of *is* and *ought*? The answer is twofold. First, efficiency is not a value-free concept; it presupposes the values previously discussed in this section. Second, economists commit an ideological sleight of hand when they use words like "optimal" and "rational" as synonyms for efficient. If citizens were told that a particular policy would create an "optimal allocation of resources," they would understandably interpret that phrase to mean the best possible allocation. However, an efficient economy is consistent with conditions that would offend most people. For example, those individuals who, because of age or infirmity, are incapable of supporting themselves or securing private charity would be left to die.

The assumption that perfect competition generates efficiency leads to a general presumption that society is better off if markets are more competitive. Yet in 1956, economists Richard Lipsey and Kelvin Lancaster demonstrated that when the conditions of perfect competition are violated in two or more parts of the economy, restoring competition to only one part may decrease efficiency. For example, if a labor union faces a monopolistic employer, then breaking up the labor union to improve competition may reduce efficiency. This "theory of the second best" makes any policy recommendations concerning market structure more difficult to justify.[9]

6. *Unanimous consent should be required for any political changes to the economic status quo.* This value is explicitly stated by only a minority of economists known as property rights theorists. However, the definition of efficiency makes unanimous consent an implicit value in economic analysis. Any policy that increases efficiency would presumably receive unanimous support because at least one person is made better off and nobody is made worse off. However, any policy that decreases efficiency will make at least one person worse off, and that person would presumably withhold consent. Because virtually all policies have redistributive effects harmful to at least one person, the unanimity rule effectively bars government action. However, John Hicks and Nicholas Kaldor attempted to loosen the criterion for efficient public policies by proposing a "compensation principle." If those who benefit from a public policy could hypothetically compensate the losers and still be better off, the policy would be considered efficient. This idea provides the theoretical basis for cost–benefit analysis used by economists to assess the effectiveness of decisions and policies. However, cost–benefit analysis entails the inevitable introduction of values as economists must make judgments about which costs and benefits to consider and how to measure them.

REJOINDERS FROM ECONOMISTS

If the foregoing critique of economics is valid, why do economists continue to defend the assumptions and scientific status of their discipline so aggressively? Consider the following arguments made by prominent economists:

1. English economist John Neville Keynes (1852–1949) admitted that economics held unrealistic assumptions and that economists had limited ability to predict specific occurrences. However, he defended the power of economists to forecast long-run tendencies because, over time, the random effects of unknown variables would offset each other. However, any theory can be defended with the claim that its predictions will eventually be confirmed in the future. The ultimate response to this line of reasoning came from Neville Keynes's son, Maynard: "in the long run we are all dead."

2. English economist Sir Dennis Robertson (1890–1963) defended the assumption of self-interest by arguing that while love, empathy, and altruism exist, they are too scarce to serve as a basis for social organization. This

judgment is most likely accurate, but Robertson concluded that markets are the ideal coordinating institution because they economize on love by relying solely on self-interest. Compassion and good will can then be reserved for personal relationships. The problem with this argument is that economizing on altruism to create a good society is a bit like refraining from exercise to maintain bodily strength. The structures and opportunities available to humans shape their capacities for particular sentiments and behaviors. A society organized solely around the principle of self-interest will generate strongly self-interested citizens. This phenomenon occurs because individuals in markets acting as isolated agents are relatively powerless to counteract market forces with noneconomic values. For example, employers who pay generous wages because of loyalty to their workers may lose customers due to higher costs.

3. Economists' assumptions about human behavior have also been defended as protecting the freedom and dignity of the individual. The self-interested pursuit of material well-being is a necessary and universal aspect of human existence. Any fuller account of human behavior, economists claim, might not be universally valid and would therefore bias economics in favor of certain lifestyles or values. This argument fails to recognize that ignoring nonmaterial values creates a bias in favor of acquisitive, materialistic lifestyles. A more objective description of human behavior would include other universal traits such as self-reflection, compassion, playfulness, creativity, and the search for meaning, purpose, and identity.

4. Economists may admit that the nineteenth century image of *homo economicus* was indeed an ideological construct, but simultaneously defend modern economic theory's portrayal of human behavior. The goal of wealth maximization has been replaced by utility maximization, and utility can be derived from any pursuit of human interests. Therefore, they claim, economic theory is relevant to any situation in which individuals pursue their interests under conditions of scarcity. This argument constitutes the most widely used defense of economics, but taken to its logical conclusion it leads to tautology. As previously noted, if utility is defined as the goal of all possible choices and behaviors, then a person could never act in a nonutilitarian manner. Tautologies are useless for practical application, so when economists apply theory to analyze real-world situations, they invariably narrow the concept of utility to focus on material interests most amenable to monetary quantification.

Economists are confronted with a dilemma. A broader concept of utility is attractive because it provides a quick defense against critics of *homo economicus* and legitimizes economic theory as a valid method of inquiry into all dimensions of human existence. However, this definition of utility is tautologous and therefore useless in practice. On the other hand, a narrower conception of utility linked primarily with material gain provides economists with a "set of tools" for advising corporations and governments in making efficient decisions. However, to explicitly acknowledge a limited scope for utility would make economics vulnerable to charges of narrowness and irrelevance to nonmaterial realms of social life. Since neither of these choices is appealing, economists simply live with the dilemma, paying lip service to a broadly defined utility while practicing with a narrower concept.

5. Milton Friedman acknowledges that many of the assumptions of economics are unrealistic but claims that predictive capability rather than realism of assumptions is the hallmark of good science.[10] In other words, if economic theory generates predictions confirmed by observation, then the realism of its assumptions should not matter. Using Friedman's criteria, the field of macroeconomics has been a dismal failure. Economists have been unable to forecast future economic conditions accurately. In fact, different economists offer such divergent forecasts that one consulting firm has developed a thriving business gathering and averaging the various forecasts to arrive at a consensus. Many corporations have reduced or eliminated their economic research departments due to unreliable forecasts of changing market trends.

In microeconomics, the relatively new field of experimental economics represents an effort to confirm the predictions of economic theory. Small groups of people are given instructions for participating in a competitive, interactive situation designed to simulate a market. These experiments usually yield results consistent with economic theory, but by placing people in a 'laboratory' with instructions about their goals and methods for achieving those goals, economists create the *ceteris paribus* conditions that make microeconomic theory largely an exercise in logic rather than a description of how humans produce, distribute, and consume goods and services. Experimental economics often simply demonstrates the obvious and therefore fails to address the deeper criticisms of neoclassical microeconomic theory.[11]

6. A final defense of the assumptions and implicit values underlying economics is based on appeals to the necessity of science. When the human mind attempts to grasp reality, the overwhelming complexity of the world dictates reliance on the methods of abstraction, simplification, logical analysis, and controlled experimentation. Simplifying assumptions may entail human judgments of the relative significance of different aspects of reality, but without them, knowledge would be at a standstill. Moreover, without science, there would be no ultimate authority for distinguishing between knowledge and mere opinion. To openly allow values into economics would, in the words of Nobel laureate James Buchanan, remove "all scientific content from the discipline and (reduce) discussion to a babel of voices making noise."[12]

The persuasive power of the foregoing argument derives from the implicit assumption that the method of the natural sciences is the only reliable avenue for expanding knowledge. The scientific method demands that researchers and theorists be skeptical, willing to reject established truths in light of new evidence, and continually open to consider new hypotheses and research findings. However, the scientific method also creates its own form of dogmatism. New ideas are given a hearing only when they are presented in a form amenable to logical analysis and empirical verification. While these processes may be useful for developing knowledge, they do not exhaust the sources of human understanding. The objectivity and detachment so prized by natural scientists actually pose a barrier to inquiries into the human condition. The natural scientific method was originally designed to yield knowledge of causes and effects among natural phenomena so that humans could better manipulate the environment to meet their needs. When this same method is applied to human activities, people are viewed as objects responding to external forces, and knowledge is geared toward prediction and control. The social scientist adhering to the method of natural science cannot generate knowledge of the requisites for a good life.

The dogmatism generated by an unwavering commitment to the natural scientific method is exemplified by Stanford economist Robert Hall, who informed an interviewer that he immediately stops reading any article in which he encounters the words "social" or "society" because he knows it will be unscientific. Perhaps the most insightful explanation for this dogmatism comes from economist Charles Schultze:

When you dig deep down, economists are scared to death of being sociologists. The one great thing we have going for us is the premise that individuals act rationally in trying to satisfy their preferences.[13]

Like all scientists, economists pride themselves on being rational, analytical, and objective. They accept an intellectual obligation to act as guardians of the economy, trying to defend the market from "irrational exuberance," ideological enthusiasm, and the machinations of politicians. Yet, no matter how well-intentioned, economists rely on a distorted vision of human behavior and social structure and therefore their analysis inevitably constitutes only a partial perspective on any situation.

THE SCIENCE OF POLITICAL ECONOMY

If economics is ultimately based on values, then it cannot be defended as a purely scientific approach to understanding social, political, and economic institutions. In contrast to the value-free stance of economics, political economy recognizes the inevitable presence of values in all social inquiry and therefore acknowledges the legitimacy of diverse approaches for gaining knowledge. Political economy does not reject science, but rather defines it more broadly as a disciplined, communicable, and nondogmatic effort to expand the knowledge base with which humans are able, both individually and collectively, to improve the conditions of their existence. Using this definition, many alternative approaches to understanding the economy can be recognized as scientific. Accepting diversity creates a hospitable climate in which adherents of different viewpoints can exchange ideas. In the words of economist Frank Hahn:

We do not possess much certain knowledge about the economic world and . . . our best chance of gaining more is to try in all sorts of directions and by all sorts of means. This will not be furthered by strident commitments of faith.[14]

Traditional social scientists have divided society into separate realms over which they claim exclusive domain. Economists deal with the economy, that portion of society characterized by voluntary exchanges among rational, self-interested individuals. Political scientists examine the polity, in which individuals and groups pursue common goals and resolve conflicting interests through laws enforceable by government. Sociologists focus on society, in which the cultural practices and behavioral norms of communities function to harmonize individual behavior and social order. These distinctions among economy, polity, and society are important but also misleading without additional attention to their interdependence. The three realms are more accurately described as different facets of an immense network of systems. No scientific guidelines exist for dividing this network into neat compartments. The boundaries of economy, polity, and society are porous and shifting because they ultimately depend on values emanating from each realm. Commercial or market values formed in the economy, political values developed through the governing process, and cultural values within community life interact with one another to determine the proper extent of economic activity, political authority, and social control.

Economy, polity, and society each contain a "governance structure" that serves as both a control mechanism and an arena for the exercise of popular sovereignty. Hence each realm is both master and servant; each contains the potential for both oppression and liberation. A governance structure aggregates individual choices, coordinates these choices in an orderly pattern, and, based on this pattern, authoritatively circumscribes future individual choices. In performing these functions, each of the three governance structures has unique capabilities and deficiencies.

The economy's governance structure is the market. Through the price mechanism, markets allocate resources in a pattern responsive to individual choices and property rights. Market outcomes limit future choices by placing budget constraints on individuals and firms. The capabilities of markets include providing a broad range of individual freedom, facilitating personal development through choice and competition, and promoting higher standards of living. On the other hand, markets have exhibited notable deficiencies including instability, an inability to provide public goods, the creation of politically unacceptable levels of inequality, and an expansionist tendency to weaken and marginalize the political and social realms, thereby undermining potential remedies for the market's deficiencies.

The polity's governance structure is the state or government. Individual values and preferences are transmitted to government through the voting process, with additional reliance on opinion polls, focus groups, town meetings, and issue forums. These values are processed by elected representatives who then formulate laws posing constraints on individual choice that are backed by the coercive authority of the state. Government's capacities include pursuing goals incapable of expression in the market, protecting individual rights, addressing failures of the market, and serving as a symbol and agent of national unity and purpose. Some notable deficiencies of democratic government include its susceptibility to manipulation by powerful private interests, its weak mechanisms for enforcing internal efficiency and accountability, and its potential for abusing public authority.

The sociocultural system, or society, has its governance structure dispersed throughout numerous communities. A community consists of people sharing sufficiently similar values, traditions, and culture to create a sense of belonging and group identity. Communities materialize gradually as individual actions coalesce into cultural practices that are affirmed and nurtured because they are perceived as valuable to the community. Communities enforce these practices through institutions including parenting and schooling of young members, cultural rituals and ceremonies, expressions of approbation, and ostracism of deviants. Because communities are so closely involved in the character formation of young persons, they exert considerable influence on the development of values. Communities are stabilizing institutions because they integrate individuals into larger social units and thereby reduce the potential for conflict among members. Communities also provide a context within which individuals develop a sense of personal identity. However, community life contains several potential deficiencies. Community identities are based on a distinction between members and nonmembers that can degenerate into discrimination, hostility, and even warfare. Communities may be narrowly parochial and stifling, leading to suppression of creativity, innovation, and diversity. Communities may not be democratic since nongovernmental leaders typically emerge without formal selection procedures and exercise power without formal constraints. Finally, communities have little control over the larger environment in which they function and are therefore fragile and vulnerable to disruptive economic and political forces.

The interaction among market, government, and community may be destructive, but the three governance structures can also be mutually supportive. This support appears in two forms—*discipline* to suppress the deficiencies of other structures and *enabling* to enhance the capacities of other structures. Discipline places restraints on self-aggrandizing behaviors such as greed, power-seeking, and opportunistic strategies to benefit oneself at others' expense. Enabling facilitates the realization of capacities contributing to individual and societal well-being. Some highlights of the positive interactions among governance structures can be briefly described.

Markets discipline governments by facilitating movement of resources away from jurisdictions with unfavorable business climates, by generating concentrations of private wealth which can finance opposition candidates or dissenting ideas, and by strengthening popular support for individual rights. On the other hand, markets enable governments by generating tax revenue, by performing a substantial portion of social coordination, and by generating rising standards of living that contribute to public satisfaction with government.

Markets discipline communities by facilitating movement of resources away from communities with unfavorable business climates, providing alternatives and choices to individuals, and encouraging self-directed, self-reliant behavior. Yet markets also enable communities by providing opportunities for employment and entrepreneurship, by allowing communities to remain economically viable through specialization and exchange, and by creating economic interdependence among individuals.

Governments discipline markets by establishing and enforcing laws prohibiting or requiring certain types of market transactions, business practices, and industry structures, and by using macro policy tools to regulate the level of economic activity. On the other hand, governments enable markets by defining and protecting property rights, enforcing contracts, and providing infrastructure within which economic activity occurs.

Governments discipline communities by establishing and enforcing laws prohibiting certain behaviors and cultural practices, by imposing curriculum and standards in education, and by protecting individual and property rights. At the same time, governments enable communities by serving as symbols of unity and shared purpose, by providing public goods such as roads and schools, and by limiting the encroachment of market forces through regulations on business activity.

Communities discipline markets by generating organized movements aimed at halting certain business practices, by shaping values that affect patterns of consumption and production, and by exerting peer pressure on members whose business practices violate community norms. On the other hand, communities enable markets by sustaining ethical standards that reduce opportunistic behavior such as shirking or fraud, by creating a climate of trust and loyalty that reduces business costs related to employee turnover, conflict resolution, and litigation, and by fostering a sense of personal identity to compensate for the impersonal nature of market activities.

Communities discipline governments by generating grassroots movements aimed at political reform and by affecting members' political opinions and voting behavior. Yet communities also enable governments by reducing crime, by fostering patriotism and loyalty, and by teaching respect for authority and laws.

The potential synergies of market, government, and community become manifest only when each governance structure is sufficiently strong to exercise its capacities. This condition, in turn, requires that no governance structure becomes so dominant that other structures are rendered ineffective. Allowing either market, government, or community to be marginalized is like building a table with only two legs. No matter how the legs are arranged, the table cannot function. A healthy society requires three mutually supportive institutional bases because humans have three essential modes of behavior. Economically, they act as autonomous individuals choosing between different actions based on calculations of personal advantage. Politically, they act as citizens to secure the kinds of laws and institutional structures they want governing their collective existence. Socially, they derive meaning and purpose by fulfilling the functions of roles defined by their relations to others. If any one of these modes of behavior is denied expression by an inadequate institutional base, individual frustration and social disorder are inevitable.

CONCLUSION

Each of the four ideological perspectives examined in this book may be faulted for neglecting one or more of the three governance structures. Classical Liberalism, in its quest to shatter the organic unity of medieval society, elevated the market at the expense of government and community. This ideology proposed that the market would assure rational individual behavior by making material self-interest consistent with the well-being of society. Government would be reduced to the role of referee, protecting property rights and enforcing contracts. What Classical Liberals fail to perceive is that strong governments and vibrant communities are essential to maintain smoothly operating markets. Without regulations and ethical norms, self-interested behavior destroys markets. When government is weak, mafias and militias arise as citizens attempt to secure through collective action what they cannot obtain individually. When community is weak, an amoral society breeds conflict, crime, and litigation, making business activities increasingly costly and difficult.

Radicals and Conservatives emphasize the role of community, but in the past, they viewed markets as divisive and disruptive to both community and government. Since World War II, Conservatives have moved closer to

Classical Liberalism by accepting markets and criticizing government. Radicals have also evolved, expressing interest in markets but remaining suspicious of governments in capitalist societies. However, both ideological perspectives have remained marginal in Western societies because of their opposition to markets and government.

Modern Liberalism became the dominant ideology in the West by proposing to balance government and market, relying on each governance structure to suppress the deficiencies of the other and anticipating the full benefits of the capacities of both structures. However, Modern Liberalism ignores community, and much of its current disarray is attributable to this oversight. In the absence of healthy communities, government and market cannot function synergistically to resolve each other's deficiencies. For example, government efforts to promote equality are undermined by fraud, abuse, and opportunism as isolated individuals seek relief from competitive market forces.

The current ideological gridlock is largely explained by the widespread presumption that only two choices are available: stronger markets or stronger governments. The deficiencies of each institution are sufficiently well-known that democratic societies are unable to move boldly in either direction. To permit markets to dominate raises fears of instability, unemployment, externalities, monopolization, lack of public goods, concentration of wealth, erosion of democratic rights, and loss of national sovereignty. Efforts to strengthen government are met with concerns about waste, inefficiency, abuse of power, manipulation by special interests, and undermining of personal freedom. This stalemate has a positive effect since a victory for either side would be self-defeating. When markets are permitted to dominate, they so weaken trust, loyalty, and honesty that government, unable to rely on individual virtue to maintain social order, necessarily becomes coercive.[15] Conversely, recent history provides plentiful evidence that overly dominant governments are eventually toppled by market forces.

A plausible resolution to this dilemma does exist. If liberalism were to explicitly incorporate community into its theorizing and policy proposals, many of the seemingly irresolvable issues confronting modern societies could be managed. However, since its inception in the political struggles against papal, royal, and aristocratic power, liberalism has been committed to individualism, viewing community as the source of parochial prejudices interfering with markets and government. Community is associated with emotional attachments, narrow-mindedness, and intolerance. Because liberalism, with its open disdain for community, has been the dominant ideology for the past two centuries, the unraveling of community life should come as no surprise. The fact that communities have managed to sustain themselves at all provides testimony to the deep human need for fellowship and shared purpose.

In 1982, Harvard political theorist Michael Sandel wrote a book entitled *Liberalism and the Limits of Justice*. His effort to introduce a communitarian perspective into liberalism gave rise to a new ideological
perspective called "communitarian liberalism" or simply "communitarianism."[16] This approach seeks to balance the individualistic focus on
rights, autonomy, and choice against the communitarian emphasis on
duties, participation, and commitment. Liberals react strongly against any
proposals that might limit individual freedom, but communitarians are
confident that commitments to and participation in communities will
enlarge freedom by creating greater civility, trust, and a sense of purpose
to guide individuals as they function in the market and practice politics.
Markets and governments, according to communitarians, actually erode
freedom by reducing all values to commercial values or laws imposed by
impersonal market forces and government. Individuals are free only in the
sense that their property rights and civil rights are protected and they may
select which transactions to make. But without a sense of purpose to give
meaning to their desires, this freedom leaves individuals unsatisfied, seeking ever-elusive fulfillment through novelty and possessions. Isolated,
amoral individuals manifest their frustration in low productivity, violence,
opportunism, and self-destructive behavior. Liberalism is blind to this phenomenon because it views all behavior as resulting from the choices of
rational individuals.

Communitarian liberalism suggests that government must take the initiative in reinvigorating communities. While markets can contribute to rising
standards of living, they are also corrosive of the values and commitments
essential to community life. Communities, by themselves, are relatively powerless to defend against the encroachments of markets and governments and
therefore cannot be the primary source of their own renewal. However, to
place responsibility for rebuilding communities with government does not
imply the need for bigger or more intrusive government. Instead of acting
primarily as an external authority regulating the actions of individuals and
businesses with threats of coercion, government can become the partner of
communities in creating "free spaces" protected from both market and government within which participatory institutions foster communication, interaction, and a renewal of civic virtue.[17]

The most appropriate balance between markets, governments, and communities is not a fixed ideal toward which nations move. The desired balance may differ from nation to nation depending on resource bases,
cultures, and existing institutional arrangements. The balance may also
evolve over time in response to changes in technology, the environment,
and values. Looking ahead to the twenty-first century, serious problems
will surely arise due to deterioration of the environment, overpopulation,
and global inequality. Another fundamental challenge is posed by the
increasing globalization of markets. Despite the capacities of markets for

advancing human purposes, free international markets will steadily erode the sovereignty of governments and communities within their jurisdictions. The political struggles of the past two centuries to place boundaries on national markets and to make their functioning consistent with the public interest must now be refought in the international arena. The available alternatives are not free international markets versus regulated international markets. If international governing bodies do not coordinate economic policies, nations will take separate measures to protect themselves because unregulated global markets make it impossible to achieve a desired balance among market, government, and community. Contributing to the formation of structures for international governance will be a major priority for twenty-first century political economy.

NOTES

1. See Daniel Bell, *The End of Ideology*, Glencoe, IL: Free Press, 1960; Chaim Waxman, *The End of Ideology Debate*, New York: Funk & Wagnalls, 1968; and Job L. Dittberner, *The End of Ideology and American Social Thought*, Ann Arbor, MI: UMI Institute Press, 1979.

2. John Stuart Mill, *Essays On Some Unsettled Questions of Political Economy* (1844), New York: Augustus M. Kelley, 1968, p. 137.

3. *Ibid*, p. 139.

4. A. C. Pigou, ed., *Memorials of Alfred Marshall* (1925), New York: Augustus M. Kelley, 1966.

5. See Lionel Robbins, *An Essay on the Nature and Significance of Economic Science* (1932), New York: New York University Press, 1984.

6. Anne O. Krueger, *et al.,* "Report of the Commission on Graduate Education in Economics," *Journal of Economic Literature*, 29:3 (1991), 1044–45. For additional assessment of graduate economic education in the United States, see Arjo Klamer and David Colander, *The Making of An Economist*, Boulder, CO: Westview Publishing, 1990.

7. Ronald H. Coase, *The Firm, the Market, and the Law*, Chicago: University of Chicago Press, 1988, p. 185.

8. Tibor Scitovsky, "A Note on Welfare Propositions in Economics," *Review of Economic Studies*, 9 (1941), 77–88.

9. Richard G. Lipsey and Kelvin Lancaster, "The General Theory of the Second Best," *Review of Economic Studies*, 24:1 (October, 1956), pp. 11–32.

10. Milton Friedman, *Essays in Positive Economics*, Chicago: University of Chicago Press, 1953.

11. Prominent works in experimental economics include Vernon L. Smith, ed., *Experimental Economics*, Brookfield, VT: Edward Elgar, 1990, and Douglas D. Davis, *Experimental Economics*, Princeton, NJ: Princeton University Press, 1993.

12. James Buchanan, "Economics and Its Scientific Neighbors," *in* Buchanan, *What Should Economists Do?*, Indianapolis, IN: Liberty Press, 1979.

13. Charles Schultze, quoted in Robert Kuttner, *Everything for Sale: The Virtues and Limits of Markets*, New York: Alfred A. Knopf, 1997, p. 41.

14. Frank Hahn, quoted in Warren J. Samuels, "The Case for Methodological Pluralism," *in* Andrea Salanti and Ernesto Screpanti, eds., *Pluralism in Economics*, Brookfield, VT: Edward Elgar, 1997.

15. William Leach, *Land of Desire: Merchants, Power, and the Rise of a New American Culture*, New York: Pantheon Books, 1993; Andrew B. Schmookler, *The Illusion of Choice: How the Market Economy Shapes Our Destiny*, Ithaca, NY: State University of New York Press, 1993; Andrew B. Schmookler, *Fools Gold: The Fate of Values in a World of Goods*, New York: HarperCollins, 1993; and Barry Schwartz, *The Costs of Living: How Market Freedom Erodes the Best Things in Life*, New York: W. W. Norton, 1994.

16. Michael Sandel, *Liberalism and the Limits of Justice*, New York: Cambridge University Press, 1982. Other prominent works in communitarianism include William A. Galston, *Liberal Purposes: Goods, Virtues, and Diversity in the Liberal State*, New York: Cambridge University Press, 1991; and Robert Bellah, *et al.*, *Habits of the Heart: Individualism and Commitment in American Life*, Berkeley: University of California Press, 1985. For comprehensive assessments of communitarianism see Robert Booth Fowler, *The Dance with Community: The Contemporary Debate in American Political Thought*, Lawrence: University Press of Kansas, 1991; Amitai Etzioni, *The Spirit of Community: Rights, Responsibilities, and the Communitarian Agenda*, New York: Crown, 1991; Stephen Mulhall and Adam Swift, *Liberals and Communitarians*, Cambridge, MA: Blackwell, 1996; Derek L. Phillips, *Looking Backward: A Critical Appraisal of Communitarian Thought*, Princeton, NJ: Princeton University Press, 1993; and Cornelius Delaney, ed., *The Liberalism-Communitarianism Debate*, Totowa, NJ: Rowman & Littlefield, 1993.

17. See Sara M. Evans and Harry C. Boyte, *Free Spaces: The Sources of Democratic Change in America*, Chicago: University of Chicago Press, 1992, and Robert Putnam, *Making Democracy Work: Civic Traditions in Modern Italy*, Princeton, NJ: Princeton University Press, 1993.

ADDITIONAL READING

Audretsch, David B. *The Market and the State*. New York: Harvester Wheatsheaf, 1989.

Boswell, Jonathan. *Community and the Economy: The Theory of Public Co-operation*. New York: Routledge, 1990.

Bowles, Samuel, and Herbert Gintis. *Democracy and Capitalism*. New York: Basic Books, 1986.

Daley, Herman E., and John B. Cobb, Jr. *For the Common Good: Redirecting the Economy Toward Community, the Environment, and A Sustainable Future*. Boston: Beacon Press, 1989.

Davidson, Greg, and Paul Davidson. *Economics for A Civilized Society*. Armonk, NY: M. E. Sharpe, 1996.

Foldvary, Fred E., ed. *Beyond Neoclassical Economics*. Brookfield, VT: Edward Elgar, 1996.

Friedland, Roger, and A. F. Robertson, eds. *Beyond the Marketplace: Rethinking Economy and Society*. Hawthorne, NY: Aldine de Gruyter, 1990.

Haslett, D. W. *Capitalism With Morality*. Oxford: Clarendon Press, 1994.

Hodgson, Geoffrey M. *Economics and Evolution: Bringing Life Back Into Economics*. Cambridge, UK: Polity Press, 1993.

Hollingsworth, J. Rogers, and Robert Boyer, eds. *Contemporary Capitalism: The Embeddedness of Institutions*. Cambridge, UK: Cambridge University Press, 1997.

Miller, David. *Market, State, and Community*. New York: Oxford University Press, 1990.

Ormerud, Paul. *The Death of Economics*. New York: J. Wiley & Sons, 1997.

Ostrom, Elinor. *Governing the Commons*. Cambridge, UK: Cambridge University Press, 1990.

Sen, Amartya. *On Ethics and Economics*. New York: Basil Blackwell, 1987.

Vickers, Douglas. *Economics and Ethics*. New York: Praeger, 1997.

Walzer, Michael. *Spheres of Justice*. New York: Basic Books, 1983.

Whalen, Charles J., ed. *Political Economy for the 21st Century*. Armonk, NY: M. E. Sharpe, 1996.

Young, James P. *Reconsidering American Liberalism*. Boulder, CO: Westview Press, 1996.

Bibliography

Aaron, Henry J., and Cameron M. Lougy. *The Comparable Worth Controversy*. Washington, DC: Brookings Institution, 1986.

Acker, Joan. *Doing Comparable Worth*. Philadelphia: Temple University Press, 1989.

Ackerman, Frank. *Reaganomics: Rhetoric vs. Reality*. Boston: South End Press, 1982.

Adelman, Irma, and Cynthia Taft Morris. *Economic Growth and Social Equity in Developing Countries*. Stanford, CA: Stanford University Press, 1973.

Adorno, Theodor W. *Aesthetic Theory*. Boston: Routledge & Kegan Paul, 1983.

Agarwala, Prakash N. *The New International Economic Order: An Overview*. New York: Pergamon, 1983.

Akerlof, G. A., and W. T. Dickens. "The Economic Consequences of Cognitive Dissonance," *American Economic Review* 72, no. 3 (June 1982): 307–19.

Alchian, Armen, and Harold Demsetz. "Production, Information Costs, and Economic Organization," *American Economic Review* 62 (December 1972): 777–95.

Alesina, Alberto, and Nouriel Roubini. *Political Cycles and the Macroeconomy*. Cambridge, MA: MIT Press, 1998.

Altbach, Edith Hoshina, ed. *From Feminism to Liberation*. Cambridge, MA: Schenkman, 1971.

Amacher, Ryan C., Gottfried Haberler, and Thomas D. Willett, eds. *Challenges to a Liberal Economic Order*. Washington, DC: American Enterprise Institute, 1979.

Amin, Samir. *Accumulation on a World Scale*. New York: Monthly Review Press, 1974.

Anderson, Terry L., and Donald R. Leal. *Enviro-Capitalists: Doing Good While Doing Well*. Savage, MD: Rowman & Littlefield, 1997.

———. *Free Market Environmentalism*. Boulder, CO: Westview Press, 1991.

Arato, Andrew, and Eike Gebhardt, eds. *The Essential Frankfurt School Reader*. New York: Continuum, 1982.

Archambault, Reginald D., ed. *Dewey on Education*. New York: Random House, 1966.

Archer, Robin. *Economic Democracy: The Politics of Feasible Socialism*. New York: Oxford University Press, 1995.

Arestis, Philip, and Victoria Chick. *Recent Developments In Post-Keynesian Economics*. Brookfield, VT: Edward Elgar, 1992.

Arestis, Philip, and Thanes Skouras, eds. *Post-Keynesian Economic Theory*. Armonk, NY: M. E. Sharpe, 1985.

Aronowitz, Stanley. *False Promises: The Shaping of American Working-Class Consciousness*. New York: McGraw-Hill, 1973.

Arren, Judith, and Christopher Jencks. "Educational Vouchers: A Proposal for Diversity and Choice," *in* George R. LaNoue, ed. *Educational Vouchers: Concepts and Controversies*. New York: Teachers College Press, 1972.

Arrow, Kenneth J. *The Limits of Organization*. New York: W. W. Norton, 1974.

———. *Some Models of Racial Discrimination in the Labor Market*. Santa Monica, CA: Rand Corporation, 1971.

Atkinson, Anthony B., Lee Rainwater, and Timothy M. Smeeding. *Income Distribution in OECD Countries*. Paris: OECD, 1995.

Bachrach, Peter, and Aryeh Botwinick. *Power and Empowerment: A Radical Theory of Participatory Democracy*. Philadelphia: Temple University Press, 1992.

Baer, M. Delal, and Sidney Weintraub, eds. *The NAFTA Debate*. Boulder, CO: Lynne Rienner, 1994.

Bailey, Elizabeth E., and Janet Rothenberg Pack, eds. *The Political Economy of Privatization and Deregulation*. Brookfield, VT: Edward Elgar, 1995.

Baily, Martin, Gary Burtless, and Robert Litan. *Growth with Equity*. Washington, DC: Brookings Institution, 1993.

Bandow, Doug, ed. *Protecting The Environment: A Free Market Strategy*. Washington, DC: Heritage Foundation, 1986.

Banfield, Edward C. *The Moral Basis of a Backward Society*. Glencoe, IL: The Free Press, 1958.

———. *The Unheavenly City: The Nature and Future of Our Urban Crisis*. Boston: Little, Brown, 1968.

Banner, Lois W. *Women in Modern America: A Brief History*, 3rd ed. Fort Worth: Harcourt Brace College Publishers, 1995.

Baran, Paul. *The Political Economy of Growth*. New York: Monthly Review Press, 1967.

Baran, Paul, and Paul Sweezy. *Monopoly Capital: An Essay on the American Economic and Social Order*. New York: Monthly Review Press, 1966.

Barber, Benjamin R. *Strong Democracy*. Berkeley: University of California Press, 1984.

Barbier, Edward, ed. *Economics and Ecology: New Frontiers and Sustainable Development*. New York: Chapman & Hall, 1993.

Barrett, Michele. *Women's Oppression Today: Problems in Marxist Feminist Analysis*. London: Verso, 1980.

Barro, Rudolph. *Building the Green Movement*. London: Green Movement Press, 1986.

Barrow, Robin. *Radical Education: A Critique of Freeschooling and Deschooling*. New York: John Wiley & Sons, 1978.

Barry, Brian, and Richard Sikora, eds. *Obligations to Future Generations*. Philadelphia: Temple University Press, 1978.

Bator, F. M. "The Anatomy of Market Failure," *Quarterly Journal of Economics* 72, no. 288 (1958): 351–79.

Bauer, Peter T. *Dissent on Development*. London: Weidenfeld & Nicolson, 1971.

———. *Reality and Rhetoric: Studies in the Economics of Development*. Cambridge, MA: Harvard University Press, 1984.

Baxter, William F. *People or Penguins: The Case for Optimal Pollution*. New York: Columbia University Press, 1974.

Becker, Gary. *The Economic Approach to Human Behavior*. Chicago: University of Chicago Press, 1976.

———. *The Economics of Discrimination*, 2nd ed. Chicago: University of Chicago Press, 1971.

———. *Human Capital*, 2nd ed. New York: National Bureau of Economic Research, 1975.

———. *A Treatise on the Family*. Cambridge, MA: Harvard University Press, 1981.

Becker, Gary S., and Guity Nashat Becker. *The Economics of Life*. New York: McGraw-Hill, 1997.

Beckerman, Wilfred. *Pricing For Pollution*, 2nd ed. London: Institute for Economic Affairs, 1990.

———. *Two Cheers for the Affluent Society: A Spirited Defense of Economic Growth*. New York: St. Martin's, 1974.

Beckwith, Francis J., and Todd E. Jones, eds. *Social Justice or Reverse Discrimination*. Amherst, NY: Prometheus Books, 1997.

Beesley, Michael E. *Privatization, Regulation and Deregulation*. New York: Routledge, 1992.

Belasich, Deborah K. *Enterprise Zones: Policy Perspectives of Economic Development*. New York: Garland Publishers, 1993.

Bell, Daniel. *The Coming of Post-Industrial Society: A Venture in Social Forecasting*. New York: Basic Books, 1973.

———. *The Cultural Contradictions of Capitalism*, rev. ed. New York: Basic Books, 1996.

———. *The End of Ideology*. Glencoe, IL: Free Press, 1960.

Belleh, Robert, et al. *Habits of the Heart: Individualism and Commitment in American Life*. Berkeley: University of California Press, 1985.

Benjamin, Walter. *Illumination*. New York: Harcourt Brace & World, 1968.

Bennett, William J. *The Devaluing of America: The Fight for Our Culture and Our Children*. New York: Summit Books, 1992.

Benodraitis, Nijole V., and Joe R. Feagin. *Affirmative Action and Equal Opportunity: Action, Inaction, and Reaction*. Boulder, CO: Westview Press, 1978.

Berger, Peter L., and Richard J. Neuhaus. *To Empower People: The Role of Mediating Structures in Public Policy*, 2nd ed. Washington, DC: American Enterprise Institute, 1996.

Bergman, Barbara. "The Economics of Women's Liberation," *Challenge* 21, no. 5 (May/June 1973): 11–17.

Bergstrand, Jeffrey H., *et al.*, eds. *The Changing Distribution of Income in an Open U.S. Economy.* New York: North-Holland, 1994.

Bernstein, Michael, and David Adler, eds. *Understanding American Economic Decline.* New York: Cambridge University Press, 1994.

Bevall, Bill, and George Sessions. *Deep Ecology: Living As If Nature Mattered.* Layton, UT: G. M. Smith, 1985.

Bhagwati, Jagdish, ed. *The New International Economic Order.* Cambridge: MIT Press, 1977.

Blau, Francine, and Carol L. Jusenius. "Economists' Approaches to Sex Segregation in the Labor Market: An Appraisal," *Signs* (Spring 1976): 181–200.

Blauner, Robert. *Alienation and Freedom: The Factory Worker and His Industry.* Chicago: University of Chicago Press, 1964.

Block, N. J., and Gerald Dworkin, eds. *The IQ Controversy.* New York: Pantheon, 1976.

Bloom, Allan. *The Closing of the American Mind.* New York: Simon & Schuster, 1987.

Bluestone, Barry, and Bennett Harrison. *The Deindustrialization of America.* New York: Basic Books, 1982.

Blum, Linda M. *Between Feminism and Labor: The Significance of the Comparable Worth Movement.* Berkeley: University of California Press, 1991.

Boddy, Raford, and James Crotty. "Class Conflict and Macro Policy: The Political Business Cycle," *Review of Radical Political Economics* 7 (Spring 1975): 1–19.

Boeke, J. H. *Economics and Economic Policy in Dual Societies.* New York: Institute for Pacific Relations, 1953.

Bookchin, Murray. *Deep Ecology and Anarchism: A Polemic.* London: Freedom Press, 1993.

———. *Remaking Society: Pathways To A Green Future.* Boston: South End Press, 1990.

Bovard, James. *The Fair Trade Fraud.* New York: St. Martin's, 1991.

Bowles, Samuel, and Herbert Gintis. "Contested Exchange: New Microfoundations for the Political Economy of Capitalism," *Politics & Society* 18, no. 2 (June 1990): 165–222.

———. "Efficient Redistribution: New Rules for Markets, States and Communities," *Politics & Society* 24:4 (December 1996): 307–342.

———. "The Problem with Human Capital Theory, A Marxian Critique," *American Economic Review* 65:2 (May 1975): 74–82.

———. "The Revenge of Homo Economicus: Contested Exchange and the Revival of Political Economy," *Journal of Economic Perspectives* 7:1 (Winter 1993): 83–102.

———. *Schooling in Capitalist America.* New York: Basic Books, 1976.

Bowles, Samuel, Herbert Gintis, and Bo Gustafsson, eds. *Markets and Democracy: Participation, Accountability and Efficiency.* New York: Cambridge University Press, 1993.

Bowles, Samuel, David M. Gordon, and Thomas E. Weisskopf. *After the Wasteland: A Democratic Economics for the Year 2000.* New York: M. E. Sharpe, 1990.

Bramwell, Anna. *The Fading of the Greens: The Decline of Environmental Politics in the West.* New Haven: Yale University Press, 1994.

Brand, Donald R. *Corporatism and the Rule of Law: A Study of the National Recovery Administration.* Ithaca, NY: Cornell University Press, 1988.

Braun, Denny. *The Rich Get Richer: The Rise of Income Inequality in the United States and the World.* Chicago: Nelson-Hall, 1991.

Braverman, Harry. *Labor and Monopoly Capital: The Degradation of Work in the Twentieth Century.* New York: Monthly Review Press, 1974.

Brennen, H. G., and James M. Buchanan. *Monopoly in Money and Inflation: The Case of a Constitution to Discipline Government.* London: Institute of Economic Affairs, 1981.

Brewer, Anthony. *Marxist Theories of Imperialism: A Critical Survey,* 2nd ed. New York: Routledge, 1992.

Brittan, Samuel. *The Economic Consequences of Democracy.* London: Temple Smith, 1977.

Buchanan, James M. *Constitutional Economics.* Cambridge, MA: Blackwell, 1991.

———. *Freedom in Constitutional Contract: Perspectives of a Political Economics.* College Station, TX: Texas A&M University Press, 1977.

———. *What Should Economists Do?* Indianapolis, IN: Liberty Press, 1979.

Buchanan, James M., Charles K. Rowley, and Robert D. Tollison, eds. *Deficits.* New York: Basil Blackwell, 1987.

Buchanan, James M., and Robert D. Tollison. *Theory of Public Choice: Political Applications of Economics.* Ann Arbor: University of Michigan Press, 1972.

Buchanan, James M., Robert D. Tollison, and Gordon Tullock, eds. *Toward a Theory of the Rent-seeking Society.* College Station, TX: Texas A&M University Press, 1980.

Buchanan, James M., and Gordon Tullock. *Calculus of Consent: The Logical Foundations of Constitutional Democracy.* Ann Arbor: University of Michigan Press, 1965.

Buchanan, James M., and Richard M. Wagner. *Democracy in Deficit: The Political Legacy of Lord Keynes.* New York: Academic Press, 1977.

Buell, Emmett H., Jr. *School Desegregation and Defended Neighborhoods.* Lexington, MA: Lexington Books, 1982.

Buhle, Mari Jo, and Paul Buhle. *The Concise History of Woman Suffrage.* Urbana, IL: University of Illinois Press, 1978.

Burawoy, Michael. *Manufacturing Consent: Changes in the Labor Process under Monopoly Capitalism.* Chicago: University of Chicago Press, 1979.

Burggraf, Shirley P. *The Feminine Economy and Economic Man.* Reading, MA: Addison-Wesley, 1997.

Burr, Richard E. *Are Comparable Worth Systems Truly Comparable?* St. Louis: Center for the Study of American Business, Washington University, 1986.

Butler, Stuart. *Enterprise Zones: Greenlining the Inner Cities.* New York: Universe Books, 1981.

Butler, Stuart, and Anna Kondratas. *Out of the Poverty Trap: A Conservative Strategy for Welfare Reform.* New York: Free Press, 1987.

Cagan, Phillip, ed. *The Economy in Deficit.* Washington, DC: American Enterprise Institute, 1985.

Callenbach, Ernest. *Ecotopia.* Berkeley, CA: Banyan Tree Press, 1975.

Campen, James T. *Benefit, Cost, and Beyond: The Political Economy of Benefit–Cost Analysis*. Cambridge, MA: Ballinger, 1986.

Canto, Victor A., Marc A. Miles, and Arthur B. Laffer. *Foundations of Supply-side Economics: Theory and Evidence*. New York: Academic Press, 1983.

Capra, Fritjof. *The Turning Point*. London: Flamingo, 1985.

Card, David, and Alan B. Krueger. *Myth and Measurement: The New Economics of the Minimum Wage*. Princeton, NJ: Princeton University Press, 1995.

Carnoy, Martin. *Schooling in a Corporate Society*. New York: McKay, 1972.

Carnoy, Martin, and Derek Shearer. *Economic Democracy: The Challenge of the 1980's*. White Plains, NY: M. E. Sharpe, 1980.

Castells, Manuel. *The Economic Crisis and American Society*. Princeton, NJ: Princeton University Press, 1980.

Chase, Allan. *The Legacy of Malthus: The Social Costs of the New Scientific Racism*. New York: Alfred A. Knopf, 1977.

Chodorow, Nancy. *The Reproduction of Mothering: Psychoanalysis and the Sociology of Gender*. Berkeley: University of California Press, 1978.

Chubb, John E., and Terry M. Moe. *Politics, Markets and America's Schools*. Washington, DC: The Brookings Institution, 1990.

Clark, John Bates. *The Distribution of Wealth*. New York: Macmillan, 1899.

Cline, William R. *Policy Alternatives for a New International Economic Order: An Economic Analysis*. New York: Praeger, 1979.

Coase, Ronald H. *The Firm, the Market, and the Law*. Chicago: University of Chicago Press, 1988.

———. "The Nature of the Firm," *Economica* 4 (November 1937): 386–405.

———. "The Problem of Social Cost," *Journal of Law and Economics* 3 (October 1960): 1–44.

Colander, David C., ed. *Neoclassical Political Economy: The Analysis of Rent-seeking and DUP Activities*. Cambridge, MA: Ballinger, 1984.

Commoner, Barry. *The Politics of Energy*. New York: Alfred A. Knopf, 1979.

Connolly, William, ed. *Legitimacy and the State*. New York: New York University Press, 1984.

Conover, Pamela Johnston, and Virginia Gray. *Feminism and the New Right: Conflict Over the American Family*. New York: Praeger, 1983.

Cookson, Peter W., Jr. *School Choice: The Struggle for the Soul of American Education*. New Haven: Yale University Press, 1994.

Copp, David, Jean Hampton, and John Roemer, eds. *The Idea of Democracy*. Cambridge, UK: Cambridge University Press, 1993.

Could, Carol. *Rethinking Democracy: Freedom and Social Cooperation in Politics, Economics and Society*. New York: Cambridge University Press, 1988.

Cowen, Tyler, ed. *The Theory of Market Failure*. Fairfax, VA: George Mason University Press, 1988.

Crane, Edward H., and David Boaz. *An American Vision: Policies for the '90's*. Washington, DC: Cato Institute, 1988.

Crouch, Colin, ed. *State and Economy in Contemporary Capitalism*. New York: St. Martin's, 1979.

Crozier, Michael, Samuel P. Huntington, and Joji Watanuki, eds. *The Crisis of Democracy*. New York: New York University Press, 1975.

Culbertson, John M. "The Folly of Free Trade," *Harvard Business Review* (Sept./Oct. 1986): 122–28.

Dahl, Robert A. *Democracy, Liberty, and Equality*. New York: Oxford University Press, 1986.

———. *Dilemmas of Pluralist Democracy: Autonomy versus Control*. New Haven, CT: Yale University Press, 1982.

———. *Pluralist Democracy in the United States*. Chicago: Rand McNally, 1967.

———. *A Preface to Economic Democracy*. Berkeley: University of California Press, 1985.

Daly, Mary. *Gyn/Ecology: The Metaethics of Radical Feminism*. Boston: Beacon Press, 1978.

Danziger, Sheldon, and Peter Gottschalk. *Uneven Tides: Rising Inequality in America*. New York: Russell Sage, 1992.

Danziger, Sheldon, Gary D. Sandefur, and Daniel H. Weinberg, eds. *Confronting Poverty: Prescriptions for Change*. Cambridge: Harvard University Press, 1994.

Danziger, Sheldon, and Daniel H. Weinberg, eds. *Fighting Poverty: What Works and What Doesn't*. Cambridge, MA: Harvard University Press, 1986.

Davidson, Nicholas. *The Failure of Feminism*. Buffalo, NY: Prometheus, 1988.

Davidson, Paul. *Controversies In Post-Keynesian Economics*. Brookfield, VT: Edward Elgar, 1991.

Davis, Douglas D. *Experimental Economics*. Princeton, NJ: Princeton University Press, 1993.

Davis, Kingsley, and Wilbert Moore. "Some Principles of Stratification." *American Sociological Review* 10 (April 1945): 242–49.

Davison, Peter, Rolf Meyersohn, and Edward Shils, eds. *Culture and Mass Culture*. Teaneck, NJ: Somerset House, 1978.

Deal, Terrence E., and Robert R. Nolan, eds. *Alternative Schools: Ideologies, Realities, Guidelines*. Chicago: Nelson-Hall, 1978.

Decter, Midge. *The New Chastity and Other Arguments against Women's Liberation*. New York: Coward, McGann and Geoghegan, 1972.

Delaney, Cornelius, ed. *The Liberalism–Communitarianism Debate*. Totowa, NJ: Fowman & Littlefield, 1993.

Dewar, Donald L. *The Quality Circle Guide to Participation Management*. Englewood Cliffs, NJ: Prentice-Hall, 1980.

Dittberner, Job L. *The End of Ideology and American Social Thought*. Ann Arbor, MI: UMI Institute Press, 1979.

Domhoff, G. William. *The Power Elite and the State*. New York: Aldine de Gruyter, 1990.

———. *State Autonomy or Class Dominance*. New York: Aldine de Gruyter, 1996.

Donahue, John D. *The Privatization Decision: Public Ends, Private Means*. New York: Basic Books, 1989.

Downs, Anthony. *An Economic Theory of Democracy*. New York: Harper & Row, 1957.

———. *Inside Bureaucracy*. Boston: Little, Brown, 1967.

D'Souza, Dinesh. *The End of Racism: Principles for A Multiracial Society*. New York: Free Press, 1995.

Dugger, William. *Corporate Hegemony*. Westport, CT: Greenwood Press, 1989.

Dupré, Louis. *Marx's Social Critique of Culture*. New Haven, CT: Yale University Press, 1983.

Durkheim, Emile. *The Division of Labor in Society*. New York: Free Press, 1933.

Easton, David. *The Political System*. New York: Alfred A. Knopf, 1981.

Echeverria, John, and Raymond Booth Eby, eds. *Let the People Judge: Wise Use and the Private Property Rights Movement*. Washington, DC: Island Press, 1995.

Echols, Alice. *Daring To Be Bad: Radical Feminism in America 1967–1975*. Minneapolis: University of Minnesota Press, 1989.

Eckes, Alfred E. *Opening America's Markets*. Chapel Hill: University of North Carolina Press, 1995.

Edgell, Stephen, Sandin Walklate, and Gareth Williams. *Debating the Future of the Public Sphere: Transforming the Public and Private Domains in Free Market Societies*. Brookfield, VT: Avebury, 1995.

Edwards, Richard C. *Contested Terrain: The Transformation of the Workplace in the Twentieth Century*. New York: Basic Books, 1979.

Edwards, Richard C., David M. Gordon, and Michael Reich, eds. *Labor Market Segmentation*. Lexington, MA: D. C. Heath, 1975.

Eichner, Alfred, ed. *A Guide to Post-Keynesian Economics*. White Plains, NY: M. E. Sharpe, 1979.

Eisenstein, Zillah R., ed. *Capitalist Patriarchy and the Case of Socialist Feminism*. New York: Monthly Review Press, 1979.

Eisner, Robert. *The Great Deficit Scares: The Federal Budget, Trade, and Social Security*. Washington, DC: Brookings Institution, 1997.

Ellerman, David P. *Property and Contract in Economics: A Case for Economic Democracy*. Cambridge, MA: Blackwell, 1992.

Elshtain, Jean Bethke. *Public Man, Private Woman: Women in Social and Political Thought*. Princeton, NJ: Princeton University Press, 1981.

Emmanuel, Arghiri. *Unequal Exchange: A Study of the Imperialism of Trade*. New York: Monthly Review Press, 1972.

England, Paula. *Comparable Worth: Theories and Evidence*. New York: Aldine de Gruyter, 1992.

Engler, Robert. *The Brotherhood of Oil: Energy Policy and the Public Interest*. Chicago: University of Chicago Press, 1977.

Epstein, Richard. *Bargaining with the State*. Princeton: Princeton University Press, 1993.

———. *Forbidden Grounds: The Case Against Employment Discrimination Laws*. Cambridge: Harvard University Press, 1992.

———. *Simple Rules for A Complex World*. Cambridge, MA: Harvard University Press, 1995.

———. *Takings: Private Property and the Power of Eminent Domain*. Cambridge: Harvard University Press, 1985.

Etzioni, Amitai. *The Spirit of Community: Rights, Responsibilities, and the Communitarian Agenda*. New York: Crown, 1991.

Evans, Richard J. *The Feminists*. Totowa, NJ: Rowman & Littlefield, 1979.

Evans, Sara M. *Born for Liberty: A History of Women in America*. New York: Free Press, 1989.

Evans, Sara M., and Harry C. Boyte. *Free Spaces: The Sources of Democratic Change in America*. Chicago: University of Chicago Press, 1992.

Firestone, Shulamith. *The Dialectic of Sex: The Case for Feminist Revolution*. New York: William Morrow, 1970.

Fletcher, Ronald. *The Abolitionists: The Family and Marriage Under Attack*. New York: Routledge, 1988.

———. *The Shaking of the Foundations: Family and Society*. New York: Routledge, 1988.

Foldvary, Fred. *Public Goods and Private Communities: The Market Provision of Social Services*. Brookfield, VT: Edward Elgar, 1994.

Fowler, Robert Booth. *The Dance with Community: The Contemporary Debate in American Political Thought*. Lawrence: University Press of Kansas, 1991.

Frank, André Gunder. *Capitalism and Underdevelopment in Latin America*. New York: Monthly Review Press, 1969.

———. *Crisis in the Third World*. New York: Holmes & Meier, 1981.

Frank, André Gunder and Barry K. Gills, eds. *The World System*. New York: Routledge, 1993.

Frank, Robert H. and Philip J. Cook. *The Winner-take-all Society*. New York: Free Press, 1995.

Frankel, S. H. *The Economic Impact on Underdeveloped Societies*. Oxford: Basil Blackwell, 1953.

Fraser, Steven, ed. *The Bell Curve Wars: Race, Intelligence, and the Future of America*. New York: Basic Books, 1995.

Freeman, Richard B., and James L. Medoff. *What Do Unions Do?* New York: Basic Books, 1988.

Freud, Sigmund. *Civilization and Its Discontents*, translated by James Strachey. New York: W. W. Norton, 1961.

Friedan, Betty. *The Feminine Mystique*. New York: W. W. Norton & Co., 1963.

———. *The Second Stage*. New York: Summit Books, 1981.

Friedman, Georges. *Anatomy of Work*. Glencoe, IL: Free Press, 1961.

Friedman, Jeffrey, ed. *The Rational Choice Controversy*. New Haven, CT: Yale University Press, 1996.

Friedman, Milton. *Essays in Positive Economics*. Chicago: University of Chicago Press, 1953.

———. "The Role of Government in Education," *in* Robert A. Solo, ed. *Economics and the Public Interest*. New Brunswick, NJ: Rutgers University Press, 1955.

Friedman, Milton, and Anna J. Schwartz. *A Monetary History of the United States 1867–1960*. Princeton, NJ: Princeton University Press, 1963.

Fuller, Bruce, and Richard F. Elmore. *Who Chooses? Who Loses?* New York: Teachers College Press, 1995.

Galambos, Louis, and Joseph Pratt. *The Rise of the Corporate Commonwealth*. New York: Basic Books, 1989.

Galbraith, John Kenneth. *Economics and the Public Purpose*. Boston: Houghton Mifflin, 1973.

———. *The New Industrial State*. Boston: Houghton Mifflin, 1967.

Galston, William A. *Liberal Purposes: Goods, Virtues, and Diversity in the Liberal State*. New York: Cambridge University Press, 1991.

Gans, Herbert. *More Equality*. New York: Vintage Books, 1974.

———. "The Positive Functions of Poverty," *American Journal of Sociology* 78, no. 2 (1972): 275–89.

George, Donald A. R. *Economic Democracy: The Political Economy of Self-Management and Participation*. Basingstoke: Macmillan, 1993.

Georgescu-Roegen, Nicholas. *The Entropy Law and the Economic Process*. Cambridge, MA: Harvard University Press, 1971.

Ghosh, Pradip K. *NIEO: A Third World Perspective*. Westport, CT: Greenwood, 1984.

Gilbreth, Frank. *Motion Study* [1911]. Easton, PA: Hive, 1972.

Gilder, George. *Men and Marriage*. Gretna, LA: Pelican, 1986.

———. *Naked Nomads: Unmarried Men in America*. New York: Quadrangle Books, 1974.

———. *Wealth and Poverty*. New York: Basic Books, 1981.

Gilligan, Carol. *In a Different Voice: Psychological Theory and Women's Development*. Cambridge, MA: Harvard University Press, 1982.

Gilpin, Robert. *War and Change in World Politics*. Cambridge: Cambridge University Press, 1981.

Giner, Salvador. *Mass Society*. London: Martin Robertson, 1976.

Gintis, Herbert. "The Political Economy of School Choice," *Teachers College Record*, 96, 3 (Spring, 1995): 492–511.

———. "Towards a Political Economy of Education: A Radical Critique of Ivan Illich's Deschooling Society," *Harvard Educational Review* 42, no. 1 (February 1972): 70–96.

Glasner, David. *Politics, Prices and Petroleum: The Political Economy of Energy*. Cambridge, MA: Ballinger, 1985.

Glazer, Nathan. *Affirmative Discrimination: Ethnic Inequality and Public Policy*. New York: Basic Books, 1975.

Glazer, Nathan, and Daniel Patrick Moynihan. *Ethnicity*. Cambridge, MA: Harvard University Press, 1975.

Goldberg, Steven. *The Inevitability of Patriarchy*. New York: William Morrow, 1973.

Goldman, Alan H. *Justice and Reverse Discrimination*. Princeton, NJ: Princeton University Press, 1979.

Gordon, David M. *Theories of Poverty and Unemployment: Orthodox, Radical and Dual Labor Market Perspectives*. Lexington, MA: D. C. Heath, 1972.

Gordon, David M., Richard C. Edwards, and Michael Reich. *Segmented Work, Divided Workers: The Historical Transformation of Labor in the United States*. New York: Cambridge University Press, 1982.

Gorz, André. *Critique of Economic Reason*. London: Verso, 1989.

———. *Paths to Paradise: On the Liberation from Work*. London: Pluto Press, 1985.

Gossett, Thomas F. *Race: The History of an Idea in America*. New York: Schocken, 1963.

Gough, Ian. *The Political Economy of the Welfare State*. London: Macmillan, 1979.

Grant, Wyn, ed. *The Political Economy of Corporatism*. New York: St. Martin's, 1985.

Graubard, Allen. *Free the Children: Radical Reforms and the Free School Movement*. New York: Random House, 1972.

Gray, H. Peter. *Free Trade or Protection?: A Pragmatic Analysis*. New York: St. Martin's, 1985.

Gray, John. *Beyond The New Right*. New York: Routledge, 1993.

Green, Donald P., and Ian Shapiro. *Pathologies of Rational Choice Theory*. New Haven: Yale University Press, 1994.

Green, Philip. *Retrieving Democracy: In Search of Civic Equality*. Totowa, NJ: Rowman & Allanheld, 1985.

Greenberg, Edward. *Workplace Democracy: The Political Effect of Participation*. Ithaca, NY: Cornell University Press, 1987.

Grinspun, Ricardo, and Maxwell A. Cameron, eds. *The Political Economy of North American Free Trade*. New York: St. Martin's, 1993.

Gross, Bertram. *Friendly Fascism: The New Face of Power in America*. New York: M. Evans, 1980.

Grundmann, Reiner. *Marxism and Ecology*. New York: Oxford University Press, 1991.

Gutman, Amy. *Liberal Equality*. New York: Cambridge University Press, 1980.

Habermas, Jurgen. *Legitimation Crisis*. Boston: Beacon Press, 1975.

Hall, Thomas E., and J. David Ferguson. *The Great Depression*. Ann Arbor: University of Michigan Press, 1998.

Harris, Nigel. *Competition and the Corporate Society*. London: Methuon, 1972.

Harrison, Bennett, and Barry Bluestone. *The Great U-Turn: Corporate Restructuring and the Polarizing of America*. New York: Basic Books, 1988.

Hartman, Heidi, ed. *Comparable Worth*. Washington, DC: National Academy Press, 1985.

Hartsock, Nancy. *Money, Sex and Power: Toward a Feminist Historical Materialism*. New York: Longman, 1983.

Hayek, Friedrich A. *The Constitution of Liberty*. Chicago: University of Chicago Press, 1960.

———. *Denationalization of Money*. London: Institute of Economic Affairs, 1976.

———. *The Mirage of Social Justice*. Vol. 2 of *Law, Legislation, and Liberty*. London: Routledge & Kegan Paul, 1982.

———. *The Road to Serfdom*. London: Routledge & Kegan Paul, 1979.

———. *Studies in Philosophy, Politics and Economics*. New York: Simon & Schuster, 1967.

———. *Unemployment and Monetary Policy: Government as Generator of the "Business Cycle."* Washington, DC: Cato Institute, 1979.

Hayes, Edward J. *Busing and Desegregation: The Real Truth*. Springfield, IL: Charles C. Thomas, 1981.

Heilbroner, Robert. *21st Century Capitalism*. New York: W. W. Norton, 1993.

Heilbroner, Robert L. *An Inquiry into the Human Prospect*. New York: W. W. Norton, 1980.

Heilbroner, Robert L., and Peter Bernstein. *The Debt and the Deficit: False Alarms, Real Possibilities*. New York: W. W. Norton, 1989.

Henderson, David R. *The Case For School Choice*. Stanford: Hoover Institution, 1993.

Henig, Jeffrey R. *Rethinking School Choice: Limits of the Market Metaphor*. Princeton: Princeton University Press, 1994.

Henry, William A., III. *In Defense of Elitism*. New York: Doubleday, 1994.

Herrnstein, Richard. *Educability and Group Differences*. New York: Harper & Row, 1973.

——. *IQ and the Meritocracy*. Boston: Little, Brown, 1973.

Herrnstein, Richard, and Charles Murray. *The Bell Curve: Intelligence and Class Structure in American Life*. New York: Free Press, 1994.

Hirschman, Albert O. *Exit, Voice and Loyalty: Responses to Declines in Firms, Organizations, and States*. Cambridge, MA: Harvard University Press, 1970.

——. *The Strategy of Economic Development*. New Haven, CT: Yale University Press, 1959.

Hirst, Paul. *Associational Democracy: New Forms of Economic and Social Governance*. Cambridge, UK: Polity, 1994.

Hobson, John A. *Imperialism: A Study* [1902]. Ann Arbor: University of Michigan Press, 1965.

Hochman, Harold M., and James D. Rodgers. "Pareto Optimal Redistribution," *American Economic Review* 59:4 (1969): 542–57.

Hochschild, Arlie. *The Second Shift*. New York: Viking, 1989.

Hogan, Lloyd. *Principles of Black Political Economy*. Boston: Routledge & Kegan Paul, 1984.

Hole, Judith, and Ellen Levine. *Rebirth of Feminism*. New York: Quadrangle Books, 1971.

Holmberg, Johan. *Making Development Sustainable: Redefining Institutions, Policy and Economics*. Washington, DC: Island Press, 1992.

Holton, Robert J., and Bryan S. Turner. *Talcott Parsons on Economy and Society*. New York: Routledge, 1989.

Hoover, Kenneth, and Raymond Plant. *Conservative Capitalism in Britain and the United States: A Critical Appraisal*. New York: Routledge, 1989.

Hughes, Robert. *The Culture of Complaint: The Fraying of America*. New York: Oxford University Press, 1993.

Hula, Richard, ed. *Market Based Public Policy*. New York: Macmillan, 1987.

Huntington, Ellsworth. *Civilization and Climate*. New York: Arno Press, 1977.

Illich, Ivan. *Deschooling Society*. New York: Harper & Row, 1971.

Jacobs, Michael. *The Green Economy: Environment, Sustainable Development and the Politics of the Future*. Concord, MA: Pluto Press, 1991.

Jacoby, Russell, and Naomi Glauberman. *The Bell Curve Debate: History, Document, Opinions*. New York: Times Books, 1995.

Jencks, Christopher. *Rethinking Social Policy: Race, Poverty and the Underclass*. Cambridge, MA: Harvard University Press, 1992.

Jenkins, Glenville, and Michael Poole. *The Impact of Economic Democracy: Profit Sharing and Employee Sharing Schemes*. New York: Routledge, 1990.

Jenness, Linda, ed. *Feminism and Socialism*. New York: Pathfinder Press, 1972.

Jensen, Arthur R. *Educability and Group Differences*. New York: Harper & Row, 1973.

——. *Genetics and Education*. New York: Harper & Row, 1972.

——. "How Much Can We Boost IQ and Scholastic Achievement?" *Harvard Educational Review* 39, no. 1 (Winter 1969): 1–123.

——. *Straight Talk About Mental Tests*. New York: Free Press, 1981.

Jessop, Bob. *The Capitalist State*. New York: New York University Press, 1982.

Jevons, W. Stanley. *The Theory of Political Economy*, 2nd ed. London: University Press, 1879.

Johansen, Elaine. *Comparable Worth: The Myth and the Movement*. Boulder, CO: Westview Press, 1984.

Johnson, Chalmers, ed. *The Industrial Policy Debate*. San Francisco: Institute for Contemporary Studies Press, 1984.

Jouvenel, Bertrand de. *The Ethics of Redistribution* (1951). Indianapolis: Liberty Press, 1990.

Kalecki, Michal. "Political Aspects of Full Employment," *Political Quarterly* 14, no. 4 (1943): 322–30.

Kaus, Mickey. *The End of Equality*. New York: Basic Books, 1995.

Kelly, Rita Mae, and Jane Bayes, eds. *Comparable Worth, Pay Equity, and Public Policy*. Westport, CT: Greenwood, 1988.

Kelman, Steven J. *What Price Incentives?: Economists and the Environment*. Boston: Auburn House, 1981.

Kelso, Louis O., and Patricia Hetter Kelso. *Democracy and Economic Power: Extending the ESOP Revolution*. Cambridge, MA: Ballinger, 1986.

Kemp, Jack. *An American Renaissance: A Strategy for the 80s*. New York: Harper & Row, 1979.

Keohane, Robert O. *After Hegemony: Cooperation and Discord in the World Political Economy*. Princeton, NJ: Princeton University Press, 1984.

Keynes, John Maynard. *The General Theory of Employment, Interest, and Money*. New York: Harcourt, Brace & World, 1964.

———. "National Self-sufficiency," *The Yale Review* 22, no. 4 (June 1933): 769–75.

Kinchloe, Joe L., Shirley R. Steinberg, and Aaron D. Gresson III. *Measured Lies: The Bell Curve Examined*. New York: St. Martin's Press, 1996.

Kirkpatrick, Jeane J. *Dictatorships and Double Standards*. New York: Simon & Schuster, 1982.

———. *Legitimacy and Force*. New Brunswick, NJ: Transaction Books, 1988.

Klamer, Arjo, and David Colander. *The Making of An Economist*. Boulder, CO: Westview Publishing, 1990.

Koedt, Anne, Ellen Levine, and Anita Rapone, eds. *Radical Feminism*. New York: Quadrangle Books, 1973.

Kohlberg, Lawrence. *Essays on Moral Development*. San Francisco: Harper & Row, 1981.

Kolko, Gabriel. *The Triumph of Conservatism: A Re-interpretation of American History, 1900–1916*. New York: Free Press, 1963.

Kornhauser, William. *The Politics of Mass Society*. Glencoe, IL: Free Press, 1959.

Kotz, David, Terence McDonough, and Michael Reich, eds. *Social Structures of Accumulation: The Political Economy of Growth and Crisis*. Cambridge, UK: Cambridge University Press, 1994.

Krauss, Melvyn B. *How Nations Grow Rich: The Case for Free Trade*. New York: Oxford University Press, 1997.

Krueger, Anne O. *Economic Policies at Cross-Purposes: The United States and Developing Countries*. Washington, DC: Brookings Institution, 1993.

———. *The Political Economy of Trade Protection*. Chicago: University of Chicago Press, 1996.

Krueger, Anne O., *et al.* "Report of the Commission on Graduate Education in Economics," *Journal of Economic Literature* 29:3 (1991): 1035–53.

Krugman, Paul. *The Age of Diminished Expectations*, 3rd ed. Cambridge, MA: MIT Press, 1997.

———. "Is Free Trade Passé," *Journal of Economic Perspectives* (1987) 131–44.

———. *Pop Internationalism.* Cambridge, MA: MIT Press, 1996.

———, ed. *Strategic Trade Policy and the New International Economics.* Cambridge: MIT Press, 1986.

Kuttner, Robert. *Everything for Sale: The Virtues and Limits of Markets.* New York: Alfred A. Knopf, 1997.

———. *Managed Trade and Economic Sovereignty.* Washington, DC: Economic Policy Institute, 1989.

Kuznets, Simon. "Economic Growth and Income Inequality," *American Economic Review* 45 (1955), 1–28.

Lal, Deepak. *Against Dirigisme: The Case for Unshackling Economic Markets.* San Francisco: ICS Press, 1994.

———. *The Poverty of Development Economics.* Cambridge, MA: Harvard University Press, 1985.

Langlois, Richard N., ed. *Economics as a Process: Essays in the New Institutional Economics.* New York: Cambridge University Press, 1986.

Larson, Edward J. *Sex, Race and Science: Eugenics in the Deep South.* Baltimore: Johns Hopkins University Press, 1995.

Lasch, Christopher. *The Culture of Narcissism: American Life in an Age of Diminishing Expectations.* New York: W. W. Norton, 1978.

Lawler, James M. *IQ, Heritability, and Racism.* New York: International Publishers, 1978.

Lazonick, William. *Business Organization and the Myth of the Market Economy.* Cambridge: Cambridge University Press, 1991.

Leach, William. *Land of Desire: Merchants, Power, and the Rise of a New American Culture.* New York: Pantheon Books, 1993.

Lee, Dwight R., and Richard McKenzie. *Regulating Government: A Preface to Constitutional Economics.* Lexington, MA: Lexington Books, 1987.

Lehmbruch, Gerhard, and Phillippe Schmitter, eds. *Patterns of Corporatist Policymaking.* Beverly Hills, CA: Sage, 1982.

Lekachman, Robert. *Greed Is Not Enough: Reaganomics.* New York: Pantheon, 1982.

Lenin, V. I. *Imperialism: The Highest Stage of Capitalism.* New York: International Publishers, 1969.

Leopold, Aldo. *The Land Ethic.* Oxford: Oxford University Press, 1949.

Levin, Michael. *Feminism and Freedom.* New Brunswick, NJ: Transaction Books, 1987.

Lewin, Kurt. *Resolving Social Conflicts.* New York: Harper & Row, 1948.

Lieberman, Myron. *Privatization of Educational Choice.* New York: St. Martin's, 1989.

Lipset, Seymour Martin, ed. *Unions in Transition.* San Francisco: Institute for Contemporary Studies Press, 1986.

Lipsey, Richard G., and Kelvin Lancaster. "The General Theory of the Second Best," *Review of Economic Studies* 24:1 (October 1956): 11–32.

Loomis, C. Douglas. *Radical Democracy.* Ithaca, NY: Cornell University Press, 1996.

Loury, Glenn C. "The Moral Quandary of the Black Community," *Public Interest* 79 (Spring 1985): 9–22.

Lovelock, James. *Gaia.* Oxford: Oxford University Press, 1979.

Lowi, Theodore. *The End of Liberalism: The Second Republic of the U.S.,* 2nd ed. New York: W. W. Norton, 1979.

Lustig, R. Jeffrey. *Corporate Liberalism: The Origins of Modern American Political Theory 1880–1920.* Berkeley: University of California Press, 1982.

Macesich, George. *The Politics of Monetarism: Its Historical and Institutional Development.* Totowa, NJ: Rowman & Allanheld, 1984.

Machlup, Fritz. *Education and Economic Growth.* Lincoln, NE: University of Nebraska Press, 1970.

MacKinnon, Catherine. *Only Words.* Cambridge, MA: Harvard University Press, 1993.

Macpherson, C. B. *The Political Theory of Possessive Individualism.* Oxford: Clarendon Press, 1962.

Magaziner, Ira C., and Robert B. Reich. *Minding America's Business: The Decline and Rise of the American Economy.* New York: Harcourt Brace Jovanovich, 1982.

Mahler, Vincent A. *Dependency Approaches to International Political Economy.* New York: Columbia University Press, 1980.

Mandeiker, Daniel R. *Environment and Equity: A Regulatory Challenge.* New York: McGraw-Hill, 1981.

Mansbridge, Jane J. *Beyond Adversarial Democracy.* New York: Basic Books, 1980.

Marable, Manning. *Beyond Black and White.* New York: Verso, 1995.

———. *How Capitalism Underdeveloped Black America.* Boston: South End Press, 1983.

Marcuse, Herbert. *The Aesthetic Dimension: Toward a Critique of Marxist Aesthetics.* Boston: Beacon Press, 1978.

———. *Eros and Civilization.* Boston: Beacon Press, 1966.

———. *One Dimensional Man.* Boston: Beacon Press, 1964.

Marglin, Stephen. "What Do Bosses Do: The Origins and Functions of Hierarchy in Capitalist Production," *Review of Radical Political Economics* 6 (Spring 1974): 60–112.

Marglin, Stephen, and Julie Schor, eds. *The Golden Age of Capitalism: Reinterpreting the Postwar Experience.* Oxford: Clarendon Press, 1990.

Marin, Peter, Vincent Stanley, and Kathryn Marin. *The Limits of Schooling.* Englewood Cliffs, NJ: Prentice-Hall, 1975.

Marshall, Ray. "The Economics of Racial Discrimination: A Survey," *Journal of Economic Literature* 12, no. 3 (September 1974): 849–71.

———. *Unheard Voices: Labor and Economic Policy in a Competitive World.* New York: Basic Books, 1987.

Marx, Karl. *Capital,* Vol. 3. New York: International Publishers, 1961.

Marx, Karl, and Friedrich Engels. *The German Ideology.* New York: International Publishers, 1947.

Maslow, Abraham H. *Motivation and Personality,* 3rd ed. New York: Harper & Row, 1987.

Mason, Ronald M. *Participatory and Workplace Democracy: A Theoretical Development in Critique of Liberalism.* Carbondale, IL: Southern Illinois University Press, 1982.

Mayer, Thomas. *Monetarism and Macroeconomic Policy*. Brookfield, VT: Edward Elger Publishers, 1990.

Mayo, Elton. *The Human Problems of an Industrial Civilization*. New York: Macmillan, 1933.

McCartney, John T. *Black Power Ideologies*. Philadelphia: Temple University Press, 1992.

McClelland, David. *The Achieving Society*. Princeton, NJ: Van Nostrand, 1961.

McElroy, Wendy, ed. *Freedom, Feminism, and the State*. Washington, DC: Cato Institute, 1982.

McKenzie, Richard B. *Competing Visions: The Political Conflict Over America's Economic Future*. Washington, DC: Cato Institute, 1985.

———. *The Fairness of Markets*. Lexington, MA: D. C. Heath, 1987.

———. *Fugitive Industry: The Economics and Politics of Deindustrialization*. San Francisco: Pacific Institute, 1984.

———. *The Political Economy of the Educational Process*. Boston: Martinus Nijhoff, 1979.

———, ed. *Constitutional Economics: Containing the Economic Powers of Government*. Lexington, MA: Lexington Books, 1985.

McKenzie, Richard B., and Gordon Tullock. *The Best of the New World of Economics*, 5th ed. Homewood, IL: Richard D. Irwin, 1989.

Mead, Lawrence. *The New Politics of Poverty*. New York: Basic Books, 1992.

Meadows, Donella H., Dennis L. Meadows, and Jorgen Randers. *Beyond the Limits: Confronting Global Collapse; Envisioning A Sustainable Future*. Post Mills, Vermont: Chelsea Green Publishing Company, 1992.

Meadows, Donella H., Dennis L. Meadows, Jorgen Randers, and William W. Behrens. *The Limits to Growth*. New York: University Books, 1972.

Mecklenburger, James, and Richard W. Hostrop. *Education Vouchers*. Homewood, IL: ETC Publications, 1972.

Meier, Kenneth J. *Regulation: Politics, Bureaucracy and Economics*. New York: St. Martin's, 1985.

Meisner, Martin. "The Long Arm of the Job: A Study of Work and Leisure," *Industrial Relations* 10 (October 1971): 239–60.

Mensh, Elaine, and Harry Mensh. *The IQ Mythology: Race, Class, Gender, and Inequality*. Carbondale, IL: Southern Illinois University Press, 1991.

Miliband, Ralph. *The State in Capitalist Society*. New York: Basic Books, 1969.

Mill, John Stuart. *Essays on Some Unsettled Questions of Political Economy* (1844). New York: Augustus M. Kelley, 1968.

———. *On Liberty*. New York: Liberal Arts Press, 1956.

Miller, Alan S. *Gaia Connections: An Introduction to Ecology, Ecoethics and Economics*. Savage, MD: Rowman & Littlefield, 1991.

Millett, Kate. *Sexual Politics*. New York: Avon, 1971.

Mills, C. Wright. *The Power Elite*. New York: Oxford University Press, 1956.

Mills, Nicolaus. *Debating Affirmative Action*. New York: Delta, 1994.

Mishan, E. J. *Cost–Benefit Analysis: An Introduction*, 3rd ed. Boston: Allen & Unwin, 1982.

Mitchell, Edward J. *Energy and Ideology*. Washington, DC: American Enterprise Institute, 1979.

Mitchell, Juliet. *Woman's Estate*. Baltimore, MD: Penguin, 1975.

Mitchell, William C., and Randy T. Simmons. *Beyond Politics: Markets, Welfare and the Failure of Bureaucracy*. Boulder, CO: Westview Press, 1994.

Mitnick, Barry. *The Political Economy of Regulation*. New York: Columbia University Press, 1980.

Monroe, Kristen R., ed. *The Economic Approach to Politics: A Critical Reassessment of the Theory of Rational Action*. New York: HarperCollins, 1991.

Montague, Ashley, ed. *Race and IQ*. New York: Oxford University Press, 1975.

Moore, Thomas S. *The Disposable Work Force*. New York: Aldine de Gruyter, 1996.

Morgan, Philip, ed. *Privatization and the Welfare State: Implications for Consumers and the Workforce*. Brookfield, VT: Dartmouth Publishing Co., 1995.

Morris, Lydia. *The Workings of the Household*. Cambridge: Polity, 1990.

Mosca, Gaetano. *The Ruling Class*, edited by A. Livingston. New York: McGraw-Hill, 1939.

Mouffe, Chantal, ed. *Dimensions of Radical Democracy: Pluralism, Citizenship, Community*. London: Verso, 1992.

Mount, Ferdinand. *The Subversive Family: An Alternative History of Love and Marriage*. London: Jonathan Cape, 1982.

Mulhall, Stephen, and Adam Swift. *Liberals and Communitarians*. Cambridge, MA: Blackwell, 1996.

Munkirs, John. *The Transformation of American Capitalism*. Armonk, NY: M. E. Sharpe, 1985.

Murray, Charles. *Losing Ground: American Social Policy 1950–1980*. New York: Basic Books, 1984.

Murray, Michael L. *". . . And Economic Justice For All": Welfare Reform for the 21st Century*. Armonk, NY: M. E. Sharpe, 1997.

Musgrave, Richard A. *The Theory of Public Finance*. New York: McGraw-Hill, 1959.

Myrdal, Gunnar. *An American Dilemma: The Negro Problem and Modern Democracy*. New York: Harper & Brothers, 1944.

———. *Development and Underdevelopment*. Cairo: National Bank of Egypt, 1956.

———. *The International Economy*. New York: Harper, 1956.

Naess, Arne. *Ecology, Community and Lifestyle*. Cambridge: Cambridge University Press, 1989.

Nelson, Cary, and Lawrence Grossberg, eds. *Marxism and the Interpretation of Culture*. Urbana, IL: University of Illinois Press, 1988.

Nisbet, Robert A. *Community and Power*. New York: Oxford University Press, 1962.

———. *The Quest for Community: A Study in the Ethics of Order and Freedom*. New York: Oxford University Press, 1953.

———. *The Twilight of Authority*. New York: Oxford University Press, 1975.

Niskanen, William A. *Bureaucracy and Public Economics*. Brookfield, VT: Edward Elgar, 1994.

———. *Reaganomics: An Insider's Account of the Policies and the People*. New York: Oxford University Press, 1988.

Novak, Michael. *The Catholic Ethic and the Spirit of Capitalism*. New York: Free Press, 1993.

———, ed. *Democracy and Mediating Structures: A Theological Inquiry*. Washington, DC: American Enterprise Institute, 1980.

Nozick, Robert. *Anarchy, State, and Utopia*. New York: Basic Books, 1974.

Nurkse, Ragnar. *Problems of Capital Formation in Underdeveloped Countries.* Oxford: Basil Blackwell, 1953.

O'Connor, James. *Accumulation Crisis.* New York: Basil Blackwell, 1984.

————. *The Fiscal Crisis of the State.* New York: St. Martin's, 1973.

O'Donoghue, Martin. *Economic Dimensions in Education.* Chicago: Aldine-Atherton, 1971.

Okin, Susan Moller. *Women in Western Political Thought.* Princeton, NJ: Princeton University Press, 1979.

Okun, Arthur M. *Equality and Efficiency: The Big Trade-off.* Washington, DC: Brookings Institution, 1975.

Oldenquist, Andrew, and Menachem Rosner. *Alienation, Community and Work.* New York: Greenwood Press, 1991.

Ollman, Bertell. *Alienation: Marx's Conception of Man in Capitalist Society.* New York: Cambridge University Press, 1971.

Olson, Mancur. *The Logic of Collective Action: Public Goals and the Theory of Groups.* Cambridge, MA: Harvard University Press, 1965.

————. *The Rise and Decline of Nations: Economic Growth, Stagflation, and Social Rigidities.* New Haven, CT: Yale University Press, 1982.

Ophuls, William. "The Politics of A Sustainable Society," *in* Gary Orfield, *Must We Bus?: Segregated Schools and National Policy.* Washington, DC: Brookings Institution, 1978.

Orme, William J., Jr. *Understanding NAFTA: Mexico, Free Trade and the New North America.* Austin: University of Texas Press, 1996.

Ortega y Gasset, José. *The Revolt of the Masses* [1932]. Notre Dame, IN: University of Notre Dame Press, 1985.

Ouchi, William G. *Theory Z: How American Business Can Meet the Japanese Challenge.* New York: Avon, 1982.

Oxley, Alex. *The Challenge of Free Trade.* New York: Harvester Wheatsheaf, 1990.

Pagano, Ugo. *Work and Welfare in Economic Theory.* New York: Basil Blackwell, 1985.

Pareto, Vilfredo. *The Mind and Society: A Treatise of General Sociology.* New York: Dover, 1935.

————. *Sociological Writings,* edited by S. E. Finer. New York: Praeger, 1966.

Parsons, Talcott. *The Social System.* Glencoe, IL: Free Press, 1951.

Partridge, Ernest, ed. *Responsibilities to Future Generations.* New York: Prometheus Books, 1981.

Paul, Ellen Frankel. *Equity and Gender.* Washington, DC: Cato Institute, 1988.

Pepper, David. *Eco-socialism: From Deep Ecology to Social Justice.* New York: Routledge, 1993.

Pestel, Edward. *Beyond the Limits to Growth.* New York: University Books, 1989.

Peterson, Wallace C., ed. *Market Power and the Economy.* Boston: Kluwer Academic Publishers, 1988.

Pheby, John, ed. *New Directions In Post-Keynesian Economics.* Brookfield, VT: Edward Elgar, 1989.

Phelps, Edmund S. "The Statistical Theory of Racism and Sexism," *American Economic Review* 62, no. 4 (September 1972): 659–61.

Phillips, Derek L. *Looking Backward: A Critical Appraisal of Communitarian Thought.* Princeton, NJ: Princeton University Press, 1993.

Phillips, Kevin. *The Politics of Rich and Poor: Wealth and the American Electorate in the Reagan Aftermath*. New York: HarperCollins, 1990.

Piaget, Jean. *The Essential Piaget*, edited by H. E. Gruber and J. J. Voneche. New York: Basic Books, 1977.

Pigou, A. C., ed. *Memorials of Alfred Marshall* (1925). New York: Augustus M. Kelley, 1966.

Pinkerton, James P. *What Comes Next: The End of Big Government—and The New Paradigm Ahead*. New York: Hyperion, 1995.

Piore, Michael J., ed. *Inflation and Unemployment: Institutionalist and Structuralist Views*. White Plains, NY: M. E. Sharpe, 1979.

Pirages, Dennis C., ed. *Building Sustainable Societies: A Blueprint for a Post-Industrial World*. Armonk, NY: M. E. Sharpe, 1996.

———, ed. *The Sustainable Society*. New York: Praeger, 1977.

Piven, Francis Fox, and Richard Cloward. *Regulating the Poor*. New York: Pantheon, 1971.

Podhoretz, Norman. *The Present Danger*. New York: Simon & Schuster, 1980.

Polychroniou, Chronis. *Marxist Perspectives on Imperialism*. New York: Praeger, 1991.

Posner, Richard A. *The Economics of Justice*. Cambridge, MA: Harvard University Press, 1984.

———. *Overcoming Law*. Cambridge, MA: Harvard University Press, 1995.

Poulantzas, Nicos. *Political Power and Social Classes*. London: New Left Books, 1975.

Prestowitz, Clyde V., Jr. *Trading Places*. New York: Basic Books, 1988.

Pujol, Michele A. *Feminism and Anti-feminism in Early Economic Thought*. Brookfield, VT: Edward Elgar, 1992.

Putnam, Carleton. *Race and Reason*. Washington, DC: Public Affairs Press, 1961.

Putnam, Robert. *Making Democracy Work: Civic Traditions in Modern Italy*. Princeton, NJ: Princeton University Press, 1993.

Putterman, Louis, ed. *The Economic Nature of the Firm: A Reader*. New York: Cambridge University Press, 1986.

Reed, Evelyn. *Problems of Women's Liberation: A Marxist Approach*. New York: Pathfinder Press, 1971.

Reich, Michael. *Racial Inequality: A Political Economic Analysis*. Princeton, NJ: Princeton University Press, 1981.

Reich, Robert B. *The Next American Frontier*. New York: Times Books, 1983.

———. *The Resurgent Liberal*. New York: Times Books, 1989.

———. *Tales of a New America*. New York: Times Books, 1987.

———. *The Work of Nations: Preparing Ourselves for 21st Century Capitalism*. New York: Vintage Books, 1992.

Remick, Helen, ed. *Comparable Worth and Wage Discrimination*. Philadelphia: Temple University Press, 1984.

Riggs, A. R., and Tom Valk, eds. *Beyond NAFTA: An Economic, Political and Sociological Perspective*. Vancouver: The Frazier Institute, 1993.

Roback, Jennifer. *A Matter of Choice: A Critique of Comparable Worth by a Skeptical Feminist*. New York: Priority Press, 1986.

Robbins, Lionel. *An Essay on the Nature and Significance of Economic Science* (1932). New York: New York University Press, 1984.

_____. *The Great Depression*. London: Macmillan, 1934.

Roberts, Paul Craig. *The Supply-Side Revolution: An Insider's Account of Policy-making in Washington*. Cambridge, MA: Harvard University Press, 1984.

Roberts, Paul Craig, and Lawrence M. Stratton. *The New Color Line: How Quotas and Privilege Destroy Democracy*. Washington, DC: Regnery Publishers, 1995.

Robinson, Joan. *The Economics of Imperfect Competition*. London: Macmillan, 1933.

Rosenstein-Rodan, Paul. *Philosophy and Practice in Latin American Development*. Cambridge: MIT Press, 1972.

Rothbard, Murray. *America's Great Depression*. Kansas City, KS: Sheed & Ward, 1975.

Rothenberg, Randall. *The Neoliberals: Creating the New American Politics*. New York: Simon & Schuster, 1984.

Rousseas, Stephen. *The Political Economy of Reaganomics: A Critique*. Armonk, NY: M. E. Sharpe, 1982.

Rowbotham, Sheila. *Woman's Consciousness, Man's World*. Baltimore: Penguin, 1973.

Rowley, Charles K., ed. *Public Choice Theory*. Brookfield, VT: Edward Elgar, 1993.

Rowley, Charles K., Willem Thorbecke, and Richard E. Wagner. *Trade Protection in the United States*. Brookfield, VT: Edward Elgar, 1995.

Rowley, Charles K., Robert D. Tollison, and Gordon Tullock. *The Political Economy of Rent-Seeking*. Boston: Martinus Nijhoff, 1988.

Rutledge, John, and Deborah Allen. *Rust to Riches: The Coming of the Second Industrial Revolution*. New York: Harper & Row, 1989.

Sackrey, Charles. *The Political Economy of Urban Poverty*. New York: W. W. Norton, 1973.

Sagan, Eli. *Freud, Women, and Morality*. New York: Basic Books, 1988.

Sale, Kirkpatrick. *Dwellers in the Land: The Bioregional Vision*. San Francisco: Sierra Club, 1985.

Samuels, Warren J. "The Case for Methodological Pluralism," *in* Andrea Salanti and Ernesto Screpanti, eds. *Pluralism in Economics*. Brookfield, VT: Edward Elgar, 1997.

Samuelson, Paul. "Wage and Interest: A Modern Discussion of the Marxian Theory of Discrimination," *Bell Journal of Economics* 10 (Autumn 1979): 695–905.

Sarup, Madan. *Marxism and Education*. Boston: Routledge & Kegan Paul, 1978.

Sawhill, Isabel V. "The Economics of Discrimination Against Women: Some New Findings," *Journal of Human Resources* 8, no. 3 (Summer 1973): 383–96.

Sawyer, Malcom C., ed. *Post-Keynesian Economics*. Brookfield, VT: Edward Elger Publishers, 1988.

Schacht, Richard. *The Future of Alienation*. Urbana: University of Illinois Press, 1994.

Schaeffer, Francis A. *Pollution and the Death of Man: The Christian View of Ecology*. Wheaton, IL: Tyndale House, 1970.

Schindler, Ronald J. *The Frankfurt School Critique of Capitalist Culture*. Aldershot: Avebury Publishers, 1996.

Schlafly, Phyllis. *The Power of the Positive Woman*. New Rochelle, NY: Arlington House, 1977.

Schmid, A. Allan. *Benefit–Cost Analysis: A Political Economy Approach*. Boulder, CO: Westview Press, 1989.

Schmitter, Philippe, and Gerhard Lehmbruch, eds. *Trends Toward Corporatist Intermediation*. Beverly Hills, CA: Sage, 1979.

Schmookler, Andrew B. *Fool's Gold: The Fate of Values in a World of Goods*. New York: HarperCollins, 1993.

———. *The Illusion of Choice: How the Market Economy Shapes Our Destiny*. Ithaca, NY: State University of New York Press, 1993.

Schor, Juliet. *The Overworked American: The Unexpected Decline of Leisure*. New York: Basic Books, 1991.

Schumacher, E. F. *Small Is Beautiful: Economics As If People Mattered*. New York: Harper & Row, 1973.

Schumpeter, Joseph. *Business Cycles*. New York: McGraw-Hill, 1939.

———. *Capitalism, Socialism, and Democracy*. New York: Harper & Brothers, 1950.

———. *The Theory of Economic Development*, 3rd ed. Cambridge, MA: Harvard University Press, 1951.

Schwartz, Barry. *The Costs of Living: How Market Freedom Erodes the Best Things in Life*. New York: W. W. Norton, 1994.

Schweickart, David. *Against Capitalism*. New York: Cambridge University Press, 1993.

Scitovsky, Tibor. *The Joyless Economy: An Inquiry into Human Satisfaction and Consumer Dissatisfaction*. New York: Oxford University Press, 1976.

———. "A Note on Welfare Propositions in Economics," *Review of Economic Studies* 9:77–88, 1941.

Scott, Hilde. *Does Socialism Liberate Women?* Boston: Beacon Press, 1974.

Scully, Gerald W. *Constitutional Economics: The Framework for Economic Growth and Social Progress*. Washington, DC: The Heritage Foundation, 1991.

Seers, Dudley, ed. *Dependency Theory: A Critical Reassessment*. London: Pinter, 1981.

Seligman, Daniel. *A Question of Intelligence: The IQ Debate in America*. New York: Carol Publishing Group, 1992.

Senna, Carl, ed. *Race and IQ*. New York: Third Press, 1973.

Shapiro, Ian. *The Evolution of Rights in Liberal Theory*. New York: Cambridge University Press, 1986.

Shaw, G. K. *Rational Expectations: An Elementary Exposition*. New York: St. Martin's, 1984.

Sherman, Howard. *Stagflation: A Radical Theory of Unemployment and Inflation*. New York: Harper & Row, 1976.

Shipman, Pat. *The Evolution of Racism: Human Differences and the Use and Abuse of Science*. New York: Simon & Schuster, 1994.

Shockley, William. "Dysgenics, Geneticity, Raceology: A Challenge to the Intellectual Responsibility of Educators," *Phi Delta Kappan* 53, no. 5 (January 1972): 297–307.

Simmie, James M. *Power, Property, and Corporatism*. London: Macmillan, 1982.

Simms, Margaret C., ed. *Economic Perspectives on Affirmative Action*. Washington, DC: Joint Center for Political and Economic Studies, 1995.

Singer, Peter. *Animal Liberation: A New Ethic for Our Treatment of Animals*. New York: Random House, 1975.

Sjostedt, Gunnar, and Bengt Sundelius, eds. *Free Trade-Managed Trade?: Perspectives on a Realistic International Trade Order*. Boulder, CO: Westview Press, 1986.

Sklar, Holly. *Trilateralism: The Trilateral Commission and Elite Planning for World Management*. Boston: South End Press, 1980.

Sklar, Martin J. *The Corporate Reconstruction of American Capitalism*. New York: Cambridge University Press, 1988.

Smith, Adam. *The Wealth of Nations*. London: Dent, 1910.

Smith, Kevin B., and Kenneth J. Meier. *The Case Against School Choice*. Armonk, NY: M. E. Sharpe, 1995.

Smith, Vernon L., ed. *Experimental Economics*. Brookfield, VT: Edward Elgar, 1990.

Sobel, Lester A., ed. *Quotas and Affirmative Action*. New York: Facts on File, 1980.

Sowell, Thomas. *The Economics and Politics of Race*. New York: William Morrow, 1983.

————. *Ethnic America: A History*. New York: Basic Books, 1981.

————. *Markets and Minorities*. New York: Basic Books, 1981.

————. *Migrations and Cultures: A World View*. New York: Basic Books, 1996.

————. *Race and Cultures: A World View*. New York: Basic Books, 1994.

————. *Race and Economics*. New York: David McKay, 1975.

Stabile, Donald. *Prophets of Order: Class, Technocracy, and Socialism in America*. Boston: South End Press, 1985.

Stassinopoulos, Arianna. *The Female Woman*. New York: Random House, 1973.

Steele, G. R. *Monetarism and the Demise of Keynesian Economics*. New York: St. Martin's Press, 1989.

Stein, Jerome. *Monetarist, Keynesian and New Classical Economics*. Oxford: Basil Blackwell, 1982.

Stigler, George J. "The Theory of Economic Regulation," *Bell Journal of Economics & Management Science* 2, no. 1 (Spring 1971): 3–21.

Storkey, Elaine. *What's Right with Feminism*. Grand Rapids, MI: William B. Erdman's, 1985.

Strike, Kenneth A. *Liberal Justice and the Marxist Critique of Education*. New York: Routledge, 1989.

Sunstein, Cass R. *Democracy and the Problem of Free Speech*. New York: The Free Press, 1993.

Tabb, William. *The Political Economy of the Black Ghetto*. New York: W. W. Norton, 1970.

Talmon, Jacob. *The Origins of Totalitarian Democracy*. New York: Praeger, 1960.

Tawney, R. H. *Equality*. London: George Allen and Unwin, 1931.

Taylor, Frederick W. *The Principles of Scientific Management* [1911]. New York: W. W. Norton, 1967.

Taylor, Joan Kennedy. *Women's Issues: Feminism, Classical Liberalism, and the Future*. Stanford, CA: Hoover Institution, 1993.

Tetreault, Mary Ann, and Charles Frederic Abel. *Dependency Theory and the Return of High Politics*. Westport, CT: Greenwood, 1986.

Thompson, E. P. *The Making of the English Working Class*. New York: Pantheon, 1963.

Thurow, Lester. *The Future Of Capitalism: How Today's Economic Forces Shape Tomorrow's World*. New York: W. Morrow & Co., 1996.

———. *Generating Inequality: Mechanisms of Distribution in the U.S. Economy.* New York: Basic Books, 1975.

———. *The Zero-Sum Society: Distribution and the Possibilities for Economic Change.* New York: Basic Books, 1980.

———. *The Zero-Sum Solution.* New York: Basic Books, 1984.

Tocqueville, Alexis de. *Democracy in America,* edited by J. P. Mayer and M. Lerner. New York: Harper & Row, 1966.

Tollison, Robert D., and Roger D. Congleton, eds. *The Economic Analysis of Rent-Seeking.* Brookfield, VT: Edward Elgar, 1995.

Toye, John. *Dilemmas of Development: Reflections on the Counter-revolution in Development Theory and Policy.* Oxford: Blackwell, 1987.

Trilling, Lionel. *The Liberal Imagination.* New York: Viking Press, 1950.

Truman, David. *The Governing Process.* New York: Alfred A. Knopf, 1951.

Tullock, Gordon. *Economics of Income Distribution.* Boston: Kluwer-Nijhoff, 1983.

———. *Private Wants, Public Means.* New York: Basic Books, 1970.

———. *Rent Seeking.* Brookfield, VT: Edward Elgar, 1993.

Turner, R. Kerry, ed. *Sustainable Environmental Economics and Management: Principles and Practice.* London: Belhaven, 1993.

Udehn, Lars. *The Limits of Public Choice.* New York: Routledge, 1996.

Usher, Dan. *The Economic Prerequisite to Democracy.* New York: Columbia University Press, 1981.

van den Bergh, Jeroen. *Ecological Economics and Sustainable Development.* Brookfield, VT: Edward Elgar, 1995.

Vatter, Harold G., and John F. Walker. *The Inevitability of Government Growth.* New York: Columbia University Press, 1990.

Vogel, Lise. *Woman Questions: Essays for A Materialist Feminism.* New York: Routledge, 1995.

Vroman, Jack J. *Economic Evolution: An Enquiry Into The Foundations of New Institutional Economics.* New York: Routledge, 1995.

Waldmann, Raymond J. *Managed Trade: The New Competition Between Nations.* Cambridge, MA: Ballinger Publishing Co., 1986.

Walker, John F., and Harold G. Vatter. *The Rise of Big Government in the United States.* Armonk, NY: M. E. Sharpe, 1997.

Wall, David, ed. *Chicago Essays in Economic Development.* Chicago: University of Chicago Press, 1972.

Wallerstein, Immanuel, and Terence K. Hopkins. *World-systems Analysis: Theory and Methodology.* Beverly Hills, CA: Sage, 1982.

Wanniski, Jude. *The Way the World Works.* New York: Basic Books, 1978.

Ward, Barbara, and Rene Dubos. *Only One Earth: The Care and Maintenance of A Small Planet.* London: André Deutsch, 1972.

Waxman, Chaim. *The End of Ideology Debate.* New York: Funk & Wagnalls, 1968.

Weidenbaum, Murray. *Rendezvous with Reality: The American Economy after Reagan.* New York: Basic Books, 1988.

Weinbaum, Batya. *The Curious Courtship of Women's Liberation and Socialism.* Boston: South End Press, 1978.

Weinstein, James. *The Corporate Ideal in the Liberal State 1900–1918.* Boston: Beacon Press, 1969.

Weisberg, Barry. *Beyond Repair: The Ecology of Capitalism*. Boston: Beacon Press, 1971.

Weitzman, Martin L. *The Share Economy: Conquering Stagflation*. Cambridge, MA: Harvard University Press, 1984.

White, Joseph, and Aaron Wildavsky. *The Deficit and the Public Interest*. Berkeley, CA: University of California Press, 1989.

White, Lawrence H. *Competition and Currency*. New York: New York University Press, 1989.

Whitfield, Dexter. *The Welfare State: Privatization, Deregulation, Commercialization of Public Services*. Boulder, CO: Westview Press, 1992.

Wilborn, Steven L. *A Comparable Worth Primer*. Lexington, MA: Lexington Books, 1986.

Wildavsky, Aaron. *The Politics of the Budgetary Process*, 4th ed. Boston: Little, Brown, 1984.

Will, George. *Statecraft As Soulcraft*. New York: Simon & Schuster, 1983.

Willett, Thomas D., ed. *Political Business Cycles: The Political Economy of Money, Inflation, and Unemployment*. Durham, NC: Duke University Press, 1988.

Williams, Eric. *Capitalism and Slavery*. New York: Putnam, 1966.

Williams, Walter. *The State Against Blacks*. New York: McGraw-Hill, 1982.

Williamson, Oliver E., "The Economics of Organizations: The Transaction Approach," *American Journal of Sociology* 87, no. 3 (1981): 548–77.

———. *The Mechanisms of Governance*. New York: Oxford University Press, 1996.

Williamson, Peter J. *Varieties of Corporatism*. New York: Cambridge University Press, 1986.

Wilson, James Q., ed. *The Politics of Regulation*. New York: Basic Books, 1980.

Wilson, William Julius. *The Declining Significance of Race: Blacks and Changing American Institutions*, 2nd ed. Chicago: University of Chicago Press, 1980.

Wittman, Donald A. *The Myth of Government Failure: Why Political Institutions are Efficient*. Chicago: University of Chicago Press, 1995.

Wolff, Edward N. *Top Heavy: A Study of the Increasing Inequality of Wealth in America*. New York: Twentieth Century Fund Press, 1995.

Wolff, Robert Paul, Barrington Moore, Jr., and Herbert Marcuse. *A Critique of Pure Tolerance*. Boston: Beacon Press, 1969.

World Commission on Environment and Development. *Our Common Future*. Oxford: Oxford University Press, 1987.

Wright, Erik Olin. *Class, Crisis, and the State*. London: New Left Books, 1978.

Zaretsky, Eli. *Capitalism, The Family and Personal Life*. New York: Harper & Row, 1976.

Zucker, Seymour, and The Business Week Team. *The Reindustrialization of America*. Boston: Houghton Mifflin, 1982.

Index

ABOUT THE AUTHOR

BARRY CLARK is Professor of Economics and former Department Chairperson at the University of Wisconsin–La Crosse. He has also taught at Pennsylvania State University, Tufts University, and Ripon College.

Dr. Clark holds a BA degree from Ohio University, an MS in Economics from the University of Wisconsin, and a Ph.D. in Economics from the University of Massachusetts–Amherst. His research and publications have focused on the ethical dimensions of public policy.

ISBN 0-275-95869-8

90000>

EAN

9 780275 958695

HARDCOVER BAR CODE